Lecture Notes in Computer Science   10372

Commenced Publication in 1973
Founding and Former Series Editors:
Gerhard Goos, Juris Hartmanis, and Jan van Leeuwen

Editorial Board

More information about this series at http://www.springer.com/series/7411

Yevgeni Koucheryavy · Lefteris Mamatas
Ibrahim Matta · Aleksandr Ometov
Panagiotis Papadimitriou (Eds.)

Wired/Wireless Internet Communications

15th IFIP WG 6.2 International Conference, WWIC 2017
St. Petersburg, Russia, June 21–23, 2017
Proceedings

 Springer

Editors
Yevgeni Koucheryavy
Tampere University of Technology
Tampere
Finland

Lefteris Mamatas
University of Macedonia
Thessaloniki
Greece

Ibrahim Matta
Boston University
Boston, MA
USA

Aleksandr Ometov
Peoples' Friendship University of Russia
  (RUDN University)
Moscow
Russia

Panagiotis Papadimitriou
University of Macedonia
Thessaloniki
Greece

ISSN 0302-9743   ISSN 1611-3349 (electronic)
Lecture Notes in Computer Science
ISBN 978-3-319-61381-9   ISBN 978-3-319-61382-6 (eBook)
DOI 10.1007/978-3-319-61382-6

Library of Congress Control Number: 2017943840

LNCS Sublibrary: SL5 – Computer Communication Networks and Telecommunications

Printed on acid-free paper

This Springer imprint is published by Springer Nature
The registered company is Springer International Publishing AG
The registered company address is: Gewerbestrasse 11, 6330 Cham, Switzerland

Preface

We welcome you to the joint proceedings of the 15th International Conference on Wired/Wireless Internet Communications (IFIP WWIC). The conference constitutes a forum for the presentation and discussion of the latest results in the field of wired/wireless networks and aims at providing research directions and fostering collaborations among the participants. In this context, the Program Committee accepts a limited number of papers that meet the criteria of originality, presentation quality, and topic relevance. IFIP WWIC is a single-track conference that has reached, over the past 14 years, a high-quality level, which is reflected by the paper acceptance rate as well as the level of attendance. Following the conference tradition, there is a best paper award.

The 15th IFIP WWIC technical program addressed various aspects of next-generation data networks. This year, special attention was given to advanced wireless networking and applications as well as to lower-layer communication enablers and circuit design. In particular, the authors demonstrated novel and innovative approaches to performance and efficiency analysis of ad hoc and machine-type systems, employed game-theoretical formulations, Markov chain models, and advanced queuing theory.

WWIC 2017 provided a forum for academic and industrial researchers to discuss new ideas and trends in the emerging areas of networking that create new opportunities for fully-customized applications and services. The conference brought together leading experts from top affiliations around the world. This year, we saw a good participation from representatives of various players in the field, including academic teams and industrial world-leader companies, particularly representatives of Russian R&D centers, which have a good reputation for high-quality research and business in innovative service creation and applications development.

We would like to thank the Technical Program Committee members, as well as the associated reviewers, for their hard work and important contribution to the conference. This year, the conference program met the highest quality criteria with an acceptance ratio of around 35%.

The current edition of the conference was organized in cooperation with RUDN University, Tampere University of Technology, National Research University Higher School of Economics, Peoples' Friendship University of Russia, St. Petersburg State University of Telecommunications, and the Popov Society. The support of these organizations is gratefully acknowledged. IFIP WWIC was held in the framework of the RUDN University Competitiveness Enhancement Program 5-100.

June 2017

Y. Koucheryavy
L. Mamatas
I. Matta
A. Ometov
P. Papadimitriou

Organization

Editorial Committee

Koucheryavy Yevgeni	Tampere University of Technology, Finland
Mamatas Lefteris	University of Macedonia, Greece
Matta Ibrahim	Boston University, USA
Ometov Aleksandr	Peoples' Friendship University of Russia (RUDN University), Moscow
Papadimitriou Panagiotis	University of Macedonia, Greece

Technical Program Committee

Sami Akin	Leibniz Universität Hannover, Germany
Francisco Barcelo-Arroyo	Universitat Politecnica de Catalunya (UPC), Spain
Paolo Bellavista	University of Bologna, Italy
Fernando Boavida	University of Coimbra, Portugal
Zdravko Bozakov	Dell EMC Research Europe, Ireland
Torsten Braun	University of Bern, Switzerland
Scott Burleigh	California Institute of Technology, USA
Maria Calderon	Universidad Carlos III de Madrid, Spain
Ana Cavalli	Telecom SudParis, France
Marinos Charalambides	University College London, UK
Stuart Clayman	University College London (UCL), UK
Marilia Curado	University of Coimbra, Portugal
Panagiotis Demestichas	University of Piraeus, Greece
Paul Gendron	University of Massachusetts Dartmouth, USA
Jarmo Harju	Tampere University of Technology, Finland
Sonia Heemstra de Groot	Eindhoven Technical University, The Netherlands
Geert Heijenk	University of Twente, The Netherlands
Andreas J. Kassler	Karlstad University, Sweden
Ibrahim Korpeoglu	Bilkent University, Turkey
Peter Langendoerfer	IHP Microelectronics, Germany
Sotiris-Angelos Lenas	Democritus University of Thrace, Greece
Pascal Lorenz	University of Haute Alsace, France
Chung-Horng Lung	Carleton University, Canada
Christian Maihfer	Daimler AG, Germany
Xavier Masip-Bruin	Universitat Politecnica de Catalunya, Spain
Paulo Mendes	COPELABS/Lusofona University, Portugal
Edmundo Monteiro	University of Coimbra, Portugal
Hassnaa Moustafa	Intel, USA
Liam Murphy	University College Dublin, Ireland

Contents

XII Contents

Circuit Design

Network Analysis and Dimensioning

Bargaining over Fair Channel Sharing Between Wi-Fi and LTE-U Networks

Andrey Garnaev[1,2($\boxtimes$)], Shweta Sagari[2], and Wade Trappe[2]

[1] Saint Petersburg State University, St. Petersburg, Russia
garnaev@yahoo.com
[2] WINLAB, Rutgers University, North Brunswick, USA
{shsagari,trappe}@winlab.rutgers.edu

Abstract. Wireless networks are increasingly moving towards a heterogeneous operating model involving the sharing of spectrum resources by different access technologies. Sharing wireless resources between different wireless technologies requires protocols that share spectrum in an equitable manner. In this paper, we examine the time-sharing of wireless channels by Wi-Fi and LTE-U networks. To design fair access protocol for the networks we use α fairness criterion. It allows to find a continuum of fair protocols (a protocol per α). To find the most fair from this continuum of fair protocols we apply Nash bargaining approach. In particular, we show that such a time-sharing bargaining protocol, in spite of the interference between signals, can lead to a gain for both networks under an increase of the transmission power to one of them.

Keywords: Wi-Fi · LTE-U · Fairness · Bargaining

1 Introduction

The demand for radio spectrum has been dramatically increasing over the last decade, in large part due to the emergence of new wireless applications and devices. In order to address the increased demand on congested bands of radio spectrum, there have been numerous proposals to make under-utilized spectrum bands open for simultaneous sharing by different wireless technologies. However, allowing different wireless access networks, such as cellular and wireless local area networks, to operate in proximity to each other while in the same frequency bands, requires the development of new technologies that can coordinate sharing and coexistence. In fact, the significant value that spectrum sharing can provide to technologies like LTE-U (LTE in unlicensed spectrum) and Wi-Fi has led to prominent discussions occurring in the standards community (notably the 3rd Generation Research Project, i.e. 3GPP, community) regarding the throughput and latency requirements needed for maintaining fair coexistence [1] even though the full specification of LTE-U has not been finalized.

The literature describing the coexistence between LTE-U and Wi-Fi technologies is very recent and thus there are only a few works investigating Wi-Fi

© IFIP International Federation for Information Processing 2017
Published by Springer International Publishing AG 2017. All Rights Reserved
Y. Koucheryavy et al. (Eds.): WWIC 2017, LNCS 10372, pp. 3–15, 2017.
DOI: 10.1007/978-3-319-61382-6_1

and LTE-U coexistence. In [2], simulation analysis was used to show that LTE system performance can be slightly affected by coexistence, while Wi-Fi performance is significantly impacted by LTE transmissions. In [3], it was pointed out that the coexistence of LTE and Wi-Fi must be carefully investigated since, as it was previously illustrated, Wi-Fi networks might be severely impacted by LTE transmissions. The performance of coexisting femtocell and Wi-Fi networks operating over a fully-utilized, unlicensed band were analytically modeled in [4]. LBT mechanisms for LAA-LTE was suggested in [5] to ensure that it operates at least as fairly as Wi-Fi in unlicensed spectrum. The effects of Wi-Fi channel access parameters on the performance of Wi-Fi and Femtocell networks were investigated in [6]. A novel system to support co-existence between Wi-Fi and LTE was developed in [7] allowing to decode the interfering signals under cross technology interference even when the interfering signals have similar power. A traffic-balancing algorithm was explored in [8], while a fair and QoS-based unlicensed spectrum splitting strategy between Wi-Fi and femtocell networks was suggested in [9]. Results of experimental evaluation on the coexistence between Wi-Fi and LAA-LTE were presented in [10]. A proportional fair allocation scheme for Wi-Fi and LTE coexistence was develop in [11]. Modeling the coexistence of LTE and Wi-Fi heterogeneous networks was performed in [12].

A goal of this paper is to design the most fair channel access protocol for a channel shared between LTE-U and Wi-Fi networks. The model studied in the paper is based on the model for coordinated dynamic spectrum management between LTE-U and Wi-Fi networks suggested in [13,14]. Namely, in [13], a system for coordinating between multiple heterogeneous networks to improve spectrum utilization and facilitate co-existence, which involves building a logically-centralized spectrum management controller using the principles of a Software Defined Networking was outlined. Based on this architecture, an optimization model to maximize the aggregated Wi-Fi+LTE throughput was designed and tested in [14]. This optimization problem was divided into two steps: in the first step, based on information about the networks and their users, power control optimization problems were solved to obtain the optimal throughput for only-Wi-Fi access, and for joint Wi-Fi+LTE access to the channels. In the second step, based on these throughputs, a maxmin problem involving time-division access between the different access technologies to the shared resources, was solved numerically. Later, in [15], an analytical solution for the family of α-fair protocols (which includes also the maxmin protocol) for shared access to the channels with equal priority of the networks was given. The evaluation of such joint coordination led to the important insight that such a dual optimization approach can actually increase the aggregated Wi-Fi+LTE throughput compared to each technology separately.

One critical challenge, though, facing the design of a system trying to support fairness between two or more parties is the selection of an appropriate fairness criterion. Even for a single criterion, such as maxmin, the resulting fair allocation strategies can be complicated, but the question of whether that was the right criterion is rarely, if ever, addressed. The matter becomes more complex, though, when one considers a continuum of fairness criteria, such as represented by the family of α-fairness schemes, and which of those resulting allocation strategies should be chosen. In this paper, we examine this problem for a communication scenario involving the fair time-division allocation between LTE-U and Wi-Fi communication systems, and arrive at an approach that allows a system engineer to chose the unique optimal protocol from a continuum of optimal protocols (i.e. an optimal protocol per α). Namely, we show that the Nash bargaining solution over this continuum of protocols can be considered as the optimal access protocol for the shared resource from point of view of both networks. We solve the problem in closed form, which allows us to illustrate the improved efficiency possible by both technologies jointly accessing the shared resource.

The organization of this paper is as follows: in Sect. 2, the basic interference model between Wi-Fi and LTE that we use is described. In Sect. 3, the fair time-division access to a shared channel is formulated and solved in closed form. Also, it is illustrated that for each of the participating networks, there is generally no monotonic dependence in benefit associated with an increase in the α fairness coefficient. Thus, a question arises: out of the associated continuum of optimal fairness access protocols, which one should be considered the *optimal* one. To answer these questions, in Sect. 4, auxiliary properties of the optimal solution are obtained. This has allowed us, in Sect. 5, to apply Nash bargaining to find the best trade-off access protocol for both networks. Finally, in Sect. 6, a discussion of the results is offered, and in Appendix, sketch of proofs is given.

2   Interference Model between Wi-Fi and LTE

We begin by briefly describing a simple analytical model suggested in [14] for the interference between Wi-Fi and LTE, which will be used as a basic model for numerical illustration in this paper. In this model both technologies utilizing the same amount of bandwidth (e.g. 20 MHz) share a single spectrum channel. Also, we assume that there is only a single Wi-Fi network and a single LTE-U cell operating on that channel, and hence we do not worry about problems involving clients choosing between multiple operators within a specific technology. Let the transmission power for the Wi-Fi and LTE cell be p_W and p_L. Then, a model for the throughput, $R_i, i \in \{W, L\}$ is given as

$$R_i = \alpha_i B \log_2 \left(1 + \beta_i h_{ii} p_i / \left(N_i + h_{ij} p_j \right) \right), i, j \in \{W, L\}, i \neq j,$$

where B is the channel bandwidth, h_{ij} are channel gains, N_i is noise power for receiver i, β_i is a factor associated with the modulation scheme, α_i is bandwidth efficiency, namely, for Wi-Fi (i.e., $i = W$) it is the bandwidth efficiency of CSMA/CA, while for LTE (i.e., $i = L$) it is the bandwidth efficiency resulting from factors such as adjacent channel leakage and practical filters design.

For coordinating between units of such multiple heterogeneous networks to improve spectrum utilization and facilitate co-existence, a Global Controller (GC) was proposed [14]. The GC receives information from each network's operating conditions in order to forecast the throughput under separate or joint access by the Wi-Fi and LTE networks to the channel. In this paper, we assume that such throughput values have been obtained and focus our research on the problem of fair access of the networks to the channels. We note that there is extensive work being done by the community on facilitating such information sharing.

3   Fair Time Division Access Optimization

In this section, we formulate the problem of determining the fraction of time that each wireless technology (Wi-Fi and LTE-U) accesses the channel so as to fairly coexist. Following [14], we assume that the total throughput of each network is proportional to the fraction of time that technology uses the channel, and that it also depends on whether the channel access is simultaneous or not. In the considered scenario, Wi-Fi has priority to access the channels, i.e., Wi-Fi always has access, while LTE-U may or may not have access. To describe the problems let us introduce the following notations:

(i) q^W is the fraction of time the channel is accessed by the Wi-Fi network only (*Wi-Fi access mode*);

(ii) q is the fraction of tine the channel is accessed by both the networks simultaneously (*joint Wi-Fi and LTE-U access mode*);

(iii) Without loss of generality, we can assume that the total time duration for access to the channels is $[0, 1]$. Thus, $q^W + q = 1$, and the vector of time fractions $\boldsymbol{q} = (q, q^W)$ can be interpreted also as a probability vector. Let $\boldsymbol{Q}$ be the set of all such vectors;

(iv) R^W is the throughput of Wi-Fi network per time unit, when the network is in Wi-Fi access mode;

(v) R_W^L and R_L^W are respectively the throughputs for LTE-U and Wi-Fi networks per time unit, when operating in joint Wi-Fi and LTE-U access mode, where both networks access the channel simultaneously. It is natural to assume that extra interference in the network reduces its throughput, i.e., $R_L^W \leq R^W$;

(vi) T^W is the total throughput of the Wi-Fi network, i.e., $T^W(\boldsymbol{q}) = q^W R^W + q R_L^W$;

(vii) T^L is the total throughput of LTE-U network, i.e., $T^L(\boldsymbol{q}) = q R_W^L$.

If $q = 0$, we call such strategy $\boldsymbol{q}$ as a *channel on/off strategy*, i.e., when the networks do not jointly access the channels simultaneously, but only one does. If $q > 0$, we call such a strategy $\boldsymbol{q}$ as a *channel sharing strategy*, i.e., when the networks might access the channel simultaneously. As an aside remark, we note that different resource sharing strategies could be applied for different network optimization problems, see for example, channel sharing [16], bandwidth scanning [17], spectrum coexistence [18], time sharing [19], and channel sharing in selfish transmission for low SNR mode [20] and general SNR mode [21].

When allocating the fraction of time for these access modes, the issue of fairness naturally arises as improving one system's throughput typically won't lead to improvement in the other system. A survey of different fairness concepts used in wireless communication is given in [22]. Generally, in the fairness problem, there are n agents and each of them has an utility that depend on its share of a common resource. The problem then involves allocating such shares fairly between the agents. Of course, the result depends on the criterion for fairness, and maxmin is one such criterion that is popular. We focus though on α-fairness, which allows one to consider, in a uniform scale, such separate fairness concepts as bargaining (for $\alpha = 1$) and maxmin (for α tending to infinity). In [23], a general problem for fair throughput assignment (α-*fairness*) was suggested. In [24], a problem of bargaining over the fair trade-off between secrecy and throughput in OFDM communications was solved. In [25], in the context of LTE-A networks, cooperative bargaining solutions for resource allocation over the available component carriers was investigated as well as the optimal tradeoff between fairness and efficiency, which allows one to select the most appropriate solution over all of the available carriers. In [26], bargaining problem over fair performing dual radar and communication task was solved. In [27], fair power control was applied for resources allocation by base station under uncertainty. In [28], a Baysian game of fair power allocation is solved.

In our scenario, the α-fair channel access problem for LTE-U and Wi-Fi networks to a shared channel, we consider the expected throughput of networks as utilities. Then, the α-fair channel access protocol $\boldsymbol{q}_\alpha$ is given as solution of the following problem:

$$\text{maximize } v_\alpha(\boldsymbol{q}), \text{ subject to } \boldsymbol{q} \in \boldsymbol{Q} \tag{1}$$

with

$$v_\alpha(\boldsymbol{q}) = \begin{cases} \left(T^W(\boldsymbol{q})\right)^{1-\alpha}/(1-\alpha) + \left(T^L(\boldsymbol{q})\right)^{1-\alpha}/(1-\alpha), & \alpha \neq 1, \\ \ln\left(T^W(\boldsymbol{q})\right) + \ln\left(T^L(\boldsymbol{q})\right), & \alpha = 1, \end{cases}$$

$$= \begin{cases} \dfrac{(q^W R^W + q R_L^W)^{1-\alpha}}{1-\alpha} + \dfrac{(q R_W^L)^{1-\alpha}}{1-\alpha}, & \alpha \neq 1, \\ \ln(q^W R^W + q R_L^W) + \ln(q R_W^L), & \alpha = 1. \end{cases}$$

Theorem 1. *The optimal α-fair strategy $\boldsymbol{q}_\alpha$ is given as follows:*

$$q_\alpha^W = \begin{cases} 0, & R_W^L\left(R_L^W/R_W^L\right)^\alpha + R_L^W \geq R^W, \\ 1 - \dfrac{\dfrac{R_L^W}{R^W - R_L^W}\left(\dfrac{R_W^L}{R^W - R_L^W}\right)^{1/\alpha-1}}{1 + \left(\dfrac{R_W^L}{R^W - R_L^W}\right)^{1/\alpha-1}}, & R_W^L\left(R_L^W/R_W^L\right)^\alpha + R_L^W < R^W, \end{cases} \tag{2}$$

$$q_\alpha = \begin{cases} 1, & R_W^L\left(R_L^W/R_W^L\right)^\alpha + R_L^W \geq R^W, \\ \dfrac{R^W}{R^W - R_L^W}\dfrac{\left(\dfrac{R_W^L}{R^W - R_L^W}\right)^{1/\alpha-1}}{1 + \left(\dfrac{R_W^L}{R^W - R_L^W}\right)^{1/\alpha-1}}, & R_W^L\left(R_L^W/R_W^L\right)^\alpha + R_L^W < R^W. \end{cases} \tag{3}$$

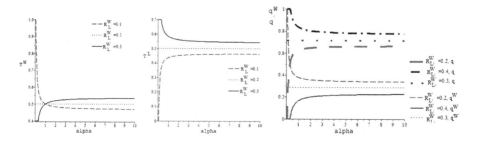

Fig. 1. Wi-Fi throughput (left), LTE-U throughput (middle) and fraction of time for only Wi-Fi network's a access and joint access the channels (right) as functions on fairness coefficient.

Thus, Theorem 1 allows one to find the optimal fraction of time for joint access the channels for each fixed fairness coefficient. Figure 1 illustrate that an increase in fairness coefficient leads generally to loss in throughput for one network and to gains in throughput for the other network with $R_W = 1$, $R_W^L = 0.7$ and $R_L^W = 0.2, 0.3, 04$. This puts forward a question: *which of these α to assign to make the most fair access the channels for the network.* Figure 1 also illustrate that under some condition the optimal fraction of time for join access to the network can be indifferent to fairness coefficient. In the considered example, if $R_L^W = 0.3$ then $q_\alpha = 5/7$ and $q_\alpha^W = 2/7$ for any α. This puts forward the other question: *to find the condition for which the optimal strategy is indifferent to fairness coefficient.*

4   Properties of the optimal solution

In this section, first we find the condition on network parameters when the optimal fair solution is indifferent to fairness coefficient. Second, we simplify the optimal solution for two boundary cases of the fairness coefficient: (a) *cooperative solution* (i.e., for $\alpha = 0$) and (b) *maxmin solution* (i.e., for α tending to infinity).

Corollary 1. *The optimal α fair strategy $\boldsymbol{q}_\alpha$ does not depend on α if and only if the following condition holds:*

$$R_L^W \geq R_W^L \text{ and } R_L^W + R_W^L \geq R^W. \tag{4}$$

Moreover, under condition (4) α fair strategy $\boldsymbol{q}_\alpha$ is constant and equals to $(0, 1)$.

In particular, if condition (4) holds then maxmin solution and cooperative solution coincide. That is why, below we assume that (4) does not hold. This assumption holds if and only if one of the inequalities in (4) does not hold, i.e.,

$$R_L^W < R_W^L \text{ or } R_L^W + R_W^L < R^W. \tag{5}$$

Corollary 2. *(a)* **Cooperative solution** q_0 *is given as follows:*

$$(q_0, q_0^W) = \begin{cases} (1,0), & R_L^W + R_W^L > R^W, \\ any\ (q_0, q_0^W)\ such\ that\ q_0 + q_0^W = 1 & R_L^W + R_W^L = R^W, \\ (0,1), & R_L^W + R_W^L < R^W, \end{cases}$$

with payoffs

$$(T_0^L, T_0^W) = \begin{cases} (R_W^L, R_L^W), & R_L^W + R_W^L > R^W, \\ \left(q_0 R_W^L, R^W - q_0(R_L^W - R^W)\right), & R_L^W + R_W^L = R^W, \\ (0, R^W), & R_L^W + R_W^L < R^W. \end{cases}$$

(b) **Maxmin solution** q_∞ *is unique and given as follows:*

$$(q_\infty, q_\infty^W) = \begin{cases} (1,0), & R_L^W \geq R_W^L, \\ \left(\dfrac{R^W}{R^W + R_W^L - R_L^W}, \dfrac{R_W^L - R_L^W}{R^W + R_W^L - R_L^W}\right), & R_L^W < R_W^L \end{cases}$$

with payoffs

$$(T_\infty^L, T_\infty^W) = \begin{cases} (R_W^L, R_L^W), & R_L^W \geq R_W^L, \\ (T_\infty, T_\infty), & R_L^W < R_W^L \end{cases}$$

with $T_\infty = (R^W R_W^L)/(R^W + R_W^L - R_L^W)$.

In particular, (a) for $R_L^W + R_W^L = R^W$, a continuum cooperative solution might arise returning the same total payoff R^W to both networks, (b) for $R_L^W < R_W^L$ both the Wi-Fi and LTE-U networks have the same maxmin payoff.

5 Trade-off Value for the Fairness Coefficient

In previous section we shown that if condition (5) holds then there is a continuum of fair solution. Namely, a solution q_α per an α. Then, a question arises: *which of these* $\{q_\alpha : \alpha \geq 0\}$ *is the most fair?* To answer on this question we are going to apply Nash bargaining approach [29].

First let us define the feasibility set L of all the fair throughput for the networks, i.e., $L := \{(T_\alpha^L, T_\alpha^W) : \alpha \geq 0\}$.

Theorem 2. *(a) The feasibility set L is a line in plane (T^L, T^W) connecting two boundary points $A_0 := (T_0^W, T_0^W)$ and $A_\infty := (T_\infty^W, T_\infty^L)$. Moreover, this line can be given in closed form as follows:*

$$T_\alpha^W = R^W - \frac{R^W - R_L^W}{R_W^L} T_\alpha^L \qquad (6)$$

with

$$(A_0, A_\infty) = \begin{cases} \left((R_W^L, R_L^W), (T_\infty, T_\infty)\right), & (R_W^L, R_L^W) \in I, \\ \left((0, R^W), (T_\infty, T_\infty)\right), & (R_W^L, R_L^W) \in II, \\ \left((0, R^W), (R_W^L, R_L^W)\right), & (R_W^L, R_L^W) \in III, \end{cases} \qquad (7)$$

where $I := \{(R_W^L, R_L^W) : R_L^W + R_W^L > R^W, R_W^W < R_W^L\}$, $II := \{(R_W^L, R_L^W) : R_L^W + R_W^L < R^W, R_L^W < R_W^L\}$ and $III := \{(R_W^L, R_L^W) : R_L^W + R_W^L < R^W, R_L^W > R_W^L\}$.

(b) An increase in one expected throughput yields a corresponding decrease in the other throughput.

(c) Each point of the feasibility set $\mathbf{L}$ is Pareto optimal.

Second let $(T_d^L, T_d^W) = \left(\min\{T_0^L, T_\infty^L\}, \min\{T_0^W, T_\infty^W\}\right)$ be the point composed by minimal throughput in $\mathbf{L}$ of each network. This point can be considered as a disagreement point [29]. Then, the Nash bargaining solution [29] is given as the unique solution of the following optimization problem:

$$\text{maximize } NP(T^L, T^W) := (T^L - T_d^L)(T^W - T_d^W),$$
$$\text{subject to } (T^L, T^W) \in \mathbf{L}, \tag{8}$$

where NP is called the Nash product.

Theorem 3. (a) The bargaining throughput (T^L, T^W) e is uniquely given as follows:

$$T^L = T_d^L/2 + (R^W - T_d^W)R_W^L/(2(R^W - R_L^W)) \tag{9}$$

with T^W given by (6), and

$$(T_d^L, T_d^W) = \begin{cases} (T_\infty, R_L^W), & (R_W^L, R_L^W) \in I, \\ (0, T_\infty), & (R_W^L, R_L^W) \in II, \\ (0, R_L^W), & (R_W^L, R_L^W) \in III. \end{cases} \tag{10}$$

(b) The bargaining value for the fairness coefficient is uniquely defined as follows:

$$\alpha = 1/\left(1 - \ln\left(\frac{R_W^L R^W}{T^L(R^W - R_L^W)} - 1\right)/\ln\left(\frac{R_W^L}{R^W - R_L^W}\right)\right). \tag{11}$$

As a numerical illustration, we consider the basic example of a single Wi-Fi and a single LTE-U cell operating on the same channel with $B = 1$, $\alpha_W = \beta_W = 1$, $\alpha_L = \beta_L = 1$, $N_W = N_L = 0.1$, $h_{WW} = h_{WL} = 1$ and $h_{LW} = h_{LW} = 0.5$. Figure 2 illustrates the bargaining fairness coefficient and the corresponding Wi-Fi throughput and LTE-U throughput as functions of the transmission power p_W of the Wi-Fi cell for a fixed transmission power $p_L = 1$ for the LTE-U cell in the example we considered previously. This figure shows that an increase in the transmission power of the Wi-Fi unit leads to an increase in Wi-Fi throughput and to a decrease in the LTE-U throughput. By (10), (T_d^L, T_d^W) has a jump at switching between cases I and II while it is continuous at switching between cases I and II, while p_W varies. In the considered basic example, switching between cases I and II, while p_W varies, takes place at $p_W = 0.6$, and this yields a jump increase in Wi-Fi throughput and to a jump decrease in LTE-U throughput. Switching between cases II and III, while varying p_W, takes place at $p_W = 1.0$.

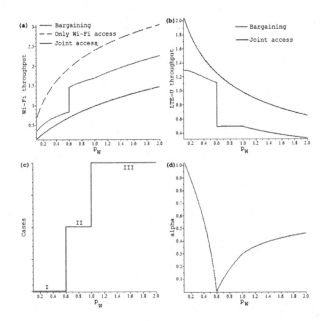

Fig. 2. (a) Wi-Fi throughput, (b) LTE-U throughput, (c) cases and (d) fairness coefficient as functions of the transmission power p_W of the Wi-Fi unit with constant transmission power p_L for the LTE-U cell with $p_L = 1$.

The bargaining fairness coefficient is decreasing and becomes zero at $p_W = 0.6$. Thus, at this point the bargaining fair solution becomes a cooperative solution. Further increase in the transmission power leads to an increase in the bargaining fairness coefficient.

Figure 3 illustrates the bargaining fairness coefficient and the corresponding Wi-Fi throughput and LTE-U throughput as functions of the transmission power p_L for the LTE-U cell for a fixed transmission power $p_W = 1$ associated with the Wi-Fi cell. In this situation, switching between cases II and III can only be observed while p_L varies. This switch takes place at $p_L = 1.0$. It is interesting to note that *both cells might achieve a gain* resulting from an increase in the LTE-U cell's transmission power, namely, throughput for both systems increase after the switching point $p_L = 1.0$ as one increases p_L.

6 Conclusions

In this paper, we examined the problem of how Wi-Fi and LTE-U networks should share access to a wireless channel. As a criterion for such joint access, α-fairness over the expected throughput was used in this paper since it provides a unifying framework for examining a wide-range of fairness schemes. Following this approach, we arrived at a formal derivation for the continuum of fair protocols (an optimal protocol per α). We also developed an approach for choosing

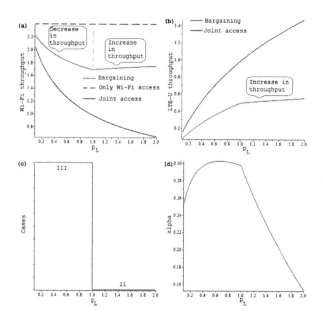

Fig. 3. (a) Wi-Fi throughput, (b) LTE-U throughput, and (c) cases and (d) fairness coefficient as functions of the transmission power p_L of the LTE-U cell with constant transmission power p_W for the Wi-Fi system with $p_W = 1$.

the unique time-sharing protocol that arises as the solution to the Nash bargaining problem over all the α-fair protocols. Under such a protocol, an increase in throughput gains for one network leads to a decrease in performance for the other network, and thus we may consider this protocol as optimal from the point of view of each network. Also, we have shown that such a time-sharing protocol, in spite of the interference between signals, can lead to a gain for both networks under an increase of the transmission power to one of them. Finally, the approach taken in this paper is general and may be applied to examine other problems involving a shared resource.

Appendix

Proof of Theorem 1. First, let us define the Lagrangian $L_\omega(\boldsymbol{q}) = v_\alpha(\boldsymbol{q}) + \omega(1 - q^W - q)$, where ω is a Lagrange multiplier. By Kuhn-Tucker Theorem, for the optimal strategy $\boldsymbol{q}$ (which is a probability vector) the following conditions have to hold:

$$\frac{R^W}{(q^W R^W + q R^W_L)^\alpha} \begin{cases} = \omega, & q^W > 0, \\ \leq \omega, & q^W = 0, \end{cases} \tag{12}$$

$$\frac{R^W_L}{(q^W R^W + q R^W_L)^\alpha} + \frac{R^L_W}{(q R^L_W)^\alpha} \begin{cases} = \omega, & q > 0, \\ \leq \omega, & q = 0. \end{cases} \tag{13}$$

Hence, the boundary strategy $\boldsymbol{q} = (1,0)$ cannot be optimal. Thus only two cases have to be considered (a) $q^W = 0$ and $q > 0$, and (b) $q^W > 0$ and $q > 0$.

(a) Let $q^W = 0$ and $q > 0$. Then, $q = 1$, and, by (12) and (13),

$$R^W/(R_L^W)^\alpha \leq \omega = R_L^W/(R_L^W)^\alpha + R_W^L/(R_W^L)^\alpha.$$

This is equivalent to the upper condition in (2) and (3), and (a) follows.

(b) Let $q^W > 0$ and $q > 0$. normalsize Then, by (12) and (13),

$$\frac{R^W}{(q^W R^W + q R_L^W)^\alpha} = \frac{R_L^W}{(q^W R^W + q R_L^W)^\alpha} + \frac{R_W^L}{(q R_W^L)^\alpha}.$$

Thus,

$$q^W R^W + q R_L^W = q R_W^L \left((R^W - R_L^W)/R_W^L\right)^{1/\alpha}. \tag{14}$$

Since $q + q^W = 1$, (14) implies that q and q^W has to be given by bottom line of (2) and (3). While the condition $0 < q, q^W < 1$ is equivalent to the bottom condition in (2) and (3), and the result follows. ∎

Proof of Corollary 1. Due to if $R_L^W < R_W^L$ then $\left(R_L^W/R_W^L\right)^\alpha < 1$ for and $\alpha \geq 0$, and if $R_L^W > R_W^L$ then $\left(R_L^W/R_W^L\right)^\alpha > 1$ for and $\alpha \geq 0$, the result follows from Theorem 1. ∎

Proof of Theorem 2. Recall that $T^W = q^W R^W + q R_L^W$ and $T^L = q R_W^L$. This, jointly with the fact that $\boldsymbol{q}$ is a probability vector, implies (6), and the result follow.

Proof of Theorem 3. Substituting (6) into Nash product given by (8) turns (8) into a maximization problem for a quadratic polynom on T^L, and (9) follows. Since $R_W^L q_\alpha = T^L$, by (3), the bargaining value for the fairness coefficient is uniquely defined by (11), and the result follows. ∎

References

1. Barbagallo, P., McElgunn, T.: 3Gpp set to study lte over unlicensed technology, sowing new spectrum battles. Bloomberg BNA, 10 September 2014. http://www.bna.com/3gpp-set-study-n17179894699/
2. Cavalcante, A.M., Almeida, E., Vieira, R.D., Choudhury, S., Tuomaala, E., Doppler, K., Paiva, R.C.D., De Sousa Chaves, F., Abinader, F.: Performance evaluation of LTE and Wi-Fi coexistence in unlicensed bands. In: IEEE Vehicular Technology Conference (VTC Spring), pp. 1–6 (2013)
3. Abinader, F.M., Almeida, E.P.L., Chaves, F.S., Cavalcante, A.M., Vieira, R.D., Paiva, R.C.D., Sobrinho, A.M., Choudhury, S., Tuomaala, E., Doppler, K., Sousa, V.A.: Enabling the coexistence of LTE and Wi-Fi in unlicensed bands. IEEE Commun. Mag. **52**, 54–61 (2014)
4. Liu, F., Bala, E., Erkip, E., Yang, R.: A framework for femtocells to access both licensed and unlicensed bands. In: 9th International Symposium on Modeling and Optimization in Mobile, Ad Hoc and Wireless Networks (WiOpt), pp. 407–411 (2011)

5. Kwan, R., Pazhyannur, R., Seymour, J., Chandrasekhar, V., Saunders, S.R., Bevan, D., Osman, H., Bradford, J., Robson, J., Konstantinou, K.: Fair co-existence of licensed assisted access LTE (LAA-LTE) and Wi-Fi in unlicensed spectrum. In: 7th Computer Science and Electronic Engineering Conference (CEEC), pp. 13–18 (2015)

6. Hajmohammad, S., Elbiaze, H., Ajib, W.: Fine-tuning the femtocell performance in unlicensed bands: case of wifi co-existence. In: International Wireless Communications and Mobile Computing Conference (IWCMC), pp. 250–255 (2014)

7. Yun, S., Qiu, L.: Supporting WiFi and LTE co-existence. In: IEEE Conference on Computer Communications (INFOCOM), pp. 810–818 (2015)

8. Liu, F., Erkip, E., Beluri, M., Yang, R.: Small cell traffic balancing over licensed and unlicensed bands. IEEE Trans. Veh. Technol. **64**, 5850–5865 (2015)

9. Hajmohammad, S., Elbiaze, H.: Unlicensed spectrum splitting between femtocell and wifi. In: IEEE International Conference on Communications (ICC), pp. 1883–1888 (2013)

10. Jian, Y., Shih, C.-F., Krishnaswamy, B., Sivakumar, R.: Coexistence of Wi-Fi and LAA-LTE: experimental evaluation, analysis and insights. In: IEEE International Conference on Communications (ICC), pp. 10387–10393 (2015)

11. Cano, C., Leith, D.: Coexistence of WiFi and LTE in unlicensed bands: a proportional fair allocation scheme. In: IEEE International Conference on Communications (ICC), pp. 10350–10355 (2015)

12. Sagari, S., Seskar, I., Raychaudhuri, D.: Modeling the coexistence of lte and wifi heterogeneous networks in dense deployment scenarios. In: IEEE International Conference on Communications (ICC), pp. 10363–10368 (2015)

13. Raychaudhuri, D., Baid, A.: NASCOR: network assisted spectrum coordination service for coexistence between heterogeneous radio systems. IEICE Trans. Commun. **E97-B**, 251–260 (2014)

14. Sagari, S., Baysting, S., Sahay, D., Seskar, I., Trappe, W., Raychaudhuri, D.: Coordinated dynamic spectrum management of LTE-U and Wi-Fi networks. In: IEEE International Conference on Dynamic Spectrum Access Network (DySPAN) (2015)

15. Garnaev, A., Sagari, S., Trappe, W.: Fair channel sharing by Wi-Fi and LTE-U networks with equal priority. In: Noguet, D., Moessner, K., Palicot, J. (eds.) CrownCom 2016. LNICSSITE, vol. 172, pp. 91–103. Springer, Cham (2016). doi:10.1007/978-3-319-40352-6_8

16. Yerramalli, S., Jain, R., Mitra, U.: Coalitional games for transmitter cooperation in mimo multiple access channels. IEEE Trans. Sig. Process. **62**, 757–771 (2014)

17. Garnaev, A., Trappe, W.: A bandwidth monitoring strategy under uncertainty of the adversary's activity. IEEE Trans. Inform. Forensics Secur. **11**, 837–849 (2016)

18. Garnaev, A., Trappe, W.: One-time spectrum coexistence in dynamic spectrum access when the secondary user may be malicious. IEEE Trans. Inf. Forensics Secur. **10**, 1064–1075 (2015)

19. Marina, N., Arslan, G., Kavcic, A.: A power allocation game in a four node relay network: An upper bound on the worst-case equilibrium efficiency. In: International Conference on Telecommunications (ICT), pp. 1–6 (2008)

20. Altman, E., Avrachenkov, K., Garnaev, A.: Transmission power control game with SINR as objective function. In: Altman, E., Chaintreau, A. (eds.) NET-COOP 2008. LNCS, vol. 5425, pp. 112–120. Springer, Heidelberg (2009). doi:10.1007/978-3-642-00393-6_14

21. Altman, E., Avrachenkov, K., Garnaev, A.: Closed form solutions for water-filling problems in optimization and game frameworks. Telecommun. Syst. **47**, 153–164 (2011)

22. Huaizhou, S., Prasad, R.V., Onur, E., Niemegeers, I.G.M.M.: Fairness in wireless networks: Issues, measures and challenges. IEEE Commun. Surv. Tutorials **16**, 5–24 (2014)
23. Mo, J., Walrand, J.: Fair end-to-end window-based congestion control. IEEE/ACM Trans. Networking **8**, 556–567 (2000)
24. Garnaev, A., Trappe, W.: Bargaining over the fair trade-off between secrecy and throughput in OFDM communications. IEEE Trans. Inf. Forensics Secur. **12**, 242–251 (2017)
25. Militano, L., Niyato, D., Condoluci, M., Araniti, G., Iera, A., Bisci, G.M.: Radio resource management for group-oriented services in LTE-A. IEEE Trans. Veh. Technol. **64**, 3725–3739 (2015)
26. Garnaev, A., Trappe, W., Petropulu, A.: Bargaining over fair performing dual radar and communication task. In: 50th Asilomar Conference on Signals, Systems, and Computers, Pacific Grove, CA, pp. 47–51 (2016)
27. Altman, E., Avrachenkov, K., Garnaev, A.: Fair resource allocation in wireless networks in the presence of a jammer. Perform. Eval. **67**, 338–349 (2010)
28. Garnaev, A., Trappe, W.: Fair resource allocation under an unknown jamming attack: a Bayesian game. In: IEEE Workshop on Information Forensics and Security (WISP), Atlanta, GA, pp. 227–232 (2014)
29. Fudenberg, D., Tirole, J.: Game Theory. MIT Press, Boston (1991)

Time-Dependent SIR Analysis in Shopping Malls Using Fractal-Based Mobility Models

Yuri Orlov[1], Elisabeth Kirina-Lilinskaya[1], Andrey Samuylov[2,3],
Aleksandr Ometov[2,3], Dmitri Moltchanov[2,3(✉)], Yulia Gaimamaka[3,4],
Sergey Andreev[2], and Konstantin Samouylov[3,4]

[1] Department of Kinetic Equations, Keldysh Institute of Applied Mathematics,
Moscow, Russia
[2] Department of Communications Engineering,
Tampere University of Technology, Tampere, Finland
dmitri.moltchanov@tut.fi
[3] Department of Applied Probability and Informatics,
RUDN University, Moscow, Russia
[4] Institute of Informatics Problems, FRC CSC RAS, Moscow, Russia

Abstract. Shopping malls are characterized by a high density of users.
The use of direct device-to-device (D2D) communications may significantly mitigate the load imposed on the cellular systems in such environments. In addition to high user densities, the communicating entities are
inherently mobile with very specific attractor-based mobility patterns.
In this paper, we propose a model for characterizing time-dependent
signal-to-interference ratio (SIR) in shopping malls. Particularly, we use
fractional Fokker-Plank equation for modeling the non-linear functional
of the average SIR value, defined on a stochastic fractal trajectory. The
evolution equation of the average SIR is derived in terms of fractal motion
of the tagged receiver and the interfering devices. We illustrate the use
of our model by showing that the behavior of SIR is generally varying
for different types of fractals.

Keywords: Mobility · Fractal stochastic motion · Time-dependent
metrics · Average SIR evolution · Device-to-device communications

1 Introduction

The numbers of hand-held devices have dramatically increased over the past
decade [1] followed by a tremendous traffic growth brought along by the emerging
spectrum consumers [2]. This trend is expected to be continued towards new growing markets of wearable electronics that integrate into the next generation (5G)
communications paradigm [3,4] and embrace direct device-to-device (D2D) connectivity as part of it [5]. At the same time, International Telecommunications

© IFIP International Federation for Information Processing 2017
Published by Springer International Publishing AG 2017. All Rights Reserved
Y. Koucheryavy et al. (Eds.): WWIC 2017, LNCS 10372, pp. 16–25, 2017.
DOI: 10.1007/978-3-319-61382-6_2

Union (ITU) has recently provided 5G requirements including several novel scenarios [6] and offered some considerations on the mobility support [7].

While the communications quality in conventional outdoor scenarios could be improved by increasing the density of wireless infrastructure nodes [8], the indoor case is much more sensitive to wireless interference [9]. It is particularly important for the enclosed offices, corridors within their premises, and shopping malls [10]. The typical environments of this type could be described as cubical areas with different sizes where the user movement is fairly predictable [11,12].

The mobility pattern of a user in the indoor premises depends on a number of factors dictating the movement trajectory, that is, it is not an entirely "random" process. A typical example of the corresponding mobility model could be described as a relatively slow movement of users inside the shops and faster movement between them. Similar behavior is observed in the dynamics of fractal sets, see, e.g., [13,14]. The analysis of stable connectivity between mobile devices in such a scenario could be considered as a challenging task in the context of 5G communications systems [15–18].

A conventional way to study the performance of wireless networks is to utilize the tools of stochastic geometry. According to this approach, the locations of communicating entities are represented by employing a static spatial point process. The metrics of interest, such as the signal-to-interference ratio (SIR) moments and distributions, are then obtained by analyzing the distances between a receiver, a transmitter, and other communicating stations [19,20]. This approach is however limited to static time-averaged measures. At the same time, accounting for the fact that communication sessions are always of finite durations, time-dependent metrics are often of interest.

In this work, a model for analyzing the dynamics of the connection quality indicator, the so-called SIR, is developed. We consider the case, where the movement of transceivers is considered as a set of paths that are random on a fractal set process. The proposed model is a representative abstraction for the aforementioned office or shopping mall scenario, where the fractal set represents the attraction points of a shopping mall (specific areas inside the shops). The analysis is based on the Fokker-Planck equation with fractional spatial derivatives. The model considers the distribution of coordinates for the receiver, the transmitter, and the interfering stations, as well as the level of mobility, and translates them into the average SIR evolution in time. The use of fractal sets allows to explicitly include the effects of spatial movement correlation thus adequately representing the real-life scenarios. We illustrate the application of the proposed model and demonstrate that the behavior of SIR is generally varying for different types of fractals, that is, spatial correlation of the movement process.

The rest of this work is organized as follows. The system model, metrics of interest, and SIR trajectory modeling are introduced in Sect. 2. The formulation for the time evolution of SIR is derived in Sect. 3. The numerical results and the conclusions are drawn in the last section.

2   System Model and Preliminaries

2.1   Random Walks over Fractal Sets

We consider a set of users moving over the fractal set. We focus on a tagged receiver and N interfering stations. The random movement trajectory of a user is represented as a random walk on the three-dimensional fractal set [17]. Fokker-Planck equation with fractional derivatives that represents the distribution function on such sets has been studied in [21]. One of the crucial assumptions in our model is that the motion of each spatial coordinate is small movements independent. With this assumption at hand, the evolution equation in the one-dimensional coordinate space can be considered as a basic model. This equation is the following

$$\frac{\delta f(x,t)}{\delta t} + \frac{\delta(u(x,t)f(x,t))}{\delta x} = B(t)\frac{\delta^{2\alpha} f(x,t)}{\delta x^{2\alpha}}, \tag{1}$$

where $f(x,t)$ is a continuously-differentiable function of the coordinates and time, $u(x,t)$ is the so-called drift velocity, which is defined as the average velocities of the respective two-dimensional distribution [17], that is,

$$u(x,t)f(x,t) = \int F(x,v,t)v dv, \tag{2}$$

where the integration is performed over the entire mobility domain by considering the boundary conditions.

The non-negative diffusion coefficient $B(t)$ is determined as

$$B(t) = \frac{1}{2}\frac{d\sigma^2}{dt} - cov_{x,u}(t), \tag{3}$$

where

$$\sigma^2(t) = \int (x - \overline{x}(t))^2 f(x,t)dx, \quad \overline{x}(t) = \int x f(x,t)dx. \tag{4}$$

The value of the fractal derivative α, $\alpha \in (0,1)$ is a parameter of the model. This fractional order derivative has several different interpretations. It can be considered in terms of Riemann-Liouville, Riesz-Feller, Caputo-Gerasimov, Grunwald-Letnikov considerations, see, e.g. [22] for further details. The function f is required to belong to L_p, $p > 1$ class with respect to x. For example, a symmetric Riesz-Feller derivative on $[a,b]$ is represented as

$$\frac{\delta^{2\alpha} f(x)}{\delta x^{2\alpha}} = \frac{1}{2cos\pi\alpha}\Big[(D_{a+}^{2\alpha}f)(x) + (D_{b-}^{2\alpha}f)(x)\Big], \tag{5}$$

where

$$\begin{aligned}
(D_{a+}^{2\alpha}f)x &= \frac{1}{\Gamma(m - 2\alpha)}\frac{d^m}{dx^m}\int_a^x f(y)(x - y)^{m-2\alpha-1}dy, \\
(D_{b+}^{2\alpha}f)x &= \frac{(-1)^m}{\Gamma(m - 2\alpha)}\frac{d^m}{dx^m}\int_x^b f(y)(y - z)^{m-2\alpha-1}dy,
\end{aligned} \tag{6}$$

and $m = [Re(2\alpha)] + 1$. We consider the special case, $m = 2$, in (1).

The fractional derivative term is conventionally represented as a convolution with an appropriate (usually singular) kernel as

$$\frac{\delta^{2\alpha} f(x)}{\delta x^{2\alpha}} = \int K_\alpha(x - y) f(y) dy. \tag{7}$$

We consider the following kernel

$$K_\alpha(z) = \frac{1}{\Gamma(1 - 2\alpha)} \frac{1}{z^{2\alpha}}.$$

The kinematic Eq. (1) can be solved numerically for any initial condition $f(x,t)|_{t=0} = p(x)$ and boundary conditions. We choose the probability of zero flow at the border as the latter.

The coordinates density distribution of users corresponding to the motion over a fractal random trajectory is described in the n-dimensional space ($n = 1, 2, 3$) by the following equation

$$\frac{\delta f(x,t)}{\delta t} + div_x\big(u(x,t)f(x,t)\big) = B(t) \int K\big(|x - y|\big) f(y,t) dy, \tag{8}$$

where $u(x,t), B(t)$, and $K(z)$ are known.

In the following sections, we study the dependence of the mean SIR value, when the mobility trajectories are samples generated from the distribution evolving according to (8).

2.2 SIR Trajectories

Observe that SIR is a functional depending on the distance between the moving points at consecutive time instants. The coordinates $(x_i(t), y_i(t), z_i(t))$ determine the position of the ith point of the trajectory in a convex three-dimensional region, $V \subset \Re^3$. The distance between the points on two randomly chosen trajectories in three-dimensional space is defined by

$$r_{ij}^2 = \big(x_i(t) - x_j(t)\big)^2 + \big(y_i(t) - y_j(t)\big)^2 + \big(z_i(t) - z_j(t)\big)^2. \tag{9}$$

Let the function of interest, depending on the distance between the spatial points and belonging to different trajectories, be denoted as $\phi_{ij} = \phi(r_{ij})$. In wireless networks, this function is known as the path loss model. In this paper, we assume the commonly accepted power law path loss model [23], i.e.,

$$\phi_{ij} \equiv \phi(r_{ij}) = \frac{1}{r_{ij}^2}. \tag{10}$$

In a field of $N + 2$ moving users, let us tag two users – one receiver and one transmitter. The remaining nodes are considered as interfering stations. The mean SIR at the tagged receiver at each time instance is given by

$$S(r_1, r_2) = \frac{\phi_{ij}}{\sum_{j=3}^{N+2} \phi_{1j}}, \tag{11}$$

where the sum in the denominator is the average value of the interference defined by using the distances between the receiver and the interfering stations, i.e.,

$$U(r,t) = \int_V \phi(|r - r'|) f(r', t) dr', \tag{12}$$

and $f(r', t)$ is the density function of distances.

Then, the mean SIR in (11) can be written as

$$q(t) = \int S(r, t) f(r, t) dr. \tag{13}$$

The mean value of SIR in (13) depends on the average environmental field $U(r, t)$ in (12). This value is a non-linear function over the trajectory sample.

2.3 Examples

The typical movement trajectories in the example obtained for the fractal walk on a two-dimensional ternary Cantor set are shown in Fig. 1(a). The modeling algorithm is described in [17]. As one may observe, the mobility process of users comprises many short travels around the attractor points as well as occasional long-distant movements. This process closely resembles the basic properties of real measurements of user mobility in shopping malls, see, e.g., [24].

The associated SIR trajectory produced by using (13) for a randomly tagged receiver is shown in Fig. 1(b). For this illustration, the number of interfering stations, N, was set to 100. Note that the autocorrelation being a result of spatial correlation caused by a fractal set is clearly observed.

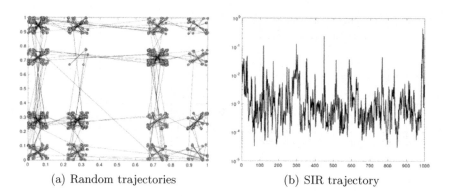

(a) Random trajectories   (b) SIR trajectory

Fig. 1. Ternary Cantor set in $\Re^2$.

3 Formulation for Evolution of Average SIR

In this section, we derive the main result of this paper, which is the evolution equation for the average value of SIR as specified in (13). Recall that the coordinates density of the communicating users evolves according to (8). Using (12)–(13), we obtain

$$N\frac{dq}{dt} = \int_V \frac{\phi(r)}{U(r,t)}\frac{\delta f(r,t)}{\delta t}dr - \int_V \frac{\phi(r)}{U^2(r,t)}\frac{\delta U(r,t)}{\delta t}f(r,t)dr. \qquad (14)$$

Substituting the first term of (14) with the derivative $\frac{\delta f(r,t)}{\delta t}$ obtained from (8), we proceed as

$$\int \frac{\phi(x)}{U(x,t)}\frac{\delta f(x,t)}{\delta t} = -\int \frac{\phi(x)}{U(x,t)}div_x\big(u(x,t)f(x,t)\big)dx+$$
$$+ B(t)\int \frac{\phi(x)}{U(x,t)}\int K\big(|x-y|\big)f(y,t)dydx =$$
$$= \int grad_x\Big(\frac{\phi(x)}{U(x,t)}\Big)u(x,t)f(x,t)dx+ \qquad (15)$$
$$+ B(t)\int \frac{\phi(x)}{U(x,t)}\int K\big(|x-y|\big)f(y,t)dydx.$$

The Eq. (15) is obtained by using the integration by parts if the distribution function vanishes on the boundary of the region. We further denote the result of the scalar product $u(x,t)grad_x\Big(\frac{\phi(x)}{U(x,t)}\Big)$ by $P(x,t)$. Due to the SIR heterogeneity and the existence of non-zero density function for the speed change, the offset in the average value of SIR is estimated by the scalar product. The second term with the altered integration order from the last line of (15) is obtained in the form of SIR fractal derivative by applying Fubini's theorem as $R(y,t) = D^{2\alpha}\big(\frac{\phi}{U}\big)(y,t)$. Hence, we now have

$$\int \frac{\phi(x)}{U(x,t)}\frac{\delta f(x,t)}{\delta t}dx = \int \Big(P(x,t)+B(t)D^{2\alpha}\Big(\frac{\phi}{U}\Big)(x,t)\Big)f(x,t)dx. \qquad (16)$$

The second term in (8) can be treated similarly. Particularly, substituting derivative in (12) with $\delta f/\delta t$ of (8), the derivative $\delta U/\delta t$ becomes

$$\frac{\delta U(r,t)}{\delta t} = \int \phi\big(|r-r'|\big)\frac{\delta f(r',t)}{\delta t}dr' =$$
$$- \int \phi\big(|r-r'|\big)div_{r'}\big(u(r',t)f(r',t)\big)dr'+ \qquad (17)$$
$$+ B(t)\int \phi\big(|r-r'|\big)K\big(|r'-r''|\big)f(r'',t)dr'dr''.$$

Integrating the first term by parts, we have

$$
\begin{aligned}
\int \phi(|r - r'|) div_{r'}\big(u(r', t)f(r', t)\big) dr' &= \\
&= \int grad_{r'}\phi(|r - r'|)\big(u(r', t)f(r', t)\big) dr' = \\
&= \int grad_r\phi(|r - r'|)\big(u(r', t)f(r', t)\big) dr' = \\
&= div_r \int grad_r\phi(|r - r'|)\big(u(r', t)f(r', t)\big) dr' = div_r J(r, t).
\end{aligned}
\tag{18}
$$

The resulting equation is obtained by replacing the derivative of $\phi(|r - r'|)$ with respect to r' by the derivative with respect to r. The second term in (8) for the fractional derivative of the $L_p([a, b])$ class of functions is represented as [22]

$$
\int_a^b h(x)\big(D_{a+}^{2\alpha}g\big)(x)dx = \int_a^b h(x)\big(D_{b-}^{2\alpha}h\big)(x)dx.
$$

As a result, we obtain

$$
\int \phi(|r - r'|) K(|r' - r''|) f(r'', t) dr' dr'' = \big(D^{2\alpha}U\big)(x, t).
\tag{19}
$$

Next, by combining (17) and (19), we arrive at

$$
\frac{\delta U(x, t)}{\delta t} = B(t)\big(D^{2\alpha}U\big)(x, t) - div_x J(x, t).
\tag{20}
$$

The latter result demonstrates that the average SIR changes over time in the same manner as the distribution function of coordinates defined in (8). Note that these changes occur with the same coefficients as in (8).

The final equation for the evolution of the mean value of SIR is obtained with (14) and (16)–(20), thus resulting in

$$
\begin{aligned}
N\frac{dq}{dt} &= \int \Big(P(x, t) + B(t)D^{2\alpha}\big(\frac{\phi}{U}\big)(x, t)\Big) f(x, t) dx - \\
&\quad - B(t)\int \frac{\phi(x)}{U^2(x, t)}\Big((D^{2\alpha}U)(x, t)\Big) f(x, t) dx + \\
&\quad + \int \frac{\phi(x)}{U^2(x, t)}\big(div_x J(x, t)\big) f(x, t) dx.
\end{aligned}
\tag{21}
$$

Observe that the above equation non-linearly depends on the distribution function of the coordinates of points. Therefore, to quantitatively assess each contribution of the term in (21) to the SIR values, the numerical simulations are required. The result in (21) is a general model of the average SIR values evolution in diffusion approximation, and it is valid not only for fractal but also for the general non-stationary random walks.

Despite the complex structure of (21), it still provides a possibility to make qualitative conclusions regarding the contributions of each component. In the scenario with $\alpha = 1$ in (8), there is an interesting special case of the so-called zero-flow average SIR. Recall that in the classic Fokker-Planck equation, the term $f(r,t)u grad\left(\frac{\phi}{U}\right)$ after integration over the region of interest represents the drift. Here, the term $\frac{\phi}{U^2}div(J)$ corresponds to the similar effect, but it affects the average field $U(r,t)$. These two terms have different signs, i.e., the total transport effect of the drift $u\nabla\frac{\phi}{U} + \frac{\phi}{U^2}div(J)$ after integration with the density $f(r,t)$ might be negligible, e.g., the average scalar product of the drift and the radius-vector ur is equal to zero. In this case, the SIR changes are due to the diffusion effect only.

4   Numerical Results and Conclusions

The result in (21) offers an opportunity for faster modeling of the average SIR values. In our numerical illustration, we consider two empirical density functions corresponding to two various Hausdorff dimensions of the fractal sets, Cantor square with $2\alpha_1 = \ln 8/\ln 3$ and Sierpinski triangle with $2\alpha_2 = \ln 3/\ln 2$. As one may observe in Fig. 2(a), these functions exhibit drastically different properties.

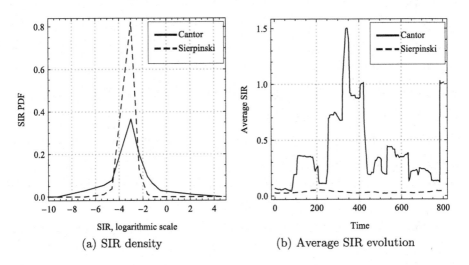

(a) SIR density   (b) Average SIR evolution

Fig. 2. SIR densities and average SIR evolution in time for two fractals.

The average SIR values for the sample lengths of 100 are demonstrated in Fig. 2(b). The number of interfering nodes in this example is $N = 10$. Note that the Cantor fractal results have much more variability implying that an appropriate choice of the underlying model is of paramount importance.

In this paper, starting from the kinematic equation that describes the evolution of the coordinates density of users, we obtained the equation for the time evolution of the average SIR value experienced at the receiver of interest that moves in a field of N interfering stations. The proposed formalism allows to address a wide variety of specific movement patterns including non-stationary ones. We then proceeded with obtaining the kinematic equation for the average SIR value. The resulting expression, although being complex, can be solved in special cases of interest, e.g., when the stationary density of the coordinates is considered. However, even in the general case of non-stationary movement, it allows for the qualitative assessment.

Our numerical illustration highlights that the average SIR evolution is drastically affected by the choice of the fractal set. One practical problem emphasized by our study is to determine the appropriate value of α for different environments. In realistic scenarios, i.e., for applications in shopping malls, stadiums, etc., there is not only non-zero time-dependent drift corresponding to e.g., a lunch break or other intermissions when the flow of people changes significantly, but also specific collective effects with non-local interaction.

Acknowledgments. The publication was financially supported by the Ministry of Education and Science of the Russian Federation (the Agreement number 02.a03.21.0008) and RFBR (research projects No. 16-07-00766, 17-07-00845).

References

1. Ericsson: Ericsson mobility report: on the pulse of the networked society, July 2015
2. Nordrum, A.: Popular internet of things forecast of 50 billion devices by 2020 is outdated. IEEE Spectrum 18 (2016)
3. Dohler, M., Nakamura, T., Osseiran, A., Monserrat, J.F., Marsch, P.: 5G Mobile and Wireless Communications Technology. Cambridge University Press, Cambridge (2016)
4. Andreev, S., Gonchukov, P., Himayat, N., Koucheryavy, Y., Turlikov, A.: Energy efficient communications for future broadband cellular networks. Comput. Commun. **35**(14), 1662–1671 (2012)
5. Orsino, A., Militano, L., Araniti, G., Iera, A.: Social-aware content delivery with D2D communications support for emergency scenarios in 5G systems. In: Proceedings of 22th European Wireless Conference European Wireless, VDE, pp. 1–6 (2016)
6. International Telecommunications Union (ITU): Framework and overall objectives of the future development of IMT for 2020 and beyond. Recommendation ITU-R M.2083-0, September 2015
7. International Telecommunications Union (ITU): Minimum requirements related to technical performance for IMT-2020 radio interface(s). DRAFT NEW REPORT ITU-R M.[IMT-2020.TECH PERF REQ], February 2017
8. Ge, X., Tu, S., Mao, G., Wang, C.-X., Han, T.: 5G ultra-dense cellular networks. IEEE Wirel. Commun. **23**(1), 72–79 (2016)
9. Haneda, K., Tian, L., Asplund, H., Li, J., Wang, Y., Steer, D., Li, C., Balercia, T. Lee, S., Kim, Y., et al.: Indoor 5G 3GPP-like channel models for office and shopping mall environments. In: Proceedings of International Conference on Communications Workshops (ICC), pp. 694–699. IEEE (2016)

10. Lin, X., Andrews, J.G., Ghosh, A., Ratasuk, R.: An overview of 3GPP device-to-device proximity services. IEEE Commun. Mag. **52**(4), 40–48 (2014)
11. Galati, A., Djemame, K., Greenhalgh, C.: A mobility model for shopping mall environments founded on real traces. Network. Sci. **2**(1–2), 1–11 (2013)
12. Samuylov, A., Moltchanov, D., Gaidamaka, Y., Begishev, V., Kovalchukov, R., Abaev, P., Shorgin, S.: SIR analysis in square-shaped indoor premises. In: Proceedings of 30th European Conference on Modelling and Simulation, ECMS, pp. 692–697 (2016)
13. Hughes, B., Montroll, E., Shlesinger, M.: Fractal random walks. J. Stat. Phys. **28**(1), 111–126 (1982)
14. Kaye, B.H.: A random walk through fractal dimensions. Wiley, New York (2008)
15. ElSawy, H., Hossain, E., Alouini, M.-S.: Analytical modeling of mode selection and power control for underlay D2D communication in cellular networks. IEEE Trans. Commun. **62**(11), 4147–4161 (2014)
16. ElSawy, H., Hossain, E., Haenggi, M.: Stochastic geometry for modeling, analysis, and design of multi-tier and cognitive cellular wireless networks: a survey. IEEE Commun. Surv. Tutorials **15**(3), 996–1019 (2013)
17. Orlov, Y., Fedorov, S., Samuylov, A., Gaidamaka, Y., Molchanov, D.: Simulation of devices mobility to estimate wireless channel quality metrics in 5G network. In: Proceedings of the ICNAAM, pp. 19–25 (2016)
18. Samuylov, A., Ometov, A., Begishev, V., Kovalchukov, R., Moltchanov, D., Gaidamaka, Y., Samouylov, K., Andreev, S., Koucheryavy, Y.: Analytical performance estimation of network-assisted D2D communications in urban scenarios with rectangular cells. Transactions on Emerging Telecommunications Technologies (2015)
19. Baccelli, F., Błaszczyszyn, B., et al.: Stochastic geometry and wireless networks: volume I. Found. Trends Network. **4**(1–2), 1–312 (2010)
20. Haenggi, M.: Stochastic Geometry for Wireless Networks. Cambridge University Press, Cambridge (2012)
21. Zenyuk, D.A., Mitin, N.A., Orlov, Y.N.: Random walks modeling on Cantor set. In: Preprints of the Keldysh Institute of Applied Mathematics, pp. 31–18 (2013)
22. Samko, S.G., Kilbas, A.A., Marichev, O.I.: Fractional Integrals and Derivatives. 1993. Gordon & Breach Science Publishers, Yverdon (1987)
23. Rappaport, T.S., et al.: Wireless Communications: Principles and Practice, vol. 2. Prentice Hall PTR New Jersey, Upper Saddle River (1996)
24. Galati, A., Greenhalgh, C.: Human mobility in shopping mall environments. In: Proceedings of the Second International Workshop on Mobile Opportunistic Networking, pp. 1–7. ACM (2010)

Analysis and Performance Evaluation of SDN Queue Model

Samuel Muhizi[1], Gregory Shamshin[1], Ammar Muthanna[1], Ruslan Kirichek[1,2(✉)],
Andrei Vladyko[1], and Andrey Koucheryavy[1]

[1] The Bonch-Bruevich State University of Telecommunication, 22 Prospekt Bolshevikov,
St. Petersburg, Russia
[2] Peoples' Friendship University of Russia (RUDN University), 6 Miklukho-Maklaya Street,
Moscow, Russia
samno1@yandex.ru, reignsword@gmail.com, ammarexpress@gmail.com,
{kirichek,vladyko}@sut.ru, akouch@mail.ru

Abstract. In this paper, we present an Openflow-SDN based network visualization and performance evaluation model that helps in network designing and
planning to examine how networks' performance will be affected as the traffic
loads and network utilization change. To achieve the aimed goal, as a research
method, we used AnyLogic Multimethod simulation tool. This is a first of its kind
where SDN performance evaluation is based on queuing model simulation to
monitor change of average packet processing time for various network parameters. Using presented in this work SDN model, network administrators and plan-
ners can better predict likely performance changes arising from traffic variation.
This allows them to make prompt decisions to prevent seemingly small issues
from becoming major bottlenecks.

Keywords: SDN controller · OpenFlow switch · Flow table · AnyLogic · Queue
model · Simulation model · Analytical model

1 Introduction

The concept of software defined networks (SDN) is a growing trend in the domain of
telecommunication network management, that offers to remove restrictions on existing
infrastructure networks by dividing the network control plane and data plane by means
of transferring control functions of network forwarding devices (routers, switches) in
the applications running on a single entity (controller), which makes the network more
centralized and improves its software management capabilities [1–3]. This simplifies
the network usability and significantly reduces the network system cost and equipment.
However, all these benefits come with a non-negligible problem in network functionality
such as packet transmission rate and network performance, which are attributed to the
use of the controller as a remote system to manage all transmission network devices
(switches). The controller can manage one or several OpenFlow switches; it contains a
network operating system that provides network services for low-level network

© IFIP International Federation for Information Processing 2017
Published by Springer International Publishing AG 2017. All Rights Reserved
Y. Koucheryavy et al. (Eds.): WWIC 2017, LNCS 10372, pp. 26–37, 2017.
DOI: 10.1007/978-3-319-61382-6_3

management, network segments, and the state of network elements and applications, implementing a high-level network management and data flow. Each controller has at least one application that manipulates switches connected to it, and can provide a global view of physical network topology under the controller management. The idea of creating a unified, independent from the network equipment manufacturer [4–6], program-controlled interface between the controller and the network transport infrastructure is defined in the OpenFlow standards and OpenFlow protocol [7], which allows users to define and control with whom, under what conditions and with what quality can interact on the network. OpenFlow is an open standard, which describes the remote management requirements to a switch that supports OpenFlow protocol. According to OpenFlow standard specifications, the interaction between the controller and the switch is carried out through OpenFlow protocol. Each switch must contain one or more flow tables and group tables, which perform packet lookups and forwarding, and support OpenFlow secured channel to a remote controller. Each flow table in the switch contains a set of flow entries; each flow entry consists of match fields, counters, and a set of instructions to apply to matching packets. Data management in OpenFlow is carried out, not on the individual packet level, but at the level of their packet streams. Rules are dynamic. Packets which have no match are sent to the controller (packet in). Controller creates appropriate rule and sends packet back to switch (packet out) for processing. The rule in the switch is set only for the first packet, and then all the other packets of the flow use it.

In this paper is introduced an analytical and simulation analysis of an SDN model where the network is modelled as queueing system to capture the time costs associated with the controller and the switches activities.

2 SDN Modelling Concept

In case of SDN deployment, the controller usually manages multiple OpenFlow switches each connecting group of host. The typical SDN architecture is shown in Fig. 1. The OpenFlow switch packet forwarding procedure is shown in Fig. 2. The switch performs flow table lookups on packet arrivals. If the lookups succeed, the switch applies the actions in the matched table entry to the packet, typically forwarding it to the specified interface. Otherwise, the packet is supposed to belong to a new flow, and the switch sends it to the upper SDN controller in a packet-in message. The controller defines the corresponding flow rules and sends to the switch it in packet-out or flow_mod packet. As a result, the SDN controller receives a flow of packet-in messages from each Open-Flow switch.

In the modern telecommunication networks, at the same time are processed different types of information (video and audio information, compressed video and audio information, and less sensitive to delay data) with different quality of service levels. Accordingly, traffic management methods play a key role in its optimization and to minimize network losses. To create a network model (topology and its elements characteristics), and dynamically simulate its operation mechanism, optimize its characteristics, analyze and manage the traffic, evaluate the performance bounds undoubtedly, it is more than necessary to use more advanced multimethod modeling and simulation tools for complex systems research [8–10].

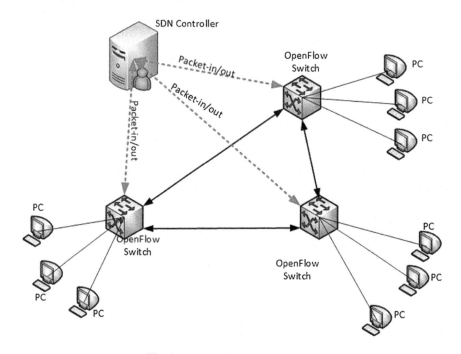

Fig. 1. A typical SDN architecture.

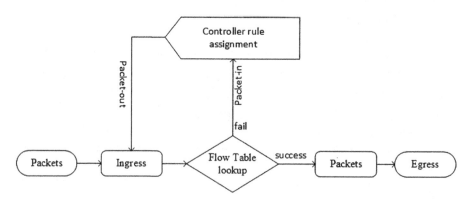

Fig. 2. The packet forwarding of an OpenFlow switch.

3 Model Description

Operations on SDN switches with different data transmission processes control capabilities lead to a significant delay change for flow entries configuration. In order to simulate different general arrival processes, describe and monitor flow exchange between the controller and the switches we presented the SDN as queuing system. The SDN queue model was built using AnyLogic Multimethod simulation modeling tool and is shown in Fig. 3. AnyLogic is a very flexible [11], dynamic simulation tool with high flexibility and unlimited expansion possibilities due to operating system-independant native Java environment. AnyLogic runs on Windows, Mac and Linux. AnyLogic initially designed to support multiple modeling methods and their arbitrary combinations it offers the modeler more flexibility than any other existing simulation tools by the means of reduction of development costs and -times: fast integration of pre-configured simulation elements with the comprehensive object libraries. It makes it possible to design various types of models with one single tool: agent-based, system dynamic, event-oriented, continuous or dynamic models.

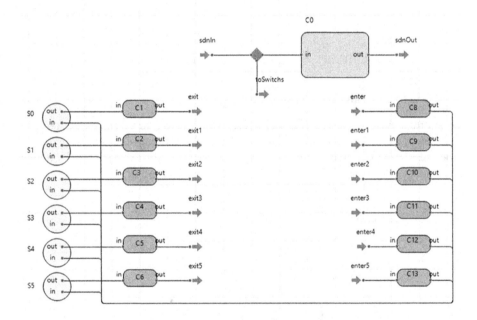

Fig. 3. SDN conceptual model in AnyLogic 7.3.6

The SDN model consists of 6 OpenFlow switches and a controller. Switches are numbered from S0 to S5 and the controller C0. Source objects generate incoming traffic with a specified arrival rate at each and every switch connected to controller.

3.1 Packet Processing on the Switch

Figure 4 shows a switch packet forwarding process. For a more accurate simulation of the information exchanges between the switch and the controller, incoming packets were divided in four categories; each of them is determined by specified occurrence probability. From the switch, packets to the controller are sent using specific communication channel. In this model the channel processing unit is built that it doesn't significantly affect on the overall evaluation of the model performance.

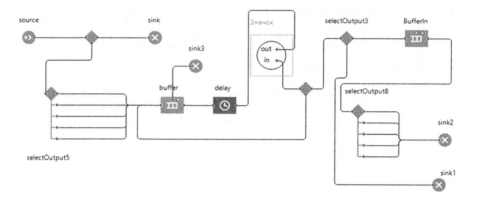

Fig. 4. OpenFlow switch conceptual model in AnyLogic 7.3.6

3.2   Packet Processing on the Controller

The controller manipulates multiple switches and therefore the arrival process of packets at the switch characterizes the packet processing rate at the controller. Accordingly, the model describes the packet transmission process management at different SDN model service units. We consider SDN controller model as shown in Fig. 5.

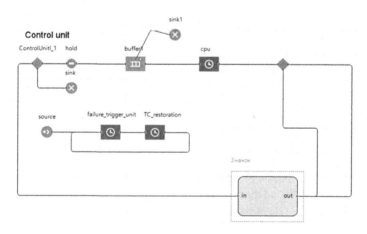

Fig. 5.   SDN controller conceptual model in AnyLogic 7.3.6

Packet-in and Packet-out messages.   On the arrival of a packet, the switch checks the flow table for presence of the destination address. The SDN model contains a central unit (controller) manage flow entries in the network. In this model switch numbers match the source and destination addresses. Forwarding rules and destination addresses for arrival packets are defined for each packets category arriving at the switch. First packet of the category is sent to the controller for rules and destination address confirmation. The controller determines the rule to assign to the respective packet category and sends it back as a response to the packet-in message to the switch. The switch then forwards the packet to the destination address. The next packets in this category then use the assigned forwarding rules and there won't be any requirement to confirm addresses. The designed controller model works with a given failure rate. If the failure occurs, the entire flow entry checking process starts again.

4   Modeling Results

Using the above described SDN model, we measured the network load, therefore for given parameters a network administrator can simply establish required quality of service for different network nodes by managing the delay, delay variation (jitter), bandwidth, and packet loss parameters on a network. Experimental processes were performed using a modeling time of 3600 s, and the memory size for the simulation was set to 1024 MB.

To illustrate the impact of various network parameters on the quality of service exist multiple options: arrival traffic rate changes, trigger sequences of packet-in messages, controller performance impact on the overall packet processing mean time, etc. In Fig. 6, the plot highlights the switch average packet processing time for different packet arrival rates. The more packet arrival rate increases, the more average packet processing time increases, thus the increasing arrival traffic rate will result in network throughput decrease. The plot can be used to determine the maximum load that the network should reach before its performance is compromised. For a fixed packet arrival rate on each switch we measured changes in average packet processing time while increasing the controller service rate. The simulation results are shown in Fig. 7. The average packet processing time significantly decreases as controller service rate increases. Therefore, the network throughput increases.

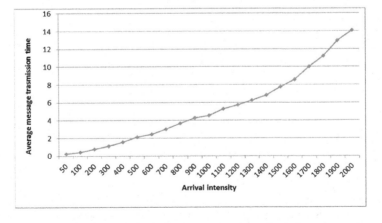

Fig. 6. Average packet processing time of switches

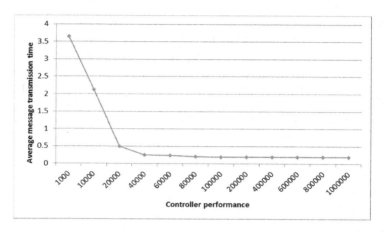

Fig. 7. Average packet processing time of the controller

5   Analytical Modeling Framework

To assert the described above SDN model we proceeded to analytically evaluation of OpenFlow switch. For that we considered a queueing model [12] for OpenFlow-based SDN [13–15] as illustrated in Fig. 8. The switches and controller are modelled as queueing systems to capture the time cost of the network.

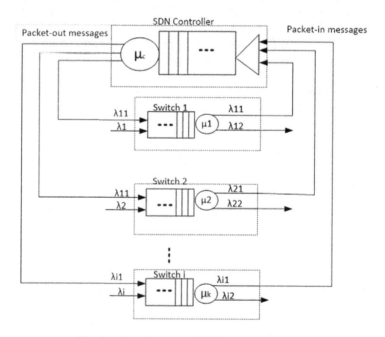

Fig. 8. OpenFlow-based SDN queueing model

We assume that the packet arrival process in the network follows a Poisson Process and the average arrival rate in the ith switch is λi, and that the arrivals in different switches are independent. Packets may not match any flow entries in which case they are forwarded to the controller via packet-in message. This happens with probability ρ. Packets are classified into two classes, both of them arrive in a Poisson process with an average arrival rate of λi*ρ and λi*(1 − ρ). The packet service time of switches is assumed to follow an exponential distribution, and the expected service time is denoted 1/μ1 and 1/μ2, respectively. The mean service time of packet-in messages in the controller is denoted 1/μc. This service time includes the transmission time from the switches to the controller. In other, to simplify this model, both controller and switches are powerful enough for the traffic in the network, and there is no limit on the queue capacity. We queue all the packets arriving at a switch in a single queue instead of a separate queue on each ingress port and all the packets are processed in order of arrival time. Moreover, we assume that when the first packet of a connection arrives at a switch, the controller installs a flow entry. After that, the remaining packets arrive to the switch and are forwarded directly. We also assume that all the switches in our model have the same service rate, and the packet-in messages arrive the switch following a Poisson process.

5.1 OpenFlow Switch Performance

The flow entry matching for all packets are assumed to be independent and the packet processing time can be supposed to follow an exponential distribution. With the assumptions above the performance of OpenFlow switches can be modeled as a M/H2/1 queue,

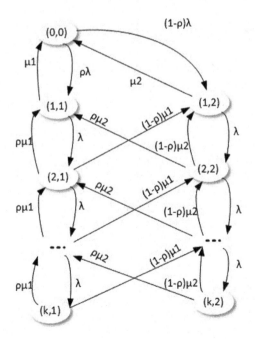

Fig. 9. State transition diagram of an M/H2/1 queue

which means packets arrive at the ith switch at rate λi and the service time is represented by a two-phase hyperexponential distribution. The state transition diagram of this queue is shown in Fig. 9. With probability ρ, a packet receives service at rate $\mu 1$, while with probability $1 - \rho$ it receives service at rate $\mu 2$.

A state is represented by a pair (a, b), where a is the total number of packets in the switch and b is the current service phase. In our case b can be only 1 or 2. The stationary distribution of this queue in the ith switch can be obtained by applying the Matrix-Geometric Method. We denote the stationary probability vector $\pi(i)$ as

$$\pi^{(i)} = (\pi_0^{(i)}, \pi_1^{(i)}, \pi_2^{(i)}, \dots, \pi_{k,}^{(i)} \dots) \tag{1}$$

$$\rho = \frac{\lambda}{\mu} < 1 \tag{2}$$

$$\pi_0 = 1 - \rho \tag{3}$$

$$\pi_k = (1 - \rho)\rho^k \tag{4}$$

Where $\pi k(i)$ is the probability of k packets in the ith switch.

Then the mean number of packets in the queueing system can be computed as:

$$N_i = \sum_{k=0}^{\infty} k\pi_k^{(i)} \tag{5}$$

$$N_i = \sum_{k=0}^{\infty} (1 - \rho)\rho^k \tag{6}$$

For k = 0, the product is zero then we can start the sum from k = 1

$$N_i = (1 - \rho) \sum_{k=1}^{\infty} k\rho^k = (1 - \rho)\rho \sum_{k=1}^{\infty} k\rho^{k-1} \tag{7}$$

Since $k\rho^{k-1}$ can be written as $k\rho^{k-1} = \frac{d\rho^k}{d\rho}$

Respectively

$$N_i = (1 - \rho)\rho \sum_{k=1}^{\infty} \frac{d}{d\rho}\rho^k$$
$$= (1 - \rho)\rho\frac{d}{d\rho}\left(\sum_{k=1}^{\infty} \rho^k\right) \tag{8}$$

Since $\sum_{k=1}^{\infty} \rho^k = \sum_{k=0}^{\infty} \rho^k - 1 = \frac{1}{1 - \rho} - 1 = \frac{\rho}{1 - \rho}$

We can write $N_i = (1 - \rho)\rho\frac{d}{d\rho}\left(\frac{\rho}{1 - \rho}\right) \tag{9}$

$$N_i = \frac{\rho}{1-\rho}, \tag{10}$$

where $(\rho < 1)$ and $\rho = \dfrac{\lambda}{\mu}$

$$N_i = \frac{\lambda}{\mu - \lambda} \tag{11}$$

According to Little's law, the average packet processing time in the ith switch can be given by

$$W_{si} = \frac{1}{\lambda}N_i = \frac{1}{\mu - \lambda} \tag{12}$$

The mean packet processing time of switches can be given by

$$W_s = \sum_{i=1}^{n} \frac{\lambda_i}{\sum_{i=1}^{n} \lambda_i} W_{si} \tag{13}$$

5.2   Numerical Evaluation and Results

With the mentioned analytical framework and presented outcomes, we can evaluate the proposed queuing model with different parameters and report the upper bound of packet processing delay in the SDN switch. The switch average packet processing time is shown

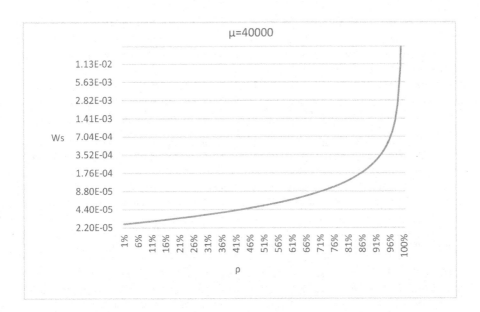

Fig. 10. Average packet processing time of switch

in Fig. 10. As packets arrival rate at the switch increases, the average packet processing time constantly increases. It sharply increases to the maximum when packet arrival rate is closer to the switch processing service rate. That matches the time when the switch runs out of resources and can't perform packet processing service.

6 Conclusion

Understanding the performances and limitations of OpenFlow-based SDN is a prerequisite of its deployment. In this work we have proposed a model for an OpenFlow SDN based on queueing theory, and resolves its average packet processing time. We reviewed the optimal parameter combinations of Openflow switch and controller to allow future network architects and administrators to be able to compute an upper bound estimation of packet delay and buffer requirement of SDN switches and controller for a given packet arrival rate.

Furthermore, we will extend the analysis to the possibility of SDN network from a single controller to the case of controller clusters to evaluate how much switches a given controller can handle in a network without much performance loss.

Acknowledgment. The publication was financially supported by the Ministry of Education and Science of the Russian Federation (the Agreement number 02.a03.21.0008), RFBR according to the research project No. 17-57-80102 "Small Medium-sized Enterprise Data Analytics in Real Time for Smart Cities Applications".

References

1. Kreutz, D., Ramos, F., Verissimo, P., Rothenberg, C., Azodolmolky, S., Uhlig, S.: Software-defined networking: a comprehensive survey. Proc. IEEE **103**(1), 14–76 (2015)
2. Xia, W., Wen, Y., Foh, C., Niyato, D., Xie, H.: A survey on software-defined networking. IEEE Commun. Surv. Tutorials **17**(1), 27–51 (2015)
3. Alsmadi, I.M., AlAzzam, I., Akour, M.: A systematic literature review on software-defined networking. In: Alsmadi, I.M., Karabatis, G., AlEroud, A. (eds.) Information Fusion for Cyber-Security Analytics. SCI, vol. 691, pp. 333–369. Springer, Cham (2017). doi:10.1007/978-3-319-44257-0_14
4. Liu, L., Zhang, D., Tsuritani, T., et al.: Field trial of an openflow-based unified control plane for multilayer multigranularity optical switching networks. J. Lightwave Technol. **31**(4), 506–514 (2013)
5. Jararweh, Y., Al-Ayyoub, M., Darabseh, A., Benkhelifa, E., Vouk, M., Rindos, A.: SDIoT: a software defined based internet of things framework. J. Ambient Intell. Humanized Comput. **6**(4), 453–461 (2015)
6. Kirichek, R., Vladyko, A., Paramonov, A., Koucheryavy, A.: Software-defined architecture for flying ubiquitous sensor networking. In: 19th International Conference on Advanced Communication Technology (ICACT), pp. 158–162 (2017)
7. OpenFlow. https://www.opennetworking.org/sdn-resources/openflow
8. Kirichek, R., Vladyko, A., Zakharov, M., Koucheryavy, A.: Model networks for internet of things and SDN. In: 18th International Conference on Advanced Communication Technology (ICACT), pp. 76–79. IEEE (2016)

9. Vladyko, A., Muthanna, A., Kirichek, R.: Comprehensive SDN testing based on model network. In: Galinina, O., Balandin, S., Koucheryavy, Y. (eds.) NEW2AN/ruSMART -2016. LNCS, vol. 9870, pp. 539–549. Springer, Cham (2016). doi:10.1007/978-3-319-46301-8_45

10. Vladyko, A., Letenko, I., Lezhepekov, A., Buinevich, M.: Fuzzy model of dynamic traffic management in software-defined mobile networks. In: Galinina, O., Balandin, S., Koucheryavy, Y. (eds.) NEW2AN/ruSMART -2016. LNCS, vol. 9870, pp. 561–570. Springer, Cham (2016). doi:10.1007/978-3-319-46301-8_47

11. Borshchev, A.: The Big Book of Simulation Modeling: Multimethod Modeling with Anylogic 6. AnyLogic North America (2013)

12. Dombacher, C.: Queueing Models for Call Centres. BDD (2010)

13. Xiong, B., Yang, K., Zhao, J., Li, W., Li, K.: Performance evaluation of OpenFlow-based software-defined networks based on queueing model. Comput. Netw. **102**, 174–183 (2016)

14. Xiong, B., Peng, X., Zhao, J.: A concise queuing model for controller performance in software-defined networks. J. Comput. **11**(3), 232–237 (2016)

15. Ansell, J., Seah, W., Ng, B., Marshall, S.: Making queueing theory more palatable to SDN/ OpenFlow-based network practitioners. In: IEEE/IFIP Network Operations and Management Symposium (NOMS), pp. 1119–1124 (2016)

Analysis of a Retrial Queue with Limited Processor Sharing Operating in the Random Environment

Sergey Dudin[1,2], Alexander Dudin[1(✉)], Olga Dudina[1,2], and Konstantin Samouylov[2]

[1] Belarusian State University, 4 Nezavisimosti Avenue, 220030 Minsk, Belarus
{dudins,dudin,dudina}@bsu.by
[2] RUDN University, 6 Miklukho-Maklaya Street, 117198 Moscow, Russia
ksam@sci.pfu.edu.ru

Abstract. Queueing system with limited processor sharing, which operates in the Markovian random environment, is considered. Parameters of the system (pattern of the arrival rate, capacity of the server, i.e., the number of customers than can share the server simultaneously, the service intensity, the impatience rate, etc.) depend on the state of the random environment. Customers arriving when the server capacity is exhausted join orbit and retry for service later. The stationary distribution of the system states (including the number of customers in orbit and in service) is computed and expressions for the key performance measures of the system are derived. Numerical example illustrates possibility of optimal adjustment of the server capacity to the state of the random environment.

Keywords: Processor sharing · Markovian arrival process · Random environment

1 Introduction

Processor sharing discipline is widely applied for modelling and analysis of communication systems and networks. For references and examples of real world applications, the recent papers [1,2] can be recommended along with the known surveys [3,4]. Generally speaking, a processor can be shared by infinitely many users. However, in many applications, especially to wireless communication networks, too small share of the bandwidth of the channel assigned to a customer may lead to poor service and its termination due to too long service. Therefore, the **limited** processor sharing is often considered. This kind of processor sharing suggests that the maximal number of users who obtain service simultaneously is fixed. This number is called as the server capacity. Customers arriving when capacity of the server is not exhausted immediately start service with the rate inversely proportional to the number of customers in service.

Y. Koucheryavy et al. (Eds.): WWIC 2017, LNCS 10372, pp. 38–49, 2017.
DOI: 10.1007/978-3-319-61382-6_4

The model considered in this paper has the following features previously not addressed or only partially addressed in the relevant literature.

(1) It is usually assumed that an arriving customer can be lost or queued to the finite or infinite buffer if the capacity of the server is exhausted. In our paper, we assume a more realistic in application to wireless networks scenario that such the arriving customer virtually moves to so-called orbit from which he/she makes the repeated attempts (retrials) to obtain service after the random time intervals. It is well-known that the phenomenon of retrials is typical in wireless communication networks and that analysis of retrial queueing models is more difficult comparing to the queues with buffers, see, e.g., [5].

(2) The customers in service can be impatient. They may leave the server before service completion after an exponentially distributed amount of time the parameter of which depends on the number of customers in service.

(3) We assume that the system operates in the random environment (*RE*). This means that the parameters of the system (pattern of the arrival rate, capacity of the server, intensities of service and impatience rate, etc.) depend on the state of the *RE*. They instantaneously change their values at the moment of a jump of the *RE* to another state. As special case, our model includes the systems with processor sharing and unreliable servers, see, e.g., [1,2,6]. Consideration of the system operating in the *RE* is important for potential applications in wireless networks because the server capacity and other parameters can be changed due to redistribution of the system resources among the existing servers due to many reasons, including the users mobility, noise in radio-channel, etc. We assume that the behavior of the *RE* does not depend on the state of the system while such a dependence is suggested in [7]. However, in that paper capacity of the system does not depend on the state of the *RE* while we allow such a dependence.

(4) As well as in [2], we assume quite general model of arrival process, namely, Markovian arrival process, while the overwhelming majority of existing papers deal with the stationary Poisson arrival process. Model considered in [8] assumes the batch Markovian arrival process. However, the number of customers, which can get service simultaneously, is not limited in that paper.

2 Mathematical Model

We consider a retrial single-server queueing system with limited server (processor) sharing discipline.

All system parameters depend on the state of the *RE*. The *RE* is defined by the stochastic process r_t, $t \geq 0$. This process is an irreducible continuous-time Markov chain with finite state space $\{1, 2, \ldots, R\}$ and the infinitesimal generator H.

The structure of the system under study is presented in Fig. 1.

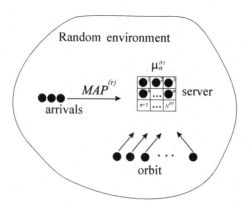

Fig. 1. Queueing system under study

Arrival of customers to the system is described by the process which is a slight generalization of the well-known Markovian Arrival Process (MAP) introduced in [9]. Arrival are governed by the underlying process $\{r_t, \nu_t\}$, $t \geq 0$, where r_t is the state of the RE and the process ν_t with finite state space $\{0, 1, \ldots, W\}$ is defined as follows. Under the fixed state r of the RE the process ν_t behaves as an irreducible continuous-time Markov chain. The sojourn time of this chain in the state ν is exponentially distributed with the positive finite parameter $\lambda_\nu^{(r)}$. When the sojourn time in the state ν expires, with probability $p_0^{(r)}(\nu, \nu')$ the process ν_t jumps to the state ν' without generation of a customer, $\nu, \nu' = \overline{0, W}$, $\nu \neq \nu'$, $r = \overline{1, R}$. With probability $p_1^{(r)}(\nu, \nu')$, the process ν_t jumps to the state ν' with generation of a customer, $\nu, \nu' = \overline{0, W}$, $r = \overline{1, R}$.

The behavior of the arrival process under the fixed state r of the RE is completely characterized by the matrices $D_0^{(r)}$ and $D_1^{(r)}$ defined by the entries

$$(D_0^{(r)})_{\nu,\nu} = -\lambda_\nu^{(r)}, \nu = \overline{0, W}, \ (D_0^{(r)})_{\nu,\nu'} = \lambda_\nu^{(r)} p_0^{(r)}(\nu, \nu'), \ \nu, \nu' = \overline{0, W}, \nu \neq \nu',$$

$$(D_1^{(r)})_{\nu,\nu'} = \lambda_\nu^{(r)} p_1^{(r)}(\nu, \nu'), \ \nu, \nu' = \overline{0, W}, r = \overline{1, R}.$$

The average arrival rate $\lambda^{(r)}$ under the fixed state r of the RE is given as $\lambda^{(r)} = \boldsymbol{\theta}^{(r)} D_1^{(r)} \mathbf{e}$ where $\boldsymbol{\theta}^{(r)}$ is the invariant vector of the stationary distribution of the Markov chain ν_t, $t \geq 0$, under the fixed state r. The vector $\boldsymbol{\theta}^{(r)}$ is the unique solution to the system $\boldsymbol{\theta}^{(r)} D^{(r)}(1) = \mathbf{0}$, $\boldsymbol{\theta}^{(r)} \mathbf{e} = 1$. Here and in the sequel $\mathbf{0}$ is the zero row vector and $\mathbf{e}$ is the column vector of appropriate size consisting of ones.

Let us introduce the following matrices: $\tilde{D}_1 = \text{diag}\{D_1^{(r)}, r = \overline{1, R}\}$, $\tilde{D}_0 = H \otimes I_{W+1} + \text{diag}\{D_0^{(r)}, r = \overline{1, R}\}$, where $\text{diag}\{\ldots\}$ denotes the diagonal matrix with the diagonal entries listed in the brackets.

The averaged (over all states of the RE) intensity of input flow of customers λ is defined as $\lambda = \boldsymbol{\theta} \tilde{D}_1 \mathbf{e}$ where the vector $\boldsymbol{\theta}$ is the unique solution of the system

$$\boldsymbol{\theta}(\tilde{D}_0 + \tilde{D}_1) = \mathbf{0}, \ \boldsymbol{\theta}\mathbf{e} = 1.$$

The squared coefficient of variation c_{var} of intervals between successive arrivals is given as $c_{var} = 2\lambda\boldsymbol{\theta}(-\tilde{D}_0)^{-1}\mathbf{e}-1$. The coefficient of correlation c_{cor} of two successive intervals between arrivals is given as $c_{cor} = (\lambda\boldsymbol{\theta}(-\tilde{D}_0)^{-1}\tilde{D}_1(-\tilde{D}_0)^{-1}\mathbf{e} - 1)/c_{var}$.

Under the fixed state r of the RE, up to $N^{(r)}$ customers can obtain service simultaneously. We call the number $N^{(r)}$ as server capacity under the state r of the RE, $r = \overline{1,R}$. Without the loss of generality, let us assume that the states of the RE are enumerated in ascending order of the server capacity, i.e.,

$$0 \leq N^{(1)} \leq N^{(2)} \leq \cdots \leq N^{(R)}.$$

We permit that the server capacity can be equal to 0 under some states of the RE. This allows us to consider the model with server breakdowns as the partial case of the model under study and use the presented below results for analysis of the model with server breakdowns.

If during an arbitrary customer arrival epoch the number of customers in service is less than $N^{(r)}$, the customer is admitted and starts obtaining service immediately. Otherwise, with probability $q^{(r)}$, $0 \leq q^{(r)} \leq 1$, the arriving customer joins orbit and retries later or leaves the system permanently with the complimentary probability. Each customer from orbit makes the repeated attempts (retrials) to obtain service after an exponentially distributed with the parameter $\gamma^{(r)}$, $0 \leq \gamma^{(r)} < \infty$, time. If the attempt will be successful, i.e. if the number of customers in service is less than $N^{(r)}$, the retrial customer is accepted for service. Otherwise, the retrial customer returns to the orbit with probability $q^{(r)}$ or leaves the system permanently with the complimentary probability.

The service rate of each customer depends on the number of customers that obtain service. Under the fixed state r of the RE, the service rate of each customer is $\mu_n^{(r)}$ where $0 \leq \mu_n^{(r)} < \infty$ if n customers are obtaining service simultaneously, $n = \overline{1,N^{(r)}}$. For the sake of mathematical generality, in our analysis we do not impose any special restrictions on dependence of values $\mu_n^{(r)}$ on n. However, it looks realistic to assume that the increase of the number n of simultaneously serviced customers implies the decrease of the individual service rate, i.e., for each state r of the RE, the following inequalities are satisfied: $\mu_1^{(r)} \geq \mu_2^{(r)} \geq \cdots \geq \mu_{N^{(r)}}^{(r)}$. The most popular in the literature form of dependence of the intensity $\mu_n^{(r)}$ on n is: $\mu_n^{(r)} = \frac{\mu^{(r)}}{n}$ where $\mu^{(r)}$ is the fixed constant characterizing the total service rate under the state r of the RE. This popular dependence satisfies our assumption as a very particular case.

The customers obtaining service can be impatient, i.e., a customer can leave server without completing service. We assume that the individual customer's intensity of impatience also depends on the number of customers in service and if there are n customers in service, each customer leaves the server due to impatience after an exponentially distributed with the parameter $\beta_n^{(r)}$ time, $\beta_n^{(r)} \geq 0$. After leaving the server due to impatience, a customer joins the orbit with probability $a^{(r)}$ or leaves the system permanently with the complimentary probability.

Because the server capacity depends on the state of the RE, the transition of the RE from one state to another one may lead to decreasing the server capacity.

We assume that in the case where n customer obtain service during the epoch of the transition of the RE from the state r to the state r', $r' < r$, and $n > N^{(r')}$, i.e. the "new" server capacity is less that the number of customers in service, then $n - N^{(r')}$ customers are forced to terminate service. If the customer is forced to terminate service, he/she leaves the system permanently with probability $1 - p^{(r)}$, $r = \overline{2, R}$, or joins orbit with the complimentary probability. If the transition of the underlying process of the RE leads to increasing the server capacity, the number of customers that obtain service at the epoch of transition does not change.

Our goal is to analyse the stationary behavior of the described queueing model under the fixed parameters of the RE and system having in mind a possibility of further use of the results of analysis for various managerial purposes, e.g., adjusting the values of capacities $N^{(r)}$ to the corresponding arrival rates and requirements to the maximal admissible value of a customer loss probability.

3   Process of System States and Its Stationary Distribution

Let $i_t, i_t \geq 0$, be the number of customers in orbit, $r_t, r_t = \overline{1, R}$, be the state of the RE, $n_t, n_t = \overline{0, N^{(r_t)}}$, be the number of customers in service, $\nu_t, \nu_t = \overline{0, W}$, be the state of the second component of the underlying process of customers arrivals at the moment t, $t \geq 0$.

It is easy to see that the process $\xi_t = \{i_t, r_t, n_t, \nu_t\}$, $t \geq 0$, is the four dimensional irreducible Markov chain.

We enumerate all states of the Markov chain ξ_t, $t \geq 0$, in the lexicographic order of the components (i, r, n, ν). Let us call the set of the states having value (i, r) of the two first components of the Markov chain as the macro-state (i, r).

Let $\mathbf{A}$ be the generator of the Markov chain ξ_t, $t \geq 0$. It is formed by the blocks $\mathbf{A}_{i,j}$, consisting of the matrices $(A_{i,j})_{r,r'}$ that define (except the diagonal entries of the matrix $\mathbf{A}_{i,i}$) the intensities of the transitions of the Markov chain ξ_t, $t \geq 0$, from the macro-state (i, r) to the macro-state (j, r'), $r, r = \overline{1, R}$. The diagonal entries of the matrix $\mathbf{A}_{i,i}$ are negative. The modulus of each element defines the intensity of departing from the corresponding state of the Markov chain ξ_t, $t \geq 0$.

Let us introduce the following notation.

- I is an identity matrix, O is a zero matrix of appropriate dimension;
- $\otimes$ is the symbol of Kronecker's product of matrices;
- $\bar{W} = W + 1$;
- $\hat{N} = \max\{N^{(R)} - N^{(1)}, 1\}$;
- E_r^-, $r = \overline{1, R}$, is the square matrix of size $N^{(r)} + 1$ with all zero entries except the subdiagonal entries $(E_r^-)_{n,n-1}$, $n = \overline{1, N^{(r)}}$, which are equal to 1;
- $\hat{I}_r$, $r = \overline{1, R}$, is the diagonal matrix of size $N^{(r)} + 1$ having the form $\hat{I}_r = \text{diag}\{0, \ldots, 0, 1\}$;

- E_r^+, $r = \overline{1, R}$, is the square matrix of size $N^{(r)} + 1$ with all zero entries except the overdiagonal entries $(E_r^+)_{n,n+1}$, $n = \overline{0, N^{(r)} - 1}$, which are equal to 1;
- M_r, $r = \overline{1, R}$, is the diagonal matrix of size $N^{(r)} + 1$ having the form $M_r = \mathrm{diag}\{n\mu_n^{(r)}, n = \overline{0, N^{(r)}}\}$;
- B_r, $r = \overline{1, R}$, is the diagonal matrix of size $N^{(r)} + 1$ having the form $B_r = \mathrm{diag}\{n\beta_n^{(r)}, n = \overline{0, N^{(r)}}\}$;
- $P_{r,r'}$, $r = \overline{1, R}$, $r' = \overline{r + 1, R}$, is the matrix of size $(N^{(r)} + 1) \times (N^{(r')} + 1)$ that has the form $P_{r,r'} = (I_{N^{(r)}+1} | O)$, i.e., $P_{r,r'}$ is obtained from the identity matrix $I_{N^{(r)}+1}$ by supplementing it from the right by zero matrix of the corresponding size;
- $p^{(r)}(n, k)$, $0 \leq n \leq k$, is the probability that n customers join the orbit and $k - n$ customers leave the system permanently when the state of the RE was r and k customers are forced to terminate service. This probability is defined as $p^{(r)}(n, k) = C_k^n (1 - p^{(r)})^{k-n} (p^{(r)})^n$, $k = \overline{1, \tilde{N}}$;
- $Z_{r,r'}^{(n)}$, $r = \overline{1, R}$, $r' = \overline{1, r - 1}$, $n = \overline{0, \tilde{N}}$, is the matrix of size $(N^{(r)} + 1) \times (N^{(r')} + 1)$ that has the following non-zero entries:

$$(Z_{r,r'}^{(0)})_{l,l} = 1,\ l = \overline{0, N^{(r')}},\ (Z_{r,r'}^{(n)})_{l,N^{(r')}} = p^{(r)}(n, l - N^{(r')}),\ l = \overline{N^{(r')} + 1, N^{(r)}}.$$

Lemma 1. *The generator* $\mathbf{A}$ *has the following block structure:*

$$\mathbf{A} = \begin{pmatrix} \mathbf{A}_{0,0} & \mathbf{A}_{0,1} & \mathbf{A}_{0,2} & \cdots & \mathbf{A}_{0,\tilde{N}} & O & O & \cdots \\ \mathbf{A}_{1,0} & \mathbf{A}_{1,1} & \mathbf{A}_{1,2} & \cdots & \mathbf{A}_{1,\tilde{N}} & \mathbf{A}_{1,\tilde{N}+1} & O & \cdots \\ O & \mathbf{A}_{2,1} & \mathbf{A}_{2,2} & \cdots & \mathbf{A}_{2,\tilde{N}} & \mathbf{A}_{2,\tilde{N}+1} & \mathbf{A}_{2,\tilde{N}+2} & \cdots \\ \vdots & \vdots & \vdots & \ddots & \vdots & \vdots & \vdots & \ddots \end{pmatrix}. \tag{1}$$

The non-zero blocks $\mathbf{A}_{i,j}$, $i, j \geq 0$, *are defined as follows:*

- $\mathbf{A}_{i,i} = (\mathbf{A}_{i,i})_{r,r'}, r, r' = \overline{1, R}$, $i \geq 0$, *where*

$$(\mathbf{A}_{i,i})_{r,r} = I_{N^{(r)}+1} \otimes D_0^{(r)} + ((1 - q^{(r)})\hat{I}_r + E_r^+) \otimes D_1^{(r)} - (M_r(I - E_r^-) +$$

$$+ B_r(I - (1 - a^{(r)})E_r^-) + i\gamma^{(r)}(I_{N^{(r)}+1} - q^{(r)}\hat{I}_r)) \otimes I_{\bar{W}} + (H)_{r,r}I_{(N^{(r)}+1)\bar{W}},$$

$$(\mathbf{A}_{i,i})_{r,r'} = (H)_{r,r'}Z_{r,r'}^{(0)} \otimes I_{\bar{W}}, r' < r,\ (\mathbf{A}_{i,i})_{r,r'} = (H)_{r,r'}P_{r,r'} \otimes I_{\bar{W}}, r' > r.$$

- $\mathbf{A}_{i,i+n} = \mathbf{A}_n^+ = (\mathbf{A}_n^+)_{r,r'}, r, r' = \overline{1, R}$, $i \geq 0$, *where*

$$(\mathbf{A}_n^+)_{r,r} = \delta_{n,1}(q^{(r)}\hat{I}_r \otimes D_1^{(r)} + a^{(r)}B_r E_r^- \otimes I_{\bar{W}}),\ n = \overline{1, \tilde{N}},$$

$\delta_{i,j}$ *indicates the Kronecker delta,*

$$(\mathbf{A}_n^+)_{r,r'} = (H)_{r,r'}Z_{r,r'}^{(n)} \otimes I_{\bar{W}}, r = \overline{1, R}, r' = \overline{1, r - 1},$$

$$(\mathbf{A}_n^+)_{r,r'} = O, r = \overline{1, R}, r' = \overline{r + 1, R}, n = \overline{1, \tilde{N}}.$$

- $\mathbf{A}_{i,i-1} = \operatorname{diag}\{i\gamma^{(r)}((1-q^{(r)})\hat{I}_R + E_r^+) \otimes I_{\bar{W}}, r = \overline{1,R}\}, i \geq 1.$

Proof of the lemma is performed by means of analysis of the intensities of all possible transitions of the Markov chain ξ_t during the time interval having infinitesimal length. Existence of $\tilde{N} + 1$ non-zero block diagonals in the matrix $\mathbf{A}$ is explained by the fact that the number $\tilde{N}$ (the maximal difference of the system capacities under various states of the RE if this difference is not equal to zero, or 1, otherwise) defines the maximal number of customers that can join orbit simultaneously due to a customer arrival when the number of customers in service is equal to the server's capacity or due to the service forced termination caused by the reduction of the server capacity.

Analysis of the Markov chain having the generator $\mathbf{A}$ defined by Lemma 1 is non-trivial due to two essential reasons. The first reason is that the matrix $\mathbf{A}$ is not the block-tridiagonal. The second reason is that this matrix does not have Toeplitz-like structure, i.e. the form of the blocks $\mathbf{A}_{i,j}$ depends not only on the difference $j - i$ but depends on i and j separately. Fortunately, the Markov chains, which have the generator in form (1), are known in the literature.

Lemma 2. *The Markov chain ξ_t, $t \geq 0$, belongs to the class of continuous-time asymptotically quasi-Toeplitz Markov chains (AQTMC), see [10].*

To prove this lemma, it is required to verify that the following limits exist:

$$Y^{(0)} = \lim_{i\to\infty} R_i^{-1}\mathbf{A}_{i,i-1}, \ Y^{(1)} = \lim_{i\to\infty} R_i^{-1}\mathbf{A}_{i,i} + I,$$

$$Y^{(n)} = \lim_{i\to\infty} R_i^{-1}\mathbf{A}_{i,i+n-1}, \ n = \overline{2, \tilde{N}+1},$$

where R_i is a diagonal matrix with the diagonal entries which are defined as the moduli of the corresponding diagonal entries of the matrix $\mathbf{A}_{i,i}$, $i \geq 0$.

By the direct calculation of these limits, it is possible to show that they exist and the matrices $Y^{(n)}$, $n = \overline{0, \tilde{N}+1}$, have the following form:

- $Y^{(0)} = \operatorname{diag}\{Y_1^{(0)}, \ldots, Y_R^{(0)}\}$, where

$$Y_r^{(0)} = \begin{cases} O, & \text{if } \gamma^{(r)} = 0, \\ E_r^+ \otimes I_{\bar{W}}, & \text{if } \gamma^{(r)} > 0, q^{(r)} = 1, \\ (E_r^+ + \hat{I}_r) \otimes I_{\bar{W}}, & \text{if } \gamma^{(r)} > 0, q^{(r)} \neq 1; \end{cases}$$

- $Y^{(1)} = (Y^{(1)})_{r,r'}, r, r' = \overline{1,R}$, where

$(Y^{(1)})_{r,r'} = R_1^{(r)}(\mathbf{A}_{0,0})_{r,r'} + \delta_{r-r',0}\hat{I}_r \otimes I_{\bar{W}}, \text{ if } q^{(r)} = 1, \gamma^{(r)} > 0,$

$(Y^{(1)})_{r,r'} = R_2^{(r)}(\mathbf{A}_{0,0})_{r,r'} + \delta_{r-r',0}I_{N^{(r)}+1} \otimes I_{\bar{W}}, \text{ if } \gamma^{(r)} = 0,$

$(Y^{(1)})_{r,r'} = O, \text{ if } q^{(r)} \neq 1, \gamma^{(r)} > 0, r, r' = \overline{1,R},$

$R_1^{(r)} = \hat{I}_r \otimes (((\mu_{N^{(r)}}^{(r)} + \beta_{N^{(r)}}^{(r)})N^{(r)} - (H)_{r,r})I_{\bar{W}} + \Sigma_0^{(r)} - (1-q^{(r)})\Sigma_1^{(r)})^{-1}, r = \overline{1,R},$

$R_2^{(r)} = ((M_r + B^{(r)}) \otimes I_{\bar{W}} + I_{N^{(r)}} \otimes (\Sigma_0^{(r)} -$

$-(H)_{r,r}I_{\bar{W}}) - (1-q^{(r)})\hat{I}_r \otimes \Sigma_1^{(r)})^{-1}, r = \overline{1,R},$

$\Sigma_0^{(r)} = \operatorname{diag}\{(-D_0^{(r)})_{l,l}, l = \overline{0,W}\}, \Sigma_1^{(r)} = \operatorname{diag}\{(D_1^{(r)})_{l,l}, l = \overline{0,W}\}.$

- $Y^{(n)} = (Y^{(n)})_{r,r'}, r, r' = \overline{1,R}, n = \overline{2, \tilde{N}+1}$, where

$$(Y^{(n)})_{r,r'} = \begin{cases} R_1^{(r)} \mathbf{A}_{n-1}^+, & \text{if } q^{(r)} = 1, \gamma^{(r)} > 0, \\ R_2^{(r)} \mathbf{A}_{n-1}^+, & \text{if } \gamma^{(r)} = 0, \\ O, & \text{if } q^{(r)} \neq 1, \gamma^{(r)} > 0. \end{cases}$$

It is possible to verify that the matrices $Y^{(n)}$, $n = \overline{0, \tilde{N}+1}$, are sub-stochastic while their sum is the stochastic. According to definition of $AQTMC$, this means that the Markov chain ξ_t belongs to the class of $AQTMC$. Lemma 2 is proven.

Therefore, it is possible to apply the theory of $AQTMC$ from [10] for analysis of the Markov chain ξ_t. First of all, it is necessary to obtain the conditions on the system parameters which guarantee existence of the steady state distribution (the ergodicity) of the Markov chain ξ_t. According to [10], the sufficient condition of the ergodicity of the chain is the fulfillment of the following inequality:

$$\mathbf{y} Y^{(0)} \mathbf{e} > \mathbf{y} \sum_{n=2}^{\tilde{N}+1} (n-1) Y^{(n)} \mathbf{e} \tag{2}$$

where the vector $\mathbf{y}$ is the unique solution to the system

$$\mathbf{y} \sum_{n=0}^{\tilde{N}+1} Y^{(n)} = \mathbf{y}, \quad \mathbf{y}\mathbf{e} = 1 \tag{3}$$

If the customers from orbit are persistent for all states of the RE, i.e. $q^{(r)} = 1$, $r = \overline{1,R}$, the procedure for verifying the existence of the steady state distribution is the following. Because system (3) is the finite system of the linear algebraic equations, its solving on computer is not the difficult task. By substituting the obtained solution to inequality (2), one can easily check whether or not the steady state distribution exist under these values of the system parameters.

If customers from orbit non-persistent ($q^{(r)} \neq 1$) at least for one state r of the RE such as $\gamma^{(r)} \neq 0$, the following statement is true.

Lemma 3. *If customers from orbit not absolutely persistent ($q^{(r)} \neq 1$) at least for one state r of the RE such as $\gamma^{(r)} \neq 0$, then the Markov chain ξ_t is ergodic for any set of the system parameters.*

Proof is implemented by analogy with Theorem 2 from [11].

In the sequel, we assume that the ergodicity condition is fulfilled. Then, the following stationary probabilities exist:

$$\pi(i, r, n, \nu) = \lim_{t \to \infty} P\{i_t = i, r_t = r, n_t = n, \nu_t = \nu\},$$

$$i \geq 0, r = \overline{1, R}, n = \overline{0, N^{(r)}}, \nu = \overline{0, W}.$$

Let us form the row-vectors $\boldsymbol{\pi}_i$ as follows:

$$\boldsymbol{\pi}(i, r, n) = (\pi(i, r, n, 0), \pi(i, r, n, 1), \dots, \pi(i, r, n, W)),$$

$$\boldsymbol{\pi}(i,r) = (\boldsymbol{\pi}(i,r,0), \boldsymbol{\pi}(i,r,1), \dots, \boldsymbol{\pi}(i,r,N^{(r)})), \ r = \overline{1,R},$$

$$\boldsymbol{\pi}_i = (\boldsymbol{\pi}(i,1), \boldsymbol{\pi}(i,2), \dots, \boldsymbol{\pi}(i,R)), \ i \geq 0.$$

It is well known that the vectors $\boldsymbol{\pi}_i$, $i \geq 0$, satisfy the system

$$(\boldsymbol{\pi}_0, \boldsymbol{\pi}_1, \dots)\mathbf{A} = \mathbf{0}, \quad (\boldsymbol{\pi}_0, \boldsymbol{\pi}_1, \dots)\mathbf{e} = 1. \tag{4}$$

System (4) is infinite. Therefore, its solution is a difficult problem. However, this problem can be successfully solved using the numerically stable algorithm developed in [10].

4   Performance Measures

Having computed the vectors of the stationary probabilities $\boldsymbol{\pi}_i, i \geq 0$, it is possible to compute a variety of the performance measures of the system.

The average number of customers in the service area is

$$N = \sum_{i=0}^{\infty} \sum_{r=1}^{R} \sum_{n=0}^{N^{(r)}} n\boldsymbol{\pi}(i,r,n)\mathbf{e}.$$

The average number of customers in orbit is $L = \sum_{i=1}^{\infty} i\boldsymbol{\pi}_i\mathbf{e}.$

The intensity of output of successfully serviced customers is

$$\lambda_{out} = \sum_{i=0}^{\infty} \sum_{r=1}^{R} \sum_{n=1}^{N^{(r)}} n\mu_n^{(r)}\boldsymbol{\pi}(i,r,n)\mathbf{e}.$$

The intensity of flow of customers who leaves the server due to impatience is

$$\lambda_{imp} = \sum_{i=0}^{\infty} \sum_{r=1}^{R} \sum_{n=1}^{N^{(r)}} n\beta_n^{(r)}\boldsymbol{\pi}(i,r,n)\mathbf{e}.$$

The probability that a customer arrives to the system when the server already reached its capacity and leaves the system is $P_{ent} = \lambda^{-1} \sum_{i=0}^{\infty} \sum_{r=1}^{R} (1 - q^{(r)})\boldsymbol{\pi}(i,r,N^{(r)})D_1^{(r)}\mathbf{e}.$

The probability that a customer leaves the system forever due to impatience is $P_{imp} = \lambda^{-1} \sum_{i=0}^{\infty} \sum_{r=1}^{R} (1 - a^{(r)}) \sum_{n=1}^{N^{(r)}} n\beta_n^{(r)}\boldsymbol{\pi}(i,r,n)\mathbf{e}.$

The probability of customers loss due to the decrease of the number of servers caused by change of the state of the RE is $P_{RE} = \frac{1}{\lambda} \sum_{i=0}^{\infty} \sum_{r=2}^{R} \sum_{r'=1}^{r-1} (1 - p^{(r)})(H)_{r,r'} \sum_{n=N^{(r')}+1}^{N^{(r)}} (n - N^{(r')})\boldsymbol{\pi}(i,r,n)\mathbf{e}.$

The probability that an arbitrary customer from orbit makes an attempt to receive service when the server capacity is exhausted and permanently leaves the system is $P_{retry} = \lambda^{-1} \sum_{i=1}^{\infty} \sum_{r=1}^{R} i\gamma^{(r)}(1 - q^{(r)})\boldsymbol{\pi}(i,r,N^{(r)})\mathbf{e}.$

The loss probability of an arbitrary customer is

$$P_{loss} = 1 - \frac{\lambda_{out}}{\lambda} = P_{retry} + P_{imp} + P_{ent} + P_{RE}. \tag{5}$$

5 Numerical Example

Let us consider the queueing system that operates in the RE having three states $(R = 3)$ with the generator $H = \begin{pmatrix} -0.06 & 0.04 & 0.02 \\ 0.0002 & -0.0005 & 0.0003 \\ 0.0004 & 0.0005 & -0.0009 \end{pmatrix}$ and stationary distribution given by the vector $\psi = (0.00439, 0.6735, 0.32211)$.

We assume that the server doesn't work (is broken, takes vacation, etc.) during the $RE's$ stay in state 1.

Under state 2 of the RE, the server can serve up to 10 customers simultaneously. When there are n customers on service, the service intensity of one customer is determined as $\mu_n^{(2)} = \frac{10.0 - 0.3n}{n}$, $n = \overline{1, 10}$.

Under state 3 of the RE, the server can serve up to 15 customers simultaneously. When there are n customers on service, the service intensity of one customer is determined as $\mu_n^{(3)} = \frac{20.0 - 0.3n}{n}$, $n = \overline{1, 15}$.

The individual intensities of impatience are given by $\beta_n^{(2)} = 0.03n$, $\beta_n^{(3)} = 0.04n$.

To define the arrival flow under various states of the RE, let us consider the MAP arrival flow that defined by the matrices

$$D_0 = \begin{pmatrix} -1.35164 & 0 \\ 0 & -0.04387 \end{pmatrix}, D_1 = \begin{pmatrix} 1.34265 & 0.00899 \\ 0.024435 & 0.019435 \end{pmatrix}.$$

This arrival flow has the coefficient of correlation $c_{cor} = 0.2$ and the coefficient of variation $c_{var} = 12.34$.

We assume that under state 1 of the RE the arrival flow is defined by the matrices $D_0^{(1)} = 2D_0$ and $D_1^{(1)} = 2D_1$, under state 2 of the RE the arrival flow is defined by the matrices $D_0^{(2)} = 5D_0$ and $D_1^{(2)} = 5D_1$, under state 3 of the RE the arrival flow is defined by the matrices $D_0^{(3)} = 8D_0$ and $D_1^{(3)} = 8D_1$. The intensities of arrivals are $\lambda^{(1)} = 2$, $\lambda^{(2)} = 5$, and $\lambda^{(3)} = 8$, correspondingly.

The rest of the system parameters are as follows: $q^{(1)} = 0.95$, $a^{(1)} = 0.5$, $\gamma^{(1)} = 0.2$; $q^{(2)} = 0.9$, $a^{(2)} = 0.4$, $p^{(2)} = 0.6$, $\gamma^{(2)} = 0.2$; $q^{(3)} = 0.9$, $a^{(3)} = 0.4$, $p^{(3)} = 0.7$, $\gamma^{(3)} = 0.2$.

As the main performance measure of the system, we will consider the loss probability of an arbitrary customer P_{loss}. The goal of the experiment is to find the values of the server capacities $N^{(2)}$ and $N^{(3)}$ which provide the minimal value of this probability. To this end, we will compute the values of this probability for various combinations of $N^{(2)}$ and $N^{(3)}$ from the set $N^{(2)} = \overline{1, \min\{N^{(3)}, 10\}}$ and $N^{(3)} = \overline{1, 15}$. Note, that because service is not provided when the RE stays in state 1 we have $N^{(1)} = 0$.

It is clear that the problem of choosing the optimal combination of $N^{(2)}$ and $N^{(3)}$ is not trivial. If these values are chosen be small, the probabilities of customers loss upon arrival P_{ent} or retrial P_{retry} may be high. This is confirmed by Fig. 2.

If the values of $N^{(2)}$ and $N^{(3)}$ are chosen be large, the probabilities of customers loss upon arrival or retrial essentially decrease. However the probabilities

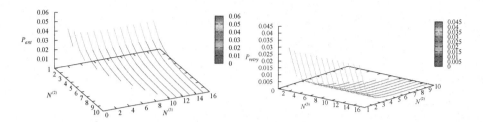

Fig. 2. Dependence of P_{ent} and P_{retry} on $N^{(2)}$ and $N^{(3)}$

of customers loss due impatience P_{imp} and due to the decrease of the server capacity P_{RE} grow. This is confirmed by Fig. 3. The loss probability P_{loss} of an arbitrary customer is the sum of the probabilities P_{ent}, P_{retry}, P_{imp}, and P_{RE}. The surface giving dependence of P_{loss} on $N^{(2)}$ and $N^{(3)}$ is presented in Fig. 4.

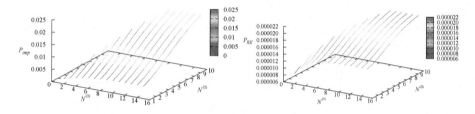

Fig. 3. Dependence of P_{imp} and P_{RE} on $N^{(2)}$ and $N^{(3)}$

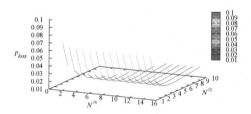

Fig. 4. Dependence of P_{loss} on $N^{(2)}$ and $N^{(3)}$

It is evidently seen from Fig. 4, that there exit the points $(N^{(2)}, N^{(3)})$ providing some trade-off in situation when the summands in expression (5) for probability P_{loss} demonstrate the opposite behavior when $N^{(2)}$ and $N^{(3)}$ increase and decrease. The minimal value of the loss probability $P_{loss} = 0.0177847$ is reached for $N^{(2)} = 5$ and $N^{(3)} = 7$. If we do not control capacity of the server and accept all customers for each state of the RE (up to 10 when the RE is in state 2 and up to 15 when the RE is in state 3), then $P_{loss} = 0.022658$. Therefore, admission for simultaneous service of less customers than the maximally possible allows essentially decrease the customer loss probability.

6   Conclusion

A retrial queueing system with limited processor sharing discipline and impatient customers, which operates in the RE, is analysed. An arbitrary dependence of the individual service and impatience rates on the number of customers in service is allowed. The behavior of the system is described by the multi-dimensional asymptotically quasi-Toeplitz Markov chain. Expressions for key performance measures of the system are presented. Feasibility of the described algorithmic results is numerically illustrated. It is shown that the results can be used for the optimal adjustment of capacity of the server at each state of the RE.

Acknowledgments. The publication was financially supported by the Ministry of Education and Science of the Russian Federation (the Agreement number 02.a03.21.0008) and by the Belarusian Republican Foundation for Fundamental Research (grant F16MV-003).

References

1. Samouylov, K., Naumov, V., Sopin, E., Gudkova, I., Shorgin, S.: Sojourn time analysis for processor sharing loss system with unreliable server. In: Wittevrongel, S., Phung-Duc, T. (eds.) ASMTA 2016. LNCS, vol. 9845, pp. 284–297. Springer, Cham (2016). doi:10.1007/978-3-319-43904-4_20
2. Samouylov, K., Sopin, E., Gudkova, I.: Sojourn time analysis for processor sharing loss queuing system with service interruptions and MAP arrivals. In: Vishnevskiy, V.M., Samouylov, K.E., Kozyrev, D.V. (eds.) DCCN 2016. CCIS, vol. 678, pp. 406–417. Springer, Cham (2016). doi:10.1007/978-3-319-51917-3_36
3. Yashkov, S.: Processor-sharing queues: some progress in analysis. Queuing Syst. **2**, 1–17 (1987)
4. Yashkov, S., Yashkova, A.: Processor sharing: a survey of the mathematical theory. Autom. Remote Contr. **68**, 1662–1731 (2007)
5. Artalejo, J.R., Gomez-Corral, A.: Retrial Queueing Systems: A Computational Approach. Springer, Heidelberg (2008)
6. Nunez-Queija, R.: Sojourn times in a processor sharing queue with service interruptions. Queueing Syst. **34**, 351–386 (2000)
7. Nunez-Queija, R.: Sojourn times in non-homogeneous QBD processes with processor sharing. Stoch. Models **17**, 61–92 (2001)
8. Ghosh, A., Banik, A.D.: An algorithmic analysis of the $BMAP/MSP/1$ generalized processor-sharing queue. Comput. Oper. Res. **79**, 1–11 (2017)
9. Lucantoni, D.: New results on the single server queue with a batch Markovian arrival process. Commun. Statist. Stoch. Models **7**, 1–46 (1991)
10. Klimenok, V., Dudin, A.: Multi-dimensional asymptotically quasi-Toeplitz Markov chains and their application in queueing theory. Queueing Syst. **54**, 245–259 (2006)
11. Dudin, A., Kim, C., Dudin, S., Dudina, O.: Priority retrial queueing model operating in random environment with varying number and reservation of servers. Appl. Math. Comput. **269**, 674–690 (2015)

Stationary Distribution of Waiting Time in $MAP/G/1/N$ Queueing System with LIFO Service Discipline

Alexander Dudin[1,2(✉)], Valentina Klimenok[1,2], and Konstantin Samouylov[2]

[1] Department of Applied Mathematics and Computer Science,
Belarusian State University, 220030 Minsk, Belarus
{dudin,klimenok}@bsu.by
[2] Department of Applied Probability and Informatics, RUDN University,
6 Miklukho-Maklaya Street, 117198 Moscow, Russia
ksam@sci.pfu.edu.ru

Abstract. In this paper, we consider single server queueing system with a finite buffer, MAP input and independent generally distributed service times. Customers are selected for the service in accordance with the LIFO (Last In – First Out) service discipline. It is well known that stationary distribution of the number of customers in such a system coincides with the corresponding distribution in the system with FIFO (First In – First Out) discipline which has been studied in the literature early. In the present research we focus on investigating the stationary distribution of waiting (sojourn) time in the system.

Keywords: Single-server queue · Finite buffer · Markovian arrival process · LIFO service discipline · Waiting time distribution · Resource management and admission control

1   Introduction

Queueing systems with inversive service discipline (Last-in-First-out, LIFO) can be used to describe the data processing in many real systems. LIFO discipline is used in cases when the last data written into the structure of data must be removed or processed first. A useful analogy with the office worker is: a person can only work with one page at a time, so a new document is added to a folder on the top of the stack of the previous documents. By analogy, in a computer we also have limitations such as the width of the data bus and every time the system can manipulate with only one memory cell. Abstract mechanism of the LIFO is used in calculations realized in the real structures of data in the form of a stack, which is obviously related to a "pack of paper", a "pile of plates", and so on. The term LIFO emphasizes that in the process of list processing and temporary storage of a limited set of data the last written data must be processed first.

Y. Koucheryavy et al. (Eds.): WWIC 2017, LNCS 10372, pp. 50–61, 2017.
DOI: 10.1007/978-3-319-61382-6_5

LIFO service discipline can be considered as the opposed one to the ordered FIFO service discipline. Queueing systems with FIFO service discipline are most popular among researches because the corresponding real systems are more common. The second reason for popularity of FIFO discipline is the fact that distributions of the queue length in the systems with FIFO and LIFO disciplines are the same. It allows sometimes to get the desired results for a queue with LIFO discipline using the results of investigation of the corresponding queue with FIFO discipline which is generally easier to study.

However, the distributions of waiting (sojourn) time in the queues with FIFO and LIFO are different. For queueing system with stationary Poisson flow, an infinite buffer and LIFO service discipline the stationary distribution of the waiting (sojourn) time has been obtained early, see, for example, [9]. But we do not know results concerning the distribution of waiting (sojourn) time for the analogous system with a finite buffer, and even much less results for the system with a finite buffer and the input flow different from the stationary Poisson one.

Both disciplines, FIFO and LIFO, are widely used in modern telecommunication and computer networks. E.g., comparison of these discipline (with variants of tail-drop and front-drop of packets) in application to modelling the delivering of live multimedia streaming over ad hoc networks is given in [11]. Application of LIFO discipline in multihop networks is discussed in [7].

The flows in modern telecommunication and computer networks can considerably differ from a stationary Poisson one. In particular, they do not possess the basic property of a stationary Poisson flow - memoryless property. Therefore, in the past decade and more queueing systems with correlated flows have a great interest among researchers in the field of telecommunications and queuing theory. At the present time, the most popular mathematical model of such flows is a Markovian Arrival Process.

In this paper we consider single server queueing system with a finite buffer, MAP input and generally distributed service time. Customers are selected for the service in accordance with LIFO service discipline. As in was mentioned above, the stationary distribution of the number of customers in such a system coincides with the corresponding distribution in the system with FIFO discipline which has been studied in [2–4]. In the present research, we focus on investigating the stationary distribution of waiting (sojourn) time of an arbitrary customer admitted into the system and arbitrary customer.

2   Model Description

We consider a single server queueing system with a finite buffer of size N and LIFO service discipline. Customers arrive into the system in accordance with a Markovian Arrival Process (MAP). The MAP is defined by the underlying process ν_t, $t \geq 0$, which is an irreducible continuous-time Markov chain with finite state space $\{0, \ldots, W\}$, and the $(W + 1) \times (W + 1)$ matrices D_0 and D_1. The entries of the matrix D_0 define the rates of the process ν_t, $t \geq 0$, transitions which are accompanied by generating a customer while non-diagonal entries of the matrix D_0 describe the rates of the process ν_t, $t \geq 0$, transitions which are not accompanied by generating a customer. The matrices D_0 and D_1 can be defined by their matrix generating function $D(z) = D_0 + D_1 z$, $|z| \leq 1$. The matrix $D(1)$ is an infinitesimal generator of the process ν_t, $t \geq 0$. The intensity (fundamental rate) of the MAP is defined as

$$\lambda = \boldsymbol{\theta} D_1 \mathbf{e}$$

where $\boldsymbol{\theta}$ is the unique solution of the system

$$\boldsymbol{\theta} D(1) = \mathbf{0}, \ \boldsymbol{\theta}\mathbf{e} = 1,$$

and the intensity of batch arrivals is defined as $\lambda_b = \boldsymbol{\theta}(-D_0)\mathbf{e}$. Here and in the sequel $\mathbf{e}(\mathbf{0})$ is a column (row) vector of appropriate size consisting of 1's (0's). The coefficient of variation, c_{var}, of intervals between batch arrivals is given by

$$c_{var}^2 = 2\lambda_b \boldsymbol{\theta}(-D_0)^{-1}\mathbf{e} - 1$$

while the coefficient of correlation, c_{cor}, of intervals between successive batch arrivals is calculated as

$$c_{cor} = (\lambda_b \boldsymbol{\theta}(-D_0)^{-1}D_1(-D_0)^{-1}\mathbf{e} - 1)/c_{var}^2.$$

Let $p_{\nu,\nu'}(k,t)$ be the probability that k customers arrive in the MAP during the interval $(0,t)$ and the state of the underlying process ν_t of the MAP at the moment t is ν' given that $\nu_0 = \nu$. Denote

$$P(k,t) = (p_{\nu\nu'}(k,t))_{\nu,\nu'=\overline{0,W}}, \ k \geq 0.$$

Then, the matrices $P(k,t)$ are defined as the coefficients of the matrix expansion

$$e^{D(z)t} = \sum_{k=0}^{\infty} P(k,t)z^k, \ |z| \leq 1.$$

For more information about the MAP see, e.g., [8].

The successive service times of customers are independent random variables with general distribution $B(t)$, Laplace-Stieltjes transform

$$\beta(s) = \int_0^{\infty} e^{-st}dB(t), \ Re \ s > 0,$$

and finite first moment $b_1 = \int_0^{\infty} tdB(t) < \infty$.

As it was noted above, in the literature there are no results regarding such important performance measure of the system under study as waiting time. This paper is devoted to finding the Laplace-Stieltjes transform of the stationary distribution of the waiting time in such a system.

3   Laplace-Stieltjes Transform of the Stationary Distribution of Waiting Time

Let us introduce the following notation:

- $\Pi_{n,\nu,\nu'}(t)$ be the probability that the length of the busy period generated by a customer, which goes to the service leaving n customers in the buffer, is less than t and at the end of this period the MAP is in the state ν' under condition that at the beginning of the busy period the MAP was in the state ν, $n = \overline{0, N}, \nu, \nu' = \overline{0, W}$;
- $\pi_{n,\nu,\nu'}(s) = \int\limits_0^\infty e^{-st} d\Pi_{n,\nu,\nu'}(t), \ Re\, s \geq 0$;
- $\Pi_n(s) = (\pi_{n,\nu,\nu'}(s))_{\nu,\nu'=\overline{0,W}}$;
- $W_{n,\nu,\nu'}(t)$ be the probability that the waiting time of a customer, which sees n customers in the system at the arrival moment, is less than t and at the end of the waiting time the MAP is in the state ν' under condition that at the arrival moment the MAP was in the state ν, $n = \overline{0, N}, \nu, \nu' = \overline{0, W}$;
- $w_{n,\nu,\nu'}(s) = \int\limits_0^\infty e^{-st} dW_{n,\nu,\nu'}(t)$;
- $W_n(s) = (w_{n,\nu,\nu'}(s))_{\nu,\nu'=\overline{0,W}}$.

Lemma 1. *The matrices $\Pi_n(s)$ of LSTs of distribution of the length of the busy period generated by a customer, which goes to the service leaving n customers in the buffer, are calculated by the formulas of backward recursion*

$$\Pi_n(s) = \{I - \sum_{k=1}^{N-n-1} Y_k(s)\Pi_{n+k-1}(s)\Pi_{n+k-2}(s)\ldots\Pi_{n+1}(s)-$$

$$-[\beta(sI - D(1)) - \sum_{k=0}^{N-n-1} Y_k(s)]\,\Pi_{N-1}(s)\Pi_{N-2}(s)\ldots\Pi_{n+1}(s)\}^{-1}\beta(sI - D_0),$$

$$n = N - 1, N - 2, \ldots, 0, \tag{1}$$

where

$$\beta(sI - D(1)) = \int\limits_0^\infty e^{-(sI-D(1))x} dB(x),$$

$$Y_k(s) = \int\limits_0^\infty e^{-sx} P(k, x) dB(x), \ k \geq 0, \tag{2}$$

I is the identity matrix. When it is needed, the dimension of the matrix is indicated as its suffix.

Proof. The proof is based on the probabilistic interpretation of the Laplace-Stieltjes transform. We assume that, independently on the system operation, the stationary Poisson input of so called catastrophes arrives. Let s, $s > 0$, be the rate of this flow.

Then $\Pi_n(s)$ is a matrix probability that during the busy period generated by a tagged customer, which goes to the service leaving n customers in the buffer, a catastrophe does not arrive.

First, consider $n = N-1$. Let us calculate $\Pi_{N-1}(s)$ using the total probability formula. To this end, consider two cases: (a) during the service time of the tagged customer no customers arrive at the system and (b) during the service time of the tagged customer one or more customers arrive at the system.

In case (a) the busy period under consideration ends at the service completion epoch. The matrix probability that during the service time no customers arrive at the system and a catastrophe does not arrive is equal to $\int_0^\infty e^{-sx} e^{D_0 x} dB(x)$.

In case (b) the length of the busy period under consideration (L_{tag}) can be represented as a sum of two independent random variables: service time of the tagged customer and the length of busy period generated by youngest customer arrived at the system during the service time (L_{youn}).

A matrix probability that during the service time one or more customers arrive at the system and a catastrophe does not arrive is equal to $\int_0^\infty e^{-sx}(e^{D(1)x} - e^{D_0 x})dB(x)$.

The distribution of the random variable L_{youn} is the same as the distribution of L_{tag}. From this it follows that a matrix probability that during the period L_{youn} a catastrophe does not occur is equal to $\Pi_{N-1}(s)$. Then a matrix probability that during the service time of the tagged customer one or more customers arrive at the system and a catastrophe does not arrive during the busy period L_{tag} is equal to the product $\int_0^\infty e^{-sx}(e^{D(1)x} - e^{D_0 x})dB(x)\Pi_{N-1}(s)$.

From all has been said and the total probability formula it follows that the matrix LST $\Pi_{N-1}(s)$ is calculated as

$$\Pi_{N-1}(s) = \int_0^\infty e^{-sx} e^{D_0 x} dB(x) + \int_0^\infty e^{-sx}(e^{D(1)x} - e^{D_0 x})dB(x)\Pi_{N-1}(s).$$

The similar arguments lead to the following relation:

$$\Pi_{N-i}(s) = \int_0^\infty e^{-sx} e^{D_0 x} dB(x)+$$

$$+ \int_0^\infty e^{-sx} \sum_{k=1}^{i-1} P(k,x)dB(x)\Pi_{N-i+k-1}(s)\Pi_{N-i+k-2}(s)\Pi_{N-i}(s)+$$

$$+ \int_0^\infty e^{-sx}[e^{D(1)x} - \sum_{k=0}^{i-1} P(k,x)]dB(x)\Pi_{N-1}(s)\ldots\Pi_{N-i}(s),\ i = 1,2,\ldots,N. \quad (3)$$

Using notation of Lemma 1 and introducing the value $n = N - i$, we obtain from (3) formula (1).

Now we are able to derive the LST of the distribution of the waiting time of a customer admitted into the system.

Lemma 2. *The matrix $W_n(s)$ of LSTs of distributions of waiting time of a customer, which sees n customers in the system at the arrival moment is calculates as follows:*

$$W_0(s) = I_{W+1},$$

$$W_n(s) = \sum_{k=0}^{N-n} \tilde{Y}_k(s) \Pi_{k+n-1}(s) \Pi_{k+n-2}(s) \ldots \Pi_n(s)$$

$$+ [\tilde{\beta}(sI - D(1)) - \sum_{k=0}^{N-n} \tilde{Y}_k(s)] \Pi_{N-1}(s) \Pi_{N-2}(s) \ldots \Pi_n(s), \ n = \overline{1, N}, \qquad (4)$$

where

$$\tilde{\beta}(sI - D(1)) = \int_0^\infty e^{-(sI - D(1))x} d\tilde{B}(x),$$

$$\tilde{Y}_n(s) = \int_0^\infty e^{-sx} P(n, x) d\tilde{B}(x), \qquad (5)$$

$\tilde{B}(t)$ *is a distribution function of residual service time,*

$$\tilde{B}(t) = b_1^{-1} \int_0^t (1 - B(x)) dx.$$

Proof. We should prove formula (4) for $1 \leq n \leq N$. Let an arriving (tagged) customer finds $n > 0$ customer in the system. It means that one customer is in the service and the rest $n - 1$ customers stay in the buffer. Suppose that during the residual service time k customers arrive at the system, $k = \overline{0, N - n}$. Then all these customers will be admitted into the system.

Using the probabilistic interpretation of the Laplace-Stieltjes transform, we interpret $\int_0^\infty e^{-sx} P(k, x) d\tilde{B}(x)$ as a matrix probability that k customers arrive at the system and during the residual service time a catastrophe does not arrive. Then, at the end of the current service, $n + k$ customers stay in the buffer. A customer which came last (the kth customer) will go to the service first. This customer leaves $n + k - 1$ customers in the buffer and initializes busy period generated by this customer. By Lemma 1, LSTs of distributions of busy period generated by the customer are given by the matrix $\Pi_{k+n-1}(s)$. After that, the $(k - 1)$th customer arrived during residual service time will go to the service. LSTs of distributions of busy period generated by this customer are given by the matrix $\Pi_{k+n-2}(s)$.

The similar reasoning lead to the conclusion that the tagged customer will go to the service, i.e. his/her waiting time is over, when the busy period generated by the first customer arrived at the system during the residual service time ends. This first customer, entering the service, leaves in the buffer n customers and distribution of the busy period, generated by this customer, has matrix LST $\Pi_n(s)$.

Since busy periods, generated by k customers arrived at the system during the residual service time and placed in the buffer in front of our tagged customer, are independent random variables then their sum has a distribution with the matrix LST $\Pi_{k+n-1}(s)\Pi_{k+n-2}(s)\ldots\Pi_n(s)$. During the residual service time, k customers can be admitted into the buffer, where $k = \overline{0, N-n}$. This explains presence of the sum over k in the first term on the right side of (4).

The second term on the right side (4) corresponds to the case when during the residual service time more than $N-n$ customers arrive at the system. The matrix probability that during the residual service time more than $N - n$ customers arrive at the system and a catastrophe does not occur is equal to $\int\limits_0^\infty e^{-sx}[e^{D(1)x} - \sum\limits_{k=0}^{N-n} P(k,x))]d\tilde{B}(x)$. Further arguments are similar to those in the derivation of the first term on the right side of (4) and lead to the corresponding expression on the right side of (4).

Introduce the notation for the joint stationary distribution of the number of customers in the system and state of the underlying process of the MAP at an arbitrary time:

$$p_i(\nu) = \lim_{t\to\infty} P\{i_t = i, \nu_t = \nu\}, \ \nu = \overline{0, W+1},$$

$$\mathbf{p}_i = (p_i(0), p_i(1), \ldots, p_i(W)), \ i = \overline{0, N+1}.$$

As it was mentioned before, the stationary distribution $\mathbf{p}_i$, $i = \overline{0, N+1}$, can be calculated as the stationary distribution of the system $MAP/G/1$ with FIFO service discipline. The corresponding result is presented in [2,3]. Then, we can calculate the LST $w(s)$ using the following theorem.

Theorem 1. *The LST $w(s)$ of the distribution of the waiting time of an arbitrary customer admitted into the system is calculated as*

$$w(s) = \sum_{i=0}^{N} \mathbf{p}_i \frac{D_1}{\lambda} W_i(s)\mathbf{e}. \tag{6}$$

Proof of the theorem follows from the total probability formula.

Corollary 1. *The LST $\tilde{w}(s)$ of the distribution of the waiting time of an arbitrary customer is calculated as*

$$\tilde{w}(s) = P_{loss} + w(s)(1 - P_{loss})$$

where the probability P_{loss} of an arbitrary customer loss is computed as

$$P_{loss} = \mathbf{p}_{N+1}\frac{D_1\mathbf{e}}{\lambda}.$$

Corollary 2. *The rth moment of the waiting time of an arbitrary customer admitted into the system is calculated as*

$$E_r\{w\} = (-1)^r\frac{d^r w(s)}{ds^r}|_{s=0}, \; r \geq 1.$$

4   Calculation of the Matrices $Y_n(s)$ and $\tilde{Y}_n(s)$

In the numerical implementation of formulas (1), (4) the problem of computing the matrices $Y_k(s)$ and $\tilde{Y}_k(s)$ defined by (2) and (5) arises.

First, we consider the problem of calculating the matrices $Y_k(s)$. In general, the elements of integration, matrices $P(k,t)$, $k \geq 0$, are not computed in explicit form, so to calculate these matrices, a procedure based on uniformization of the matrix exponent can be used. Such a procedure is described, e.g., in [6,8]. In our case, we use this procedure with minor modification, and obtain the following formula for the calculation of the matrices $Y_n(s)$:

$$Y_n(s) = \sum_{j=0}^{\infty}\gamma_j(s)K_n^{(j)}, \; n \geq 0,$$

where $\gamma_j(s) = \int_0^{\infty} e^{-(\varphi+s)x}\frac{(\varphi t)^j}{j!}dB(x)$, $j \geq 0$, φ is a maximum of modules of the diagonal entries of the matrix D_0, the matrices $K_n^{(j)}$, $n \geq 0, j \geq 0$, are computed using the recurrent formula given in [6,8].

Calculation of the matrices $Y_n(s)$, $n \geq 0$, is greatly simplified when the service time has Phase type (PH) distribution. Class of such distributions is sufficiently general and is dense in the set of nonnegative distributions, see, e.g., [1,10]. The reader can find the definition and properties of PH distribution e.g., in [10]. Here we suppose that the reader is generally conversant with definition and properties of PH distribution and suggest that service time has PH distribution with an irreducible representation $(\mathbf{g}, G)$ where $\mathbf{g}$ is a stochastic M-size row vector and G is a matrix of size M which has the property of a sub-generator. Then the distribution function $B(t)$ has the following form:

$$B(t) = 1 - \mathbf{g}e^{Gt}G_0$$

where $G_0 = -G\mathbf{e}$.

Substituting in (2) the expression for $B(t)$ and using the mixed product rule, we have

$$Y_k(s) = \int_0^{\infty} e^{-sx}P(k,x)dB(x)$$

$$= \int_0^\infty e^{-sx} P(k, x) \boldsymbol{g} e^{Gx} \mathbf{G}_0 dx$$

$$= (I_{\bar{W}} \otimes \boldsymbol{g}) \int_0^\infty P(k, x) \otimes e^{(G-sI)x} dx (I_{\bar{W}} \otimes \mathbf{G}_0) \tag{7}$$

where $\otimes$ is a symbol of Kronecker product of matrices, see [5].

Now we try to calculate the integral in (7).

For $n = 0$, we have $P(0, x) = e^{D_0 x}$ and we obtain the following formula

$$\int_0^\infty P(0, x) \otimes e^{(G-sI)x} dx = -[D_0 \oplus (G - sI)]^{-1} \tag{8}$$

where $\oplus$ is a symbol of Kronecker sum of matrices, see [5].

To calculate the integrals for $n > 0$, we use the formula for integration by parts and the well known from the theory of $MAPs$ the matrix differential equations:

$$P'(k, x) = \sum_{l=0}^k P(l, x) D_{k-l}, \ k \geq 0. \tag{9}$$

Then the following relations take place

$$\int_0^\infty P(k, x) \otimes e^{(G-sI)x} dx = P(k, x) \otimes (G - sI)^{-1} e^{(G-sI)x} |_0^\infty$$

$$- \int_0^\infty P'(k, x) \otimes e^{(G-sI)x} dx [I_{\bar{W}} \otimes (G - sI)^{-1}]$$

$$= -\sum_{l=0}^k \int_0^\infty P(l, x) D_{k-l} \otimes (sI - G)^{-1} e^{(G-sI)x} dx. \tag{10}$$

Denote

$$F_l(s) = \int_0^\infty P(l, x) \otimes e^{(G-sI)x} dx, \ l \geq 0. \tag{11}$$

Using this notation, after some algebra we derive from (10) the following recursive formula for calculating the matrices $F_k(s)$:

$$F_k(s) = -\sum_{l=0}^{k-1} \int_0^\infty F_l(x)(D_{k-l} \otimes I_M)[D_0 \oplus (sI - G)^{-1}]^{-1}, k > 0, \tag{12}$$

with boundary condition (8).

Having the matrices $F_n(s)$ been calculated, we are able to calculate the required matrices $Y_k(s)$ by formula (7) which takes the form

$$Y_k(s) = (I_{\bar{W}} \otimes g)F_k(s)(I_{\bar{W}} \otimes \mathbf{G}_0), k \geq 0. \tag{13}$$

Now we focus on calculating the matrices $\tilde{Y}_k(s), k \geq 0$, introduced in (5). We will show that, for arbitrary distribution function $B(t)$ such that $B(0) = 0$, these matrices can be calculated via the matrices $Y_k(s)$ defined by formula (13).

Let $n = 0$.

$$\tilde{Y}_0(s) = \int_0^\infty e^{-sx} P(0,x) d\tilde{B}(x) = b_1^{-1} \int_0^\infty e^{(D_0-sI)x}(1 - B(x))dx. \tag{14}$$

Using integration by parts, we have

$$\int_0^\infty e^{(D_0-sI)x}(1 - B(x))dx =$$

$$= (D_0 - sI)^{-1}e^{(D_0-sI)x}(1 - B(x))|_0^\infty + (D_0 - sI)^{-1}\int_0^\infty e^{(D_0-sI)x}dB(x).$$

whence it follows that

$$\int_0^\infty e^{(D_0-sI)x}(1 - B(x))dx$$

$$= (D_0 - sI)^{-1}[-I + \int_0^\infty e^{(D_0-sI)x}dB(x)]. \tag{15}$$

Note that

$$\int_0^\infty e^{(D_0-sI)x}dB(x) = \int_0^\infty e^{-sx}P(0,x)dB(x) = Y_0(s).$$

Then it follows from (14), (15) that

$$\tilde{Y}_0(s) = b_1^{-1}(D_0 - sI)^{-1}(Y_0(s) - I). \tag{16}$$

Let now $n > 0$. Using integration by parts, we have

$$\int_0^\infty (e^{-sx}P(k,x))'(1 - B(x))dx$$

$$= e^{-sx}P(k,x)(1 - B(x))|_0^\infty + \int_0^\infty e^{-sx}P(k,x)dB(x)$$

whence it follows that

$$Y_k(s) = -\int\limits_0^\infty (e^{-sx}P(k,x))'(1-B(x))dx. \tag{17}$$

Differentiating in (17) and using the formula (9), we get relation

$$Y_k(s) = -s\int\limits_0^\infty e^{-sx}P(k,x)(1-B(x))dx + \int\limits_0^\infty e^{-sx}P(k,x)D_0(1-B(x))dx$$

$$+ \sum_{l=0}^{k-1}\int\limits_0^\infty e^{-sx}P(l,x)D_{k-l}(1-B(x))dx.$$

Using notation, we can rewrite this formula as

$$Y_k(s) = -sb_1\tilde{Y}_k(s) + b_1\tilde{Y}_k(s)D_0 + \sum_{l=0}^{k-1}\tilde{Y}_l(s)D_{k-l}.$$

From the last relation we obtain the following recursive formula for calculation of the matrices $\tilde{Y}_k(s)$:

$$\tilde{Y}_k(s) = b_1^{-1}(D_0 - sI)^{-1}(Y_k(s) - \sum_{l=0}^{k-1}\tilde{Y}_l(s)D_{k-l}), \ k > 0,$$

with boundary condition (16).

5   Conclusion

In this paper, we derived the Laplace-Stieltjes transform $w(s)$ of the stationary distribution of the waiting time in the queueing system $MAP/G/1/N$ with LIFO service discipline. Since the waiting time and service time are the independent random variables, the Laplace-Stieltjes transform $v(s)$ of sojourn time in the system can by trivially calculated using the formula $v(s) = w(s)\beta(s)$. Using the formulas for the Laplace-Stieltjes transform, we can calculate the expectation and the higher order moments of the waiting time and the sojourn time in the system.

The results can be used for optimization of resource and buffer space management and admission control in telecommunication networks, e.g., ad hoc networks with finite buffers and in multihop networks with end-to-end deadline-constrained traffic with reliability requirements, and for performance evaluation and capacity planning of various real data structures where the last written data must be processed first.

Acknowledgments. This publication was financially supported by the Ministry of Education and Science of the Russian Federation (the Agreement number 02.a03.21.0008).

References

1. Buchholz, P., Kriege, J., Felko, I.: Input Modeling with Phase-Type Distributions and Markov Models: Theory and Applications. SpringerBriefs in Mathematics. Springer, Heidelberg (2014)
2. Dudin, A.N., Shaban, A.A., Klimenok, V.I.: Analysis of a $BMAP/G/1/N$ queue. Int. J. Simul. Syst. Sci. Technol. **6**, 13–23 (2005)
3. Dudin, A.N., Klimenok, V.I., Tsarenkov, G.V.: Characteristics calculation for a single server queue with the batch Markovian arrival process, semi-Markovian service and finite buffer. Autom. Remote Contr. **63**, 1285–1297 (2002)
4. Dudin, A., Shaban, A.: Analysis of the $BMAP/SM/1/N$ type system with randomized choice of customers admission discipline. Commun. Comput. Inf. Sci. **638**, 44–56 (2016)
5. Graham, A.: Kronecker Products and Matrix Calculus with Applications. Ellis Horwood, Cichester (1981)
6. Kim, C.S., Klimenok, V., Taramin, O.: A tandem retrial queueing system with two Markovian flows and reservation of channels. Comput. Oper. Res. **37**, 1238–1246 (2010)
7. Li, R., Eryilmaz, A.: Scheduling for end-to-end deadline-constrained traffic with reliability requirements in multihop networks. IEEE/ACM Trans. Netw. **20**, 1649–1662 (2012)
8. Lucantoni, D.M.: New results on the single server queue with a batch Markovian arrival process. Commun. Statist. Stoch. Models **7**, 1–46 (1991)
9. Matveev, V.F., Ushakov, V.G.: Queueing systems. The Moscow University Press, Moscow (1984). (in Russian)
10. Neuts, M.F.: Matrix-Geometric Solutions in Stochastic Models. The Johns Hopkins University Press, Baltimore (1981)
11. Nzouonta, J., Ott, T., Borcea, C.: Impact of queuing discipline on packet delivery latency in ad hoc networks. Perform. Eval. **66**, 667–684 (2009)

5G Communications

Distributed Sleep Mode Power Control in 5G Ultra Dense Networks

Christos Bouras[1,2(✉)] and Georgios Diles[2]

[1] Computer Technology Institute and Press "Diophantus",
N. Kazantzaki, 26504 Rio, Greece
bouras@cti.gr
[2] Computer Engineering and Informatics Department,
University of Patras, Building B, University Campus, 26504 Rio, Greece
diles@ceid.upatras.gr

Abstract. The upcoming 5G networks are characterized by ultra dense deployments of small cells. These structures are capable of providing the much desired increase in capacity and data rates. The limited resources though present challenges on how they will be shared among the high number of base stations. Distributed coordination will play a big part in resource allocation. In this paper, we present a power control mechanism for dense femtocell deployments which utilizes sleep mode strategies and spectrum sharing among users. The mechanism exhibits increased throughput for the femtocell subscribers, preserving non-subscribers performance and increasing the network's energy efficiency.

Keywords: Femtocells · Sleep mode · Power control

1 Introduction

There is a consensus that in order to reach the massive targets of next generation mobile networks, a tremendous amount of base stations will be required. Some have even estimated that at some point the access points will surpass the number of users [1]. However, this massive deployment can be problematic in terms of interference and power consumption especially for the macrocells and small cells which usually compete for the available resources, they often adopt restrictive access policies and in contrast with the M2M communications, they have a high power consumption. Thankfully, this is recognized by the community which therefore has made crucial the issue of interference mitigation for better performance and the reduction of energy consumption of new mobile networks both for cutting costs for the operators and ecological sustainability [2].

A combination of the above goals can be seen in base stations' sleep mode. Sleep mode is a major part of energy reduction in the macrocell tier. This is when the macrocell base stations decide to turn into a low power node when traffic demand does not justify their operation (i.e. at night) and can be met

© IFIP International Federation for Information Processing 2017
Published by Springer International Publishing AG 2017. All Rights Reserved
Y. Koucheryavy et al. (Eds.): WWIC 2017, LNCS 10372, pp. 65–76, 2017.
DOI: 10.1007/978-3-319-61382-6_6

by the adjacent macro base stations. Due to the massive penetration of small cells, it is evident that these techniques will have to address the small cell tier too. While micro or pico cells are easy to handle, since for the majority they are deployed and controlled by the operator who can determine their operation in a centralized way, femtocells are not.

Due to their ad-hoc deployment and the exclusive access permissions, the macro cell strategies are not that easily transferable in the femto tier. For example, one cannot centrally determine that a private owned femtocell must be deactivated, both because such action is considered invasive and because traffic cannot be easily passed to adjacent femtocells due to the Closed Subscriber Access policy of most femtocells. However, this can be facilitated if we find a way to combine the sleep mode of one femtocell with the interference mitigation for the users of another one.

Sleep mode of femtocells is an active research field. In [3] the authors propose energy-efficient algorithms that lead small cell base stations to sleep mode in a bid to reduce cellular networks' power consumption. Three different strategies for algorithm control are discussed, relying on small cell driven, core network driven, and user equipment driven approaches each leading to different energy savings. The authors in [4] also compare different sleep mode mechanisms in dense small cell networks to conclude that sleep mode can lead to significant energy efficiency especially with the careful selection of the base stations.

A cluster-based approach is incorporated in [5] to improve the energy efficiency of small cell networks. Specifically, the clusters use an opportunistic base station sleep-wake switching mechanism to strike a balance between delay and energy consumption with gains that reach 40% in energy consumption and 23% in load. The work in [6] on the other hand, utilizes sleep mode strategy but focuses on mitigating interference for macrocell users. The evaluation showed that the strategy achieved better performance along with significant power savings.

In this paper, we extend the mechanism that we introduced in [7] that aims to reduce the number of active femtocells in the area without compromising their subscribers performance. The novelty of the mechanism is that it strives for deactivating a base station even when its subscribers are active by combining sleep mode and hybrid access operation in femtocell clusters and enforcing a restriction policy that guarantees performance gains. In our initial approach we were based only in spectrum sharing waiting for the restrictions to be met. This led to a very small number of cases that met the requirements which resulted in a small number of deactivated femtocells.

Instead in this paper, we introduce power control in order to increase that number by investigating what the power level of the femtocells should be in order to meet the performance restrictions. If such level exists and it is feasible, subscribers of the femtocell that turns to sleep mode are handed over to the neighbour femtocells. On the other hand, subscribers of the femtocell accepts willingly the non-subscriber users since the increased power level of their base station and the reduced interference due to inactivation of the nearby femtocell should cause a boost to their performance. We also expand the mechanism requirement set in order to protect femtocell users that belong to the same cluster but do not participate in the user exchange. Ultimately, the addition of power control leads to fewer concurrently active base stations leading to increased capacity gains for the subscribers and increased energy efficiency.

The structure of the rest of the paper is as follows: The next section presents the model of interference between the base stations in the femto and macro tier and we describe how sleep mode works in femtocells. The third section provides a detailed analysis of our proposed mechanism. In the fourth section, the evaluation of our proposal is taking place, providing extensive results obtained through simulations. Finally, the last section summarizes our conclusions and draws future research steps.

2   System Model

For the evaluation of our method we focus on users' performance gains regarding the impact in data rate for femtocell subscribers and macrocell users. Below we describe the model we used as basis for the formation and evaluation of our proposed scheme presented in the following section and the details of the sleep mode operations.

2.1   Pilot Power

In order to evaluate the performance repercussions of our setup to users data rate, we utilize Long Term Evolution Advanced (LTE-A) architecture, and its Orthogonal frequency-division multiple access (OFDMA) technology. OFDMA is characterized by flexible allocation of available spectrum resources to users, allowing complex spectrum allocation strategies. Since dense small cell deployments will mostly back up the demands of dense populated area, we follow the LTE-A directives for urban environments for the calculation of necessary parameters, such as path loss and gain [8].

For the power levels of each femtocell, we take into account the position of the femtocell inside the macrocell. Since we examine most co-channel transmission between the macro and femto tier, the effective range of the femtocells would be totally different between a femtocell near the edge and near the center of the macrocell due to interference. Thus, we adjust femtocells' power levels towards a constant radius of coverage [9], by taking into account the power received from the closest macrocell at a target femtocell radius r. A maximum power level $Pmax$ is also set:

$$P_f = min\left(P_m + G_\theta - PL_m(d) + PL_f(r), Pmax\right). \tag{1}$$

with $PL_f(r)$ denoting the line of sight path loss at the target cell radius r, P_m the transmit power of the closest macrocell and G_θ the antenna gain. $PL_m(d)$ is the average macrocell path loss at the femtocell distance d (excluding any additional wall losses).

2.2   Sleep Mode

The sleep mode model considered in this paper is based in [3,10]. During this mode, most components of the femtocell switch off, thus contributing to the power savings, apart from the ones needed for connection with the back-haul network and the ones required for sensing when a nearby subscribed user is transmitting in order to set the femtocell to full operational mode when needed. Sensing is done with an additional component-"sniffer" that is able to sense rises in received power on the uplink frequency band. Such rise would indicate a connection established between a user and the macrocell. Setting a threshold on the sensed rise accordingly to reflect the desired coverage radius of the femtocell, the sniffer wakes up the femtocell if the threshold is surpassed and the user is allowed to access it through a handover procedure.

This approach allows multiple components of the femtocell to be switched off such as the radio frequency (RF) transmitter and receiver leading to a reduction in power consumption close to 40%. Drawbacks of this approach include the requirement of a handover from macrocell to femtocell and that it is limited by the fact that underlying macrocell infrastructure must be present. However, this limitation falls within the scope of our paper since we explore dense urban scenarios. Also, the additional signaling due to sleep mode integration and handover requirement is more than compensated by the reduction of femtocell functionalities in sleep mode, resulting in the reduction of overall signalling compared to the same scenarios if femtocells would always operate in full mode [10].

2.3   Throughput Calculation

When the power of the femtocells has been determined (either the pilot or the proposed) we derive the Signal-to-interference-plus-noise ratio (SINR) of each user. The SINR of a user u on each sub-carrier k, served by either macrocell or a femtocell, is given by:

$$SINR_{u,k} = \frac{P_{B,k}G_{u,B,k}}{N_0\Delta f + \sum_{B'} P_{B',k}G_{u,B',k}}. \tag{2}$$

where $P_{B,k}$ is the transmit power of user's serving base station B on subcarrier k, and $G_{u,B,k}$ is the channel gain between user u and its serving cell B on sub-carrier k. Similarly, $P_{B',k}$ and $G_{u,B',k}$ denote respectively the power of every other interfering base station (either femtocell or macrocell) and the gain between them and the user u. N_0 is the white noise power spectral density, and Δf the sub-carrier spacing.

From the SINR we then calculate the capacity of the user u on that subcarrier k by [11]:

$$C_{u,k} = \Delta f \cdot log_2 \left(1 + \alpha SINR_{u,k}\right). \tag{3}$$

where α is defined by $\alpha = -1.5/ln(5BER)$. Based on the spectrum allocation and the subcarriers utilized by the user, we evaluate the overall throughput of serving base station by [12]:

$$T_B = \sum_u \sum_k \beta_{u,k} C_{u,k}. \tag{4}$$

where, $\beta_{u,k}$ notifies the sub-carrier assignment for the users. When $\beta_{u,k} = 1$, the sub-carrier k is assigned to user u. Otherwise, $\beta_{u,k} = 0$.

3 Proposed Scheme

The ad hoc nature of femtocells deployments is a critical factor that depending on the circumstances may lead to a success or a failure. On the one hand, the flexibility they provide and the targeting of very specific local needs is very helpful. On the other hand, the lack of central coordination for their placement may lead to severe problems. The deployment of macrocell layer base stations is carefully planned regarding the location and the spectral usage, in order to gain the maximum of their utilization and avoid large interference issues. If no such planning took place, and base stations happened to be in very close distance and using same frequencies, the interference would be catastrophic and handovers would quite frequently occur.

Unfortunately, in femtocell layer this could be a usual scenario for the upcoming ultra dense networks. The situation gets worse, if we also consider that private owned femtocells operate mostly in closed access mode, making the handover option to other femtocells impossible. The accumulative interference of multiple nearby femtocells for an apartment residents in a building would easily lead to the acquirement of a femtocell by that household, too. It is easy to conclude that with every deployment of a femtocell in a building, the need of the neighbors for their own femtocell increases, thus eventually, every apartment in that building will have a femtocell.

This however represents a disparity, because the number of femtocell base stations will not reflect the actual needs in data rates, capacity or connections but solely the exclusivity of usage between separate apartments. This situation causes mainly three problems. Firstly, the subscribers of a femtocell will suffer by the accumulative interference of all the other nearby femtocells. Secondly, any individual not belonging to any of the femtocells access list, would also suffer tremendously. Thirdly, the energy consumption of the practically redundant base stations should be avoided.

We address the above by proposing a scheme that combines two operating modes of the femtocell: The hybrid access mode and the sleep mode. Sleep mode as explained in Sect. 2, is a mode used in base stations where most but not all of their functionalities have been turned off. On one hand this provides energy efficiency when full operation is not required, and on the other hand the transition to full operating state is rapid. A waking signal is usually used in order for the femtocell to return to full operation, either from the user, from the network or from the femtocell itself [3,4] with every approach resulting in different advantages and disadvantages in energy efficiency and in functional requirements. In sleep mode we consider zero interference towards non-subscribed users and no serving of subscribed ones.

Hybrid access mode is an operation state for a femtocell where it adapts an intermediate policy regarding which users it will admit. While closed access restricts access to users enlisted to its Closed Subscriber Group (CSG) of the femtocell, and open access allows everyone in its range, hybrid access presents a golden mean. While it preserves its main portion of resources for its CSG users, it may allow external users in their range as well, usually under custom policy restrictions. The main problem for the adoption of hybrid or open access is that owners of private femtocells are justifiably reluctant to offer their resources to external users. Hybrid access admission policies usually tackle this problem through pricing schemes where the owners are compensated for their resources' provision. The same is true for the owners of the femtocell that goes to sleep mode. In most papers, sleep mode is activated only when the traffic demands of their users is zero because otherwise they will experience performance disruptions. Instead, in our case, we follow a different approach that uses a combination of hybrid access and sleep mode to provide incentives of energy savings and data rate gains. Femtocells with active users may turn to sleep, while their users' reallocation is possible through the hybrid access of their neighboring femtocells. This exchange allows the users to willfully adopt these modes, since policy restrictions require performance improvement. As a result fewer base station will be active, while user experience stays the same or improves.

Thus, the mechanism first investigates if a femtocell is eligible to turn to sleep mode, by examining clusters of femtocells and test if a reallocation to a neighboring femtocell is possible. Incentives for the femtocell to turn to sleep mode or to hybrid access are provided through requirements. First, each user belonging to the candidate for sleep mode femtocell has to at least regain its performance when reallocated to another femtocell. This is expressed by:

$$THR_{New} \geq THR_{Old}. \tag{5}$$

The user will of course try to connect to an active femtocell, which will be serving his own subscribers at the time. That means it will probably get a portion of spectrum resources of what it enjoyed by its own femtocell. A part of this reduction is compensated by the reduced interference in the area since a close by femtocell will turn to sleep. The rest might require an increment in the power levels of the new base station in order to reach the user's prior performance. Searching for the required power increment, according to Sect. 2, based on the previous equation we have:

$$P_{Inc} \geq \frac{R * \left(\Delta f + \sum_{B'} P_{B'} G_{u,B'} \right) - P_{Old} * G_{u,N}}{G_{u,N}}. \tag{6}$$

where $\Delta f + \sum_{B'} P_{B'} G_{u,B'}$ denotes the interference in the user when connected to the new femtocell, $G_{u,N}$ his/her gain relative to the base station he might migrate, P_{Old} the power of that station and R is:

$$R = \frac{(1 + aSINR_{Old})^{(N_2+1)/N_1} - 1}{a}. \tag{7}$$

where $SINR_{Old}$ is the SINR that the user would experience if served by the original femtocell. N_2 is the number of users served by the neighbour and N_1 is the number of users served by the origin femtocell. Power increment is also subject to a maximum allowed power transmission of the femtocell.

A similar incentive is required for the users of a femtocell candidate to adopt hybrid access. Thus hybrid access is adopted only for users that come from a neighboring sleeping femtocell. In addition, the gains of it turned to sleep mode due to less interference must compensate the reduced spectrum utilization due to hybrid access. Again, added to the reduction of interference due to the sleeping neighbour, a power increment may be required to compensate for the reduction of further spectrum resources:

$$P_{Inc} \geq \frac{R * \left(\Delta f + \sum_{B'} P_{B'} G_{u,B'} \right) - P_{Old} * G_{u,N}}{G_{u,N}}. \tag{8}$$

where $\Delta f + \sum_{B'} P_{B'} G_{u,B'}$ denotes the interference of the subscriber, $G_{u,N}$ his/her gain as before, P_{Old} the power of the femtocell and R this time:

$$R = \frac{(1 + aSINR_{Old})^{(N_2+1)/N_2} - 1}{a}. \tag{9}$$

Estimating the required power level that will meet both of the demands, a final check is taking place for the rest of the femtocells of the same cluster that do not participate in that particular user exchange. The check makes sure that no subscriber of these femtocells experiences decrease in his/her throughput. This is possible when these users benefit by the deactivation of the slept femtocell at least as strongly as they are affected by the increase on their neighbour's power transmission. If this check returns successful the deactivation and the user exchange is finalized.

4   Performance Evaluation

4.1   Simulation Parameters

In our simulations, we considered a network of 9 macrocells with the base station located at the center of each cell and transmitting at 46 dBm. The cells' radius was 250 m. In this area we randomly deployed multiple femtocells and their subscribers. Each femtocell could have up to three transmitting subscribers at the same time. Macrocell users were also randomly deployed. Parameters values (Table 1) have been based on 3GPP directives from LTE-A and the LTE simulator in [13]. Results depicting cumulative distribution function (CDF) show the average obtained by 20 repeated simulations. An instance of the simulation topology is shown in Fig. 1.

Table 1. Simulation parameters

Parameter	Value
Macrocells	9
Macrocell radius	250 m
Femtocells	250–550
Subscribers per femtocell	1–3
Macrocell users	140
Bandwidth	20 MHz
Carrier frequency	2 GHz
BS transmit power	46 dBm
FBS max transmit power	18 dBm

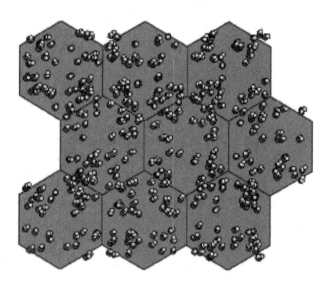

Fig. 1. Instance of the network

4.2   Simulation Results

Figure 2 shows the number of slept femtocells for different densities when the simple form is adopted and when it is enhanced with power control. Simple form represents our initial approach where no power increase was allowed in order to meet the performance requirements. The results are somewhat expected, since initially the restriction for better performance for every user with one less base station is quite strict making the possibility for a slept femtocell thin (i.e. 5 femtocells turned to sleep mode when 50 clusters were formed). Power control causes a dramatic increase in slept femtocells quadrupling the number to 20. Even if we neglect the capacity gains that we present later, and consider the worst case where users' data rate did not experience either an increase or a decrease, the energy gains of the mechanism as a result of the deactivated femtocells are substantial.

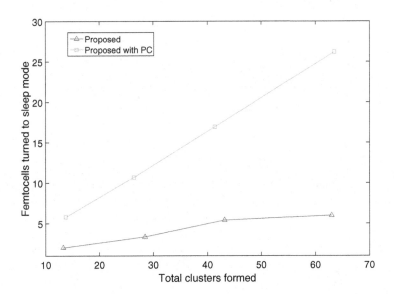

Fig. 2. Number of femtocells turned to sleep mode depending on the femtocell deployment density

However, the worst case regarding the users' throughput does not happen. Since the mechanism requires every user involved in the slept or hybrid femtocell experience the same performance, if the exchange is feasible, it adopts to the user who is in more danger to experience deterioration. That provides a margin of improvement for the users who were not in the danger zone, i.e. users who would not face decrease in their data rate even with the initial power transmission levels. This improvement can be clearly seen in Fig. 3 which displays the CDF of the throughput exhibited by subscribers of femtocells that are part of a cluster (independently of having eventually a slept femtocell in its members or not). The mechanism in its simple form showcases an improvement compared to the initial state where every femtocell is activated and operates in CSG, whereas the power control version increases the performance substantially.

Since these scenarios are characterized heavily by their tendency in trade-offs, there are also users who are going to be influenced negatively. Figure 4 depicts

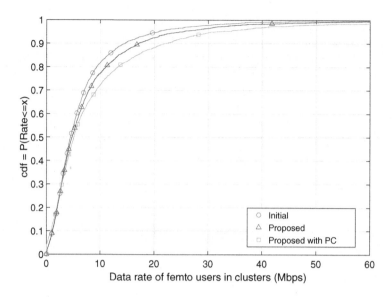

Fig. 3. CDF of the data rate of femto users that are subscribers to femtocells that are members of clusters.

the CDF of the macrocell users that were found in the range of one (or more) femtocell that belong in a cluster. The simple strategy mainly resulted in the deactivation of femtocells within a cluster. Remaining operating stations did not increase their power levels, at least not due to the mechanism requirements. This had a beneficial effect on this type of users who saw the overall interference in the

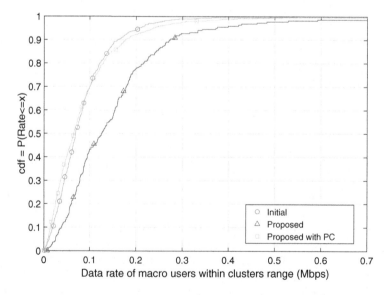

Fig. 4. CDF of the data rate of macro users that are affected by femtocells that are members of clusters

area to mitigate. Unfortunately, in the power control version, any mitigation due to femtocell deactivation is balanced by an equal increase due to power transmission increase. Therefore, the macro users' throughput is significantly behind the simple sleep strategy version. It is worth to note however, that compared to the initial state macro users mostly retain their performance without experiencing any downfall.

5   Conclusions and Future Work

In this paper we investigated performance gains for our proposed sleep mode and hybrid access mechanism extending its benefits by introducing a power control strategy. The mechanism tries to overcome the base station density caused by the exclusivity of femtocell resources, providing performance incentives to their users in order to turn their femtocell into sleep mode or adapt hybrid access policies.

We managed to increase substantially the number of femtocells turned to sleep mode by simply allowing the increase in power transmission in the hybrid access femtocells that admit neighbour femtocell's users. Balance is enforced by seeking the maximum increase in power control that retains the performance of the subscribers involved in the user exchange and at the same time avoiding negative influence to the close-by subscribers of the same cluster's femtocells. As a result the overall capacity provided by the femtocells to their subscribers is increased substantially without compromising any individual subscribed user. The increased energy efficiency of the enhanced approach is also noted. On the downside, macrocell users lose the benefit they enjoyed by the deactivation of some nearby femtocells due to the increase in power transmission of the remaining operating stations. However, compared to their initial state, no substantial decrease is observed.

Future extensions of this work could include the estimation of energy efficiency and performance gains of the algorithm, adding user mobility, and examining different traffic models.

References

1. Okino, K., Nakayama, T., Yamazaki, C., Sato, H., Kusano, Y.: Pico cell range expansion with interference mitigation toward LTE-advanced heterogeneous networks. In: IEEE International Conference on Communications Workshops (ICC), pp. 1–5, June 2011
2. Wu, J., Zhang, Y., Zukerman, M., Yung, E.K.N.: Energy-efficient base-stations sleep-mode techniques in green cellular networks: a survey. IEEE Commun. Surv. Tutorials **17**(2), 803–826 (2015)
3. Ashraf, I., Boccardi, F., Ho, L.: Sleep mode techniques for small cell deployments. IEEE Commun. Mag. **49**(8), 72–79 (2011)
4. Mugume, E., So, D.K.C.: Sleep mode mechanisms in dense small cell networks. In: IEEE International Conference on Communications (ICC), pp. 192–197, June 2015

5. Samarakoon, S., Bennis, M., Saad, W., Latva-aho, M.: Dynamic clustering and sleep mode strategies for small cell networks. In: 11th International Symposium on Wireless Communications Systems (ISWCS), pp. 934–938, August 2014

6. Ali, S., Ismail, M., Nordin, R.: Femtocell sleep mode activation based interference mitigation in two-tier networks. Procedia Technol. **11**, 1088–1095 (2013). 4th International Conference on Electrical Engineering and Informatics, fICEEIg 2013

7. Bouras, C., Diles, G.: Sleep mode performance gains in 5G femtocell clusters. In: 8th International Congress on Ultra Modern Telecommunications and Control Systems, October 2016

8. 3GPP TR 36.814 V9.0.0, Evolved Universal Terrestrial Radio Access (E-UTRA); Further advancements for E-UTRA physical layer aspects (Release 9), 3rd Generation Partnership Project, Technical report (2010)

9. Claussen, H.: Performance of macro- and co-channel femtocells in a hierarchical cell structure. In: IEEE 18th International Symposium on Personal, Indoor and Mobile Radio Communications, PIMRC 2007, pp. 1–5, September 2007

10. Claussen, H., Ashraf, I., Ho, L.T.W.: Dynamic idle mode procedures for femtocells. Bell Labs Tech. J. **15**(2), 95–116 (2010)

11. Lei, H., Zhang, L., Zhang, X., Yang, D.: A novel multi-cell OFDMA system structure using fractional frequency reuse. In: IEEE 18th International Symposium on Personal, Indoor and Mobile Radio Communications, PIMRC 2007, pp. 1–5 (2007)

12. Lee, P., Lee, T., Jeong, J., Shin, J.: Interference management in LTE femtocell systems using fractional frequency reuse. In: 12th International Conference on Advanced Communication Technology 2010 (ICACT 2010), vol. 2, pp. 1047–1051 (2010)

13. Simsek, M., Akbudak, T., Zhao, B., Czylwik, A.: An LTE-femtocell dynamic system level simulator. In: International ITG Workshop on Smart Antennas (WSA), pp. 66–71, February 2010

System Model for Multi-level Cloud Based Tactile Internet System

Abdelhamied A. Ateya[1]([✉]), Anastasia Vybornova[1],
Konstantin Samouylov[2], and Andrey Koucheryavy[1]

[1] St. Petersburg State University of Telecommunication,
22 Prospekt Bolshevikov, St. Petersburg, Russia
a_ashraf@zu.edu.eg, a.vybornova@gmail.com,
akouch@mail.ru
[2] Peoples' Friendship University of Russia (RUDN University),
6 Miklukho-Maklaya Street, Moscow 117198, Russia

Abstract. With the realization of 5G system which will become a fact by 2020, there is a great demand to achieve the Tactile Internet system. Tactile Internet system should handle a 1 ms communication latency, which is the main problem of the system realization. One of the proposed system structures to achieve such latency is to build the system based on the multilevel cloud architecture and the 5G network structure. In this work, we build a system model for a multi-level cloud based Tactile Internet system. The model is used to find the system latency and evaluate the system performance. The proposed system is simulated and the results show that the system will achieve a lower latency than other known architectures. The proposed model also reduces the overall network congestion. It can be used to optimize the number of clouds in the system to achieve the best system performance.

Keywords: Tactile internet · Cloud · System model · Mobile edge computing · Ultra-low latency · 5G

1 Introduction

Unlike the existing cellular networks, the future 5G cellular system will support new machine type communication services. By achieving the waited cellular system in 2020, Tactile Internet may become a reality. Tactile Internet will enable human -to-machine (H2 M) communication and interaction, which consequently will enable a new era for the communication networks [1]. Tactile systems will have massive applications in many fields such as smart cities, education, health care, augmented reality and smart grid [2]. The main challenge with the design and development of the Tactile Internet is the 1 ms round trip delay.

Mobile edge computing (MEC) is one of the key features that will enable the development and realization of the 5G system. MEC merge the three technologies of the mobile Internet, mobile computing and cloud computing [3]. The first technology is the mobile Internet which represents the wireless communication network or the cellular network. The second technology is the mobile computing that is represented by

© IFIP International Federation for Information Processing 2017
Published by Springer International Publishing AG 2017. All Rights Reserved
Y. Koucheryavy et al. (Eds.): WWIC 2017, LNCS 10372, pp. 77–86, 2017.
DOI: 10.1007/978-3-319-61382-6_7

the techniques used for executing wireless communications. Mobile computing includes both hardware and software involved in the communication process such as protocols, user equipment and the network infrastructure. The last part is the cloud-computing that provides a way for resources sharing or in other word deliver every-thing for the user as a service at the time and place the user need it.

Moving clouds closer to the user (approximately one hope away from the user) will allow to achieve lower latency and thus enable the realization of real time haptic communication that is known as Tactile Internet, which becomes a very promising area of research. MEC replaces the large and expensive data centers with small distributed cloud units connected to the cellular network [4]. These small cloud units have limited capabilities in terms of processing and storage. There are a lot of studies that suggest places for the edge computing unit in order to achieve better latency.

In [5] we suggest a multi-level cloud based Tactile Internet system. The system consists of three cloud levels: Micro-cloud, Mini-cloud and Core network cloud level as shown in Fig. 1. Micro-clouds are employed in each cellular cell and connected to the radio access network (RAN), and thus they are one hop away from users. Each group of Micro-clouds is connected to a Mini-cloud unit which has higher capabilities and can process much complex tasks. The second level of clouds (Mini-clouds) act as the controller for the first level (Micro-clouds) connected to it. They also can perform tasks that exceed the workload of the Micro-clouds connected to it and tasks that need processing capabilities greater than that of the Micro-cloud. Mini-clouds are connected to the core network cloud that represents the third level of clouds [5].

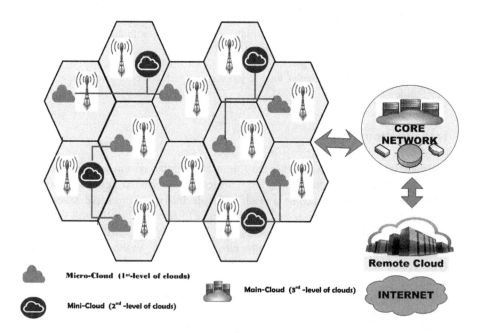

Fig. 1. Tactile Internet system [5].

Presenting a new level of higher capability clouds in the way between core network and RAN's clouds reduces the communication latency and the throughput. Thus, multi-level cloud based Tactile Internet system reduces the round trip delay by applying multilevel hierarchical of cloud units. In this paper, we build a mathematical model for the multi-level cloud based Tactile Internet system. The model is used to find the latency of the system and evaluate the system performance. In Sect. 2 the mathematical model of the system is discussed and the total latency is calculated. In Sect. 3 the system model is simulated over Java environment. Section 4 concludes the paper and describes the future work.

2   Mathematical Model

In this section, we introduce a mathematical model for the multi-level cloud based Tactile Internet system introduced in [5]. The model is used to find the latency and evaluate the system performance. In order to design a low latency Tactile Internet system with the desired performance, a mathematical model for this case is introduced and all the important parameters are defined. Figure 2 illustrates the system model for the Tactile Internet based on the multi-levels of cloud units.

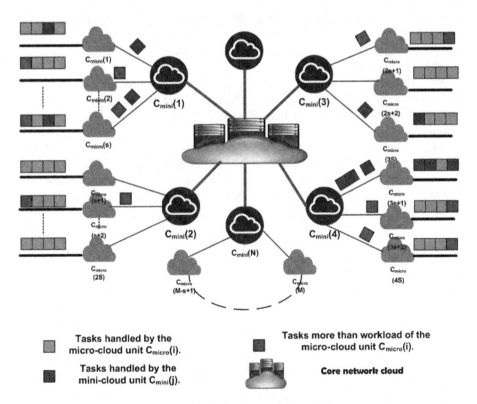

Fig. 2. System model for the Tactile Internet system.

In our system, each cellular cell eNB is connected to a small cloud unit (Micro-cloud) $C_{micro}(i)$ with acceptable processing elements, where, $i \in \{1, 2... M\}$ and M is total number of Micro-clouds in the network. Each group of Micro-clouds are connected to larger cloud unit known as Mini-cloud $C_{mini}(j)$, where, $j \in \{1, 2... N\}$ and N is the total number of Mini-clouds in the network. The Mini-cloud has higher processing and storage capabilities, and used to handle higher performance tasks that cannot be handled by Micro-clouds. Each Mini-cloud also acts as a controller for Micro-clouds connected to it. Mini-clouds represent the gateway between Micro-clouds and the core network. In our model, we assume that each Mini-cloud unit is connected to a fixed number S of Micro-cloud units.

The rate of tasks offloaded to the Micro-cloud unit changes based on the cell users demands. Thus, we assume the tasks randomly arrived based on the Poisson process with a Poisson rate of λ_i. Each cell produces a workload W_i to the connected edge computing unit $C_{micro}(i)$ with a Poisson rate λ_i. Every Micro-cloud can handle tasks offloaded by the corresponding eNB, but in case the processing demands of the current tasks is equal or higher than the maximum workload $W_{cmax}(i)$, new tasks are moved to the Mini-cloud unit, until the resources of the Micro-cloud are released. Therefore, each Micro-cloud unit holds $W_{micro}(i)$ workloads and other non-handled tasks are shifted to the Mini-cloud unit. The computing time of Micro-cloud unit depends on the delivered work load $W_{dmicro}(i)$.

Each Mini-cloud unit can handle up to $W_{mmax}(j)$ of the work load, where, $W_{mmax}(j)$ is the maximum workload of the Mini-cloud unit $C_{mini}(j)$. Tasks that require higher processing capabilities than current free processing resources of the Mini-cloud unit are shifted to the core network cloud.

We consider the multi-server queuing model M/M/s [6] to model the Micro- and Mini-clouds. For Micro-clouds the model is $M/M/S_{mic}$ and for Mini-clouds $M/M/S_{min}$, where S_{mic} and S_{min} are the numbers of servers in the Micro and Mini-cloud unit respectively.

The total latency consists of the task's response time and the communication delay. The average response time for the tasks at the Micro and Mini-clouds is the sum of the queuing time and the processing time of the tasks. The average processing time of the tasks in the Micro and Mini-cloud units can be calculated as a function of the arrival rate λ, based on the M/M/S queuing model and the Erlang's C formula as deduced in [7, 8].

$$T_{micro-i}(\lambda) = \frac{C\left(s_i, \frac{\lambda_i}{\mu_i}\right)}{s_i \mu_i - \lambda_i} + \frac{1}{\mu_i} \tag{1}$$

$$T_{mini-j}(\lambda) = \frac{C\left(s_j, \frac{\lambda_j}{\mu_j}\right)}{s_j \mu_j - \lambda_j} + \frac{1}{\mu_j} \tag{2}$$

$$C(n, \rho) = \frac{\left(\frac{(s\rho)^c}{n!}\right)\left(\frac{1}{1-\rho}\right)}{\sum_{k=0}^{n-1} \frac{(n\rho)^k}{k!} + \left(\frac{(n\rho)^c}{n!}\right)\left(\frac{1}{1-\rho}\right)} \tag{3}$$

Where $T_{micro-i}$ is the average processing time of tasks in Micro-cloud unit i, T_{mini-j} is the average processing time of tasks in Mini-cloud unit j, S_i is the total number of servers in the Micro-cloud unit i, S_j is the total number of servers in the Mini-cloud unit j, λ_i and λ_j are the arrival rates of the Micro-cloud unit i and Mini-cloud unit j and μ_i and μ_j are the corresponding service rates.

To simplify the calculation of the total latency we can assume that the latency function is a linear function and as indicated in [9] this assumption is acceptable and verified. The total latency can be calculated simply as following:

a- If the task is handled by Micro-cloud unit:

$$T_{T-micro-i}(w_i) = f_c(w) + d_{cell} = [\alpha(w_{dmicro-i}) + \beta] + d_{cell} \qquad (4)$$

Where $T_{T-micro-i}$ is the total latency for the offloaded tasks of the Micro-cloud unit i, f_c is the linear function that is used to determine the processing delay for the current work load and d_{cell} is the communication latency inside the cellular cell.

b- If the task is moved and handled by the Mini-cloud unit:

$$T_{T-mini-j}(w_j) = f_c(w) + d_{cell} = [\alpha(w_{dmini-j}) + \beta] + d_{cell} + d_{C_{Micro-i}, C_{Mini-j}} \qquad (5)$$

Where $T_{T-mini-j}$ is the total latency for the offloaded tasks of the Mini-cloud unit j and $d_{C_{Micro-i}, C_{Mini-j}}$ is the communication delay between micro-cloud unit i and Mini-cloud unit j.

3 Simulation and Results

In this section, we analyze the suggested system model for the Tactile Internet system in a simulation environment, after the mathematical model is defined in the previous section.

a- Simulation environment and simulation parameters

There are many simulation environments that are used to simulate and deploy Micro-cloud and Clouds with different facilities and capabilities [10, 11]. These environments are able to create virtual machines (VM), remote procedure execution and web services with different capabilities. We developed a tool kit based on the CloudSim framework to analyze the system. The simulator is based on Java language and on the IDE NetBeans. The simulation is run on Window 7 basic (64-bit) and i7 Processor with 3.07 GHz of speed and memory of 8 GB.

We build a system consists of 300 Micro-cloud units distributed randomly and connected to 20 Mini-cloud units. Each Micro-cloud unit represents the offload to a cellular cell. Each Mini-cloud unit is connected and controls 15 Micro-cloud units. This number is a design parameter and should be optimized in terms of achieving the lowest latency and best performance of the system. We assume that all Micro-clouds have equal capabilities and also all Mini-clouds are the same. The application tasks are sent and distributed to the Micro-clouds randomly. All important simulation parameters are illustrated in Table 1.

Table 1. Simulation parameters.

Parameter	Description	Value
M	Number of Micro-clouds in the network	300
N	Number of Mini-clouds in the network	20
S	Number of Micro-cloud units connected to each Mini-cloud unit	15
W_{mmax}	Maximum work load of the Mini-cloud unit per second	100 events/s
W_{cmax}	Maximum work load of the Micro-cloud unit per second	(20, 30, 40) events/s
λ_i	Arrival rate of the Micro-cloud unit	15
μ_i	Service rate of the Micro-cloud unit	5 Mbps
μ_j	Service rate of the Mini-cloud unit	8 Mbps
d_{cell}	The communication latency inside the cellular cell	1 ms/hop
$d_{C_{Micro-i},C_{Mini-j}}$	The communication delay between micro-cloud unit and Mini-cloud unit	1.5 ms
α	Gradient of computing function	10
β	Constant of computing function	0
RAM,HDD	Micro-cloud RAM, Storage Mini-cloud RAM, Storage	1024 Mb,1 Gb 2048 Mb, 5 Gb

b- Simulation results and analysis

We consider three simulation cases with three different values for Wcmax. In each case the latency for each Micro and Mini- cloud unit is calculated two times. The first is for the simulated system and the second is the theoretical one. The theoretical latency of Micro and Mini-cloud units is calculated using Eqs. (4) and (5) based on the amount of workload delivered to the cloud unit.

In the first case, we assume a workload of 20 events per second and tasks higher than this workload will be directed to Mini-cloud unit. This will put a load on the Mini-cloud units. Figure 3 shows the total latency for each Micro-cloud unit for both theoretical and simulation models. The average latencies for the theoretical and simulation cases are 0.698 and 0.70 ms respectively, and it seems to be very near for all Micro-clouds because they are of the same parameters. Theoretical latency varies from one cloud unit to another based on the amount of delivered workload since the tasks are distributed randomly. Figure 4 indicates the total latency for each Mini-cloud unit and the average total latencies for theoretical and simulation cases are 1.127 and 1.13 ms. It is clear that the latency for Mini-cloud units is much higher as there is an additional communication hop between the Mini and Micro-cloud units. Without Mini-clouds, the latency is supposed to be much higher as the tasks would be delivered to the core network and the core network would be loaded with more workload.

In the second case, we increase the maximum work load of the Micro-cloud units to 30 and thus it should reduce the total load on the Mini-cloud units. This is because Micro-cloud units in this case handle many tasks and therefore reduce the number of tasks moved to Mini-cloud units. Figure 5 shows the total latency for each Micro-cloud unit compared to the delay according to the theoretical model. The average latencies for

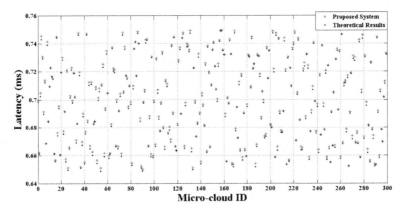

Fig. 3. Latency of Micro-cloud units in case (1).

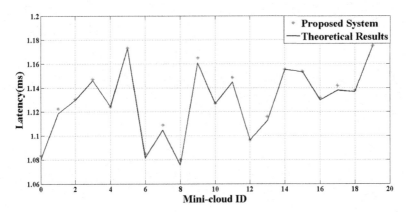

Fig. 4. Latency of Mini-cloud units in case (1).

the theoretical and simulation cases are 0.838 and 0.84 ms respectively and it increased because of the increased workload. Figure 6 indicates the total latency for each Mini-cloud unit. The average latencies are 0.978 and 0.98 ms and this is less than the first case as the tasks moved from Micro-cloud units are less than that in the first case.

In the third case, the maximum work load of all Micro-cloud units is set to 40 and the delay for Micro and Mini- clouds is recorded and compared to the delay according to the theoretical model as indicated in Figs. 7 and 8.

The time delay for each of Micro and Mini-clouds in the previous cases can be found to be relatively near to the theoretical results. The average delays for all Micro-cloud units and Mini-cloud units in the three cases are compared with that of the theoretical model in Table 2. Finally, the average workload for all Micro and Mini-clouds for each of the previous cases is illustrated in Fig. 9.

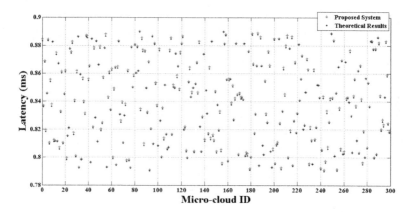

Fig. 5. Latency of Micro-cloud units in case (2).

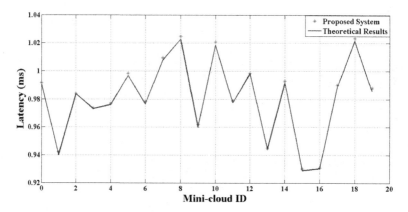

Fig. 6. Latency of Mini-cloud units in case (2).

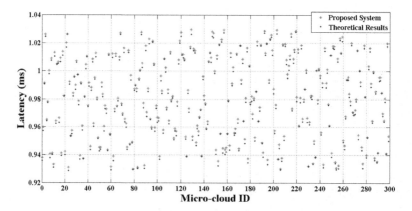

Fig. 7. Latency of Micro-cloud units in case (3).

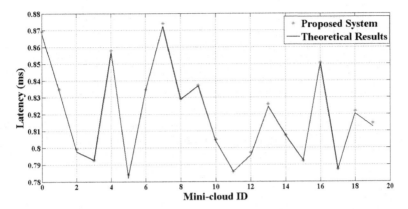

Fig. 8. Latency of Mini-cloud units in case (3).

Table 2. Average delay for Micro- and Mini-clouds.

		Case (1)	Case (2)	Case (3)
Micro-cloud level	Theoretical result	0.698 ms	0.838 ms	0.978 ms
	Simulation result	0.70 ms	0.84 ms	0.99 ms
Mini-cloud level	Theoretical result	1.127 ms	0.978 ms	0.828 ms
	Simulation result	1.13 ms	0.98 ms	0.83 ms

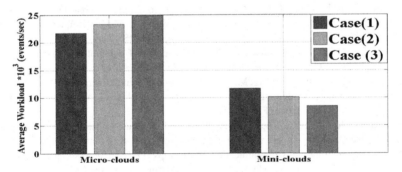

Fig. 9. Average workload for each cloud level.

4 Conclusion and Future Work

One of the efficient ways to reduce the round trip latency of data is to introduce a cloud level in the way between the eNB's cloud and the core network cloud. Multi-level cloud based Tactile Internet system introduces the Micro and Mini-cloud levels before the core network cloud. These two levels, as it was illustrated before, provides a useful and efficient way to reduce the round trip latency of data and produce away for offloading to reduce the workload delivered to the core network. The paper introduces a mathematical model for the Multi-level cloud based Tactile Internet system that is used to calculate the system latency. Simulation results verify the model and thus it can be used as a valid structure for the Tactile Internet system. The proposed system model can be used to solve the optimization problems of the Tactile Internet in terms of latency and energy efficiency.

Our future vision is to use the mathematical model to optimize the number of first level clouds connected to each Mini-cloud unit to reduce the round trip delay.

Acknowledgement. The publication was financially supported by the Ministry of Education and Science of the Russian Federation (the Agreement number 02.a03.21.0008).

References

1. Aijaz, A., Simsek, M., Dohler, M., Fettweis, G.: Shaping 5G for the tactile internet. In: Xiang, W., Zheng, K., Shen, X. (eds.) 5G Mobile Communications, pp. 677–691. Springer, Cham (2017)
2. ITU-T Technology Watch Report, The Tactile Internet, August 2014
3. Gai, K., Qiu, M., Zhao, H., Tao, L., Zong, Z.: Dynamic energy-aware cloudlet-based mobile cloud computing model for green computing. J. Network Comput. Appl. **59**, 46–54 (2016). Elsevier
4. Aijaz, A., Dohler, M., Aghvami, A.H., Friderikos, V., Frodigh, M.: Realizing the tactile internet:haptic communications over next generation 5G cellular networks. Wirel. Comm., IEEE (2015)
5. Ateya, A., Vybornova, A., Kirichek, R., Koucheryavy, A.: Multilevel cloud based Tactile Internet system. In: IEEE-ICACT2017 International Conference, Korea, February 2017
6. Nair, A., Jacob, M.J., Krishnamoorthy, A.: The multiserver M/M/(s,S) queueing inventory system. Ann. Oper. Res. **233**, 321–333 (2015). Springer, US
7. Harchol-Balter, M.: Performance Modeling and Design of Computer Systems: Queueing Theory in Action. Cambridge University Press, Cambridge (2013)
8. Jia, M., Liang, W., Xu, Z., Huang, M.: Cloudlet load balancing in wireless metropolitan area networks", Computer Communications. In: The 35th Annual IEEE International Conference on IEEE INFOCOM 2016. IEEE (2016)
9. Intharawijitr, K., Iida, K., Koga, H.: Analysis of fog model considering computing and communication latency in 5G cellular networks. In: 2016 IEEE International Conference Pervasive Computing and Communication Workshops (PerCom Workshops) (2016)
10. Wang, S., Tu, G., Ganti, R., He, T., Leung, K., Tripp, H., Warr, K., Zafer, M.: Mobile micro-cloud: application classification, mapping, and deployment. In: Proceeding of Annual Fall Meeting of ITA 2013, October 2013
11. Bahwaireth, K., Tawalbeh, L., Benkhelifa, E., Jararweh, Y.: Experimental comparison of simulation tools for efficient cloud and mobile cloud computing applications. EURASIP J. Info. Secur. (2016). Springer

Task Scheduling Scheme Based on Cost Optimization in 5G/Hetnets C-RAN

Olfa Chabbouh[1(✉)], Nazim Agoulmine[2(✉)], Sonia Ben Rejeb[1(✉)],
and Zied Choukair[1(✉)]

[1] Mediatron Laboratory, High School of Communication of Tunis (Sup'com),
Ariana, Tunisia
{olfa.chabbouh, Sonia.Benrejeb, z.choukair}@supcom.tn
[2] IBISC – IBGBI Laboratory, University of Evry-Val - d'Essonne, Evry, France
Nazim.Agoulmine@ibisc.univ-evry.fr

Abstract. With the increase of data traffic in global mobile network, data computing close to the edge is going more and more memorandum to deal with the resources limitations. This paper, addresses Cloud Radio Access Network (C-RAN) architecture and proposes to provide extra computing and storage resources in the edge in order to allow the offloading of a set of mobile users services from the remote cloud computing infrastructure to a cloud computing infrastructure deployed in the edge next to Remote Radio Heads (RRHs). This approach raises many challenges. One of the challenges is the scheduling strategy of the offloading. Therefore, the main contribution described in this paper is a novel cost based service scheduling (CBSS) mechanism which takes into account deployment cost, deadline and available resources in order to make offloading decisions more efficient and to increase user experience. The solution was implemented in a simulator to highlight the benefit of the approach compared to existing approach.

Keywords: Cloud RAN · Offloading · Cloud-RRH · Task scheduling

1 Introduction

The evolution toward global mobile networks is characterized by an exponential growth of traffic. It is estimated that the data traffic will grow at a compound annual growth rate of 47% from 2016 to 2021 [1]. This growth is mainly due to the huge success of smart phones and tablet. Nowadays, smartphones and tablets are real computers capable to run a large variety of applications in all areas of backend: entertainment, health care, business, social networking, traveling, news… More and more applications are virtualized and running in the cloud overcoming the limited capacities of the end-user devices. However, this necessitates an end to end communication from the mobile terminal to the application or service deployed in the far end cloud computing infrastructure. With the concept of Mobile Cloud Computing (MCC), the idea is to deploy additional cloud computing resources to allow some parts of the applications/services to run locally and offload the communications from the backend towards this local cloud to save resources and increase end users experience.

© IFIP International Federation for Information Processing 2017
Published by Springer International Publishing AG 2017. All Rights Reserved
Y. Koucheryavy et al. (Eds.): WWIC 2017, LNCS 10372, pp. 87–98, 2017.
DOI: 10.1007/978-3-319-61382-6_8

More precisely, cloud-based radio access network has been already proposed in the 5G to decouple the Base Band Units (BBUs) from remote radio heads (RRHs) and to move them into the cloud enabling a centralized processing and management. With this approach, traditional complicated base stations can be simplified to cost-effective and power-efficient radio units (RRHs) by centralizing the processing allowing the efficient management of large-scale small-cell systems. Centralized processing power enables indeed more advanced and efficient network coordination and management.

On the other side, mobile data offloading to external extra resources (such as using wifi) is also an important and popular issue in the cellular network. This consists on offloading the data communication from the mobile network access to another wireless access network (wifi, femto, etc.) using therefore additional resources. This offloading can also target the processing using alternative storage and processing capabilities close to the end users. Several state of art proposals exploit therefore cloud computing technology for this purpose [2].

Our work is related to this context. We propose a novel Cloud RAN heterogeneous architecture where we introduce an edge cloud: the Cloud-RRH. It consists on additional computational and storage resources added to High RRHs (macro-cells) close to mobile end users. Using this infrastructure, mobile users will be able to offload their applications/services from the far end cloud computing infrastructure close to them in Cloud-RRH. The technology to support this offloading is containers [3] that provides a higher level of abstraction in terms of virtualization and isolation compared to other virtualization techniques. Therefore, in order to fully profit from this architecture we need to efficiently schedule offloading requests among different containers. That's why we propose a cost based task scheduling scheme. Especially we focus on overload and migration costs. Moreover, load balancing between containers has been taken into consideration.

This paper is organized as follows. After this introduction, Sect. 2 describes the related works. In Sect. 3, we present a model of the system, the formulation of the problem, and the basic idea of the proposed solution. The following Sect. 4 presents a simulation of the system and the solution as well as initial results. Finally, Sect. 5 concludes this paper.

2 Related Work

Scheduling user's computing tasks is a hot challenge in cloud computing environment. Optimal resource allocation or offloading request scheduling helps to guarantee application performance and to reduce operating costs. A set of existing works are discussed in this section.

Authors in [4] have proposed a selective algorithm that uses standard deviation to decide between the two scheduling algorithms Min-Min and Max-Min in order to minimize the total execution time of tasks. In [5], the improved Max-Min algorithm is modified to define two new algorithms based on the average execution time. Unlike the Max-Min, the task with a just above average run time is selected and assigned to the resource that gives a minimum run time. The average run time is calculated using the arithmetic mean for independent tasks and the geometric mean for dependent tasks.

The main objective is to reduce tasks makespan. Authors in [6] have proposed a task scheduling algorithm based on priority. They have defined three levels of priorities: the scheduling level which represents the objective to be achieved by the planner, the level of resources which represents the attributes available to achieve the desired goal and the level of tasks which represents the available alternatives among which the best task should be scheduled first. Therefore, each task will require resources with a given priority and the priorities of the different tasks are compared with each other in order to be scheduled. In [7], authors have proposed a task scheduling algorithm based on credits. The proposed approach is based on two parameters: the priority of the user and the duration of the task. A credit is assigned to each task according to its duration and priority. The task with the highest credit value is executed first. In [8], an optimized algorithm for task scheduling based PSO (Particle Swarm Optimization) is proposed. PSO is a population-based search algorithm inspired by bird flocking and fish schooling, where each particle learns from its neighbors and itself during the time it travels in space. However, like any other metaheuristic method, this algorithm does not give any guarantees on finding the most optimal solution. Consequently, whenever the search space expands, the chance of finding an optimal solution becomes harder and harder. Authors in [9] have proposed a cost-deadline based task scheduling algorithm (CBD). The cost is calculated according to the task length, deadline and the number of processing elements required. Then, a sorting mechanism is used to decide the order of execution of tasks. Their mapping with virtual machines is given by the Min-Min heuristic algorithm. Therefore, the proposed approach is used to minimize missed deadlines. Authors in [10] have investigated cost based scheduling using linear programming. They have proposed a task scheduling algorithm based on delay bound constraint (SAH-DB) in order to improve the task execution concurrency: when a task is received all the resources (CPU, memory and network) are sorted in descending order based on the resources processing capacity, then the task is dispatched to resources with the minimum execution time.

In this paper, we propose a novel C-RAN architecture and corresponding resource management mechanism, where a Cloud-RRH is introduced in the edge of the mobile network. While most previous works have focused on jobs' completion time, we propose in this work a scheduling optimization mechanism that aims to reduce the cost of tasks scheduling. Unlike previous works, we model the cost of tasks as function of overloading and migration. The scheduling process takes mainly into account the available resources, resource requirements, deadlines and load balancing in Cloud-RRH.

3   Offloading Scheduling Mechanism Proposal

In this section, we will discuss the considered scenario and problem statement before presenting our system model and formulate the optimization problem for the offloading requests scheduling.

3.1 Scenario and Problem Statement

The scenario is depicted in Fig. 1. We consider a C-RAN heterogeneous architecture composed of H-RRHs (High RRHs) which acts as macro cells and L-RRHs (Low RRHs) which acts as small cells. In our scenario, we introduce the Cloud-RRH which represents cloud capacity in the edge network. While in a traditional C-RAN architecture all the RAN functionalities are centralized in BBU pools, we propose to flexibly split of these functionalities between edge and central cloud. We suppose also that additional computation and storage resources are available in the Cloud-RRH for computation offloading. These resources are represented by cloud containers.

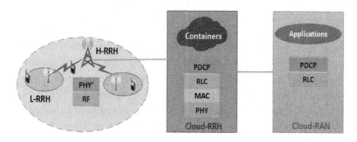

Fig. 1. Proposed C-RAN architecture

We propose to use cloud containers instead of VM because of performance gain. Indeed VM are usually larger than containers since they include the whole operation system and their startup is much slower than containers. A container is essentially a packaged self-contained, ready-to-deploy set of parts of applications, that might even include middleware and business logic in the form of binaries and libraries to run the applications [11], see Fig. 2. Containers are characterized by: (i) a lightweight portable runtime, (ii) the capability to develop, test and deploy applications to a large number of servers and (iii) the capability to interconnect them.

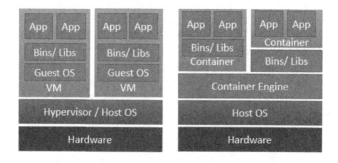

Fig. 2. VM vs Container virtualization architecture

In current data centers the control of virtual machines (VM) requires a Virtual Infrastructure Manager (VIM), which is the entity in charge of VM lifecycle management. In our approach and as part of the cloud management, we propose to add a new functional entity called Cloudlet Manager (CM). The main functionalities of the CM are the following:

- Containers placement/deployment
- Containers monitoring
- Applications scheduling

Mobile users can access their services directly in the edge cloud. The CM could instantiate containers in the edge and offload (part of) the service logic computation in these containers. Containers are not always active, rather they are activated or deactivated accordingly. Different interactions schema are represented in Fig. 3.

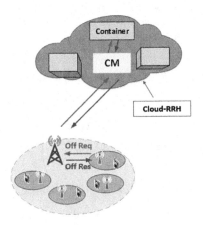

Fig. 3. Cloudlet manager interactions

Mobile users' application tasks can be offloaded in the Cloud-RRH to achieve better performances. The cloudlet manager is responsible to decide in which container application tasks will be executed. A container is characterized by a triplet of allocated resources (CPU, RAM, and Network Bandwidth). Each offloading request is considered as a set of tasks to instantiate in the Cloud-RRH. Each task has a delay constraint and resource requirements in terms of CPU, RAM and Network Bandwidth.

However, it is necessary to well design the scheduler of tasks and the offloading decision based on the available resources and the concurrent requests. The research questions that we are trying to respond are the following:

1. How to find the most suitable container for application tasks offloading that minimizes the total cost, comprising overloading cost and migration cost?
2. How to schedule offloading requests while respecting load balancing between containers in Cloud-RRH?

3.2 System Model

We assume that each Cloud-RRH infrastructure is able to run N predefined containers. Each container is characterized by its available capacity resources CPUi, RAMi and Neti, $i \in N$. An offloading request is specified as a set of M tasks to execute with a deadline D. Each task is characterized by its CPUj, RAMj and Netj requirements, and has an expected execution time Texj, $j \in M$ (time execution if all resources are satisfied). We consider a binary variable $t_{(i,j)}$ to indicate if a task is allocated to a container or not:

$$t_{(i,j)} = \begin{cases} 1 & \text{if task } j \text{ is allocated to container } i \\ 0 & \text{otherwise} \end{cases}$$

We associate to each pair container-task allocation a cost C which value depends on whether the container is overloaded after the execution of the task or not and also whether a task migration was necessary due to user mobility. In this work we did not consider the energy consumption cost. The details of the considered costs are presented in the following:

Overload cost. Let us denote by C_cap_i the computational capacity of container i at time t:

$$C\_cap_i = \begin{pmatrix} C\_cap_i^{CPU} \\ C\_cap_i^{RAM} \\ C\_cap_i^{Net} \end{pmatrix} \quad (1)$$

$C\_ut_{j,i}$ the average resource utilization of task j on container i:

$$C\_ut_{j,i} = \begin{pmatrix} C\_ut_{j,i}^{CPU} \\ C\_ut_{j,i}^{RAM} \\ C\_ut_{j,i}^{Net} \end{pmatrix} \quad (2)$$

The utilization rate μ_i of container i corresponding to the actual system configuration is given by the following formulation:

$$\mu_i = \begin{pmatrix} \mu_i^{CPU} = \dfrac{\sum t_{(i,j)} \cdot C\_ut_{j,i}^{CPU}}{C\_cap_i^{CPU}} \\[3ex] \mu_i^{RAM} = \dfrac{\sum t_{(i,j)} \cdot C\_ut_{j,i}^{RAM}}{C\_cap_i^{RAM}} \\[3ex] \mu_i^{Net} = \dfrac{\sum t_{(i,j)} \cdot C\_ut_{j,i}^{Net}}{C\_cap_i^{Net}} \end{pmatrix} \quad (3)$$

Therefore, container i is considered as overloaded when $Max\ (\mu_i^{CPU}, \mu_i^{RAM}, \mu_i^{Net}) > 1$. When a task j is allocated to an overloaded container, we associate a penalty which we also assume to be positively proportional to the level of overloading. We define the overload cost $ov\_\cos t_i$ a metric as follows:

$$ov\_\cos t_i = \begin{cases} (\mu_i - 1)^\lambda & if \quad Max\ (\mu_i^{CPU}, \mu_i^{RAM}, \mu_i^{Net}) > 1 \\ 0 & otherwise \end{cases} \tag{4}$$

Indeed, λ allows to accentuate the overload cost when approaching the saturation. Therefore, the closer we go to the maximum capacity and the more the cost will increase and the choice will go for another container in order to avoid saturation.

The overall overload cost for the Cloud-RRH system to execute all the tasks can be calculated as follows:

$$ov\_\cos t = \sum_{i=1}^{N} ov\_\cos t_i, \quad N: \text{set of containers} \tag{5}$$

Migration cost. When a mobile user is moving from one cell to another one, the corresponding tasks may be migrated. We associate a penalty r_j when a user task j is migrated, from one container to another one, to capture the service downtime incurred by the migration. The overall migration cost is defined as:

$$mig\_\cos t = \sum_i \sum_j t_{(i,j)} \cdot r_j \tag{6}$$

In this paper, we only consider a migration of the tasks in the same Cloud-RRH and that migration penalty only depends on the type of task. (Migration in the whole network will be considered in future works)

Intuitively the two variables, overload cost and migration cost, are correlated. For example, if we completely optimize the overload cost, task will be distributed over all available containers which will increase the migration cost. Therefore, we need to get a trade-off between the two variables.

Optimization model. Therefore, the goal of the scheduler is to minimize the total cost of overloading and migration in the entire system when executing all the submitted requests. We considered two parameters α and β that represents the importance of weight given to each cost.

Objective function

$$Minimize \quad \text{Cost} = \sum \alpha\ ov\_\cos t + \beta\ mig\_\cos t \tag{7}$$

Subject to

$$\sum_j t_{(i,j)} \cdot Tex_j \leq D \tag{8}$$

$$\begin{cases} \sum_j t_{(i,j)} \cdot C\_ut_{j,i}^{CPU} \leq CPU_i \\ \sum_j t_{(i,j)} \cdot C\_ut_{j,i}^{RAM} \leq RAM_i \\ \sum_j t_{(i,j)} \cdot C\_ut_{j,i}^{Net} \leq Net_i \end{cases} \tag{9}$$

$$\frac{\left| \mu_i - \frac{\sum_i \mu_i}{N} \right|}{\mu_i} \leq \varepsilon \tag{10}$$

$$\sum_j t_{(i,j)} = 1 \tag{11}$$

The optimization is subject to constraints given by (8) through (11). Constraint (8) guarantees that each offloading request is executed before the application's deadline. Constraint (9) enforces that all tasks' requirements including number of CPU, amount of memory and network bandwidth are lower than container resources. Constraint (10) guarantees load balancing between containers in the same Cloud-RRH where ε denotes for the maximum tolerance of load balancing. Finally, constraint (11) ensures that each task is scheduled on only one container.

First we set $\alpha = \beta = 0.5$ which means that equal weight is given for the different types of resources. We also consider that all tasks are executed in parallel and the deadline D constraint is therefore fixed for the worst case when all tasks are executed in serial.

This problem is a MIP and can therefore be solved as a linear program since the objective function is linear to all variables.

4   Simulation and Results

In order to evaluate the scheduling performance on tasks' execution cost for the proposed cost based scheduling scheme (CBSS), we have compared its results with SAH-DB scheduling mechanism. SAH-DB is a task scheduling algorithm based linear programming. It aims to schedule tasks while reducing the total execution cost within the user-expected delay bound. When a task t is utilizing a resource k, the execution cost is expressed as the cost of the resource k executing the task t.

Table 1. Parameters setting

Entity	Parameter	Value
Container	Number of containers	25–100
	CPU	1–10
	Memory (RAM)	128–512 Mbytes
	Network bandwidth	100–200 Kbps
Task	Total number of tasks	20–140
	CPU	1–4
	Memory (RAM)	128– 1024 Kbytes
	Network bandwidth	1–20 Kbps

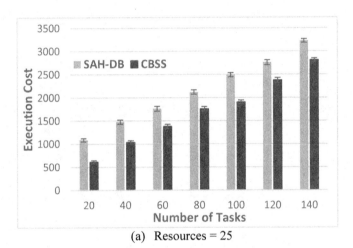

(a) Resources = 25

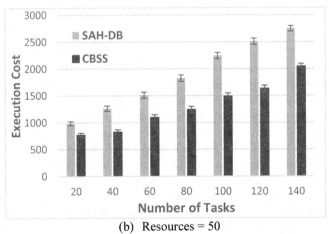

(b) Resources = 50

Fig. 4. The execution cost with different resources

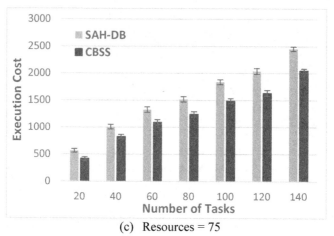

(c) Resources = 75

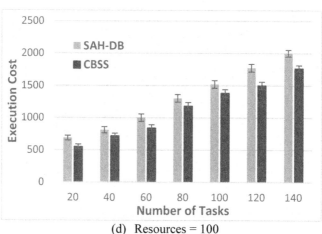

(d) Resources = 100

Fig. 4. (*continued*)

We considered a Cloud-RRH with N = {25, 50, 75, 100} containers having heterogeneous resources. The computing capacity of containers varies from 1 to 10 CPUs. The memory is set from 128 Mbytes to 512 Mbytes and the network bandwidth is set from 100 Kbps to 200 Kbps. The number of tasks is set as M = {20, 40, 60, 80, 100, 120, 140}. Tasks have heterogeneous requirements: CPU varies from 1 to 4, memory is between 128 and 1024 Kbytes and network bandwidth is varying between 1 and 20 Kbps. Offloading requests are embedded sequentially and their requirements are generated randomly. Simulation parameters are summarized in Table 1. As we have mentioned before, we set α = β = 0.5 and λ = 2.

We have used IBM's linear programming solver CPLEX [12], and solved the problem with multiple data inputs.

We have evaluated the scheduling efficiency in terms of execution cost under a varying number of associated tasks. Figure 4 represents the execution cost and its standard deviation by applying the proposed cost based scheduling scheme and SAH-DB scheduling algorithm with 25 to 100 cloud containers respectively. The proposed scheduling algorithm can reduce total execution cost compared with SAH-DB algorithm in the different number of associated tasks. Moreover, the total scheduling cost decreases with the increase of the number of resources and increases with the number of associated tasks. Therefore, the more resources are available the more the scheduling process is efficient.

5   Conclusion and Perspectives

This paper proposes a cost based scheduling scheme (CBSS) that aims to minimize scheduling cost while considering available resources, resource requirements, deadline and load balancing in Cloud-RRH. We consider a scenario where users can offload tasks to Cloud-RRH. We focus on scheduling tasks that requests several resources such as CPU, memory and disk. We formulate the problem as cost optimization problem which takes into account user performance in terms of system overload and migration cost. Simulation results show that the proposed scheme is able to schedule offloading requests while minimizing the total execution cost.

As future works, we will try consider mobility between different Cloud-RRHs while scheduling offloading request.. Furthermore, we will try to better investigate and evaluate the network performances by handling the interference and mobility management in C-RAN.

References

1. Cisco: Cisco Visual Networking Index: Global Mobile Data Traffic Forecast Update, 2016–2021 White Paper, Cisco. http://www.cisco.com/c/en/us/solutions/collateral/service-provider/visual-networking-index-vni/mobile-white-paper-c11-520862.html. Accessed 29 Apr 2017
2. Kumar, K., Liu, J., Lu, Y.-H., Bhargava, B.: A survey of computation offloading for mobile systems. Mob. Netw. Appl. **18**(1), 129–140 (2013)
3. Dua, R., Raja, A.R., Kakadia, D.: Virtualization vs containerization to support PaaS. In: 2014 IEEE International Conference on Cloud Engineering, pp. 610–614 (2014)
4. Katyal, M., Mishra, A.: Application of selective algorithm for effective resource provisioning in cloud computing environment. Int. J. Cloud Comput. Serv. Archit. **4**(1), 1–10 (2014)
5. Santhosh, B., Manjaiah, D.H.: An improved task scheduling algorithm based on max-min for cloud computing. Int. J. Innov. Res. Comput. Commun. Eng. **2**(2), 84–88 (2015)
6. Patel, S.J., Bhoi, U.R.: Improved priority based job scheduling algorithm in cloud computing using iterative method. In: 2014 Fourth International Conference on Advances in Computing and Communications, pp. 199–202 (2014)
7. Thomas, A., Krishnalal, G., Jagathy Raj, V.P.: Credit based scheduling algorithm in cloud computing environment. Procedia Comput. Sci. **46**, 913–920 (2015)

8. Khalili, A., Babamir, S.M.: Makespan improvement of PSO-based dynamic scheduling in cloud environment. In: 23rd Iranian Conference on Electrical Engineering, pp. 613–618 (2015)
9. Zhao, T., Zhou, S., Guo, X., Zhao, Y., Niu, Z.: A cooperative scheduling scheme of local cloud and internet cloud for delay-aware mobile cloud computing. In: 2015 IEEE Globecom Workshops (GC Workshops), pp. 1–6 (2015)
10. Yingchi, M., Ziyang, X., Ping, P., Longbao, W.: Delay-aware associate tasks scheduling in the cloud computing. In: IEEE Fifth International Conference on Big Data and Cloud Computing, pp. 104–109 (2015)
11. Soltesz, S., Pötzl, H., Fiuczynski, M.E., Bavier, A., Peterson, L.: Container-based operating system virtualization: a scalable, high-performance alternative to hypervisors. In: Proceedings of the 2nd ACM SIGOPS/EuroSys European Conference on Computer Systems 2007, New York, pp. 275–287 (2007)
12. IBM ILOG CPLEX Optimization Studio, 01 Janruary 2016. https://www.ibm.com/software/products/fr/ibmilogcpleoptistud. Accessed 29 Apr 2017

Energy Efficiency Performance for 5G Cellular Networks

Afef Bohli[1,2](✉) and Ridha Bouallegue[1](✉)

[1] Engineering School of Tunis, University of Tunis El Manar, Tunis, Tunisia
afef.bohli@gmail.com, ridha.bouallague@gmail.com
[2] Innov'Com Laboratory, Higher School of Communications (Sup'Com) of Tunis,
University of Carthage, Tunis, Tunisia

Abstract. The next generation of wireless connectivity-the fifth generation, or 5G will show an intense demand for data rates. Densified heterogeneous cellular networks, where a large number of small cell stations is deployed on traditional cellular topologies, is defined as one among the most important solutions in order to sustain both data volume and capacity demands. However, energy consumption in such network deployment goes up in proportion along with the rise of small cell station numbers. Thus, enhancing Energy Efficiency (EE) becomes an important aim to implement future wireless mobile networks. In this paper, a dynamic spectrum access scheme is suggested in an ultra-dense heterogeneous network based on a cognitive monitor sensing strategy to improve the EE while meeting the required capacity. The EE analytical expression is derived based on the stochastic geometry theory. Through the simulation results, the performance of the suggested scheme are conducted.

Keywords: Dense heterogeneous networks · Spectrum efficiency · Common channel protocol · Inter-cell-interferences · Cognitive radio · Stochastic geometry · Coverage probability

1 Introduction

The growth of communication traffic from 50% to 100% will contribute to an increase in the energy consumption in the communication networks [1]. Given that information and communication technologies systems and devices account for about 2% of global CO_2 emissions [2,3] and this contribution is expected to increase to 4% by the year 2020 [4], energy consumption will be an important economic cost factor for the Ultra-Dense Heterogeneous Network (UDHetNet). According to some studies, the main source of energy consumption in the mobile network is the base stations. In fact, the base station is the most energy-intensive element, given that 80% [5] of the mobile networks CO_2 contribution came from the base stations.

Therefore, and given the swelling in the number of cell stations in the UDHetNet, future communications will experience a crucial challenge introduced under the slogan of green network aiming to reduce the CO_2 emission.

© IFIP International Federation for Information Processing 2017
Published by Springer International Publishing AG 2017. All Rights Reserved
Y. Koucheryavy et al. (Eds.): WWIC 2017, LNCS 10372, pp. 99–111, 2017.
DOI: 10.1007/978-3-319-61382-6_9

To this end, future networks based on the UDHetNet deployment must be designed to be as energy efficient as possible while keeping in mind the principle spectrum efficiency.

Various aspects for saving energy in the communication systems, such as energy efficient wireless transmission technologies, interference mitigation concepts, network architecture, protocols and opportunistic cognitive spectrum-sharing schemes, are under consideration.

Given that, the higher power consumption portions were related to the circuits of the active base stations, [6] suggested a base station's deactivation technique. Accordingly, deactivation of the non-utilized base stations was evaluated as a promising approach for reducing the energy consumption in mobile networks. The simulation results prove a significant improvement in terms of energy efficiency compared to the traditional sleeping mode. Nevertheless, under the consideration of a multiple input, multiple output-orthogonal frequency division multiplexing small cells network, the Inter-Cell-Interferences (ICIs) are neglected assuming a non-overlapped sharing carrier.

In order to reduce the amount of energy consumption in a dense cell station (considered as access points), [7] put forward the on-demand resource methods strategy. This technique allowed switching, dynamically, on or off, the stations according to their number of users, which was based on the loaded traffic volume as well the set of active users in the coverage zone. A green cluster was conceived based on a set of nearby cell stations. These stations recognized themselves through the use of controlled beacons. Although the use of this strategy improved energy efficiency, it faced a trade-off between service quality and saved power. As the cell sizes were large, the overall cluster coverage was bigger, resulting in higher energy savings but at expense of lower quality service.

A solution based on the dynamic adjustment of the size of cell station coverage area was proposed in [8]. Three parameters, the estimated user demands, traffic load and channel conditions, were utilized for cell station size adaptation. Both distributed and centralized algorithms were conducted. In each case of them, the cell zone service could be implemented in the central station or distributed in all stations, respectively. The main function of this service was to detect and collect information relative to the three defined parameters. Once done, a decision about the cell zooming concept was conducted. Cooperation techniques and relaying methods were considered in the design of this strategy. This concept would provide benefits in terms of energy efficiency by saving the consumed power. Yet, it was challenging to estimate the traffic load, given the significant variations of traffic volume due to fluctuations.

A user's association and power allocation concept to maximize the energy efficiency metric in a two-tier heterogeneous uplink network was proposed in [9]. Unlike the classical mechanism that would allocate the rate to the subcarrier based on an equal manner, this method attributed the highest minimum rate to the subcarrier with the highest channel-to-noise ratio. The numerical results indicated that the rate-proportional method considerably enhanced the energy efficiency.

However, given the dense cell station deployment, the user association in a future UDHetNet will face additional challenges related to the interference management.

It is agreed that the conventional Inter-Cell-Interference-Coordination (ICIC) techniques – defined in the LTE 8/9 releases [10] and aiming to control the ICI through the use of the radio resource management approaches – and the enhanced ICIC – introduced in the LTE R10 [11] and aiming to coordinate the transmissions of multiple cell stations in the frequency and time domains based on the on-power control mechanisms using Almost Blank Subframes (ABS) – are not considered as fully effective solutions in UDHetNets. This, result, first, from the nature of these networks which are arbitrarily planned and dynamically deployed [12]. And second, from the fact that, when all the small cells share the same ABS and are so closely, intra-cell-interferences become a serious problem. A dynamic ABS for each small stations, is proposed by some previous studies, to avoid this type of intra cell interference [13–15]. Yet, in an ultra-dense heterogeneous network, keeping the macro base station silent during all the ABS that are accorded dynamically to various small cell stations bringing about the reduction of the allocated macro-users resources for data transmission, yielding in a spectrum inefficiency.

Thus, the problem of interference is addressed by [16] which coped with the problem of co/cross-tiers ICI issue in the heterogenous network through the use of the cognitive radio concept. The Small Cell Stations (SCSs) presented the secondary system and the macro base station were the primary system. Each SCS senses the free channels of the MBS and the remaining SCSs to serve their users. A semi and full cognitive models are assumed, where in the first case only a perfect MBSs sensing is assumed. However in the second case, in addition to the previous assumption, the perfect SCSs sensing is also considered. Although this technique reduces the interference, it does not reflect the realistic network state given that, in an unplanned SCSs deployment, the miss detection probability should be taken into account. [17] took the same previous issue considering an imperfect SCSs sensing model. However, the case of non existence (perfect or imperfect) sensing idle channels, the SCSs will not have spectrum resources to serve their users.

In our previous work, [18] a dynamic spectrum access scheme, was suggested, to cope with the co/cross ICI in a two-tier heterogeneous network and improve the energy efficiency. Based on the cognitive radio approach with a novel sensing strategy [19], the amount of interference was reduced compared to other traditional scenarios.

This paper presents an extension of our previous work [18]. Thus, an interference mitigation scheme in an ultra-dense heterogeneous network is conceived leading to improve the energy efficiency while guaranteing a required throughput. The rest of this paper is organized as follows. First, in Sect. 2, the system model is described and the suggested protocol is defined. Then, in Sect. 3, the coverage probability expression is derived, based on the stochastic geometry model. In Sect. 4 the Energy Efficiency (EE) formula is derived. After that, the performance of the suggested framework is quantified and proved, in Sect. 5, through the numerical results. Finally, the paper is concluded in Sect. 6.

2 System Model and Assumption

We consider an UDHetNet consisting of independent K tiers of randomly located SCSs, which differ, across tiers, in terms of spatial densities and transmit powers. We assume that the SCSs belonging the ith tier, with $i \in \{K\}$ and $K \geq 1$, follow a stationary independent marked poisson point process (i.m.p.p.p) of a spatial density λ_i. These SCSs have the same transmit power P_{RS_i}, the same static power P_{SS_i} and the same $SINR$ threshold $\widetilde{SINR}_i$. To simplify the derivation of the coverage probability expression, we assume that $\widetilde{SINR}_i > 1(0dB)$ [20]. In fact, using this assumption, [20] proved that at most one SCS in the entire network could provide a $SINR$ greater than the required threshold. Furthermore, and motivated by the same reference, the thermal noise was neglected given that it had a very limited effect on the coverage probability. A Rayleigh fading model is assumed with a gain channel h that follows an exponential distribution with a mean $\eta = 1$. In addition, an omnidirectional path-loss model $l(|x|) = x^\alpha$ is adopted, where α presents the path loss exponent. We consider that for each tier a set of M_i sub-channel are assigned and that the $\bigcap\limits_{i \in \{K\}, k \geq 1} M_i \neq \emptyset$. We note p_{coll_i} the collision probability defining the fact that a subset of the M_i sub-channel is utilized simultaneously by some SCSs (either in the same tier or the other tiers). Let us assume that this set of SCSs follows an i.m.p.p.p, which is a thinning of the i.m.p.p.p ϕ_i of the intensity measure λ_i with the retention probability p_{coll_i}, yielding an i.m.p.p.p of the intensity measure $\xi_i = p_{\text{coll}_i} \lambda_i$. Moreover, we assume $\zeta \in [0, 1]$ the probability that beacons are broadcasted and complementally $1 - \zeta$ the probability that the SCSs are not sending beacons. Therefore, using the thinning method [21], the number of beacons N_i broadcasted by the SCSs will follow an i.m.p.p.p of an intensity measure $\Xi_i = \zeta \lambda_i$ and will be provided by the probability $P_{N_i} = \frac{(A\Xi)^{N_i}}{N_i!} exp(-A_i \Xi_i)$, where A_i is the ith SCS considered area.

Furthermore, the DCCMC (Dynamic Common Cognitive Monitor Channel) MAC layer protocol, proposed and described in [18], is assumed, which means that, each station, after measuring the holding time (vacant channel time) distribution of each idle channel [22], selects the one with the highest maximum probability density function value as the common control channel DCCMC and broadcasts this information as beacons through all the detected idle channel. The user, which is listening on the idle channels, once received the broadcasted beacons, will select the one with the maximum $SINR$ and adapts its transmission parameters in order to switch into this channel.

3 Coverage Probability

The coverage probability for a typical user in the K-tiers heterogenous network, based on the DCCMC concept, represents the Complementary Cumulative Distribution Function (CCDF) of the $SINR$ distribution reached from the best selected DCCMC, which is given as follows [20]:

$$SINR_{x_i} = \frac{P_i h x_i^{-\alpha}}{\sum\limits_{k=1}^{K} I_{x_{k(k \neq i)}}} \tag{1}$$

where x_i is the users position, $I_{x_{k(k \neq i)}}$ is the noise term coming from the aggregate inter-tier interferences from the kth tier.

Setting M_i as the assigned carrier for the ith tier, a typical user UE_i, linked to a station from the ith tier will suffer from the interferences coming from the set of the stations from the same tier as well the other tiers that use some of the M_i allocations resources of its tagged station.

Let take p_{coll_i} as the probability of collision given as follows:

$$p_{\text{coll}_i} = 1 - \prod_{j=1}^{K} \left(1 - \frac{1}{M_i}\right)^{M_j} \tag{2}$$

In fact, the probability of collision, defining the event that "At least one subcarrier from M_i is used simultaneously by the other tiers" is formulated as follows:

$$
\begin{aligned}
p_{\text{coll}_i} &= \mathbb{P}\left[\text{at least one same subcarrier is used by at least two of the } K \text{ tiers}\right] \\
&= 1 - \mathbb{P}\left[\text{No subcarrier is used simultaneously by } K \text{ tiers}\right] \\
&= 1 - \prod_{j=1}^{K} \mathbb{P}\left[\text{No subcarrier is used simultaneously from the } i^{th} \text{ tier}\right] \\
&= 1 - \prod_{j=1}^{K} \left(1 - \frac{1}{M_i}\right)^{M_j}
\end{aligned} \tag{3}
$$

Thus, the interfering station in the ith tier follows an i.m.p.p Φ_i with the intensity measure ξ_i, given as:

$$\xi_i = p_{\text{coll}_i} \lambda_i \tag{4}$$

The proof results from the overlapped resources assumption and from the thinning propriety of the Poisson Point Process (PPP) [21].

Let us denote p_{rbc} as the probability of the event "At least one beacon is received from all tiers." which is derived as follows:

$$
\begin{aligned}
p_{\text{rbc}} &= \mathbb{P}\left[\text{At least one beacon is received from all tiers}\right] \\
&= 1 - \mathbb{P}\left[\text{No beacons are received from the } k \text{ tiers}\right] \\
&= 1 - \prod_{i=1}^{K} [\mathbb{P}\left[\text{No beacons are received from the } i^{th} \text{ tiers}\right] \\
&= 1 - \prod_{i=1}^{K} (1 - \zeta)^{N_i}
\end{aligned} \tag{5}
$$

Therefore, the received beacons from the ith tier follow an i.m.p.p Φ'_i with the intensity measure Ξ_i, given as:

$$\Xi_i = p_{\text{rbc}}\zeta\lambda_i \tag{6}$$

Finally, a deduction from the previous equation conduct to express the CCDF as follows:

$$p_{\text{cvg}} = \frac{\pi p_{\text{rbc}}\zeta}{G(\alpha)} \frac{\sum_{i=1}^{K} \lambda_i \left(\frac{\widetilde{SINR_i}}{P_i}\right)^{\frac{-2}{\alpha}}}{\sum_{i=1}^{K} p_{\text{coll}_i}\lambda_i P_i^{\frac{2}{\alpha}}} \tag{7}$$

where

$$G(\alpha) = \frac{2\pi^2}{\alpha\sin(\frac{2\pi}{\alpha})} \tag{8}$$

To proved this results, we start by calculated:

$$p_{\text{cvg}} = \mathbb{P}\left[\bigcup_{i\in K, x_j\in\Phi'_i} SINR_{x_j} > \widetilde{SINR_i}\right] \tag{9}$$

$$= \mathbb{E}\left[\mathbb{1}\bigcup_{i\in K, x_j\in\Phi'_i} SINR_{x_j} > \widetilde{SINR_i}\right] \tag{10}$$

$$= \sum_{i\in K}\mathbb{E}\sum_{x_j\in\Phi'_i}\left[\mathbb{1}\left(SINR_{x_j} > \widetilde{SINR_i}\right)\right] \tag{11}$$

$$= \sum_{i\in K}\Xi_i\int_{\mathbb{R}^2}\mathbb{P}\left(SINR_{x_j} > \widetilde{SINR_i}\right)dx \tag{12}$$

$$= \sum_{i\in K}\Xi_i\int_{\mathbb{R}^2}\left(1 - \mathbb{P}\left(SINR_{x_j} \leq \widetilde{SINR_i}\right)\right)dx \tag{13}$$

$$= \sum_{i\in K}\Xi_i\int_{\mathbb{R}^2}\mathcal{L}_{I_{x_j}}\left(\frac{x^\alpha\widetilde{SINR_i}}{P_i}\right)dx \tag{14}$$

where (11) yields from the sum of the probabilities of mutually exclusive events resulting from the assumption $\widetilde{SINR_i} > 1(0dB)$, (12) follows the Campbell Mecke theorem [21] and (14) results from the expression of the outage probability given in [18] where $\mathcal{L}_{I_{x_j}}$ is the Laplace transform of the cumulative interference from all the tiers when the typical user is being served by the ith tier. Therefore,

$$\mathcal{L}_{I_{x_j}}(s) = \prod_{i=1}^{K} \mathbb{E}_{\Phi_i, h} \left[exp \left(-s \sum_{k=1, k\neq i} P_k h x_k^{-\alpha} \right) \right] \tag{15}$$

$$= \prod_{i=1}^{K} \mathbb{E}_{\Phi_i} \left[\prod_{x_k \in \phi_i / x_j} \mathbb{E}_h \left[exp \left(-s P_k h x_k^{-\alpha} \right) \right] \right] \tag{16}$$

$$= \prod_{i=1}^{K} exp \left[-\xi_i \int_{o}^{infty} \left(1 - \mathbb{E}_h \left[exp \left(-s P_i h x_i^{-\alpha} \right) \right] \right) dx \right] \tag{17}$$

$$= \prod_{i=1}^{K} exp \left[-\xi_i \int_{o}^{infty} \left(1 - \frac{1}{1 + s P_i h x_i^{-\alpha}} \right) dx \right] \tag{18}$$

$$= exp \left[-s^{\frac{2}{\alpha}} G(\alpha) \sum_{i=1}^{K} \xi_i P_i^{2/\alpha} \right] \tag{19}$$

where (16) results from the assumption of the independence between the fading and the PPP which yields to move the expectation over h inside the product, and (17) follows the generating functional [21] for the PPP. A simple deduction leads to:

$$p_{cvg} = \sum_{i \in K} \Xi_i \int_{\mathbb{R}^2} \left[1 - \mathbb{P} \left(SINR_x \leq \widetilde{SINR}_i \right) \right] dx \tag{20}$$

$$= \sum_{i \in K} \Xi_i \int_{\mathbb{R}^2} exp \left[- \left(\frac{\widetilde{SINR}_i}{P_i} \right)^{\frac{2}{\alpha}} G(\alpha) x_i^2 \sum_{k=1}^{K} \xi_k P_k^{\frac{2}{\alpha}} \right] dx \tag{21}$$

$$= \frac{\pi}{G(\alpha)} \frac{\sum_{i=1}^{K} \Xi_i \left(\frac{\widetilde{SINR}_i}{P_i} \right)^{-2/\alpha}}{\sum_{i=1}^{K} \xi_i P_i^{\frac{2}{\alpha}}} \tag{22}$$

$$= \frac{\pi p_{rbc} \zeta}{G(\alpha)} \frac{\sum_{i=1}^{K} \lambda_i \left(\frac{\widetilde{SINR}_i}{P_i} \right)^{\frac{-2}{\alpha}}}{\sum_{i=1}^{K} p_{coll_i} \lambda_i P_i^{\frac{2}{\alpha}}} \tag{23}$$

Taking the simplest case where $\widetilde{SINR}_i = \widetilde{SINR}, \forall i \in \{K\}$, we observe that the coverage probability is given by:

$$p_{cvg} = \frac{\pi p_{rbc} \zeta}{G(\alpha)} \widetilde{SINR} \frac{\sum_{i=1}^{K} \lambda_i P_i^{\frac{2}{\alpha}}}{\sum_{i=1}^{K} p_{coll_i} \lambda_i P_i^{\frac{2}{\alpha}}} \tag{24}$$

which differs from the conventional model that only depends on the SINR threshold $\widetilde{SINR}$. It is clear that the maximization p_{cvg} goes up by increasing the bandwidth M_i (given that $p_{\text{coll}_i} \xrightarrow[M_i \to +\infty]{} 0$) as well as the density of stations in the tiers (given that $p_{\text{rbc}} \xrightarrow[\lambda_i \to +\infty]{} 1$).

4   Energy Efficiency

The energy efficiency was presented by the ratio between the area's spectral network and the average network power consumption, as Θ_{EE}, given by:

$$\Theta_{EE} = \frac{\text{Area spectral efficiency}}{\text{Total network area power consumption}} \tag{25}$$

where the area spectral efficiency defined as the sum of the average throughput is given as follows:

$$R = p_{cvg} \sum_{i=1}^{K} Blog(1 + \widetilde{SINR_i}) \tag{26}$$

and, the total consumption power P_T is expressed by:

$$P_T = \sum_{i=1}^{K} \lambda_i (\tfrac{1}{\beta_i} P_{RS_i} + P_{SS_i}) \tag{27}$$

where P_{RS_i} and P_{SS_i} are the ith SCS radiated power and static power, respectively, and β_i is the ith SCS power amplifier efficiency.

Based on these results, the following EE formula is conducted:

$$\Theta_{EE} = \frac{p_{cvg} \sum_{i=1}^{K} Blog(1 + \widetilde{SINR_i})}{\sum_{i=1}^{K} \lambda_i (\tfrac{1}{\beta_i} P_{RS_i} + P_{SS_i})} \tag{28}$$

5   Results and Discussion

In a first step, in terms of coverage probability, the analyses are shown based on the simulation results. After that, the difference between the suggested DCCMC scheme and the conventional model, which is subject to a severe ICI, is illustrated. The performance of the proposed protocol is proved compared to the eICIC, which is based on the ABS concept. As a second step, in terms of energy efficiency, the performances of the suggested scheme in a three-tier network are proved compared to the imperfect sensing SCS model.

To this end, we first, consider three different network deployments as follows: 2-tier, 3-tier and 4-tier located over an approximately zone with an area $A > \sum(A_i)$. Each tier has different SCSs that follow an independent PPP with the density measure λ_i, respective to the ith tier and assuming that $\lambda_i = i\lambda$,

$i \in \{2, 4\}$. To facilitate the analysis, we take the case where the considered tiers have the same *SINR* threshold $\widetilde{SINR}$, which is greater than 1(0dB). In addition, we treat the case where $\alpha = 3.2$, the noise power $W = 0$, and the probability $\zeta = 0.3$.

As shown in Fig. 1 which depicts the coverage probability considering different case network deployments (2-tier, 3-tier and 4-tier) for both proposed and conventional scenarios, the DCCMC scheme scenario with 4 tiers yields the most optimistic coverage probability p_{cvg}. This result matches reasonably with the analysis results. Hence, it is clearly observed that the coverage probability goes up resulting on the interference decrease when the number of tiers rise, unlike the conventional model that depends neither on the number of tiers nor on the number of cell-stations because it is similar to a single tier with a fixed threshold $\widetilde{SINR}$. Obviously, the coverage probability under the DCCMC approach increases with the rise of the cell-station density, until reaching a constant optimized p_{cvg} value. However, for a small cell station density, applying the DCCMC methods seems not reliable, which result from the rise of the collision probability.

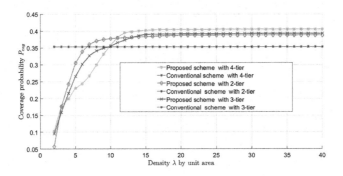

Fig. 1. Coverage probability vs SCSs density with 2, 3 and 4 tiers

Furthermore, Fig. 2 illustrates the performance in terms of coverage probability under various numbers of *SINR* threshold $\widetilde{SINR}$. A significant performance improvement in terms of coverage probability, relative to the DCCMC scheme for all the mentioned cases (2 tier, 3 tier and 4 tier) can be observed compared to the conventional model. Unlike the conventional scenario that does not depend on the number of tiers, the same remark regarding the growth of coverage probability with the increase in the number of tiers is noticed. Indeed, when the number of tiers goes up the collision probability goes down yielding on the reduction of the amount of interference.

The case of 2-tier heterogenous network deployment, where the tier of the SSs is overlaid under the macro base station tier, the classical enhanced ICIC is compared with the proposed DCCMC concept, in terms of coverage probability, as in Fig. 3. Obviously, the DCCMC protocol may be more beneficial than the

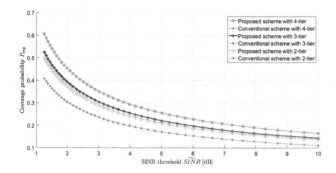

Fig. 2. Coverage probability vs $\widetilde{SINR}$ with 2, 3 and 4 tiers

eICIC approach which is based on the ABS technique. This is because the intra cell interference between SCSs is not taken into account in the eICIC. Therefore, the DCCMC, can achieves as better performance given that the cell-edge users will not suffer from coverage degradation thanks to the use of the virtual coordination based on the cognitive monitoring strategy.

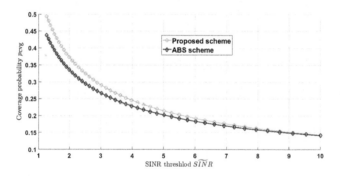

Fig. 3. Coverage probability vs $\widetilde{SINR}$ with 2 tiers

As a second step, in order to depict the performance of the suggested DCCMC protocol compared to other models, in terms of energy efficiency, a three-tier network is considered. Figure 4, shows the impact of the SCSs density λ on the energy efficiency metric and compares the performance of the suggested model with the SCSs imperfect sensing one. For a lower density value, as the density increases, the EE goes up until achieving a maximum value for an optimal SCS density. Therefore, for a density greater than the optimal value, even if the number of SCSs rises the EE remains constant. Thus, there exist a limit for the network densification and an optimal SCS density that should be defined in order to achieve the maximum EE with the minimum deployment costs. Most importantly, the EE relative to the proposed model outperforms that of imperfect SCS sensing one. In fact, about 58% of gain performance is noticed.

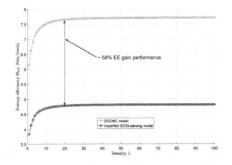

Fig. 4. Energy efficiency vs SCSs density λ

Figure 5, presents the performance gains of the suggested model, in terms of EE, under various $SINR$ thresholds $\widehat{SINR}$. The SCS density λ is equal to $0.6 \times 10^{-4}/\text{m}^2$. For a low value of $\widehat{SINR}$, the EE performance – with the increasing of $\widehat{SINR}$ – grows until reaching an optimal value. However, for a larger value of $\widehat{SINR}$, the EE declines. Clearly, the performances of the suggested framework are proved compared to the imperfect SCS sensing scenario. About 66% of again performance is noticed compared to the other scenarios.

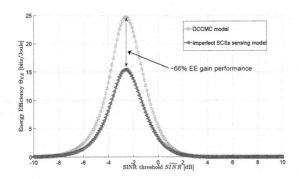

Fig. 5. Energy efficiency vs $\widehat{SINR}$

6   Conclusion

This paper proposes a novel approach to manage the interference in ultra-dense heterogeneous cellular networks. The suggested DCCMC protocol is modeled and developed, based on the stochastic geometry model. Under some general assumptions, the resulting expressions for coverage probability as well energy efficiency are involved as a closed-form expression. The numerical results are illustrated, proving the analysis and improving the performance of the proposed framework compared to the conventional model and the eICIC one as well as the

SCSs imperfect sensing scenario. However, it is proved that an optimal number of deployed SCSs is necessary to achieve a maximum energy efficiency network design. Thus, densifying the network with a number of SCSs beyond this optimal value will not improve the energy efficiency performances in an UDHetNet.

References

1. Blume, O., Zeller, D., Barth, U.: Approaches to energy efficient wireless access networks. In: 4th International Symposium on Communications, Control and Signal Processing (ISCCSP), pp. 1–5. IEEE (2010)
2. Webb, M.: Smart 2020: enabling the low carbon economy in the information age, a report by the climate group on behalf of the Global eSustainability Initiative (GeSI), Global eSustainability Initiative (GeSI), Technical report (2008)
3. Gruber, M., Blume, O., Ferling, D., Zeller, D., Imran, M.A., Strinati, E.C.: Earth–energy aware radio and network technologies. In: IEEE 20th International Symposium on Personal, Indoor and Mobile Radio Communications, pp. 1–5. IEEE (2009)
4. ICT Sustainability Outlook: an assessment of the current state of affairs and a path towards improved sustainability for public policies, Report, BIO Intelligence Service and Alcatel-Lucent (2013)
5. Richter, F., Fehske, A.J., Fettweis, G.P.: Energy efficiency aspects of base station deployment strategies for cellular networks. In: IEEE 70th Vehicular Technology Conference Fall (VTC 2009-Fall), pp. 1–5. IEEE (2009)
6. Oh, E., Krishnamachari, B., Liu, X., Niu, Z.: Toward dynamic energy-efficient operation of cellular network infrastructure. IEEE Commun. Mag. 49(6), 56–61 (2011)
7. Fettweis, G., Zimmermann, E.: ICT energy consumption-trends and challenges. In: Proceedings of the 11th International Symposium on Wireless Personal Multimedia Communications, Lapland, vol. 2(4), p. 6 (2008)
8. Su, L., Yang, C., Xu, Z., Molisch, A.F.: Energy-efficient downlink transmission with base station closing in small cell networks. In: IEEE International Conference on Acoustics, Speech and Signal Processing (ICASSP), pp. 4784–4788. IEEE (2013)
9. Lin, Y., Bao, W., Yu, W., Liang, B.: Optimizing user association and spectrum allocation in hetnets: a utility perspective. IEEE J. Sel. Areas Commun. 33(6), 1025–1039 (2015)
10. Parkvall, S., Furuskar, A., Dahlman, E.: Evolution of LTE toward IMT-advanced. IEEE Commun. Mag. 49(2), 84–91 (2011)
11. Abdullah, M., Yonis, A.: Performance of LTE release 8 and release 10 in wireless communications. In: International Conference on Cyber Security, Cyber Warfare and Digital Forensic (CyberSec), pp. 236–241. IEEE (2012)
12. Damnjanovic, A., Montojo, J., Wei, Y., Ji, T., Luo, T., Vajapeyam, M., Yoo, T., Song, O., Malladi, D.: A survey on 3GPP heterogeneous networks. IEEE Wirel. Commun. 18(3), 10–21 (2011)
13. Deb, S., Monogioudis, P., Miernik, J., Seymour, J.P.: Algorithms for enhanced inter-cell interference coordination (eICIC) in LTE hetnets. IEEE/ACM Trans. Networking 22(1), 137–150 (2014)
14. Dhungana, Y., Tellambura, C.: Multichannel analysis of cell range expansion and resource partitioning in two-tier heterogeneous cellular networks. IEEE Trans. Wireless Commun. 15(3), 2394–2406 (2016)

15. Mendrzik, R., Castillo, R.A.J., Bauch, G., Seidel, E.: Interference coordination-based downlink scheduling for heterogeneous LTE-a networks. In: Wireless Communications and Networking Conference (WCNC), 2016 IEEE, pp. 1–6. IEEE (2016)

16. ElSawy, H., Hossain, E.: On cognitive small cells in two-tier heterogeneous networks. In: 11th International Symposium on Modeling & Optimization in Mobile, Ad Hoc & Wireless Networks (WiOpt), pp. 75–82. IEEE (2013)

17. Panahi, F.H., Ohtsuki, T.: Stochastic geometry modeling and analysis of cognitive heterogeneous cellular networks. EURASIP J. Wirel. Commun. Networking **2015**(1), 141 (2015)

18. Bohli, A., Bouallegue, R.: Stochastic geometry model to analyze 5G energy efficiency based on a novel dynamic spectrum access scheme. Trans. Emerg. Telecommun. Technol. **27**(12), 1715–1728 (2016)

19. Bohli, A., Bouallegue, R.: A new sensing strategy for 5G mobile networks: towards spectral and energy efficiency trade off. In: IEEE 30th International Conference on Advanced Information Networking and Applications (AINA), pp. 155–159. IEEE (2016)

20. Dhillon, H.S., Ganti, R.K., Baccelli, F., Andrews, J.G.: Modeling and analysis of k-tier downlink heterogeneous cellular networks. IEEE J. Sel. Areas Commun. **30**(3), 550–560 (2012)

21. Baccelli, F., Błaszczyszyn, B., et al.: Stochastic geometry and wireless networks: volume ii applications. Found. Trends® Networking **4**(1–2), 1–312 (2010)

22. Jedrzycki, C., Leung, V.C.: Probability distribution of channel holding time in cellular telephony systems. In: IEEE 46th Vehicular Technology Conference, Mobile Technology for the Human Race, vol. 1, pp. 247–251. IEEE (1996)

Network Design and Planning

Interaction of the IoT Traffic Generated by a Smart City Segment with SDN Core Network

Artem Volkov[1], Abdukodir Khakimov[1], Ammar Muthanna[1],
Ruslan Kirichek[1,2(✉)], Andrei Vladyko[1], and Andrey Koucheryavy[1]

[1] State University of Telecommunication, St. Petersburg, Russia
v.artem.nikolaevich@yandex.ru,
{abdukadir94,akouch}@mail.ru, ammarexpress@gmail.com,
{kirichek,vladyko}@sut.ru
[2] Peoples' Friendship University of Russia (RUDN University),
6 Miklukho-Maklaya St, Moscow, Russia

Abstract. The main purpose of this article is to test IoT management system based on SDN core network, as well as interaction IoT traffic with SDN-switches. To conduct investigation of management system and network infrastructure behavior we carried out several IoT traffic tests, which were generated based on partnership project oneM2M specification. In this work, we considered "Smart city" model for Central district of Saint-Petersburg (Russia). During the testing of the network infrastructure were identified several parameters such as number of simultaneously supported sessions by the Mikrotik switch using different transport protocols, was proposed a recommendation for dynamically changing virtual buffers. During the testing of the IoT management system, we define reliability of IoT data management service for determined equipment in traffic conditions of the "Smart City". Also, we estimate relationship between RTT parameter using various IoT protocols and heterogeneous traffic in conjunction with "Smart city" segment in SDN network. In order to investigate the influence of the SDN network on the RTT traffic parameter of a large number of IoT and the condition of its transmission in conjunction with heterogeneous traffic in the network, a full-scale experiment was conducted on the developed model, which in turn reflected a possible distribution scheme of a certain monitoring and control system for the Central District Saint-Petersburg. The aim of the study is also to consider the possibility of implementing the IoT data management service as a central management system for monitoring urban ecological parameters in a dense buildings environment.

Keywords: IoT · SDN · Data management · API · Smart city · Round trip time · Mikrotik switches

1 Introduction

Smart City - a futuristic idea or an inevitable future? Smart City, also known as "smart city" [1], "digital city" - a concept in which there is still no unambiguous definition. It can be stated as, smart city - a city that uses information and communication technology for

© IFIP International Federation for Information Processing 2017
Published by Springer International Publishing AG 2017. All Rights Reserved
Y. Koucheryavy et al. (Eds.): WWIC 2017, LNCS 10372, pp. 115–126, 2017.
DOI: 10.1007/978-3-319-61382-6_10

the efficient use of resources, resulting in cost savings and energy, improving the quality of life of inhabitants [2], improving the ecological environment, etc. In recent years, many cities began to implement projects related to with the use of smart city technologies. For example, Singapore (use ERP «intelligent traffic system» to deal with traffic jams.), Vancouver (Power systems organized on the principle of renewable sources), Helsinki (program to increase the availability of information resources and to attract residents to their use) and so on. Course this is only the first step toward optimizing resources and saving their possible replacement by other, less harmful to the environment, information society. However, the first step has been taken. Services such as automatic collection of indications of house energy meters [3], automation of urban transport service [4], which allows you to watch the buses moving, trolley buses and the like, and to know the approximate time of their arrival, the city multifunctional centers with electronic queue, e-health care [5], geographic information systems, and other systems that facilitate a person's life in the big city. But it's certainly not all aspects that includes the concept of "Smart City". For the full realization of these ideas, require new network infrastructure, new approaches to data organization, to meet the new requirements. As a result of these issues, there is such a thing as Big Data. It can be concluded that for effective work Smart City requires a deep integrated system consisting of many subsystems, which will take into account both the current needs of various city services, and taking into account the prospects of development in terms of new factors.

This system should be resistant to different types of impact, for example, in terms of information security; this system must be protected, so in case of fails, the work of many city services will be difficult or limited. Resistant to various force majeure, that is to be provided back-up system ready from the first time to take over the functions of failed management system "Smart City". An important aspect that should be fulfilled is the organization of such systems on the basis of generally accepted standards throughout the telecommunications world. This enables many third-party companies to provide their services on general terms and protects them from monopoly in this area.

In this paper, as one of possible services examples for "Smart City", will be considered a system for monitoring environmental parameters of air in three types of sensors, for monitoring and to develop appropriate methods to optimize the ecological situation in the dense urban and highway traffic. Just ecological picture can be useful not only in terms of the environmental situation, but also for automation of control in the field of fire and gas safety.

The approach of software-defined networks (SDN) [6] allows to significantly automate and facilitate network management by allowing them to write management applications. This approach involves the separation levels and data transmission and control, wherein the operation to determine the packet transmission route identifies a controller (the "brain" in the concept), which has information about the topology of the network status for easy monitoring and network control [7]. This functionality is determined by the controller API.

2   Specifications in the M2M and the Proposed Management System

The rapid pace of urbanization poses new challenges for city services, which certainly needs to be addressed to ensure the stable operation at such a high load. For centralized collection and management of Internet of Things, an appropriate service is required that will provide the necessary management functions. Also, for the further development of the "Smart City" architecture, required a system, which built, as already mentioned before, based on certain standards of interaction.

The need for standardization in field of machine-machine communications (M2M) has sharply increased recently in the development of infocommunications [16, 17]. To solve the set tasks, was created global partner project oneM2M [8]. The initiators of the creation were seven regional telecommunication standardization organizations ETSI, ARIB, TTC, CCSA, TIA, ATIS and TTA. Currently partnership oneM2M actively developing specifications in the field of machine to machine and the Internet of Thing, which was last updated on September 29, 2016. In total, by September 29, 2016, 24 specifications have been developed, for example TS 0001 specification - describes the functional architecture of oneM2M interaction, in TS 0003 - it displays security issues, and in TS 0009, TS 0010, implements transmission based on HTTP and MQTT protocols, respectively. Community Opendaylight, which includes a considerable number of infocommunication companies, based on the specifications of oneM2M was developed the implementation of a broker (data warehouse) with Internet of Things management functions, organized using the REST API. Internet of Things Data Management is an open source software that acts as an intermediary between oneM2M resources and related applications, with the organization having a specific application access policy to appropriate resources. All resources (Internet Things) are displayed as a hierarchical tree. Typically, the interaction with the resource tree occurs using HTTP protocols (TS 0009), CoAP (TS 0008), MQTT (TS 0010). Where TS 0008, TS 0009, TS 0010 are the corresponding oneM2M specifications. By default, applications for extracting data can work with the resource tree. But it is also possible to use control systems for devices or large data, for analytical systems. Also, are possible applications for device configuration. In this paper, as the management of "Smart City" systems to test both the services and protocols of the Internet of Things, with data organization over SDN network service IoTDM, developed Opendaylight community was chosen because of its organization in accordance with the specifications oneM2M.

The study of interaction of Internet of Things traffic with SDN [9–12] and on condition to transfer it together with heterogeneous traffic, was formed the task - to conduct SDN testing for speed the establishment of network infrastructure at the primary connecting of switches, organization of the switch buffers.

The study of the IoTDM system based on SDN was formulated the main task - to carry out testing the service in view of the real potential traffic load Internet of Things using protocols: HTTP, CoAP, MQTT, based on the model of the real area of St. Petersburg city. Testing essentially reduces to checking the interaction between IoT devices, the network infrastructure and the IoTDM service.

3   Testing Results

3.1   Testing of the Network Infrastructure

As a network infrastructure, an SDN network was built, based on Mikrotik switches supporting the openflow v.1.0 protocol and the OpenDayLight Berillium SR4 controller. As a service management acted IoTDM version Boron SR1. As data sources - developed traffic generators that implement the interaction in three protocols (HTTP, CoAP, MQTT), taking into account the specifications of the partnership project oneM2M and organization model district of St. Petersburg city.

Figure 1 and Table 1 shows the network infrastructure, organized in the SDN laboratory of the St. Petersburg State University of Telecommunications.

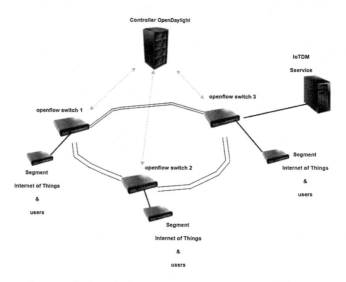

Fig. 1. The structure of the laboratory stand

As a load generator for testing the core of the SDN network, the iperf3 generator was used, which allows flexible configuration of traffic parameters. In this test, the generator was configured to simulate the load with IoT traffic [13–15]; this was reflected in the number of packets: less than 190 bytes.

In the process of work to increase the number of sessions that pass through each switch simultaneously. Testing was performed using the protocols: UDP and TCP.

The test results are shown in Figs. 2 and 3, with each of the graphs showing the dependency on each of the switches.

Table 1. The laboratory stand Structure

Hardware	Features	Functions
RAM: 16 Гб CPU: intel Xeon(R) CPU E3-1220V2	Controller	The «Brainr» for network
RAM: 12 Гб CPU: intel Xeon(R) CPU E3-1220V2	Service IoTDM	Management service for Internet of Things
Mikrotik RB201 1ui AS-RM	Network	SDN core
Cisco Catalyst 3750G Series	Network	Aggregation layer

As shown on the graphs in Figs. 2 and 3, by increasing the number of connections increases dramatically loss after a certain number of simultaneous connections in each of the SDN switches.

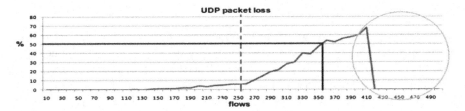

Fig. 2. Graph of UDP packet loss by increasing the number of sessions

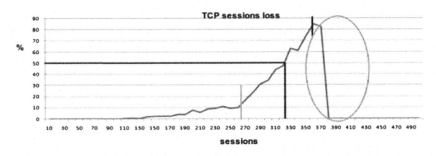

Fig. 3. Graph of the number of dangling sessions on the network by increasing their number.

Thus, it can be concluded that by using TCP, the number of possible simultaneous connections is smaller (the peak at ∼360) than when using a UDP protocol (peak at ∼400–410). A break in the graphs means the failure of the network infrastructure (shutdown of Mikrotik switches and their unplanned overload). According to the test results, we can conclude that this type of switch is possible only with the organization of internal corporate networks for small size.

Also after studying responses to switch the same type of traffic, we concluded on the use of buffers in the SDN switches. As we know, to fine-tune the buffer size in network nodes use the formula B = P * RTT where B is the buffer size, P is the throughput, and RTT is the (Round Trip Time). With this formula, you can easily configure the optimal buffer size (queue). However, this formula does not take into account the number of parallel flows that can be different types (independent of each other).

In classical networks uses the addition to this formula $\frac{RTT*P}{\sqrt{N}}$, where N - the number of independent sessions. According to this law, determine the optimal size of the buffer. Moreover, the number N is taken as the averaged value from the exponential distribution, where P => 0.7. This method gives an error of up to 30%.

As a result of tests conducted on mikrotik equipment, we came to the conclusion that we can specify virtual buffers for each session. This will reduce the RTT parameter values for both normal network services and possibly for the tactile Internet. Since OpenFlow protocol allows to control the full resource of a network device, this task can be assigned to him, in the organization of the corresponding plug on the SDN controller.

3.2   IoTDM Service Testing as "Smart City" Service Management System

For IoTDM service testing, we created a model that highlights possible Internet of Things interaction to monitor ecological situation in the city in dense urban development. For an accurate research, we chose Saint-Petersburg central district, which has a more good shape for modelling and is divided into 6 municipal divisions: #78, Dvortsovy, Ligovka-Yamskaya, Liteyny, Smolninskoye and Vladimirsky. This allows to evenly distributing sensors when building the model. Figure 4 shows a map of the central district of St. Petersburg and its municipal divisions.

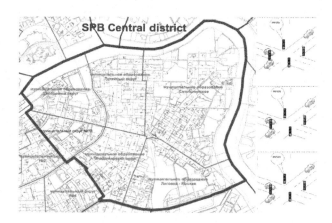

Fig. 4. Central district of St. Petersburg

We used SDN as network infrastructure, whose structure is shown in the first section.

The Smart city hierarchical model designed as follows:

- For a uniformly load distribution on network device, we connected two municipal divisions to each and every OpenFlow switch.
- In every division is involved around 40 crossroads.
- Every crossroad has four traffic lights, which serve as Internet of Thing.
- Every Internet of Thing contains three types of sensor for air ecological state control.

The model working mechanism was build based on the following algorithm:

1. Building resources tree, taking into account hierarchical division into Municipalities, crossroads, traffic lights.
2. Internet of Thing Initialization. When the IoTDM service is initialized to the resources tree, every Internet of Thing sends a request containing information about sensors readiness when connecting. Information from GPS sensor comes once.
3. Internet of Things traffic generation. Every Internet of Thing sends a request every second (Constant Instances, according to M2M specification) to the resources tree. The request contains sensors data, their registration time, value number and other metadata.

We also organized the transmission of every Internet of Thing successively from every crossroad while request to sources tree (IoTDM service) were sent simultaneously from every crossroad. Finally, we got a model with 960 Internet of Things while during one-time interval working with service of 240 Internet of Things. To build resource tree we wrote a corresponding script. To generate traffic, we developed an Internet of Thing traffic generator according to oneM2M specification and the designed "Smart city" model architecture based on HTTP, CoAP, MQTT protocols which sends requests containing, in the message body, JSON format. The IoT traffic generator was developed in Python programming language and API IoTDM.

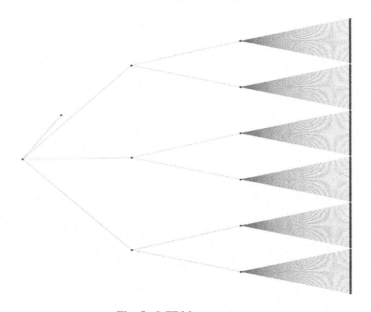

Fig. 5. IoTDM resource tree.

The built resource tree is shown in Fig. 5.

Multiple endpoints of the tree in Fig. 5, the simulated display all intersections with it at every crossroads there are 4 internet Things that are not shown in Fig. 5, with a view to properly display the tree scale. During the experiment, the RTT (Round Trip Time) parameter was calculated for each of used protocols.

The value of RTT for the HTTP protocol is displayed in Fig. 6, for CoAP in Fig. 7, for MQTT in Fig. 8.

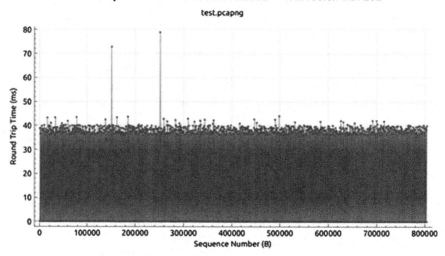

Fig. 6. RTT for HTTP.

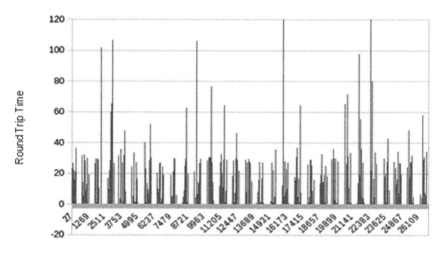

Fig. 7. RTT for CoAP.

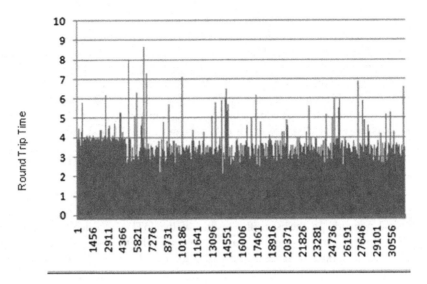

Fig. 8. RTT for MQTT.

Where the number of established sessions is displayed on the abscissa, the value of Round Trip Time is displayed directly along the ordinate axis. Emissions on the graphs show the unstable operation of the service, after a certain time of testing, which consisted in closing the service ports, as a result, the delay in the successful registration of data on the IoTDM service increased. Based on the test results, we concluded which protocol is better to use for various purposes, when considering this architecture. The conclusions are shown in Table 2.

Table 2. Recommendations on the used protocols for the interaction IoT with the IoTDM service over the SDN network

Functions	HTTP	CoAP	MQTT
Internet of things registration	+	−	−
Data transmission	−	−/+	+
RTT/average value for stable operation	+($\sim$40 ms)	+($\sim$30–40 ms)	+($\sim$4 ms)

According to the data displayed in Table 2, we concluded that for the registration of Internet things to the IoTDM service, the HTTP protocol is more appropriate than others due to its work in conjunction with the transport protocol TCP, which guarantees the transmission of the registration message over the network. If, when creating the main structure or registering the Internet of Things itself, a packet will be lost on the network, this will cause a failure in the structure of the resource tree, and eventually work with the resource tree (with the entities of this branch) will be difficult. Because The IoTDM service will not be able to register the dependent entities or the data belonging to this branch and will issue an error about the unavailability of the resource.

The CoAP protocol works in conjunction with the UDP transport protocol, which eventually failed and the error described above, therefore this protocol proved to be not stable for the organization of this function. To organize the work through the protocol, the registration of the MQTT broker is required first, that is, i.e., initially work through HTTP protocol is required to organize the MQTT workflow. However, when transmitting the data itself from the Internet of Things (sensors), the MQTT protocol proved to be on the best hand, if to perform a basic comparison based on the RTT parameter. With the same load (960 IW), it was possible to achieve an RTT of 4 ms. It should also be taken into account that after prolonged operation of the generators via the HTTP protocol, the IoTDM service began to behave unstably (closing ports), which led to delays in processing the package in the service.

As a result of the Round Trip Time values, we can safely conclude that the SDN network reduces the value of the RTT parameter several times over the organization of the classical network. In the issue the testing of the IoTDM service with this load profile, the instability of its operation was revealed, namely, the ports were closed, also in result was developed generators gave an appropriate network error about the unavailability of the receiver's ports. At the same time, the further the test passed, the response time from the service increased.

We conclude that IoTDM service has a big plus that is organized in accordance with the specifications project oneM2M, but the organization of it as a management system of a service "Smart City" is required to design a distributed server architecture and thus the resource tree for the stability of its work. It also requires an accurate calculation of the hardware used in the servers for the successful processing of this amount of traffic.

4 Conclusion

The paper examined the IoTDM service as a single service for organizing a smart city management system, also in the process of experiment, taking into account that the generated IoT traffic was transmitted over an SDN network organized on the basis of Mikrotik switches, switches were tested for stable operation under heterogeneous conditions Traffic and traffic IoT smart city. As a result of the work, it was found out that the concept of building SDN networks allows to reduce such a traffic parameter as RTT by organizing the control in the form of an SDN controller, namely: the processes of creating records in the flow table and the principle of message switching (record search). As a result, the delay in switching depends only on the physical capabilities of the switch itself (ports, memory, processor speed, etc.), with the already generated flow table, most of the delay was made by the service itself, while processing requests from Internet of Things.

Recently exponential growth of Internet connected devices and network management issues have become one of the most difficult tasks. Once IoT came to life, the volume of traffic in modern communication networks is drastically changed. The lately emerged SDN approach could bring us ineluctable benefits by automating daily network engineer's chores and facilitating overall network management through its programming. In this paper were considered the advantages of SDN for management simplification of IoT by introduction of Internet of things data management system as a service for "Smart city". The developed model, that reflected the possible distribution scheme of monitoring and management systems for the Central District of Saint-Petersburg, was used to conduct full-scale experiment.

Acknowledgment. The publication was financially supported by the Ministry of Education and Science of the Russian Federation (the Agreement number 02.a03.21.0008), RFBR according to the research project No. 17-57-80102 "Small Medium-sized Enterprise Data Analytics in Real Time for Smart Cities Applications".

References

1. Naphade, M., Banavar, G., Harrison, C., Paraszczak, J., Morris, R.: Smarter cities and their innovation challenges. Computer **44**(6), 32–39 (2011)
2. Bowerman, B., Braverman, J, Taylor, J., Todosow, H., von Wimmersperg, U.: The vision of a smart city. In: 2nd International Life Extension Technology Workshop, Paris (2000)
3. Zanella, A., Bui, N., Castellani, A., Vangelista, L., Zorzi, M.: Internet of Things for smart cities. IEEE Internet Things J. **1**(1), 22–32 (2014)
4. Fujdiak, R., Masek, P., Mlynek, P., Misurec, J., Muthanna, A.: Advanced optimization method for improving the urban traffic management. In: 18th Conference of Open Innovations Association and Seminar on Information Security and Protection of Information Technology (FRUCT-ISPIT), pp. 48–53. IEEE (2016)
5. Kirichek, R., Pirmagomedov, R., Glushakov, R., Koucheryavy, A.: Live substance in cyberspace — biodriver system. In: 18th International Conference on Advanced Communication Technology (ICACT), pp. 274–278. IEEE (2016)
6. Alsmadi, I.M., AlAzzam, I., Akour, M.: A systematic literature review on software-defined networking. In: Alsmadi, I.M., Karabatis, G., AlEroud, A. (eds.) Information Fusion for Cyber-Security Analytics. SCI, vol. 691, pp. 333–369. Springer, Cham (2017). doi:10.1007/978-3-319-44257-0_14
7. Kirichek, R., Vladyko, A., Paramonov, A., Koucheryavy, A.: Software-defined architecture for flying ubiquitous sensor networking. In: 19th International Conference on Advanced Communication Technology (ICACT), pp. 158–162 (2017)
8. oneM2M. http://www.onem2m.org/about-onem2m/why-onem2m
9. Akyildiz, I.F., Lee, A., Wang, P., Luo, M., Chou, W.: A roadmap for traffic engineering in SDN-OpenFlow networks. Comput. Netw. **71**(9–10), 1–30 (2014)
10. Vladyko, A., Muthanna, A., Kirichek, R.: Comprehensive SDN testing based on model network. In: Galinina, O., Balandin, S., Koucheryavy, Y. (eds.) NEW2AN/ruSMART - 2016. LNCS, vol. 9870, pp. 539–549. Springer, Cham (2016). doi:10.1007/978-3-319-46301-8_45
11. Jararweh, Y., Al-Ayyoub, M., Darabseh, A., Benkhelifa, E., Vouk, M., Rindos, A.: SDIoT: a software defined based Internet of Things framework. J. Ambient Intell. Humaniz. Comput. **6**(4), 453–461 (2015)
12. Kirichek, R., Vladyko, A., Zakharov, M., Koucheryavy, A.: Model networks for Internet of Things and SDN. In: 18th International Conference on Advanced Communication Technology (ICACT), pp. 76–79. IEEE (2016)

13. Kirichek, R., Koucheryavy, A.: Internet of Things laboratory test bed. In: Zeng, Q.-A. (ed.) Wireless Communications, Networking and Applications. LNEE, vol. 348, pp. 485–494. Springer, New Delhi (2016). doi:10.1007/978-81-322-2580-5_44

14. Koucheryavy, A.: State of the art and research challenges for USN traffic flow models. In: 16th International Conference on Advanced Communication Technology (ICACT), pp. 336–340. IEEE (2014)

15. Muthanna, A., Prokopiev, A., Koucheryavy, A.: The mixed telemetry/image USN in the overload conditions. In: 16th International Conference on Advanced Communication Technology (ICACT), pp. 475–478. IEEE (2014)

16. Himayat, N., Yeh, S.-P., Panah, A.Y., Tawar, S., Gerasimenko, M., Andreev, S., Koucheryavy, Y.: Multi-radio heterogeneous networks: architectures and performance. In: Proceeding International Conference on Computing, Networking and Communication (ICNC), pp. 252–258. IEEE (2014)

17. Gerasimenko, M., Petrov, V., Galinina, O., Andreev, S., Koucheryavy, Y.: Energy and delay analysis of LTE-advanced RACH performance under MTC overload. In: Globecom Workshops (GC Wkshps), December 2012, pp. 1632–1637. IEEE (2012)

Evaluation of Geocast Routing Trees on Random and Actual Networks

Bernd Meijerink[✉], Mitra Baratchi, and Geert Heijenk

University of Twente, Enschede, The Netherlands
{bernd.meijerink,m.baratchi,geert.heijenk}@utwente.nl

Abstract. Efficient geocast routing schemes are needed to transmit messages to mobile networked devices in geographically scoped areas. To design an efficient geocast routing algorithm a comprehensive evaluation of different routing tree approaches is needed. In this paper, we present an analytical study addressing the efficiency of possible routing trees for geocast packets. We evaluate the Shortest Path Tree, Minimum Spanning Tree and a Steiner Heuristic based routing tree for geocast packet distribution on real world networks and random graphs. We compare the results to those for multicast routing for which such evaluations have been performed in the past. Our results show that due to the correlation of geographic distance and network distance in most wired networks, Shortest Path forwarding efficiency can come close to an ideal Steiner Tree. We also identify a correlation between the forwarding efficiency and network characteristics such as the node degree and betweenness. This information could be useful in deciding on a choice of routing method or even help with network design.

Keywords: Geocast · Multicast · Routing · Shortest Path Tree · Steiner tree

1 Introduction

With the increase in the number of networked devices in the world, be it intelligent vehicles or household appliances, new communication methods are needed to allow efficient communication to and from these devices with a certain geographical constraint such as a street or district [1]. This can be achieved through geocast, first proposed by Navas and Imielinski [2]. Geocast is the transmission of packets towards a geographical area instead of a fixed address, devices receive packets purely based on their location.

An alternative and more explored method to geocast is multicast. Both of these schemes transmit packets to multiple destinations. They also share forwarding characteristics in that packets are only duplicated when the path in the network diverges. Unlike multicast the destination of packets in geocast share a geographical region and they are not distributed throughout the network. Furthermore, unlike multicast a device cannot simply subscribe to a group to receive

© IFIP International Federation for Information Processing 2017
Published by Springer International Publishing AG 2017. All Rights Reserved
Y. Koucheryavy et al. (Eds.): WWIC 2017, LNCS 10372, pp. 127–142, 2017.
DOI: 10.1007/978-3-319-61382-6_11

a geocast packet. The geocast packet is transmitted to all devices on a network in a specific geographic region. These characteristics are especially beneficial for transmission towards vehicular networks, where nodes are mobile and keeping track of membership information and location is inefficient [1].

The routing requirements for geocast differ from multicast in several ways: (1) There is a logical correlation between the geocast address and the area a packet needs to be forwarded to. (2) Routing is based on an geocast address, not membership information.

In a multicast scenario the routers that need to be reached can be distributed throughout a network. In the geocast case, these routers would be located close to each other geographically. While geographic distance does not directly correlate to network distance, a strong link between both of them can be observed in a large number of real world networks. Our hypothesis is that this geographic clustering will lead to a situation were a geocast source has an obvious forwarding path to the destination routers. This could result in a significant portion of Shortest Path routes from the source to the destination being shared. Therefore, due to the geographically scoped nature of geocast, traditional routing methods such as unicast or multicast will not potentially provide the required efficiency. A new set of routing algorithms specifically designed for geocast is needed to provide an effective geocast solution in Internet-scale networks [1].

To design an efficient geocast routing algorithm we require information on the efficiency of different possible forwarding trees. Our hypothesis is that more optimal methods like Steiner trees are not as relevant when destinations are located close to each other and simpler but computationally less expense methods such as naive Shortest Path forwarding are more attractive. Our assumption is that routers that are responsible for areas in close geographical proximity, are also close to each other in the network with a small amount of hops between them.

The main contribution of this paper is to identify a forwarding tree that can be used for the design of an efficient geocast routing algorithm. This is done by performing an extensive evaluation of different forwarding trees in a gecoast scenario. We use the average cost and path utilization over multiple (source, destination) pairs as our main metrics. We compare the results with results from multicast based evaluations. The multicast case has been extensively researched in the past [3,4], but the effect of geographical clustering on the forwarding tree efficiency is an open question. This information can be used in later work do design an efficient routing system for geocast traffic. In our previous work we proposed an addressing system for Internet wide geocast [5]. This system can address rectangular areas with a minimum size of 7 by 3.5 cm and is logically routable using a form of prefix matching. Combined with an efficient routing mechanism this could potentially allow geocast in Internet-scale networks.

This paper is structured in the following way: In Sect. 2 we explore previous work on the topic of multicast Shortest Paths and random graphs. Section 3 explains our evaluation approach and which metrics we use. Our results are described and discussed in Sect. 5. Finally we draw our conclusions and discuss future work in Sect. 6.

2   Previous Work

In our previous work on geocast addressing we proposed an addressing scheme for geocast [5]. This addressing scheme allows routing based on a type of prefix matching. To implement an efficient routing method we would need to know which type of routing tree has the best characteristics in terms of links used for geocast routing in real world networks.

Previous papers have explored the benefit of using different forwarding mechanisms for multicast traffic. The authors of [3] show that a naive Shortest Path Tree from the source is not that much more inefficient than a Steiner tree heuristic method. Their evaluation focuses on multicast performance in Waxman graphs.

In [4] the authors evaluate different multicast trees for their properties in overall cost and delay. They show that a Shortest Path Tree based approach can come close to the Steiner tree heuristics in terms of performance.

More recently the focus of this kind of evaluation has been in the realm of ad-hoc wireless networks. In [6] Nguyen et al. show that Shortest Path Trees provide benefits over minimum cost trees in wireless ad-hoc networks. According to the authors these benefits outweigh the downside of higher tree cost.

Knight et al. have published a database of public network topologies at the PoP level [7]. They perform a statistical analysis on the data and map the properties such as node degree of these network. We use the actual networks published in the Topology Zoo in our evaluation and use the statistical data to generate random geometric graphs.

Constructing a Steiner Tree over a graph is a NP-complete problem. Kou et al. have presented a fast Steiner Heuristic algorithm [8]. We use the algorithm to find the Steiner Tree for our route evaluations. This allows our evaluation to contain a larger number of graphs than would otherwise be possible. It also has the benefit of being more close to a solution that could be used in an actual router for tree construction.

3   Approach

In this section, we will explain our approach to evaluate the three routing trees. We will first present the trees with their advantages and drawbacks, followed by a short presentation of the tools and sources used. To perform a fair evaluation of the three different routing tree approaches in a geocast scenario we will use two graph models. We will generate random geometric graphs to create a set of networks on which we can perform evaluations, and we will use actual network topologies used in the real world. Information relevant to these graphs will be presented at the end of this section.

3.1   Routing Trees

We evaluate three methods of geocast and multicast trees that can be realistically used for routing: (1) Shortest Path Tree from source, (2) Minimum Spanning Tree, (3) Steiner Tree from source.

Each of these approaches have different benefits and drawbacks that will make them more or less suitable depending on the goals of the network administrator or even the layout of the network.

The Shortest Path Tree is simply a combination of all Shortest Paths from the source to the destination nodes. We count a link that is used multiple times as one usage, as we assume an underlying routing protocol can prevent duplicate packets over the same link. For example: Router A needs to forward a message to a specific area which includes router B, C and D. The Shortest Path Tree would be the union between the shortest paths $(A \rightarrow B)$, $(A \rightarrow C)$ and $(A \rightarrow D)$. Using Fig. 1a as an example: Using node 6 as the source and nodes 8, 9 and 10 as destinations the Shortest Path Tree would consist of $6 \rightarrow 7 \rightarrow 8, 6 \rightarrow 10 \rightarrow 9$ with a total cost of 4. This approach requires a per (source, destination) pair forwarding calculation for each router. A simple per destination forwarding calculation as would be the case for unicast is not possible. As it is probable that the destination area includes multiple routers, a forwarding router needs at least some knowledge of how it fits in the distribution tree to make an efficient forwarding decision. We suspect that this approach will be efficient for geocast as the geographic closeness of destination likely strongly correlates to closeness in the network leading to a large number of shared links.

For the Minimum Spanning Tree, we simply calculate the Minimum Spanning Tree of the network (based on hop count). This subgraph is used to reach all destination nodes from the source. This approach has the benefit that the distribution tree for any geocast (or multicast) message can be precomputed. The major downside is that several links will carry all the traffic, while others are never used. This approach will also not lead to the lowest overall path cost as the most efficient route will almost never be used in most networks. It can however, perform equal to the Steiner tree in situations were the source and destination nodes are ideally distributed on the Minimum Spanning Tree. However, this situation is not likely to occur often and will be offset by all the destinations that are not ideally distributed on the tree.

A Steiner tree is the least cost tree between source and destination nodes. Because this is a NP-complete problem we use a well known heuristic algorithm [8] to construct it. This algorithm works by first finding the metric closure of the

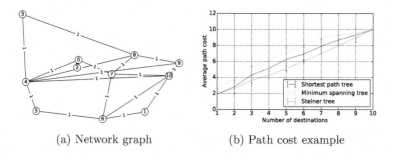

(a) Network graph   (b) Path cost example

Fig. 1. A real world network (Color figure online)

nodes we are interested in. The Minimum Spanning Tree is calculated over the metric closure graph and we map this back to the actual network. This approach will lead to a close to optimal graph but like the Shortest Path approach we need to compute a tree for each (source, destination) pair, with higher computational overhead. Again using Fig. 1a as an example, with node 6 as the source and nodes 8, 9 and 10 as destinations: The Steiner tree would consist of $6 \rightarrow 10 \rightarrow 9 \rightarrow 8$ with a total cost of 3 (one less compared to the Shortest Path Tree). As mentioned before, the Steiner tree is the least cost tree but has the downside of requiring more overhead to computer compared to the other two trees. In the geocast scenario a forwarding router would need knowledge of the source router and all destination routers to know its place in the ideal forwarding tree.

3.2   Tools and Sources

To perform our evaluation, we used several preexisting tools. To model and evaluate graphs we used the NetworkX package [9] for the python programming language. The random graphs used were also generated using this package. All the real world graphs we evaluated are taken from the Topology Zoo [7].

3.3   Networks

For the rest of this paper, we will refer to a graph $G = (V, E)$, with V the vertices or nodes (representing routers), E the edges (representing links). We use both real word networks and randomly generated graphs in our evaluation.

Real Networks. To perform a fair evaluation of the different approaches we need to consider real world networks, both as a control sample and a validation of the random geometric graphs. A computer network is by definition a designed system that is built in a certain way for specific reasons such as cost, performance or necessity. This also means that nodes close to each other are not always connected due to reasons such as geography or politics that we cannot easily fit into a graph.

We use several network graphs that have been made available through the Topology Zoo project [7]. We import these graphs and remove all nodes that are not connected to other nodes. When the resulting graph is still disconnected, we take the largest subgraph as the graph to run our evaluation on. In the majority of cases the graphs can be imported without these operations. One example of such a graph is the one depicted in Fig. 1a. This graph will be used later to explain our evaluation process.

Random Geometric Graphs. To supplement the actual networks used and provide a basis for more general conclusions we have also generated a set of random geometric graphs to run our evaluation on. We chose to use random geometric graphs because the presence of edges between vertices is based on geometric distance. This property is helpful in geocast evaluation as it provides a strong correlation between network distance and the relative distance between nodes. We acknowledge that a random geometric graph may not represent an actual network with high accuracy, but the set of actual networks should sufficiently cover this, allowing the random networks to focus on an ideal geocast case.

The graphs were generated using varying numbers of nodes and accepted as valid based on three criteria:

1. The graph is connected (every node is reachable by every other node).
2. The average betweenness centrality is similar to the studied real graphs (between 0 and 0.3). The betweenness centrality is a measure of the importance of a node, it is the fraction of shortest paths between node pairs that pass through it [10]. The average gives an indication of how centralized a network is.
3. The average node degree is distributed similar to the actual graphs. Node degree is the number of links a node has. The average node degree we use is the average of the node degree of all nodes in a network.

For the majority of random graphs, we choose to generate them in such a way that they closely resemble values from the real world networks As noted above, these values are comparable to real networks found in the topology-zoo [7]. We have also generated some outliers, such as fully connected graphs and graphs that resemble a star topology to evaluate those specific scenarios.

4   Evaluation

To perform our evaluation we use the same approach and evaluation metrics for both network sets, and the three routing trees. In this section, we will present the methods and metrics we use, and how we use them to test the usefulness of the different approaches in a geocast scenario.

4.1   Evaluation Method

To evaluate multicast and geocast destinations in the graphs we use different methods. Both methods share the source node selection. Every node in the network is selected exactly once as the source for every possible destination set, the set of source nodes is equal to the set of nodes V. Runs are done for all destination sets containing 1 node, 2 nodes, up until the total number of nodes in the network (excluding the source). The destination set generation method differs between the multicast and geocast case.

Multicast: In the case of multicast these destinations are every possible combination of all other nodes in the network. If we take the example network given in Fig. 2, using node 0 as the source, the destination set would be {1, 2, 3, (1, 2), (1, 3), (2, 3), (1, 2, 3)}.

$$DS^s_{|V|-1} = \{\{d_1, ..., d_{|V|-1}\}, ...\} \in P(V - s)$$

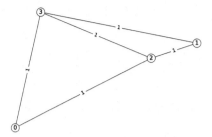

Fig. 2. 4 node example graph

The destination set $\mathbf{DS_n^s}$ is the set of all sets with length n from all distinct permutations of the node set without the source node $(\mathbf{V} - \mathsf{s})$. The maximum length of a destination set is $|V| - 1$, all nodes except the source node.

Geocast: The geocast evaluation selects each (non source) node as destination once and selects extra nodes that are geographically closest depending on the number of destinations required. For each of these destination nodes, 0 to N – 1 extra nodes are selected. The extra nodes are always selected based on their geographical distance, the first node added is always the closest, the second node is the second closest and so on. Destination sets are distinct, generated sets that are identical to already existing sets are ignored as they would represent the same geocast area. In the example network shown in Fig. 2 this would be {1, 2, 3, (1, 2), (3, 2), (1, 2, 3)} for source node 0. Note again that we do not use the same destination set twice here. In this case node 1 is also the closest other node to 2, we do not include (2, 1) as this will replicate (1, 2).

$$GS_{|V|-1}^{s,d} = \{d, v_1^d, v_2^d, ..., v_{|V|-1}^d\} | d, v \in (V - s)$$

$$GS_{|V|-1}^s = \bigcup_{d \in (V-s)} \{GS_{|V|-1}^{s,d}\}$$

In these equations $GS_{|V|-1}^{s,d}$ represents the geographic destination set with d as the initial destination and s the source, v_n^d are the other nodes in the network sorted by their geometric distance from d. $GS_{|V|-1}^s$ is the set of all distinct destination sets for source node s.

4.2   Evaluation Metrics

We evaluate the performance of the three different routing trees using the following metrics: (1) Path cost, (2) Edge usage.

To present the way we will interpret our graphs we will use the network in Fig. 1a as an example. This network has 11 nodes and 18 links.

The graphs used to present our results are generated using a consistent color coding scheme. *Blue* data belongs to the Shortest Path Tree, *red* data belongs to the Steiner heuristic and *green* data represents the Minimum Spanning Tree.

4.3   Path Cost

The average path cost in a network gives an indication of the cost to reach a number of destinations. We use all possible destination combinations to simulate multicast and clustered destinations for geocast.

$$GS_{|V|-1} = \bigcup_{s\in V} \{GS^s_{|V-1|}\}$$

$$DS_{|V|-1} = \bigcup_{s\in V} \{DS^s_{|V|-1}\}$$

We present the path cost as the average path cost for specific destination set sizes ($GS_{|V|-1}$ for geocast, $DS_{|V|-1}$ for multicast). This average is calculated over all possible source to destination trees with a certain destination size.

As an example with destination size 1: There are 11 nodes in the network shown in Fig. 1a. These 11 nodes each have 10 destinations giving us 110 (source, destination) sets. We take the average cost of these 110 routing trees for each of the three routing tree approaches.

We will start presenting our results as graphs that show the average cost for a number of destination per routing tree type. In Fig. 1b the results for network in Fig. 1a are shown. The error bars represent the standard deviation. For this specific network we can see that the Shortest Path Tree cost is close to that of the Steiner heuristic when the destination set is small. We can also observe that when the destination set includes all nodes the routing costs of all trees converge.

Later in the paper we show an average normalized path cost per graph. This cost has been normalized by the number of edges in a graph to allow comparison between graphs of different sizes.

4.4   Edge Usage and Fairness

To determine how 'fair' the link utilization is, we evaluate it for different networks. The link utilization metric describes how evenly the load is distributed in the network. If a few links are used for almost every combination of source and destination nodes it could get overloaded. Overloading a few links and leaving others completely unused is not likely to be a desirable property, and should be something to take into account.

We define edge usage as the normalized times per number of runs an edge was used when evaluating a graph. For example, if we did 10 runs and a certain edge was used in 6 of those runs, its edge usage would be 0.6. We believe the fairness of edge usage to be an important factor as it describes the load distribution within the network. A situation where few links carry almost all traffic might not be desirable from a cost and load distribution standpoint.

Using Fig. 3 we will explain how our stacked bar charts for edge usage are constructed. Figures 3a, b, and c show the edge usage fraction per edge for the network in Fig. 1a. Each of the bars represents an edge, with the height representing the fraction of runs this edge was included in the tree. These edges were

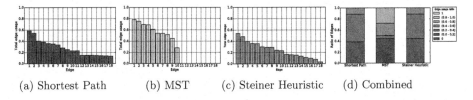

(a) Shortest Path   (b) MST   (c) Steiner Heuristic   (d) Combined

Fig. 3. Edge usage of the network in Fig. 1a

sorted with decreasing edge usage for viewing convenience. We can see that the Shortest Path and Steiner Heuristic trees use all edges and the Minimum Spanning Tree only uses 10 out of a total of 18. Figure 3d combines these graphs into a single stacked bar chart per routing tree. We can clearly see that the usage is more evenly distributed in the Shortest Path and Steiner Heuristic methods and that for the Minimum Spanning Tree a considerable fraction of edges is never used and another significant fraction is almost always in use.

5   Results

In this section we will present the results over all the graphs we have evaluated. We start with the general results and go into specific cases later in the section.

5.1   General Results

Average Path Cost. As shown in Fig. 4, on average, almost all networks we evaluated show similar results. There are a few outliers visible in the results that we will discuss later. Figure 4 shows the results for the 85 networks taken from the Topology Zoo [7] that have less than 20 nodes with all edges having weight 1. It was not feasible to compute the multicast performance for the larger networks due to the large number of destination combinations. The graphs show the number of destinations on the x-axis (starting with 1) and the average cost on the y-axis. Each line in the graph represents one network.

In Figs. 4a and b we show the average cost of routing a packet in a multicast and geocast situation using Shortest Path forwarding on networks where all edges have cost 1. The case for using a Minimum Spanning Tree and a Steiner Heuristic can be seen in Figs. 4c, d and Figs. 4e, f respectively.

In general, we can see that the geocast scenario is more efficient in terms of forwarding cost than multicast in situations where the number of destinations is around a third of the total number of nodes in the network. We can also observe that the Steiner Heuristic is the most efficient forwarding method as expected. The Shortest Path method is however not that much less efficient while using significantly less computational resources. We can see that the Minimum Spanning Tree approach shows less than optimal results but is not necessarily much less efficient depending on the network. It also has the benefit of being precomputed so forwarding costs would be extremely low. The more well connected a

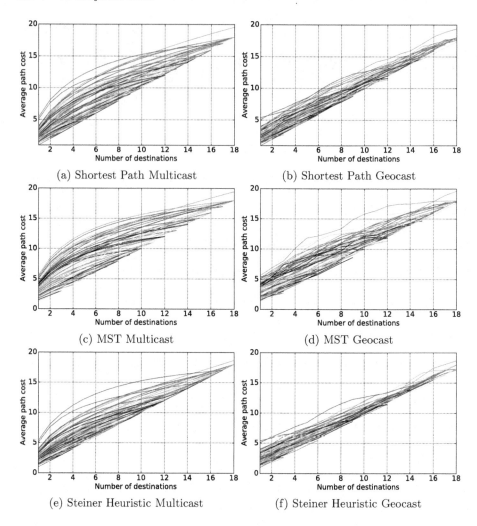

Fig. 4. Results over 85 real networks smaller than 20 nodes

graph is, the smaller the cost difference of geocast compared to general multicast becomes. In less well connected graphs that are more common in real world networks and in extreme cases such as line topologies, the geocast scenario is most optimal.

We evaluated geocast results for all networks in the Topology Zoo [7]. These graphs are an extension of the graphs in Fig. 4, also including the networks with more than 20 nodes found in the Topology Zoo. These results can be seen in Figs. 5a, c and e for the Shortest Path Tree, Minimum Spanning Tree and Steiner tree respectively. In these graphs we can see the linear relation between the number of destination nodes and the average cost more clearly. On average the number of nodes is equal to the average cost (or links used) to reach them for

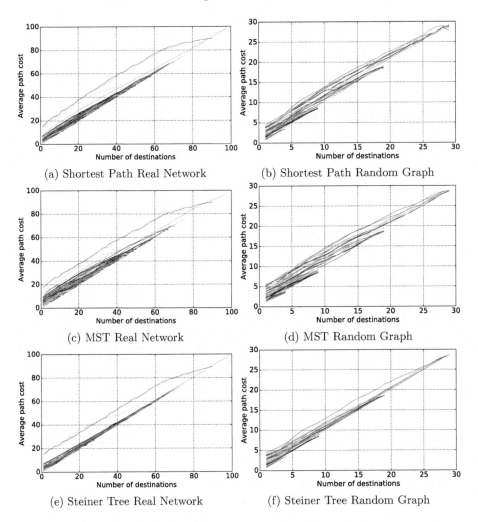

Fig. 5. Geocast results over 225 real networks and 98 random graphs

Shortest Path and close to optimal Steiner heuristic. The three obvious outliers here are networks that consist of several rings of large amounts of nodes. This leads to high overall cost to reach these destinations unless a significant portion of the network is used as destination.

Figures 5b, d and f show the geocast cost for the random geometric graphs we evaluated. These results are comparable to the results for the actual networks. We only observe a small difference in the lower maximum costs found, likely caused by the stronger correlation between geographic distance and network distance in the random geometric graphs.

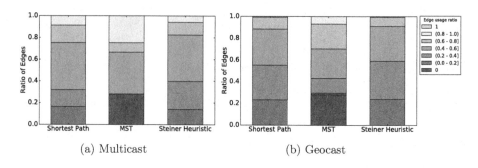

Fig. 6. Edge usage

Edge Usage and Fairness. In an ideal environment we would like to distribute the distribution tree in the network in such a way that every edge is used equally. This is under the assumption that (source, destination) pairs are also evenly distributed throughout the network.

In Fig. 6 we show the fraction of runs that a certain fraction of edges has been used. Each graph shows the results for Shortest Path, Minimum Spanning Tree, and Steiner Heuristic. In Fig. 6a and b we compare the results for all multicast runs with geocast runs over the same set of networks with less than 20 nodes. We can clearly see the difference between the multicast and geocast scenario. With multicast there is a number of edges that are almost always used, while this effect is diminished when destinations are geographically clustered. We observed the same results for geocast on the full set of real networks.

In general we can conclude that the fairness of the Minimum Spanning Tree approach is the lowest as a significant number of edges is never used. Of course this result was to be expected as the same tree is used for every (source, destination) set.

Generally, we observe that the more connected a network is the more equal the load is distributed. This makes sense as there are more possible paths in the network to reach all destination. On average multicast forwarding seems to use more edges compared to geocast. This result can be explained by the geographic clustering of the destinations, making the path from source to destinations share more edges.

5.2   Correlation with Network Characteristics

Some network characteristics have influence on the performance of forwarding trees. In other words, the way some networks are designed lead to a certain forwarding performance and give them specific values for these characteristics. The characteristics of particular interest are the average node degree of the network and the betweenness. We calculate the average normalized path cost per graph for the following results. The path costs are normalized by dividing them by the number of edges present in the graph.

Node degree is the number of edges a node has. In the case of a fully connected network this is equal to $N_{deg} = |G| - 1$. The minimum node degree is 1, as can be found in a node that is only connected to a single other node (for example in a star topology). The average node degree of a network is simply the average of all node degrees in that network.

Figure 7 shows the normalized average path cost of a network for the different routing trees plotted against the average node degree of the network. As expected we see a strong correlation between the two values. We can conclude that the different routing trees converge when the node degree is higher. When the node degree is lower, more efficient forwarding trees are more beneficial to use.

The betweenness centrality of a node is the fraction of shortest paths the node is on in the network. Figure 8 shows that when the average betweenness centrality of a network is high, the average normalized path cost is also higher.

5.3   Special Networks

As mentioned before, the general topology of a network has a large effect on how efficient geocasting is in the network. A few types of networks that occur in the real world give interesting results. The shape of these networks might affect the choice of routing method that should be used in those networks.

We show the results of some these networks in Table 1. In this table we present the average link cost as fraction of the Steiner tree cost. We generated

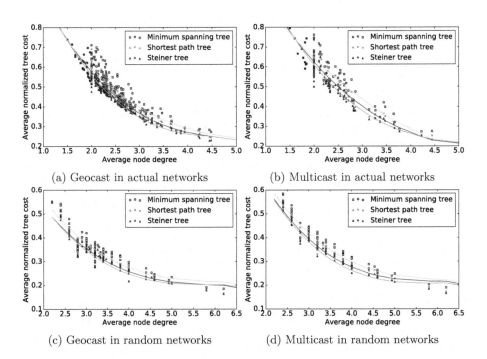

(a) Geocast in actual networks   (b) Multicast in actual networks

(c) Geocast in random networks   (d) Multicast in random networks

Fig. 7. Node degree against cost

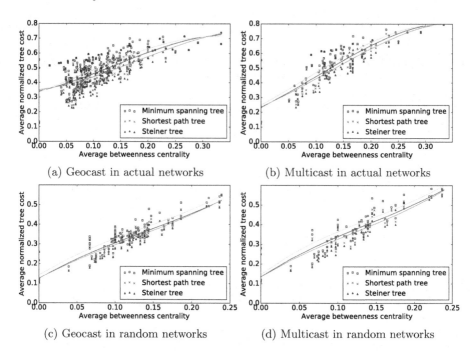

(a) Geocast in actual networks

(b) Multicast in actual networks

(c) Geocast in random networks

(d) Multicast in random networks

Fig. 8. Average betweenness against cost

networks off each network type 'Line', 'Ring', 'Star' and 'Fully connected' with 5, 10 and 20 nodes. In Table 1 these are shown as 'L', 'R', 'S' and 'F' followed by the number of nodes.

'Line' Networks: These networks simply look like strings with routers on them. Due to every router only having one link towards the geocast region in most cases the Shortest Path approach is very efficient here. In a 'true' line network the Minimum Spanning Tree is identical to the network and performs the same as Shortest Path and the Steiner heuristic as can be seen in Table 1.

Ring Networks: In networks that are designed as a ring the Shortest Path method is less efficient. This is likely caused by using both sides of the ring to reach a geocast area if the source is located on the opposite side of the destination in the ring. The Steiner heuristic always produces an optimal tree in such a network while the Minimum Spanning Tree can be extremely suboptimal depending on the destination nodes.

Star Networks: These networks generally have one or more hubs that have the majority of other routers connected to them in a star pattern. The effect is a few heavily used links between the hubs. If we consider a network that has only one hub we see that there is no difference in the performance between multicast and geocast routing. This makes sense as all routers (excluding the hub router) are two hops away from every other router (again excluding the hub). There is no

Table 1. Relative tree cost for special networks

Graph	L 5	L 10	L 20	R 5	R 10	R 20	S 5	S 10	S 20	F 5	F 10	F 20
SPT	1.0	1.0	1.0	1.081	1.155	1.191	1.0	1.0	1.0	1.0	1.0	1.0
ST	1.0	1.0	1.0	1.0	1.0	1.0	1.0	1.0	1.0	1.0	1.0	1.0
MST	1.0	1.0	1.0	1.205	1.253	1.291	1.0	1.0	1.0	1.215	1.170	1.132

possibility to optimize the distribution tree in this situation, every tree performs identical as seen in Table 1.

Fully connected Networks: An unlikely network to occur in reality, but an interesting theoretical situation to evaluate is the fully connected network. Here every router has a direct link to every other router. The result is a network in which every node can reach every other node in one hop. The Shortest Path and Steiner tree are always optimal (and identical) in this situation. The Minimum Spanning Tree will lead to two hops between most node pairs as it creates a star network. This result logically corresponds to the node degree graph, the higher the node degree (equal to $|V| - 1$ in this case) the lower the average cost.

6 Conclusion and Future Work

We set out the find the efficiency and fairness of Shortest Path, Steiner tree and Minimum Spanning Tree forwarding for geocast packets.

Based on our results we can conclude that for a relatively small number of destination nodes the Minimum Spanning Tree approach is the least efficient, using more edges and having, on average, a larger total cost. The differences between the Shortest Path Tree and Steiner tree is visible for small numbers of destinations but it is not that great.

We have shown that the average cost of a routing tree towards a geographically scoped destination is lower than that of a randomly distributed destination set. This result can be explained by the relation between geographical distance and network distance. The effect is most visible when the number of destinations is close to a third of the number of nodes in a given network.

We have also shown that a Steiner tree shows the most equal distribution of edge usage, closely followed by the Shortest Path Tree. As expected the Minimum Spanning Tree does not perform favorably on the edge usage metric due to the fixed distribution tree used. We do note that this behavior might be desired in certain situations.

It seems that networks with a high average node degree and low average betweenness centrality have the lowest forwarding costs. These characteristics can be used when deciding on a routing tree to use in a specific network.

Overall we conclude that a Shortest Path Tree is the most efficient choice for a geocast routing algorithm. Its performance and link fairness are close to that of the Steiner tree while requiring less computational resources.

For future work we will use the outcomes of this evaluation in the design of a routing algorithm for geocast based on the addressing scheme we developed earlier [5]. We will attempt to develop a Shortest Path geocast routing algorithm.

References

1. Karagiannis, G., Heijenk, G., Festag, A., Petrescu, A., Chaiken, A.: Internet-wide geo-networking problem statement (2013). https://tools.ietf.org/html/draft-karagiannis-problem-statement-geonetworking-01
2. Navas, J.C., Imielinski, T.: GeoCast - geographic addressing and routing. In: Pap, L., Sohraby, K., Johnson, D.B., Rose, C. (eds.) MOBICOM, pp. 66–76. ACM (1997)
3. Doar, M., Leslie, I.: How bad is naive multicast routing? In: Proceedings of the Twelfth Annual Joint Conference of the IEEE Computer and Communications Societies. Networking: Foundation for the Future (INFOCOM 1993), pp. 82–89. IEEE (1993)
4. Salama, H.F., Reeves, D.S., Viniotis, Y.: Evaluation of multicast routing algorithms for real-time communication on high-speed networks. IEEE J. Sel. Areas Commun. 15(3), 332–345 (1997)
5. Meijerink, B., Baratchi, M., Heijenk, G.: An efficient geographical addressing scheme for the internet. In: Mamatas, L., Matta, I., Papadimitriou, P., Koucheryavy, Y. (eds.) WWIC 2016. LNCS, vol. 9674, pp. 78–90. Springer, Cham (2016). doi:10.1007/978-3-319-33936-8_7
6. Nguyen, U.T., Xu, J.: Multicast routing in wireless mesh networks: minimum cost trees or shortest path trees? IEEE Commun. Mag. 45(11), 72–77 (2007)
7. Knight, S., Nguyen, H., Falkner, N., Bowden, R., Roughan, M.: The internet topology zoo. IEEE J. Sel. Areas Commun. 29(9), 1765–1775 (2011)
8. Kou, L., Markowsky, G., Berman, L.: A fast algorithm for Steiner trees. Acta Informatica 15(2), 141–145 (1981)
9. Hagberg, A.A., Schult, D.A., Swart, P.J.: Exploring network structure, dynamics, and function using NetworkX. In: Proceedings of the 7th Python in Science Conference (SciPy 2008), Pasadena, pp. 11–15, August 2008
10. Freeman, L.C.: A set of measures of centrality based on betweenness. Sociometry 40, 35–41 (1977)

A NURBS Based Technique for an Optimized Transmit Opportunity Map Processing in WLAN Networks

Mehdi Guessous$^{(\boxtimes)}$ and Lahbib Zenkouar

Mohammadia Engineering School, Rabat, Morocco
mehdiguessous@research.emi.ac.ma, zenkouar@emi.ac.ma

Abstract. Dynamic Radio Resource Management helps overcome interferences in dense WLAN deployments. By processing data from upper-layers services, it could optimize and enrich end-to-end wireless client experience. This experience may be tight to a transmit opportunity function that hints on the radio interface condition, and effectiveness of the transmission itself from different points of view: application, service and underlying network infrastructure. Transmit opportunity calculations that are done at WLAN central intelligence level are resource consuming due to processing of huge amount of raw data from lower and upper system layers. One major part of this processing is the establishment of a coverage map that indicates in real-time and at any point the quality of a radio transmission. This work helps optimize transmit opportunity map calculations by exploring a novel approach based on NURBS Bézier surface technique. It demonstrates that map processing's time and changes to radio environment could be enhanced.

Keywords: Interferences · NURBS surfaces · Radio resource management · WIFI · Wireless Local Area Networks

1 Introduction

Among all issues that a wireless network may face interferences and their impact on the overall network performance are a major one as they occur at a very low system layer and are unpredictable. To tackle these issues three strategies are adopted in general: centralized decision-making intelligence, coordinated intelligence processing, and dynamic radio resource management.

A centralized decision-making intelligence processor, appliance or distributed, software or hardware, is necessary to ensure that network-wide applied radio strategy is coherent among all participating nodes in one hand, and that raw data used for decision-making itself is reliable on the other hand. The need for dynamic radio resource management arises from the fact that network configuration should react quickly to unpredictable changes in radio environment and trigger necessary actions to overcome any issues. These techniques may also help

© IFIP International Federation for Information Processing 2017
Published by Springer International Publishing AG 2017. All Rights Reserved
Y. Koucheryavy et al. (Eds.): WWIC 2017, LNCS 10372, pp. 143–154, 2017.
DOI: 10.1007/978-3-319-61382-6_12

optimize overall network performance by processing transmission opportunities, as an example.

Dynamic Radio Resource Management (RRM) is the focus of this work and considers mainly these two inputs: lower layer physical inputs (RSSI, SNR, EIRP, noise, etc.) and upper layer service inputs (MAC layer, TCP/IP services and applications, etc.). Other complementary inputs may be provided by passive and active on-field site surveys. In addition to survey inputs, techniques such as Transmit Power Control, Dynamic Channel Assignment, Direction of Arrival estimation and Transmit Opportunity processing provide RRM with necessary data and tools to overcome interferences and adapt efficiently to changes.

Processing of this huge amount of raw data and estimation of transmit opportunity at every point under coverage area in a timely manner is very resource consuming. It depends on: the number of points of interest under coverage area and external or internal events that may require a recalculation of all the topology. In this work we discuss a Bézier surface technique for optimizing coverage area transmit opportunity map calculations in frequently changing dense environment.

In the upcoming section, we present a foundation on unified WIFI architectures, opportunity map calculations and NURBS surfaces. In Sect. 3, we discuss more formally the problem and in Sect. 4, we present our solution. Section 5, is dedicated to our solution results evaluation and interpretation. In the end, we conclude and further our work.

2   Theoretical Background

This section gives an overview of methods used to process transmit opportunity maps as they relate to unified WIFI architectures. Additionally they introduce NURBS, a generalization of Bézier surface technique, for the same purpose of establishing a transmit opportunity map.

2.1   Unified WIFI Architecture

Autonomous or standalone access points' architectures do not scale well with high number of access points and mobile devices networks that require high-class quality of service and security. Controller-based ones gradually replace these architectures. "Unified" architectures are managed centrally by a decision-making entity and integrate well with other end-to-end network parts: LAN, WAN, etc. from a QoS and Security point of view. Industry implements such central decision making processors mainly in three ways: physical controller-based, virtual controller-based, or access point distributed-based. In the latter implementation access points take over the controller role. The first two implementations require a controller, a virtual or physical appliance that is reachable by all network access points.

A good example of unified WIFI architectures is Cisco vendor physical WLC 5500 series controller-based one. It defines a communication protocol, CAPWAP, used by access points to build protocol associations to the main controller. It defines another over-the-air communication protocol, OTA, for access points to exchange some proprietary and standard patterns for management or control purposes. In addition, it integrates, at access point level, a set of on-chip proprietary RRM new features: Clientlink or Cleanair that are meant to monitor and measure radio environment characteristics and report them back to the controller via the already established CAPWAP tunnels. Based on this gathered information, the controller decides on channel assignment and corresponding power level tunings network-wide. Its decision conform to a pre-configured set of policies that define many configurable variables such as acceptable signal strength levels, tolerable noise levels, range of usable power levels, range of usable channel frequencies, etc. Then raw data, gathered by controllers, is forwarded to both Cisco Prime Infrastructure (PI) and Mobility Service Engine (MSE) platforms for different purposes mainly interferences spotting and analytics. Generated heat maps represent interferences occurence estimation and analytics on customer's presence at a covered location.

2.2   Transmit Opportunity Map

In this work we focus mainly on transmit opportunity map calculations that represent co-channel interferences and upper-layer SLA inputs. Co-channel interferences are considered to have more impact on network performance than cross-channel ones, and are inversely proportional to transmit opportunity. SLA inputs, corresponding to upper-layer services QoS measurements, help minimizing processing hysteresis and errors.

Methods, to calculate radio coverage characteristics (interferences, signal strength, etc.), could be categorized as:

1. predictive: distance [1–3], barycenter [4], direction based [5] or variants,
2. experimental that are based on on-field site surveys,
3. or hybrid that are a mix of both approaches.

In distance-based models distance estimation of two interfering nodes is necessary to evaluation the amount of interferences. Barycenter-based methods tend to reflect weighted impact of each transmitting point on the others. It results in partitioning of the overall coverage area into zones that are under unique control of each node and that are dependent on the weight each transmitting point may have over time which is not the case of distance based ones. Direction-based methods add more granularity and scalability to previous methods by reconsidering transmission in some areas that were considered as no-talk by other models. In addition, they hint more precisely on hidden interferers and maximize transmission opportunities by qualifying and multiplying transmit directions.

Experimentally based methods have the advantage of reflecting the real measurements. These methods are based on specialized equipments and products such as AirMagnet or Ekahau. However, they lack the ability to adapt to dynamically changing radio environments over time and require important human, financial and system resources.

To evaluate a method over another one, three criterions may be used: accuracy of transmit opportunity calculations at any point, calculation time, and recalculation time in case of network change.

Heuristic methods seem to offer the highest accuracy level. Barycenter-based models seem to have advantage over distance-based ones in terms of measurement accuracy. However, neither of them can scale with frequently changing network processing. In the upcoming sections, we explore a new method that is NURBS surface based, and evaluate how it can scale with frequently changing dense network deployments.

2.3   NURBS Surface

This subsection is an introduction to a widely used technique in computer aided graphical design fields that are NURBS surfaces which are a generalization of the much known Bézier-Bernstein and B-Spline curves. A NURBS surface of degree p and q is defined as:

$$S(u,v) = \frac{\sum\limits_{i=0}^{m}\sum\limits_{j=0}^{n} N_{i,p}(u)N_{j,q}(v)w_{i,j}P_{i,j}}{\sum\limits_{i=0}^{m}\sum\limits_{j=0}^{n} N_{i,p}(u)N_{j,q}(v)w_{i,j}} \tag{1}$$

where,

u, v — are variables in $[0, 1]$

$P_{i,j}, w_{i,j}$ — are control points and corresponding weights

m, n — correspond to number of control polygons and points

$\{t_0, t_1, ..., t_{m+p+1}\}, \{t_0, t_1, ..., t_{n+q+1}\}$ — are knots that correspond to control polygons and points respectively

p, q — function degree that corresponds to number of polygon, point knots minus number of control polygons, points minus 1

$N_{i,p}$ and $N_{j,q}$ are the B-Spline basis functions that describe surface control polygons, that are matched by u variable, and curves control points that are matched by v variable. They are given by these formulas:

$$N_{i,0}(t) = \begin{cases} 1 & \text{if} \quad t_i \le t < t_{i+1} \\ 0 \text{ otherwise} \end{cases} \tag{2}$$

$$N_{i,j}(t) = \frac{t - t_i}{t_{i+j} - t_i}N_{i,j-1}(t) + \frac{t_{i+j+1} - t}{t_{i+j+1} - t_{i+1}}N_{i+1,j-1}(t) \tag{3}$$

where, t is a variable in $[0, 1]$ and j an integer different from 0.

Our solution takes advantage of introduction of these new core concepts:

1. control points that are a special set of coverage area points that do influence radio characteristics,

2. weighting of control points that allows impact classification of these control points for a specific measurement or at upper-layer, control over the transmit opportunity,
3. knots that can be tight to the accuracy of our calculations: the more knots we work with and their distribution, the more accurate is our processing of environment attributes.

To ease our preliminary work we consider these simplifications: control polygons and control points numbers are the same, corresponding knots numbers are the same, and knot vector is uniform.

3   Problem Statement

In this section, we formally state the problem. For the rest of this paper let us define,

A_s, A_d, A_c — sets of network mobility devices: mobile stations and access points, measurement points referred as distribution points in this paper and points under the whole coverage area,

AP_i, STA_j — i^{th} access point and j^{th} mobile station respectively,

$P_{c,i}, P_{d,i}, P_{s,i}$ — are i^{th} points corresponding to A sets respectively on a 2-D plan grid,

$O()$ — function, is the transmit opportunity at every coverage area point.

Each AP_i has a communication path to a WLAN controller for radio measurement and reporting purposes. In addition, we consider that each STA_i has a virtual communication path to the controller via corresponding AP_i of attachment and for the same purpose. $P_{d,i}$ are defined as virtual points on grid such as to confine each STA_i or AP_i to the smallest possible square obtained by dividing uniformly the grid horizontally and vertically. It is to note that the number of $P_{d,i}$ depend on the distribution of AP_i and STA_i on the grid and not on their number. A_s is a subset of A_d that is itself a subset of A_c. To ease this preliminary work we consider that A_d set is sufficient for accurate $O()$ calculations.

Let us define,

$T_m, T_{ch}, T_{m,intf}, T_{m,cpu}$ — coverage map processing time, map change processing time, time to report a measure, and time to process a transmit opportunity,

T, T_n — whole cycle and n-cycle processing times,

N, M — number of control points and mobility devices respectively.

T_m and T_{ch} are required for complete map calculation and recalculation in case of changes in environment. A requirement for map calculations is that all control points report data in a timely manner. In addition, changes to radio environment should be paced enough to allow stable transition from an old map condition to a new stable one. T_m could be further divided into two times: $T_{m,intf}$ and $T_{m,cpu}$. $T_{m,intf}$ corresponds to the situation where a control point is an AP or STA and it includes necessary time for radio measurement at point level and reporting it back to the controller. On the other side $T_{m,cpu}$ corresponds to the estimated time for transmit opportunity calculation by algorithms at controller level. T_{ch} may correspond to a periodic interval at which a new map calculation is triggered and necessary time for it. $T_{m,intf}$ is a real-time measure and is dependent on vendor's hardware and control plane network condition. Then this work focuses on $T_{m,cpu}$ and T_{ch} times. $T_{m,cpu}$ depends on the used algorithm at controller level.

If distance-based or beam direction-based, transmit opportunity at any given control point except from AP or STA could be approached by a weighted function of intersections with all other transmitting sources radio patterns. In case of barycenter-based algorithms, the transmit opportunity is more related to point localization within a discovered coverage zone.

Then,

$$T_{m,cpu}(DISTANCE) = (N - M) * M * T_{intersection} \tag{4}$$
$$T_{m,cpu}(BARYCENTER) = (M - 2) * T_{iteration} + N * T_{zone} \tag{5}$$

where $T_{intersection}$ is the required time for processing an intersection between two transmit patterns in the coverage area. $T_{iteration}$ is the required time for an algorithm iteration. In case of Delaunay triangulation based calculations, iteration may correspond to a circumcircle center calculation. T_{zone} is the time required to locate a point in a defined zone and to deduce its corresponding transmit opportunity value.

The total time for a whole calculation cycle that include $k - 1$ change is equal to:

$$T(DISTANCE) = T_{m,intf} + k * (N - M) * M * T_{intersection} \tag{6}$$
$$T(BARYCENTER) = T_{m,intf} + k * ((M - 2) * T_{iteration} + N * T_{zone}) \tag{7}$$

Barycenter algorithms calculations time is negligible to distance-based one when N and M are low. For high N and M values, distance-based algorithms are more scalable. We notice also that barycenter algorithms performs better when the M is roughly a half of N. The upcoming section describe our solution aimed at scaling barycenter-based algorithms like processing times using generalized Bézier NURBS surfaces calculations. It aims also at reducing processing time for higher equivalent N and M numbers that is more relevant to distance-based algorithms like processing.

4   Our NURBS-Based Solution

Our transmit opportunity calculations are based on Bézier NURBS surfaces notions. Two algorithms run for this purpose. The first one, NTO-CP, processes transmit opportunity at every coverage area point. The second one, NTO-CH, processes changes to the current transmit opportunity map.

4.1   NTO-CP Algorithm

The aim of this algorithm is to calculate the transmit opportunity at every coverage area point and:

1. to reduce the number of control points and still obtain the same results,
2. optimize knots number corresponding to variables u and v.

Let's A be the set of $P_{i,j}$ control points. First, this set initializes to correspond to mobility devices: AP and STA as they have the ability to report raw radio data measurements and are, at the same time, the main source of interferences. To ease this work, let's correspond $P_{i,j}$ values to nodes transmission power levels. Then we reorder A set by increasing power levels, weight at maximum the first node, calculate $S()$ at all the other A set nodes and, compare them to reported measures. If reported measures after and before weight change are the same and if $S()$ at these points is the same, then we move this node from A set to a new set A_{ineff} of "ineffective" control points. A_{ineff} defines a monitoring points set that are coverage area points that do not have "effective" control over the transmission opportunity map but still monitor radio interface and report radio raw data. If $S()$ is not the same as reported measures, we define a new hysteresis value, ERR or variance that can be seen as a calibration of the actual transmit opportunity function calculations. A_i correspond to the set of P_j node that are affected by P_i maximum weighting.

For this preliminary work we consider that knot vector is the same for u and v variables. We divide the coverage area into a maximum of three zones: one central and two suburbans. In each region, we elect a zone control point that matches these two criteria:

1. covers the all-corresponding zone,
2. and is the farthest point from the central zone or central zone control point.

Then we set these three zone control points transmit power level at maximum and we turn other control points to monitoring state that corresponds to the lowest transmit power level. We initialize next, knots number to match control points number. If the reported measures at these points are the same as the calculated ones we keep the current number, otherwise we double it until the acceptable hysteresis is satisfied. Further work may consider knots distributions that are different per zone and per direction u or v. The following algorithm details this procedure:

This procedure is done only at system initialization and subsequently for any newly added control point or at sufficiently large periodic time interval to guarantee that A set is refreshed with accurate information. The second part of calculations focuses on processing of control points zones that are meant at optimizing knots numbers for calculations accuracy. For the rest of this algorithm let us define:

$w_{avg,reported}$ — the average of reported measure of P_i as seen by all other nodes,
$P_{0,pseudo}$ — the nearst point of $A - A_{ineff}$ from the processed pseudo-node,

Algorithm 1. NTO-CP algorithm: Part1

```
 1: procedure EFFECTIVE-A(A, w_max)
 2:     for i ← 0, |A|, i + + do
 3:         w_i ← w_max
 4:         A_ineff ← ∅
 5:         A_i ← ∅
 6:         for j ≠ i ← 0, |A|, j + + do
 7:             if w_{j,after} = w_{j,before} then
 8:                 A_ineff = A_ineff ∪ {P_i}
 9:                 if S_{j,after} ≠ S_{j,before} then
10:                     ERR = max(ERR_new, ERR_old)
11:                 end if
12:             else
13:                 A_i = A_i ∪ P_j
14:                 if S_{j,after} = S_{j,before} then
15:                     w_j = w_j + 1
16:                 end if
17:             end if
18:         end for
19:     end for
20: end procedure
```

$Z_{0,pseudo}$ — the central zone control points set covered by pseudo control point at maximum weight,

Processing of effective control points requires one by one node weighting at maximum and measurement of its effect over other control points. This weighting may be: an increase of transmit power level, a high QoS classification, etc. a mix of them or other variables that are under system management control and that can maximize the opportunity function. Zones processing and determination of pseudo control points helps optimizing $S(u, v)$ knots number for calculation accuracy purposes.

We double the initial number of knots until $S()$ calculation hysteresis is satisfied in each zone. We then update the current optimized knots number to match the maximum among all defined zones.

4.2 NTO-CH Algorithm

A change may affect a zone, multiple zones or the entire network. This algorithm task is to scope the change impact so that only pertaining set's control points are processed to reflect the new change. It is to note that zones used in NTO-CH are different from ones used in NTO-CP algorithm, as the purpose is different. The idea here is to find an optimized number of zones that hints on the impact of a given change.

Algorithm 2. NTO-CP algorithm: Part2

21: **procedure** CP-ZONES(A, w_{max})
22:    $\forall P_i \in A - A_{ineff}, w_i \leftarrow w_{max}$
23:    **for** $i \leftarrow 0, |A|, i++$ **do**
24:        $w_i \leftarrow \frac{w_i}{w_i + w_{avg,reported}}$
25:    **end for**
26:    $P_{0,pseudo} \leftarrow \frac{\sum w_i * P_i}{\sum w_i}$
27:    $\forall P_i \in A - A_{ineff} - P_{0,pseudo}, w_i \leftarrow w_{min}$
28:    $P_{0,pseudo} \leftarrow w_{max}$
29:    **if** $Z_{0,pseudo} = A - A_{ineff}$ **then**
30:        $P_{1,pseudo} \leftarrow P_i \in Z_{0,pseudo}$
    s. t. $\forall j, j \neq i, w_i = min(w_i, w_j)$
31:    **else**
32:        $P_{1,pseudo} \leftarrow P_i$
    s. t. $P_i \in A - A_{ineff} - Z_{0,pseudo}$
33:    **end if**
34:    $P_{2,pseudo} \leftarrow P_i$
    s. t. $P_i \in A - A_{ineff} - Z_{0,pseudo} - Z_{1,pseudo}$
35: **end procedure**

Not all changes are relevant and maybe classified to match one of this set of categories: minor, medium, or high. To ease this preliminary work only high effect changes are considered and all other changes are considered insignificant. A change may correspond to a newly reported RSSI or any other relevant variable.

4.3   Algorithm Time

Calculation time corresponds to one initialization and $k-1$ changes. This time is compound of effective control processing time, optimum knots number processing time, and change processing time. Effective control point processing is unique to this method and it requires running $S()$, $M*(M-1)$ times. Optimum knots number processing time corresponds to $S()$ calculations at every zone control points and iterations until required accuracy is achieved. Then if α, μ, and β, are number of iterations, number of zones and number of ineffective controls points respectively, the time is given by: $\frac{\alpha}{\mu} * (M - \beta)$. It is to note that the first purpose of zoning is to allow parallel processing in every zone.

$$T_{(NURBS)} = M^2 - (1 + \frac{k - \alpha}{\mu})M + k\eta N + (k\frac{\mu + \beta}{\mu} - \alpha\frac{\beta}{\mu}) \qquad (8)$$

where η is a value that represents the scope of the change.

We apply these numerical simplifications: $\alpha = 1$, $\mu = 3$, $\eta = 0.25$. $\alpha = 1$ as one iteration is sufficient for an acceptable accuracy with regards to other algorithms, and because at initialization, the number of knots could be set to

Algorithm 3. NTO-CP algorithm: Part3

36: **procedure** ZONES-KNOTS
37:     **for** $i \leftarrow 0, 1, 2$ **do**
38:         $w_{i,pseudo} \leftarrow w_{max}$
39:         **for** $j, j \neq i, P_j \in Z_{i,pseudo}$ **do**
40:             $w_j \leftarrow w_{min}$
41:             **if** $S_j \neq measure$ **then**
42:                 **while** $|S_J - measure| \geq ERR$ **do**
43:                     $Knots_{i,pseudo} = 2 * Knots_{i,pseudo}$
44:                 **end while**
45:             **end if**
46:         **end for**
47:     **end for**
48: **end procedure**

Algorithm 4. NTO-CH algorithm

1: **procedure** CH-ZONES
2:     $j \leftarrow 1$
3:     **for** $i \leftarrow |A - A_{ineff}|$ **do**
4:         **if** $w_i \geq w_{C1}$ **then**
5:             $P_{j,change} \leftarrow P_i$
6:             $Z_{j,change} \leftarrow \{P_i\}$
7:             $j = j + 1$
8:         **else if** $w_{C1} > w_i \geq w_{C2}$ **then**
9:             $Z_{j,change} \leftarrow \{P_i\} \bigcup \{P_{i+1}\}$
    $P_{i+1} \in A_i, w_{C1} > w_{i+1} \geq w_{C2}$
                                                        ▷ Otherwise break
10:             $i = i + 1, j = j + 1$
11:         **else if** $w_{C2} > w_i \geq w_{C3}$ **then**
12:             $Z_{j,change} \leftarrow \{P_i\} \bigcup \{P_{i+1}\} \bigcup \{P_{i+2}\}$
    $P_{i+1}, P_{i+2} \in A_i, w_{C2} > w_{i+1}, w_{i+2} \geq w_{C3}$
                                                        ▷ Otherwise break
13:             $i = i + 2, j = j + 1$
14:         **end if**
15:     **end for**
16: **end procedure**

---

a higher level. It influences only $S()$ calculation time in case of higher knots number which is considered insignificant in this paper but may be considered in further work if necessary. $\mu = 3$ is more to allow parallel processing when computing zones and may correspond to non-overlapping channels. $\eta = 0.25$ supposes that most changes affect only specific zones and do not span multiple zones. It is sufficient for this preliminary work that shows our solution design advantages.

5   Results Evaluation and Conclusion

At this level, our evaluation is based on Matlab simulations of our solution, distance and barycenter based ones. Next step would consider implementing this solution on Linux based AP and STA in environments including vendor-working solutions. At the same time, we consider that at coding level we could get concluding results with regard to competitors and other related work.

First, in Fig. 1, we vary N and M numbers and observe the variation of processing times of the three methods. For higher N numbers our solution starts performing better than both other solutions when M is almost greater than 10% of N. At higher M values, barycenter-based solution is no more scalable. For lower M and N numbers barycenter-based solution is better than our solution and distance-based ones. Then it is more suitable for lower density and sparse deployments. For high-density deployments which correspond to higher N numbers and with lower M number our solution starts performing better than barycenter-based ones when N number is roughly four times the M number.

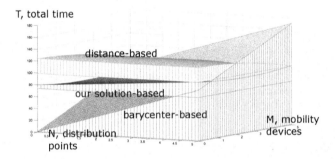

Fig. 1. Opportunity processing time comparison between our solution, distance and barycenter based algorithms

Next, we evaluate the impact of number of changes over our solution and the two other solutions. Figure 2 shows results for the three algorithms. Changes' impact over barycenter-based algorithms is very noticeable for higher numbers of distribution points and increasing number of mobility devices. Distance-based algorithm seems to depend solely on the number of affecting changes. Our solution algorithm seems to depend slightly on both the number of changes and mobility devices. We see clearly that for lower number of mobility devices, mainly access points, and significant number of distribution points our solution performs better in case of frequent changes.

Based on evaluation results we conclude that:

1. our solution performs better than both other solutions when number of mobility devices is almost greater than 10% of the number of distribution points,
2. our solution performs better than barycenter-based one when N number is roughly four times the M number.

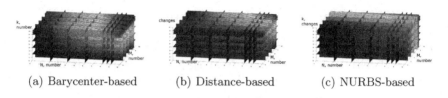

(a) Barycenter-based   (b) Distance-based   (c) NURBS-based

Fig. 2. Impact of number of changes over algorithms: (a) describes barycenter-based algorithm; (b) describes distance-based one; and, (c) describes our solution.

Further work may consider these elements to evaluate deeply our solution over the other ones:

1. accuracy of calculations,
2. feasibility of parallel multiple opportunity functions processing using our solution model,
3. zoning based on different point's distributions, knot number...
4. handling of obstacles in radio environment and its impact on processing accuracy and time,
5. dynamic or in movement obstacles' impact in terms of calculations accuracy and time.

Acknowledgment. We would thank colleagues: researchers, engineers, and anonymous reviewers for sharing their precious comments and on-field experience that improved the quality of this paper.

References

1. Ruslan, R., Wan, T.C.: Cognitive radio-based power adjustment for Wi-Fi. TENCON 2009–2009 IEEE Region 10 Conference (2009)
2. Ahmed, N., Keshav, S.: A successive refinement approach to wireless infrastructure network deployment. In: IEEE Wireless Communications and Networking Conference (2006)
3. Qiao, D.,Choi, S., Jain, A., Shin, K.G.: Adaptive transmit power control in IEEE 802.11a wireless LANs. In: Vehicular Technology Conference (2003)
4. Kapadia, P.R., Damani, O.P.: Interference-constrained wireless coverage in a protocol model. In: Proceedings of the 9th ACM International Symposium on Modeling Analysis and Simulation of Wireless and Mobile Systems (2006)
5. Guessous, M., Zenkouar, L.: Cognitive directional cost-based transmit power control in IEEE 802.11 WLAN. In: Proceedings of the 31th International Conference on Information Networking (ICOIN) (2017)

Network Protocols

Load-Balancing Adaptive Clustering Refinement Algorithm for Wireless Sensor Network Clusters

Gal Oren[1,2(✉)], Leonid Barenboim[3], and Harel Levin[2,3]

[1] Department of Computer Science, Ben-Gurion University of the Negev,
POB 653, Beersheba, Israel
orenw@post.bgu.ac.il

[2] Department of Physics, Nuclear Research Center-Negev,
P.O.B. 9001, Beersheba, Israel
harellevin@gmail.com

[3] Department of Mathematics and Computer Science,
The Open University of Israel, P.O.B. 808, Ra'anana, Israel
leonidb@openu.ac.il

Abstract. Energy efficiency is a crucial performance metric in sensor networks, imminently determining the network lifetime. Consequently, a key objective in WSN is to improve overall energy efficiency to extend the network lifetime. Its conservation influences the topology design of many WSN-based systems, especially the clustering of the network. Unlike other WSN clustering algorithms, that do not re-cluster the network after deployment, our hypothesis is that it is advisable, in terms of prolonging the network lifetime, to adaptively re-cluster specific regions that are triggered significantly more than other regions in the network. By doing so, it is possible to minimize or even prevent the premature death of CHs, which are heavily burdened with sensing and transmitting actions – much more than other parts of the WSN. In order to do so we introduce the Adaptive Clustering Refinement (ACR) algorithm, which is based on the Adaptive Mesh Refinement algorithm by Berger and Oliger [14] and the Hierarchical Control Clustering algorithm by Banerjee and Khuller [13]. We prove that the ACR algorithm complexity is linear in the total size of the graph, and that we manage to optimize the WSN cluster connectivity and prolong its lifetime. We also devise a local version of the algorithm with improved complexity.

Keywords: Wireless sensor networks · Adaptive clustering refinement · Energy optimization · Networks connectivity

1 Introduction

Background

In the past few years, rapid advances in the area of micro and nano technology have taken place with implication to all of the scientific research fields. As a result, micro-sensors have been developed for various needs. Subsequently, this has led to the

Y. Koucheryavy et al. (Eds.): WWIC 2017, LNCS 10372, pp. 157–173, 2017.
DOI: 10.1007/978-3-319-61382-6_13

development of Wireless Sensor Networks (WSNs). WSNs are composed of a variety of nodes, and they include abilities of data sensing and data processing, as well as wireless transmission such as Bluetooth or radio technology. The invention of WSNs has led to the development of various serviceable applications, including control, tracking and monitoring of large areas [1]. The introduction of WSN presents much superiority over orthodox sensing doctrines. A large-scale, dense spreading improves the spatial coverage and obtains much better resolutions; moreover, it also extends the fault tolerance and sturdiness of such a system. The deployment of sensor nodes is performed in an ad-hoc fashion and occasionally does not include sufficient planning and engineering in many WSN applications. Once the nodes are deployed in their positions, it is essential that the sensors will independently organize themselves into a unified wireless network. The nodes are powered by battery and are designed to operate without supervision for a relatively long duration of time. However, it is often problematic to replace or recharge the sensor node batteries, due to the fact that most of the deployments are in large fields (e.g. animal control) or inaccessible places (e.g. war zones) [2].

The fundamental consideration in some other networks (such as mobile networks) not always take into account the energy consumption, while it is still a significant design factor that directly influences the network lifetime; this is because those energy resources can be easily replaced or rechargeable by the users or the operators. Hence, a higher concern is given in those networks to quality of service such as higher performances. However, energy efficiency is a crucial performance metric in sensor networks, imminently determining the network lifetime. In order to tackle this array of considerations, some protocols may be used to handle the trade-off of performance metrics such as network overall postponement against energy efficiency [3].

Energy may be obtained by utilizing the external environment (for example, by using photovoltaic cells as an energy source). Nevertheless, the behavior of external energy source is usually non-persistent, which makes it unreliable and requires the use of batteries [4]. However, batteries also create a problem because of their finite amount of stored energy and the frequent need to replace or recharge them. Consequently, a main goal in WSN is to improve overall energy efficiency to extend the network lifetime. Energy conservation influences the design of many WSN-based systems. Comprehensive studies have examined this issue [5] and suggested energy optimization techniques in order to manage the WSN topology accordingly.

The most important observation from those studies [6] to our study is that the energy consumption of the transmission unit is significantly higher than the energy needed to make any kind of computation in a node, and the current estimations are that there is an order of magnitude difference in energy consumption between the two. This shows that transmission should always be traded for computation when possible, in order to preserve power. Following this observation, these factors should be considered and are vital for understanding the energy consumption problem. The most basic and common way to implement this knowledge in WSNs is by using clustering, as we explain below.

WSN Clustering

Nodes in multi-hop ad-hoc sensor networks play a dual role as a data originator and data router at the same time. Some of the nodes may not operate properly, which may lead to major topological changes and require the rerouting of some packets and network reconstruction. This further emphasizes the importance of energy efficiency and energy control. Because of this, the focus of many researchers of WSN is to develop protocols and algorithms that consider scalability and energy efficiency by grouping the network nodes into clusters in order to form a hierarchical topology and eliminating any redundant data. This process consists of the following steps: Nodes transmit their sensed data to a master node in a distributed fashion; the master node aggregates the data; after computation the master node forwards the new calculated data to its master or to the sink node after discarding of the superfluous data.

A formalized approach [7] to demonstrate this concept assumes that a WSN cluster includes two main components: A base station (BS) and a number of sub-clusters (which also can have sub-clusters). Each of the sub-clusters have a leader (usually referred to as the cluster head, or CH), as well as other nodes (non-cluster-head nodes, or NCHs) that are all within a same transmission range around the CH. The transmission range is defined as the maximal distance between a receiver and a sender – in this case, CH and NCH respectively – and there is a correlation between the length of the transmission range and the energy consumed in this topology.

A CH has various responsibilities: It gathers data from NCHs, processes it in order to minimize its volume as much as possible and transmit it to the master node or the base station. A CH forwards the information in two possible ways: Directly or by using numerous relay nodes. The relay nodes focus on carry forward the data transmitted from other nodes, rather than local sensing. The CH in each sub-cluster may be chosen in distributed fashion by the sensors themselves, or pre-determined by the network configurator. These approaches can be classified into two groups: static clustering and dynamic clustering. The difference between these two clustering algorithms is that static clustering-based algorithms do not modify clusters after formation, while dynamic algorithms may choose a new CH after a given period of time.

Another vital factor in determining the performance and network lifetime is based on the location that each CH is set in. As previously mentioned, the energy consumption is highly derived by the transmission span, and if a proper CH position is chosen, the CH node may not be forced to communicate with the master node/BS directly over a distant distance; instead, it will be able to preserve its stored energy for a long period of time. Other studies and developments in the field show heterogeneous network topologies, in which the CHs have additional energy capacity compared to NCHs, which obviously increases the network lifetime. These fields also introduce network topologies with multiple layers ($L > 2$), such as adding a meta-CH layer, which may help reducing the load of the other CHs in the layer above and so forth [8]. In this paper we adopt the idea of multi-layers CHs with a uniformed energy capacity, and devise an algorithm that turns NCHs to CHs and vice versa, in order to preserve energy.

The lifetime maximization problem has been addressed in many algorithms, and the current outcomes can be classified into two main groups: centralized doctrines vs. distributed doctrines. For centralized doctrines, the sensors' position must be available and known in order to obtain comprehensive optimizations according to some performance metrics. In contrast, distributed doctrines make resolutions according to the local data that approximate nodes manage to know about each other. In recent years, various WSN algorithms have been introduced, in attempt to minimize energy consumption using central clustering doctrine in order to extend the network lifetime [9]. These studies, however, mainly focused on reducing the number of CHs or their energy consumption, rather than focusing on NCHs.In contrast, in this paper we adopt the distributed fashion from the same reasons mentioned before: our suggested algorithm has to consider the two entities equally because of the fluidity of rules of the nodes in the WSN, from NCHs to CHs and vice versa.

2 The Adaptive Clustering Refinement (ACR) Algorithm

Energy-Efficient Schemes and Factors

Energy-efficient schemes can be mainly divided into two classes according to their purposes: reducing the energy consumption of all nodes in a WSN, and increasing the WSN lifespan and connectivity. While these two objectives are highly interdependent, they are not the same. Indeed, decreasing overall energy consumption is solely a minimization problem, while increasing network lifespan is a min-max problem, as network life spans may often be fixed or influenced by the network nodes that have the shortest lifespan [3]. The nodes with the shortest lifespan are referred to as *bottleneck nodes* and in the case of clustered WSNs they are often the CHs. These two objectives of energy-efficient schemes derive different optimizations. The term *network lifespan* has been given various definitions that mostly fit into two categories [2]: (1) The amount of time until some X percentage of nodes consume most or all of their energy supply, and (2) The amount of time until a specific coverage or connectivity setting conditions in a specific region cannot be realized.

In this paper, we adopt the idea of minimizing the overall energy consumption in conjunction with the idea of maximizing the network lifetime. We investigate the amount of time until some X percentage of nodes consume most or all of their energy supply in a **specific region**, and how is that affects the specific coverage or connectivity of the region nodes - which in this case are probably the most triggered ones. By adopting such a definition, maximizing network lifetime leads to a **localized** max-min problem with the objective of making those sensors with shortest lifespan survive as long as possible, while trying to minimize the overall energy consumption of the specific triggered area.

Research Goals

Unlike other WSN clustering algorithms, which cannot or prefer not to re-cluster the network after deployment except the necessary case of death of nodes, our hypothesis is that it is advisable, in terms of prolonging the network lifetime, to adaptively re-cluster specific regions that are **triggered significantly** more than other regions in the network in a distributed fashion. By doing so, it is possible to minimize or even prevent the premature death of CHs (in comparison to the other nodes in the network), which are heavily burdened with sensing and transmitting actions –much more than other parts of the WSN.

For example [10], imagine that the South-African government decided to hermetically map the movement of the Blue Wildebeest in Kruger national park, one of the largest game reserves in Africa, which covers an area of 19,485 km^2 in the provinces of Limpopo and Mpumalanga in northeastern South Africa. It is known that the Blue Wildebeest take part in a long-distance migration, synchronize to overlap with the yearly pattern of rainfall and herbiage sprouting on some several specific plains where they can trace the nutrient fodder [11]. Because of the huge masses of the Blue Wildebeest herds, it is impracticable to collar their members with wireless sensors. Consequently, in order to do trace those herds, at the center of each 100 m^2 a wireless sensor with animal sound recognition [12] has been placed, and initially all of those nodes created a uniform hierarchical WSN cluster. Now, because the Blue Wildebeest tend to move in large-scale herds and not in individual fashion, it means that soon there is going to be a massive load on parts of the network, while other parts of the network will not be triggered at all; a state which shortly will cause, as previously explained, the premature death of CHs in this region and the reduction of the connectivity in the network. Therefore, in order to ease the load on the burdened CHs, a re-clusterization of those specific triggered sub-clusters of the whole WSN can prolong the total lifespan of the network. This way it is possible to achieve the goal of minimizing the overall energy consumption in conjunction with the goal of maximizing the network lifetime. We refer to our re-clustering algorithm as the *Adaptive Clustering Refinement* (henceforth, ACR), which is based on the Hierarchical Control Clustering (HCC) Algorithm.

Through this paper n will represent the number of CHs and m will represent the number of sub-WSN grids to be refined.

The Hierarchical Control Clustering (HCC) Algorithm

In order to devise the ACR algorithm, we need to determine which clustering scheme will take place along with the refinement method. Unlike most of the published schemes, the goal of Banerjee and Khuller scheme is to form a multi-tier hierarchical clustering using proximity-traversing-based algorithm named Hierarchical Control Clustering [13] (henceforth, HCC). HCC is a distributed multi-hop hierarchical clustering algorithm which also effectively manages to create a multi-level cluster hierarchy. The algorithm works in a distributed fashion, meaning that each node in the WSN can initiate the cluster formation process. The HCC progress in two main sub-processes, when the first is the Tree Discovery process and the second is the Cluster Formation process.

The first process is essentially a distributed formation of a BFS tree, which is rooted is the initiator node. In this process, every single node broadcasts a message signal (which includes the parent identification, the BFS tree root identification, and the sub-tree size) at every predetermined unit of time, transporting the data regarding its shortest hop distance to the BFS tree root. This is done by the following routine: A node n_i which is adjacent to node n_j will select n_j to be its parent, and also will bring up-to-date its hop distance to the root of the BFS tree, if the route via n_j is shorter. Obviously, each node brings up-to-date its sub-tree size when its children sub-tree size modifies. The second process is initiated when a sub-tree on a node rise above the size parameter k. Then the node starts cluster formation on its sub-tree. If the sub-tree size is less than 2 k it will form a single cluster for the whole sub-tree. Otherwise, it will form multiple clusters.

This two step process has a time complexity of O(n). Nevertheless, it has managed to obtain balanced clustering, and additionally to deal with non-stable environments quite effectively. This time complexity is calculated as follows: The BFS tree formation of the first process of GRAPH CLUSTER ($T \leftarrow BFS\ tree\ of\ G$), takes $O(|E|)$. The computation time at every vertex n_i, in post-order traversal, is $O(deg_T(n_i))$, meaning the degree of n_i in the tree. Therefore, the total cost for the whole post-order traversal is $\sum_n deg_T(n_i) = O(|V|)$. Thus, the complexity of the algorithm is $O(|E| + |V|)$.

The Adaptive Mesh Refinement (AMR)and Adaptive Clustering Refinement (ACR) Algorithms

The Adaptive Mesh Refinement (AMR) is a type of multi-scale algorithm that achieves high resolution in localized regions of dynamic, multi-dimensional numerical simulations [14, 15]. The AMR algorithm has been implemented with large success to model large-scale scientific simulations in a variety of disciplines, mainly astrophysics. In principle, the AMR algorithm manages to place large high-resolution grids exactly where they are needed, meaning where the high computational cost and overheads requires. The AMR algorithm adaptability achieve a state in which it is possible to simulate multi-scale resolutions that are impossible otherwise because of computational power limits with the traditional techniques which use a global uniform fine grid.

The motivation of combining the AMR concept into clustering comes from the observation that a very fine mesh can be required for clustering on a highly irregular or concentrated data distribution, if a grid-based clustering algorithm that employs a single uniform mesh is used. This motivation also exists in the case of clustering WSNs, which are under fluid amount of load and need to re-cluster themselves in order to create a more uniformed load-balancing among the CHs nodes. In this paper, we demonstrate this re-clustering by using the HCC algorithm [13] as a building block, especially because of its hierarchical clustering fashion and the dynamic and distributed abilities to 'refine' areas when reaching some parameter (k), which for simplicity of explanation will be set to 2 through this paper.

Figure 1 shows an example of an ACR WSN-Graph tree formation in which every intersection represents a CH and every square represent the field in which the NCHs nodes are located. Each refined CH creates k^2 child-CHs. It is possible to see that each tree node uses a different resolution WSN-Graph. The root WSN-Graph with the coarsest granularity (i.e. the WSN-Graph cluster at the beginning) covers the entire domain, which contains two sub-WSN-Graphs, sub-WSN 1 and sub-WSN 2, which were refined – meaning that from each square at the previous step, an NCH turns into a CH in order to ease the load pressure of the other CHs around it (i.e. the corners of the previous square). Sub-WSN 2 at level 1 also contains two sub-WSN-Graphs that are discovered using a finer graph. The deeper the node is located in the tree, the finer the WSN-Graph is used.

In general, the ACR load-balancing-based algorithm tries to find the load burdened regions, and the number of the discovered load burdened regions determines the number of regions that will need to re-cluster themselves. Because the refinement is based on the load factor, the ACR method can recursively identify the load burdened regions and represent them in a hierarchical tree structure in which the tree nodes near the leaves indicate the more load burdened regions and the nodes close to the root have

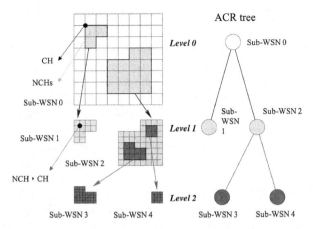

Fig. 1. An ACR WSN-Graph Tree formation example with 2 levels of refinement. A finer resolution WSN-Graph is applied each time a sub-WSN is created.

lower rates of load burden. The ACR tree construction is a top-down process starting from the root node that covers the entire problem volume.

The Adaptive Clustering Refinement Algorithm

```
ACR(WSN-Graph, level)
1. Traverse the WSN-Graph using BFS: Calculate the top
   k²-quantile of the load on the entire WSN-Graph and
   set it to be the threshold.
2. For each non-marked CH:
   2.1.     If the CH-load is greater than the threshold:
      2.1.1.     Mark this CH to be refined
      2.1.2.     Connect this CH to all of its neighbor
         CHs in the WSN-Graph that are also greater than
         the threshold and mark them too
      2.1.3.     Create a new sub-WSN-Graph containing
         all of these nodes
   2.2.     Else if the CH-load is smaller than half of
      the threshold :
      2.2.1.     Mark this CH to be coarsen
      2.2.2.     Connect this CH to all of its neighbor
         CHs in the WSN-Graph that are also smaller than
         half of the threshold and mark them too
      2.2.3.     Create a new sub-WSN-Graph containing
         all of these nodes
3. For each sub-WSN-Graph:
   3.1.     If sub-WSN-Graph set to be refined:
      3.1.1.     Refine sub-WSN-Graph
      3.1.2.     Call ACR(sub-WSN-Graph, level+1)
   3.2.     If sub-WSN-Graph set to be coarsen:
      3.2.1.     Coarse sub-WSN-Graph
```

Given a WSN-Graph (initially it assumed to be the HCC output tree), the ACR tree construction starts at the BS or the main CH node that uses the WSN-Graph with an initial granularity to cover the entire problem domain as given from the hierarchical WSN clustering algorithm [13]. While traversing the WSN-Graph in a BFS fashion, a calculation is being made in order to determine the average load on the WSN-Graph. Afterwards, each node is examined to check if the load exceeds the given threshold (we chose a k^2-quantile of the nodes because this ensures that the number of CH nodes produced at each round is less than the nodes that originally exceed the threshold. This fact helps us to bound the size of the produced tree). The nodes whose load is larger than the threshold are marked to be refined, and a new sub-WSN-Graph is created from all marked nodes that are connected (adjacent) with each other. The algorithm recursively refines the sub-WSN that has been found, and goes to the child nodes while a hierarchical tree is built. Whenever the load is lower than some pre-defined lower bound, a coarsening (un-refinement) should be performed. The algorithm stops when the maximum level of tree depth is reached or there are no nodes with load that are larger than the threshold. The process of constructing the ACR tree is a top-down operation. This is also the main difference of our ACR approach from the other grid-based algorithms whose hierarchical trees are built in a bottom-up fashion, especially because of the need to start at the BS or the main CH, which receives most of the information regarding the load. Next, we analyze the running time of the algorithm in Theorem 1, and the construction complexity of the algorithm in Theorem 2. An upper bound on the total number of CHs in the ACR tree is provided by Theorem 3.

Theorem 1: *The running time of the algorithm is* $O(dm\frac{1-p^h}{1-p})$:

Proof. Assuming m is the number of the sub-WSNs grids which need to be refined, the dimensionality of those grids is fixed to 2 dimensions of an Euclidean space ($d = 2$), h is the ACR tree height, and p represents the average percentage of data objects to be refined at each level, the complexity for scanning the database is almost the same as in the AMR algorithm, and it is bounded by $O(dm + dmp + dmp^2 + \cdots + dmp^{h-1}) = O(2m\frac{1-p^h}{1-p}) \leq O(\frac{2m}{1-p})$. ∎

Theorem 2: *The construction complexity of the algorithm is* $O(dm\frac{1-p^h}{1-p} + 6^d n\frac{1-q^h}{1-q})$.

Proof. The complexity of finding the sub-WSN-Graphs highly depends on the size of the graph in each sub-WSN-Graph. We assume the graph size at the root is n and q is the average ratio of graph sizes between two levels of graphs. Assuming m is the number of the sub-WSNs grids which need to be refined. The complexity for marking the CHs nodes that exceed the threshold and connecting the other marked CHs to form the sub-WSN-Graph is $O(2^d 3^d nq + 2^d 3^d nq^2 + \cdots + 2^d 3^d nq^{h-1}) = O(6^2 n\frac{1-q^h}{1-q})$ assuming the refinement factor is 2, meaning that we split any cluster to 2^d sub-clusters, and each node must check at most its $(3^2 - 1)$ neighbors for connected sub-WSN-Graph. Therefore the complexity for constructing the AMR tree is $O(2m\frac{1-p^h}{1-p} + 6^2 n\frac{1-q^h}{1-q})$. ∎

Theorem 3: *The total number of CH nodes in the ACR is bounded by $O(n^2)$, where n is the number of CHs in the input ACR tree.*

Proof. At every step, there are less than $\frac{n'}{k^2}$ CHs chosen to be refined (by the threshold quantile definition), where n' is the number of CHs received as an argument and k is the refinement factor. Each refined CH creates k^2 child-CHs. It means that at every iteration, the algorithm will create $\left(\frac{n'}{k^2} - 1\right)k^2 = n' - k^2$ new CHs. It is clear that after i iterations, the algorithm will produce $n' - ik^2$ new CHs, which means that after $\frac{n'}{k^2}$ iterations it will stop producing new CHs. Hence, the total number of CHs after the algorithm run is at most $n' + \sum_{i=1}^{\frac{n'}{k^2}} (n' - ik^2) = n' + \left(\frac{n'^2}{k^2} - \frac{n'}{2k^2}(k^2 + n')\right) =$ $n' + \left(\frac{n'^2}{2k^2} - \frac{n'}{2}\right) = \frac{n'}{2} + \frac{n'^2}{2k^2}$, and therefore the total complexity of the ACR tree is $O(n^2)$ while k is a constant.   ∎

3   The ACR Algorithm Energy Consumption Model

WSN Energy Consumption Model

We consider two different types of energy consumption for data transmission and receiving, respectively: a transmitter consumes energy to run both the radio electronics and the power amplifier, while a receiver only consumes energy to drive the radioelectronics. The mobile radio channels on typical sensor nodes are predominantly in the VHF (frequency from 30 MHz to 300 MHz, wavelength from 1 m to 10 m) and UHF (frequency from 300 MHz to 3 GHz, wavelength from 10 cm to 1 m), respectively [1, 2]. We employ the free space (*fs*) fading channel model for wireless communication that incurs a d^2 power loss, some outdoor deployments [2]. In a real communication system, the transmission power could be adjusted by suitably configuring the power amplifier. Therefore, the energy dissipation in transmitting one unit of data message over a directed wireless communication link can be modeled as $E_t(i)$, when $E_t(i) = E_{elec} + E_{amp}(d_{i,j}) = E_{elec} + \epsilon_{fs} \cdot d_{i,j}^2$, where E_{elec} denotes the energy for driving the electronics, which depends on various factors including digital coding, modulation, filtering, and spreading of the signals, for both transmitter electronics and receiver electronics; and ϵ_{fs} is the coefficient for calculating the amplifier energy E_{amp}, which depends on the Euclidean distance $d_{i,j} = \sqrt{(x_i - x_j)^2 + (y_i - y_j)^2}$ between transmitter v_i located at (x_i, y_i) and receiver v_j located at (x_j, j) as well as the acceptance bit-error rate. The energy consumed by a sensor v_i in receiving one unit of data packet is denoted as $E_r(i) = E_{elec}$. Note that the above transmission and receiving energy models assume a contention free MAC protocol, where interferences from simultaneous transmission can be avoided.

A CH, which also collects environment sensing data, receives data messages from NCHs within the cluster and sends all the data to a main CH or BS after performing a certain type of data processing (such as data aggregation and data compression). We use a constant E_p to represent the energy spent in processing each unit of received or sensed data. We assume that the CH performs complete data aggregation, that is, an input of two k-bit messages produces an output of one k-bit message after aggregation. Furthermore, we use a parameter α, $0 < \alpha \leq 1$, to denote the data compression ratio: an input of k bits results in an output of $\alpha \cdot k$ bits after compression.

Problem Formulation

The problem of determining the optimal number and location of CHs for minimum TEC in sensor networks is formulated as follows. We consider a WSN where n sensor nodes have been deployed in a bounded $L \times L (m^2)$ square. The location of each sensor $v_i, i \in 0, 1, \ldots, n - 1$, is denoted as (x_i, y_i). We assume a one-hop communication model, and the transmission energy is calculated using the free space (fs) model mentioned above. We consider a sensor deployment scenario in a uniform node distribution. The optimization problem is to strategically refine parts of the entire WSN by designating an appropriate subset of sensor nodes in the network as CHs base on the sensing load, each of which forms a cluster with its neighbor nodes, such that there will be a reduce of pressure on the entire CHs in the WSN. Thus, (1) the total energy consumption for the transmission of each unit of data message from all NCHs to CHs and so forth is minimized, and (2) the total energy consumption of the entire WSN will reduce, and it will be achievable to maximize the WSN lifetime and connectivity at once.

We consider the following general conditions or assumptions in our problem formulation: All sensors are pre-deployed and have constrained energy supply; The network is static, that is, neither the sensors nor the CHs has mobility once deployed; The total number of sensors is known; Each CH forms exactly one cluster, and besides data processing, also performs the same task of environmental sensing and data collection as a regular sensor node; There exists a contention free MAC protocol for wireless communication. We consider the energy consumption for data transmission of each NCH, and for data receiving, processing, and transmission of each CH. Since the energy cost for environment sensing is generally much less than communication and processing tasks, we do not consider sensing energy cost here. Obviously, the total energy consumption depends on the network distribution, the number and location of CHs, and the compression ratio α at CHs.

ACR Algorithm Energy-Efficiency Proof

In this paper, we use an analytical formula for calculating the optimal value of refinement of loaded parts of the WSN in order to achieve the minimum total energy consumption of data transfer from NCHs to the BS or the main CH through their corresponding CHs. The optimal number of refinement determined by our approach can be used to guide the execution of the HCC clustering algorithm that requires such information.

The total energy consumption per round, denoted by E_{Tot}, is the sum of the energy consumption E_{NCH} of all NCHs for data transmission and the energy consumption E_{CH} of all CHs for data receiving, processing, and transmission in one round, which can be defined as $E_{Tot} = E_{NCH} + E_{CH}$. The E_{NCH} only includes transmission energy cost E_T, when E_{CH} includes the energy cost E_r for receiving, E_p for processing, and E_t for transmission. Each of NCHs transfers one unit of data to its corresponding CH, which performs processing (aggregation and compression) on the received data and its own sensing data, and sends the compressed aggregated result to other CH or BS.

In order to prove that our algorithm reduces the total energy consumption of the whole WSN and also increases the connectivity of the network we need to show that (I) the total energy consumption of the refined zone is actually lower than the previous state, and (II) that the distances of the NCHs to their new CHs in the refined zones were reduced and became more uniform than the previous state. Therefore, we need first to formulate the energy consumption of the NCHs and the CHs in our model. Based on the previous knowledge of E_{Tot}, for each NCH in our model the energy consumption per bit will be:

$$E_{NCH} = E_t = E_{elec} + \in_{fs} \cdot d^2_{NCH \to CH} \tag{1}$$

When $d_{NCH \to CH}$ is the distance between the NCH to its CH, and for each CH in our model the energy consumption will be:

$$
\begin{aligned}
E_{CH} &= n_{NCH \to CH} E_r + (n_{NCH \to CH} + 1) E_p + \alpha E_t \\
&= n_{NCH \to CH} E_{elec} + (n_{NCH \to CH} + 1) E_p + \alpha \left(E_{elec} + \in_{fs} \cdot d^2_{CH \to InitCH} \right)
\end{aligned} \tag{2}
$$

When $n_{NCH \to CH}$ is the number of NCH that communicate with the CH, and $d_{CH \to HigherCH}$ is the distance between the CH to its higher CH in the hierarchy (the BS is the top node is the hierarchy). Hence, a refinement of the WSN is always worthwhile if the current energy consumption in the intended to refinement zone is higher than the energy consumption of the same zone after the refinement. A formulation of this condition, based on the previous formulas to E_{NCH} and E_{CH} will be:

$$\sum_{i=1}^{n_{NCH \to InitCH}} E_{NCHi} + E_{InitCH} > \sum_{i=1}^{n_{CHs}} \left(E_{CHi} + \sum_{j=1}^{n_{NCH \to CHi}} E_{NCHj} \right) + E_{InitCH} \tag{3}$$

When the *InitCH* is the CH in the hierarchy from which a refinement should start, and $\{CHi | i \in \{1, \ldots, n_{CH \to InitCH}\}\}$ is the group of NCHs which turns into CHs in the refinement process.

It is possible to see that although each refinement shortens the distance between the NCHs and the CHs, an E_p overhead accumulates due to the additional CHs in the WSN. Base on the known energy consumption parameters [7], $E_{elec} = 5 \cdot 10^{-8}$J/bit, $E_p = 5 \cdot 10^{-9}$J/bit/signal, and $\in_{fs} = 10^{-10}$J/bit/m^2, although there is an order of magnitude difference between E_p and $\in_{fs}$, which makes it look like it is not energetically efficient to add CHs to the WSN, E_p is multiplied by $(n_{NCH \to CH} + 1)$, while $\in_{fs}$ is multiplied by $d^2_{CH \to HigherCH}$, hence even a relatively small distance between the NCHs to their CH can overcome the data aggregation overhead. This means that a good refinement using the ACR algorithm, which will take into consideration this balancing, will achieve a reduction in the total energy consumption and an increase in the connectivity of the WSN simultaneously. We prove this in Theorem 4.

Theorem 4: *The total squared distances in the entire WSN constantly reduced by 70% using the refinement algorithm in WSN grid.*

Proof. An exemplification of the balancing that the ACR algorithm performs, and the energy factors out performances, are demonstrated in WSN in Fig. 2. The figure presents a 5X5 WSN grid before and after an ACR refinement, with one CH to 24 NCHs before refinement with 2 hierarchy level (right), and the same grid after refinement with 4 NCHs turned into CHs with 3 hierarchy levels.

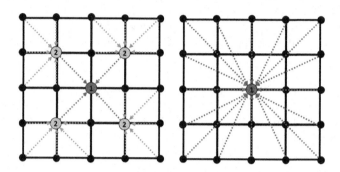

Fig. 2. A 5X5 WSN grid with one CH to 24 NCHs before refinement (right), and the same grid after refinement with 4 NCHs turned into CHs.

We reached those results using the following formulas (I-IV), which present the calculation for the pre-refine squared distances (I), the post-refine squared distances (II), the value of the distances saving (III) and the percentage of the distance saving (IV).

$$\text{PreRefineSqDist}[d, n] = 4 \cdot \sum_{i=1}^{\lfloor n/2 \rfloor} \left((i \cdot d)^2 \cdot (1+2) + 2 \cdot \sum_{j=1}^{i-1} \left((d \cdot i)^2 + (d \cdot j)^2 \right) \right) \quad \text{(III)}$$

$$\text{PostRefineSqDist}[d, n] = 4 \cdot \left(\text{PreRefineSqDist}\left[d, \left\lceil \frac{n}{2} \right\rceil \right] - \left(\left\lfloor \frac{n}{4} \right\rfloor d \right)^2 \right.$$
$$\left. - 2 \cdot \sum_{i=1}^{\lfloor \frac{n}{4} \rfloor} \left((i \cdot d)^2 + \left(\left\lfloor \frac{n}{4} \right\rfloor \cdot d \right)^2 \right) + 2 \left(\left\lfloor \frac{n}{4} \right\rfloor d \right)^2 \right) \quad \text{(IV)}$$

$$\text{DistanceSavingVal}[d, n] = \text{PreRefineSqDist}[d, n] - \text{PostRefineSqDist}[d, n] \quad \text{(V)}$$

$$\text{DistanceSavingPer}[d, n] = \frac{\text{DistanceSavingVal}[d, n]}{\text{PreRefineSqDist}[d, n]} \quad \text{(VI)}$$

Where d is the height (and width) of each tile in the mesh and n^2 is the amount of tiles.

Hence, the reduction of the total squared distances in the example above can be easy calculated. For example, if $d = 1$ the total squared distances of the pre-refinement WSN are equal to 100, while the total distances of the post-refinement are equal to 30,

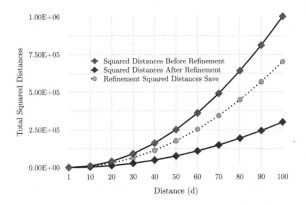

Fig. 3. The total squared distances in the WSN as function of the distance coefficient (d) before the ACR-HCC refinement (red), after the ACR-HCC refinement (blue) and the saving between the two (green). (Color figure online)

meaning 70% reduce. This reduction exists in all positive optional value of d as shown in Fig. 3. Figure 3 shows that this reduction of percentage is constant, and that the total squared distances before and after the refinement are linear.   ∎

As previously explained, in order to examine if the refinement achieved its goals, we need to focus on the distances between the nodes in the WSN. In this case study, each black line between two nodes is equal for ease of explanation (d), and we assume the *InitCH* transmitting to a specific space in both cases (distance x). According to formulas (1) and (2) before refinement of the WSN is equal to:

$$24 \cdot \left(E_{elec} + \in_{fs} \cdot d^2_{NCH \to InitCH}\right) + n_{NCH \to InitCH} E_{elec} + \left(n_{NCH \to InitCH} + 1\right)E_p$$
$$+ \alpha\left(E_{elec} + \in_{fs} \cdot d^2_x\right) \tag{I}$$

While after refinement, the WSN is equal to:

$$(5 \cdot 4) \cdot \left(E_{elec} + \in_{fs} \cdot d^2_{NCH \to CH}\right) + 4 \cdot \left(n_{NCH \to CH} E_{elec} + \left(n_{NCH \to CH} + 1\right)E_p + \right.$$
$$\alpha\left(E_{elec} + \in_{fs} \cdot d^2_{CH \to InitCH}\right)\right) + \left(n_{CH \to InitCH} E_{elec} + \left(n_{CH \to InitCH} + 1\right)E_p \tag{II}$$
$$+ \alpha\left(E_{elec} + \in_{fs} \cdot d^2_x\right)\right)$$

It is possible to see that even if $\alpha = 1$, although the total amount of E_{elec} is the same in both calculation, the transformation of the 4 NCHs into CHs created an additional overhead of $5E_p((5+1) \cdot 4)E_p + (4+1)E_p$ instead of $(24+1)E_p$. Nevertheless, Because of the ACR-HCC algorithms hierarchy creation, the total squared distances in the entire WSN constantly reduced by 70%.

Therefore, in order to determine if an ACR refinement if worthwhile, the difference between the total E_t of the WSN before and after a refinement should be bigger than the difference between the total E_p of the WSN before and after a refinement. This refinement balance can be formalized as the following formula (4):

$$\in_{fs} \cdot \left(\sum d^2_{BeforeRefinement} - \sum d^2_{AfterRefinement} \right)$$
$$> (4 \cdot ((n_{NCH \to CH} + 1) + (n_{CH \to InitCH} + 1)) - (n_{NCH \to InitCH} + 1)) \cdot E_p \tag{4}$$

It is possible to see that the saving between before the refinement and after the refinement cross the $4E_p$ (i.e. $4 \cdot 5 \cdot 10^{-9}$) at the very beginning of the measurements, when $d = \frac{4 \cdot 5 \cdot 10^{-9}}{10^{-10}} = \sqrt{200} = \sim 14$ (m), meaning that the ACR-HCC refinement algorithm proven to be efficient in many cases.

4   A Local Version of the Adaptive Clustering Algorithm

In this section we present an alternative algorithm that makes decision based on local behavior of clusters, rather than taking into account the behavior of the entire network. In this way we can significantly improve the running time of our algorithm without compromising energy efficiency significantly. The algorithm is executed by all CHs in parallel. Initially, each CH is provided with a threshold value t of a plausible energy use. If these values are unknown in the beginning of the execution, they can be computed using a single execution of the ACR algorithm of Sect. 2. This combination of an initial global execution with numerous local executions following it, is still more efficient than performing several executions of the global ACR algorithm of Sect. 2. In the initial configuration all these values t are the same, and represent a balanced environment. The algorithm can start from any cluster-hierarchy tree, where the simplest configuration is a single CH, which is the root (equivalently, a single leaf). Once an energy use of a leaf v reaches $3t$, we perform a local refinement in the cluster of v. This results in adding new CHs to the tree as leafs that become the children of v. These new leafs correspond to the newly formed clusters. This refinement results in a better energy use in each such newly formed cluster, specifically, bounded by $3t \cdot \frac{3}{10} < t$ instead of $3t$ (See Theorem 4). In other words, we balance clusters of excess energy-use by decomposing them into smaller clusters that require less energy.

Once the average energy consumption in the children of a CH node u whose all children are leafs becomes less than $t/5$, a coarsening operation is performed. (This operation is the opposite of refinement). Specifically, the clusters represented by u and its children are merged into a single cluster. Then u becomes its CH, and former children of u become NCHs. Consequently, the energy use of the newly-formed larger cluster grows, but the tree-distance between the root to some leafs decreases. This completes the description of the algorithm. Its pseudo-code is provided below, and it is executed periodically by each CH.

The Local Version of the Adaptive Clustering Algorithm

```
Local-ref(Node v, Threshold t)
1. If v is a leaf and energy_use(v) >= 3t
        1.1 Refine(v)
        1.2 Add new CHs as children of v
2. If all children of v are leafs and
   average_energy(children(v)) < t/5
             2.1 Coarsen(v)
             2.2 Remove the children of v from the tree and
   mark v as a leaf.
```

Theorem 5: *Each execution of Local-ref requires a constant number of communication rounds.*

Proof. A refinement operation adds a set of children to the tree. All these children have a common parent, which is the executing cluster, and thus their creation requires a constant number of communication rounds. A coarsening operation is performed on a node whose all children are leafs. Therefore, the node can communicate with all nodes in its sub-tree within a single round. Hence, a constant number of rounds is required to complete the operation. ∎

Theorem 6: *Local-ref preserves a balance of energy use between t/5 and 3t in each cluster.*

Proof. Each cluster whose energy use exceeds 3t performs the refinement procedure which improve energy use by 70% (See Theorem 4). Thus, after refinement of a cluster, the energy use in all its sub-clusters reduces.

If the average energy use of the leafs of a cluster goes below t/5, it means that each of the four leafs has energy use at most 4t/5. Therefore, after coarsening, we have a single cluster instead of four clusters, and its energy use is at most 3t. ∎

Theorem 7: *All longest paths from the root to a leaf contain a cluster with energy use at least t/5.*

Proof. Suppose for contradiction that there is a longest path P from the root to a leaf, for which all clusters have energy use less than t/5. Then there is a node on the path P whose all children are leafs. Since the energy use of all these children is less than t/5, the coarsen procedure would be invoked, which would eliminate these leaf. In particular, one of these leafs is an endpoint of P which would be eliminated. Hence the path P does not remain in the tree. This is a contradiction. ∎

When L is the maximum load in the network, consider the following theorem.

Theorem 8: *The maximum depth of a tree is bounded by $O\left(\log \frac{L}{t}\right)$, and the maximum tree size is bounded by $2^{O\left(\log \frac{L}{t}\right)}$.*

Proof. Suppose we have maximum load L. The load may be divided to sub-clusters. Every such step will decrease the load, allowing no more then $L/3$ load. The algorithm will repeat this division q times, until the load will be less than 3t. Thus, we obtain the following formula: $L \cdot \left(\frac{1}{3}\right)^q \leq 3t \Rightarrow q \leq O\left(\log\frac{L}{t}\right)$. Because each node may have only 4 children, the total size of the tree is bounded *by* $2^{O\left(\log\frac{L}{t}\right)}$. ∎

These theorems demonstrate a correlation between the size of the tree and the load in the network. Specifically, whenever the load is light, the tree remains small. If the loads of certain areas become heavy, the tree grows branches that correspond to these areas. Therefore, the size of the tree corresponds to the load in the entire network. In other words, the tree grows only when needed, which allows reducing the cost of maintaining the tree structure. This is in contrast to a fixed tree that does not take into account the load in the network.

5   Conclusions and Future Work

Those results and analysis lead to the conclusion that it would be beneficial to use the ACR algorithm along with the HCC algorithm in WSNs with differential load for maximization of the network lifetime as wellas connectivity.

This paper opens a number of prospective directions for future research. One immediate direction is to explore how the ACR algorithm is reacting along with different WSN hierarchical clustering algorithms, and what exactly does that mean in aspects of cost, complexity, energy-efficiency and connectivity of the network. Another direction is to understand how to optimize other WSN clustering algorithms which are not based on a hierarchical formation of the WSN using ACR algorithm.

Finally, we also expect that in the near future the ACR-HCC will be implemented for the specific problem that the algorithm was designed for. A comparison of the empirical benchmark results to those presented in this paper would be a fertile ground for further research and development.

Acknowledgments. This work was supported by the Lynn and William Frankel Center for Computer Science, the Open University of Israel's Research Fund, and ISF grant 724/15.

References

1. El Emary, S., Ibrahiem, M., Ramakrishnan, S. (eds.): Wireless Sensor Networks: From Theory to Applications. CRC Press, New York (2013)
2. Dargie, W., Poellabauer, C.: Fundamentals of Wireless Sensor Networks: Theory and Practice. Wiley, New York (2014)
3. Rault, T., Bouabdallah, A., Challal, Y.: Energy efficiency in wireless sensor networks: a top-down survey. Comput. Netw. **67**, 104–122 (2014)
4. Basagni, S., Naderi, M.Y., Petrioli, C., Spenza, D.: Wireless sensor networks with energy harvesting. Mobile Ad Hoc Netw. Cutting Edge Dir. **5**, 701–736 (2013)

5. Tuna, G., Gungor, V.C., Gulez, K.: Energy harvesting techniques for industrial wireless sensor networks. In: Hancke, G.P., Gungor, V.C. (eds.) Industrial Wireless Sensor Networks: Applications, Protocols, Standards, and Products, pp. 119–136 (2013)
6. Sachan, V., Imam, S., Beg, M.: Energy-efficient communication methods in wireless sensor networks: a critical review. Int. J. Comput. Appl. **39**(17), 35–48 (2012)
7. Zhang, P., Xiao, G., Tan, H.P.: Clustering algorithms for maximizing the lifetime of wireless sensor networks with energy-harvesting sensors. Comput. Netw. **57**(14), 2689–2704 (2013)
8. Younis, M., Senturk, I.F., Akkaya, K., Lee, S., Senel, F.: Topology management techniques for tolerating node failures in wireless sensor networks: a survey. Comput. Netw. **15**(58), 254–283 (2014)
9. Li, M., Li, Z., Vasilakos, A.V.: A survey on topology control in wireless sensor networks: taxonomy, comparative study, and open issues. Proc. IEEE **101**(12), 2538–2557 (2013)
10. Viswanathan, S., Jayakumar, D.: The role of wireless sensor network in tracking wild animals crossing forest boundaries. Program. Device Circ. Syst. **8**(5), 105–107 (2016)
11. Voeten, M.M., Van De Vijver, C.A., Olff, H., Van Langevelde, F.: Possible causes of decreasing migratory ungulate populations in an East African savannah after restrictions in their seasonal movements. Afr. J. Ecol. **48**(1), 169–179 (2010)
12. Liu, N.-H., Wu, C.-A., Hsieh, S.-J.: Long-term animal observation by wireless sensor networks with sound recognition. In: Liu, B., Bestavros, A., Du, D.-Z., Wang, J. (eds.) WASA 2009. LNCS, vol. 5682, pp. 1–11. Springer, Heidelberg (2009). doi:10.1007/978-3-642-03417-6_1
13. Banerjee, S., Khuller, S.: A clustering scheme for hierarchical control in multi-hop wireless networks. In: Twentieth Annual Joint Conference of the IEEE Computer and Communications Societies (INFOCOM 2001), Proceedings, vol. 2, pp. 1028–1037. IEEE (2001)
14. Berger, M.J., Oliger, J.: Adaptive mesh refinement for hyperbolic partial differential equations. J. Comput. Phys. **53**(3), 484–512 (1984)
15. Liao, W.K., Liu, Y., Choudhary, A.: A grid-based clustering algorithm using adaptive mesh refinement. In: 7th Workshop on Mining Scientific and Engineering Datasets of SIAM International Conference on Data Mining, 22 April, pp. 61–69 (2004)

Simulation and Testing of a Platooning Management Protocol Implementation

Bruno Ribeiro$^{(\boxtimes)}$, Fábio Gonçalves, Alexandre Santos$^{(\boxtimes)}$, Maria João Nicolau,
Bruno Dias, Joaquim Macedo, and António Costa

Department of Informatics, Algoritmi Center, University of Minho,
Campus de Gualtar, 4710-057 Braga, Portugal
{b7214,b7207}@algoritmi.uminho.pt, joao@dsi.uminho.pt,
{alex,macedo,bruno.dias,costa}@di.uminho.pt
http://algoritmi.uminho.pt

Abstract. *VANETs (Vehicular Ad Hoc Networks)* are networks of moving vehicles equipped with devices that allow spontaneous communication. Developing collaborative applications for *VANETs* has currently an increasing popularity in the *Intelligent Transportation Systems (ITS)* domain. This paper proposes a *Platooning Management Protocol (PMP)*, whose implementation and testing is carried out by means of simulation, using the *V2X Simulation Runtime Infrastructure (VSimRTI)* framework (coupling *Simulation of Urban MObility (SUMO)* and *Network Simulator 3 (ns-3)*). Results show that *PMP* works in a efficient manner: maneuvers happen during an acceptable time interval, the proposed communication requirements are met and the lane capacity is increased.

Keywords: Platooning · ITS · Simulation · VANETs

1 Introduction

ITS consist of an intricate set of technologies applied to vehicles and infrastructures that ensure an efficient and smart usage of the roads in general, which potentially improve safety, efficiency and productivity or even decrease levels of pollution. *ITS* enable the rise of several applications relying on the exchange of information between vehicles themselves and infrastructures, allowing drivers to make smarter driving choices. The goal of this work is to develop and test a *PMP* that defines several maneuvers to allow platooning (create, join, leave, merge and dissolve), including the set of messages that allow their operation. The structure of this paper is as follows: first, the state of the art regarding *ITS* application development is presented. Next, the *PMP* is introduced, analyzed and tested. The simulation environment is also discussed, along with the results obtained from the simulations.

2 Related Work

This section provides a brief overview on available publications that cover subjects related to V2X applications, specially advanced applications. The work in

© IFIP International Federation for Information Processing 2017
Published by Springer International Publishing AG 2017. All Rights Reserved
Y. Koucheryavy et al. (Eds.): WWIC 2017, LNCS 10372, pp. 174–185, 2017.
DOI: 10.1007/978-3-319-61382-6_14

[1] presents a *Cooperative Adaptive Cruise Control (CACC)* system that aims to reduce significantly the gaps between the vehicles, taking advantage from information exchanged using *Dedicated Short-Range Communications (DSRC)* wireless communication. In [2] is presented a *CACC* implementation at the *Grand Cooperative Driving Challenge (GCDC)*, based on *Vehicle to Vehicle (V2V)* communication. In [3], the interference of non-automated vehicles, when a given vehicle is joining a platoon is analyzed. It is defined a protocol that supports the join maneuver and it is validated using *PLEXE* from *Vehicles in Network Simulation (VEINS)*. A *CACC* management protocol based on IEEE 802.11p communication, including three basic maneuvers (merge, split and lane change) is presented in [4]. In [5], communication strategies for *Platooning* are investigated and compared to typical beaconing protocols, resorting to *PLEXE*. In [6], an application that aims to advise danger on emergency situations on *VANETs* resorting to IEEE 802.11p is proposed. Additionally, there are some important projects focused on the study of advanced *ITS* applications, such as *COMPANION*, *iGAME* or *SARTRE*.

Fig. 1. Platoon of trucks

3   Platooning Management Protocol

Platooning is a solution that allows vehicles to travel very close to each other in groups with automated velocity and steering control. Driving in *platoons* with automatic control enables the enhancement of safety, traffic flow and highway capacities, while providing drivers with a more convenient and comfortable driving experience. Furthermore, it helps to save energy and fuel, while reducing emissions [7,8]. Figure 1 illustrates a platoon of trucks in an highway. The simplest way of implementing *Platooning* is through the use of *V2V* communication, where vehicles only share information with their immediate predecessor. More advanced solutions disseminate information from vehicles that are not in line of sight, providing the driver with situational awareness feedback. Vehicles possessing group information in advance helps to predict the behavior of the platoon. *Platooning* requires a very efficient *PMP* that specifies all the required maneuvers and proper communication behaviors. The proposed *PMP* is described next, including a description of the maneuvers and the specification of their requirements based on European standards.

3.1   Maneuvers

The **Create** maneuver starts when a given vehicles tries to join a platoon but there are no available strings around him. The process of creating a platoon is: (i) *Leader* vehicle starts a new *Platoon*; (ii) *Leader* vehicle propagates the *Platoon* existence, broadcasting its *ID* every second.

The **Join** maneuver is triggered when a vehicle wants to join a *platoon*. An important aspect of the *Join* maneuver is the string ordering. The simplest solution is to make vehicles join the *platoon* tail. Allowing vehicles to join in any position, enables the string to be ordered by several parameters: e.g. braking performance. In these cases, vehicles open a gap that allows the joining vehicle to merge, which requires more coordination. A vehicle is able to join a *platoon* if the string does not exceed its maximum length and if no other maneuver is occurring. The joining process is: (i) *Joiner* sends a periodical *Join Request broadcast*; (ii) *Leader* responds with a *Join Acknowledgment* if it's possible to join. Otherwise, it responds with a *Join Reject*; (iii) *Joiner* moves to the correct position to change lane and informs the *Leader* with a *Distance Achieved* message; (iv) *Leader* notifies the *Followers* to open up a gap, with a *Adjust Gap* message (unless the joining is by the rear); (v) *Followers* notify the *Leader* when the adjusting process is completed with *Adjust Gap Acknowledgments*; (vi) *Leader* sends a *Start Maneuver* message, informing the *Joiner* that the maneuver can be accomplished; (vii) *Joiner* changes lane and enters automatic mode, notifying the *Leader* with a *Maneuver Completed* message. viii) *Leader* sends a *Platoon Update* message for all *Followers* with updated information.

The **Leave** maneuver is initiated when a *Follower* needs to exit the *platoon*. It informs the *Leader* and waits for its response, before assuming manual control. Only one vehicle may leave the platoon at a time and only if the other followers have confirmed to adjust their gap. The maneuver steps are: (i) *Follower* sends a *Leave Request*; (ii) *Leader* orders *Followers* to open a gap with *Adjust Gap* messages; (iii) *Followers* acknowledge their adjustments, resorting to *Adjust Gap Acknowledgment* messages; (iv) *Leader* returns a *Start Maneuver* message for the *Leaver*; (v) *Leaver* shifts to manual driving and changes lane; (vi) *Leaver* notifies the *Leader* with a *Maneuver Completed* message; (vii) *Leader* notifies *Followers* that the maneuver is finished with *Platoon Update* messages.

The **Dissolve** maneuver happens when the *Leader* decides to disassemble the string. The *Leader* may only dissolve after all *Followers* acknowledge the command. The steps are: (i) *Leader* sends a *Dissolve Request*; (ii) *Followers* enter manual driving mode and send a *Dissolve Acknowledgment* to the *Leader*; (iii) When all *Followers* respond (if any), the *Leader* dissolves the *platoon*.

The **Merge** maneuver consists on joining two *platoons*. This maneuver is only possible if the size of the *platoons* is less than the maximum length and the process is initiated by the *Rear Leader*. The following steps show how the *Merge* maneuver is performed. The front *Leader* and *platoon* are referred as *Leader A* and *Platoon A*, while the rear *Leader* and *platoon* are referred as *Leader B* and *Platoon B*: (i) *Leaders* send *Merge Requests* every 10 s; (ii) *Leader A* receives the request and responds with a *Merge Acknowledgment*; (iii) *Leaders* exchange *Platoon Info* messages with information regarding their *platoons*; (iv) *Leader A* sends a *Adjust Gap* message to *Leader B*; (v) *Leader B* moves *Platoon B* to the rear of *Platoon A*; (vi) *Leader B* acknowledges the distance with a *Adjust*

Gap Acknowledgment message; (vii) *Leader B* sends a *New Leader* message to its *Followers*; (viii) *Leader B* assumes a *Follower* role.

3.2 Platooning Requirements

The most important requirements for the *platooning* application are based on the **ETSI TR 102 638** standard [9], which provides the main requirements for a *Co-operative vehicle-highway automation system (Platoon)* use case. The *latency* is defined to have a maximum value of *100* ms, the relative *position accuracy* should be better than *2* m, and the platoon group messages should have a minimum frequency of *2* Hz. The vehicles should be prepared to transmit *V2V* messages in *unicast* and *broadcast* mode.

4 Simulation Deployment

The development of efficient *VANETs* systems requires the determination of its main properties and consequent evaluation of its performance. Performing field tests is a tough challenge: the large number of existent vehicles and scenarios makes it harder to collect data, the development of prototypes is expensive, etc. Simulation is a popular solution to evaluate the performance of *ITS* systems - tests are easily repeated and researchers are able to control parameters, configurations, conditions and input data. However, it normally assumes the use of simpler models, which may reduce the system realism. To perform a proper simulation of *VANETs*, both a traffic and a network simulator are required. Network simulation is one of the most prominent evaluation methods in computer networks, and *ns-3* and *OMNeT++* are two major tools used to model realistic V2X environments. Some of the most important tools used in to simulate mobility and traffic are *SUMO*, *VISSIM* and *VanetMobiSim*. Additionally, there are some tools that allow their interconnection, which enables them to interact with each other in a transparent way, such as *VEINS*, *iTETRIS* or *VSimRTI*.

The first step towards deployment is the choice of the simulation tools. Among all solutions, the most complete and realistic way is through the use of coupled simulators. According to [10], *iTETRIS*, *VEINS* and *VSimRTI* are strong solutions and there is no clear winner, since they all cover the required aspects for *VANETs* simulation. Despite *iTETRIS* potential, the project is finished and there is no available support. *VEINS* simulator already includes a platooning module denominated as *PLEXE*. However, since *VSimRTI* is more flexible on the choice of the simulators and allows the use of *JAVA* programming, the choice falls for *VSimRTI*. To simulate transportation, the choice is *SUMO*, since it is able to support detailed representations of large scale traffic scenarios. To support accurate simulation of communication for *ITS* systems, the choice is *ns-3*, since it includes all models to reproduce functionalities and protocols for the ITS communications stack. According to [11], a very suitable wireless technology available today to interconnect vehicles is *IEEE 802.11p*. Since it was specifically built for vehicular environments, it was the technology chosen to allow communication. The intra-platoon distance was based on the values used in [4] for homogeneous vehicles. Another important aspect of this *PMP* is that maneuvers can happen at any point but only one maneuver is allowed at a time. Allowing more than one maneuver would make the management task extremely complex. Finally, and regarding security concerns, a basic and simple security mechanism for messaging exchanging was implemented. The vehicles are statically assigned one public key pair and one symmetric key and all public keys are pre-shared between the vehicles. The symmetric cipher algorithm used was *AES* (128 bits key) and for public key scheme it was used a *RSA* (1024 bits key). The exchanged message is composed of the encrypted payload and the signature. The signature is obtained using SHA-256 and the RSA key.

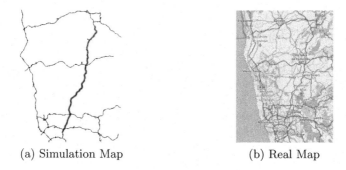

(a) Simulation Map   (b) Real Map

Fig. 2. Braga-Porto highways

4.1   Simulation Scenario and Decisions

This subsection describes some important deployment decisions. The selected simulation scenario (illustrated in Fig. 2) area comprises the highways that connect the Portuguese cities of *Braga* and *Porto*, obtained from a *Open Street Map (OSM)* file using the *osmosis* tool. The vehicles in the simulation that are running the *PMP* are *Trucks*, while other vehicles are simple *Passenger* cars. Additionally, there are some *reference Trucks* that do not run the *PMP*, to allow a comparison between them and *Platooning-enabled Trucks*. The application uses only one of the available ITS-G5 service channels and there are no additional applications running, which implies that there are no congestion problems, nor interferences. To broadcast information on *platoons*, *Leaders* use *Geocast* messages, and *V2V* Unicast on requests/replies between *Leaders* and *Followers*. When receiving a Join Request, the *Leader* computes a performance value and the position the vehicle should assume on the string based on its performance, sending this information back to the requester. Before starting dismembering the *platoon*, *Leader A* goes through a phase of velocity fluctuation, to test the *Followers* ability to adjust their velocities based on the messages received from the *Leader* every 100 ms. When the *Dissolve* process is complete and all vehicles have left *platoon A*, the simulation reaches its final state. The *ns-3* configuration was built to include values that match the communication characteristics of the *Cohda MK5 On Board Units (OBUs)*, as seen on Table 1 to allow more realistic results regarding the communications. In [12], the advised size of the string is 15 vehicles. However, two different sizes were defined for the two different *platoon* strings created in the simulation (15 and 3 vehicles). Additionally, the two strings travel with different speeds: 20 and 25 m/s, respectively. This happens so that it is easier to test the cases where the string is already full, and to study the impact of the speed on the results. The vehicles running the application are homogeneous, defined with the following parameters: *Class* - Truck; *Maximum Acceleration* - 1.1 m/s^2; *Maximum Deceleration* - 4.0 m/s^2; *Maximum Speed* - 36.11 m/s; *Length* - 16.5 m; *Width* - 2.55 m.

Table 1. NS-3 WiFi configuration established for Cohda MK5 OBU

Wifi configuration	
Wifi Mac	ns3::OcbWifiMac
Physical mode	OfdmRate6MbpsBW10MHz
Wifi manager	ConstantRateWifiManager
Received signal energy threshold	−99 dbm
Received signal energy threshold (CCA Busy)	−85 dbm
Transmission gain	10.0 dB
Reception gain	−16.0 dB
Maximum available transmission level	23 dbm
Minimum available transmission level	−10 dbm
Transmission power levels	Step 0.5 dB
Signal-to-Noise-Ratio loss	3.2 dB

5   Results and Analysis

In general, the behavior of the vehicles in *ITS* applications simulation tends to be extremely dynamic: typically, the mobility simulator runs with hundreds of vehicles equipped with applications at a given penetration rate and they follow computer generated routes. However, the simulation deployment on this work was proposed to be slightly more static, in the sense that the dissolve and leave maneuvers start timings and routes are predefined. Furthermore, the vehicles running the application and the platoon string they should join is also predefined. This causes the lane capacity results to be almost the same from simulation run to simulation run. Still, given the fact that the remaining maneuvers behavior is random, essentially due to the fact that the joining process will cause vehicles to join random positions on the string, independent runs will generate independent results. Although not being the most desired situation, this happens due to the high difficulty level of controlling and evaluating the vehicles and application behavior during the complex maneuvers that result from the *PMP*. The *PMP* generates result logs regarding maneuver durations, the exchanged messages, vehicles distance, speed values and lane capacity, which are discussed next.

5.1   Lane Capacity

The first results that can be obtained from the use of *Platooning* is increased lane capacity. According to [13], the typical lane capacity value is $C = 35$ and the formula to compute it is:

$$C = v \times \frac{n}{ns + (n-1)d + D} \quad \text{vehicles/lane/min,} \quad (1)$$

where v is the steady state speed (*meters/min*), d the intra-platoon spacing (*meters*), D the inter-platoon spacing (*meters*), s the vehicle length (*meters*) and n the number of cars composing the string. In the *PMP* deployment, the maximum theoretical capacity is $C = 71.88$ vehicles/lane/min. To compare this analytical value to the simulation, the capacity was logged every second and the mean results are presented on Fig. 3. As expected, the capacity is typically lower than the theoretical value, due to the dynamic values of the string (e.g. speed, number of vehicles). Also, these values differ in both *platoons*, which implies that the capacity values are different between them.

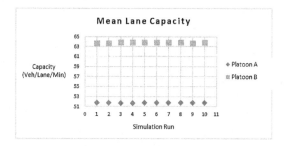

Fig. 3. Lane Capacity during simulation time

5.2   Maneuvers

This subsection describes the behavior of the *Platoons* during the application runtime, focusing and discussing on the duration of the maneuvers.

Join Maneuver. With exception to the *Leaders*, every vehicle must perform a *Join* maneuver in order to become part of a *platoon*. The mean duration of these maneuvers are presented in Table 2. The *Waiting* value represents the amount of time a vehicle awaits until it receives a *Join Acknowledgment* after sending a *Join Request*. The first conclusion one draws is that joining a *platoon* at the rear is faster than joining a *platoon* by the side, where other

Table 2. Join maneuver mean durations

Join Type	Operation (s)	Waiting (s)	Total (s)
Rear	54.6	30.3	69.0
Side	70.6	43.6	114.2
Mean	60.3	37.5	85.1

vehicles are required to adjust their gaps, making the maneuver last longer. Still regarding the *Join* maneuver, it is also important to analyze the duration of a negative response to a *Join Request*. A reject situation happens when a platoon is already at his maximum size. On average, between the request and response, only 62.2 ms elapse. This happens because the *Leader* is able to respond almost immediately if a given requester is able (or not) to perform the maneuver, even if another is already occurring.

Leave Maneuver. In side *Leaves*, vehicles that follow behind the leaving vehicle are required to open up gaps, so the maneuver is safer. In rear *Leaves*, the leaving vehicle simply changes lane and leaves. For these reasons, there is a huge difference in the duration of the maneuver, depending on the type: on average, side *Leaves* last 23.3 s, while rear *Leaves* last 1.0 s (on the simulator, the operation is immediate, making the result unrealistic).

Adjusting Gaps. Although these situations are not qualified as maneuvers, they play an important role on their duration times. On average, the *Adjust Gap* operation lasts 12.6 s on *Joins* and 17.4 s on *Leaves*.

Merge Maneuver. The merge maneuver (exemplified on Fig. 4) can be divided in three steps: exchanging the information between *Leaders*, the adjusting gap operation and the *New Leader* information dissemination. On average, the *Merge* maneuver was accomplished with a similar duration to the operations in *Join maneuvers* (a *Merge* operation can almost be seen as one *Leader* joining another *platoon*). The adjust gap operation takes most of the time (62.7 s on average) while the maneuver set up and finishing steps are very fast (72.0 ms).

Dissolve. The *Dissolve* maneuver duration time is estimated from the moment when the *Dissolve Request* is issued until the last *Dissolve Acknowledgment* is received. The maneuver performs quickly −3.8 s. This happens because, on the simulator, vehicles acknowledge the request and start manual driving instantaneously, making the result somewhat unrealistic. Hence, these durations only concern the communications part of the maneuver.

5.3 Messages

The results regarding the delay of the messages are now presented on Table 3 and Fig. 5. The calculated values present a very satisfactory result. They indicate that the *PMP* is mostly able to deliver the messages on time, and it is able to conform with the communication requirements of the *PMP* - the messages are

Fig. 4. Merge maneuver

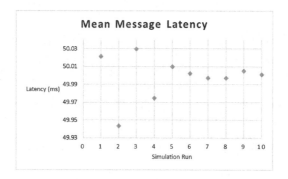

Fig. 5. Mean message latency values

Table 3. Statistic results from messages exchange

Messages latency (ms)	
Mean	50.0
Median	49.1
Standard Deviation	28.7
Minimum	0.6
Maximum	100.9
Mean Number of Messages	
709181	

able to be generated every 100 ms and the requirement for the maximum delay allowed (100 ms) can be fulfilled. This also means that the impact of the security mechanisms used to encrypt and sign the messages is almost unnoticeable (content is secure and the communication is not compromised). However, there are on average 1073 messages that are delivered with a latency greater than 100 ms. Despite the results not being perfect, the results are still acceptable, since these messages represent a universe of only 0,2%.

5.4   Distances and Speed

The *Distances* log allows the analysis of the *distance to go* value - the distance towards the computed minimum gap (when positive, the vehicles should accelerate, and vice-versa). Figure 6 illustrates the mean values of the *distance to go* for all followers in each simulation run (*Leaders* do not keep distances). These values start to be recorded during the forced fluctuation phase, in order to study the platoon stability. The error bars on the chart represent the standard deviation values. During the speed fluctuating phase, the *distance to go* is stable, which means that the vehicles can rapidly adjust their speed to reach the correct position based on the information sent by the *Leader* in the frequent *Platoon Group* messages. The *Speed* log also allows the study of the platoon stability during the same fluctuation phase. Figure 7 shows the average of the difference between the actual speed and the required speed for all followers in each simulation run. Vehicles can smoothly adjust their speed to meet the *Leader* speed. Another important aspect of the speed values that the vehicles assume during the simulation is that they are intimately related to *distance to go* values. This

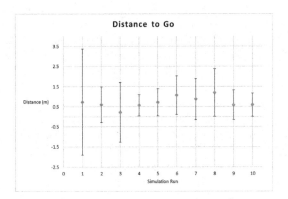

Fig. 6. Vehicle's *distance to go* value during simulation

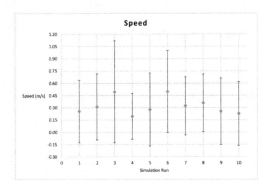

Fig. 7. Vehicle's *speed* deviation during simulation

means that the vehicle must increase its speed when the *distance to go* value its positive and vice-versa.

6   Conclusions and Future Work

ITS are systems that aim to assure a more efficient and improved usage of the roads by controlling traffic operations and drivers behavior. *ITS* enables the creation of many applications that use the information from vehicles and infrastructures to implement better driving practices and to improve traffic flow.

This paper discusses related work and general *ITS* simulation important tools. Then, the *PMP* is presented, containing the description of the maneuvers, general considerations and some important requirements (based mostly on *ITS* standards). The second part details the process of deploying the *PMP* implementation and obtaining the results from the simulation runs. The application was implemented using *VSimRTI*, coupling *SUMO* and *ns-3*. The choice of the tools was not a difficult decision, taking into account that these tools are proven to be very powerful and well-established within the research community. The deployment section describes the simulation scenario and associated decisions as well. The deployment was not an easy task - from the study on the state of the art, it was possible to conclude that the application is immensely complex and sometimes very subjective. For each particular problem that arises from *Platooning*, there are usually a lot of different proposed solutions. This seems to be an indicator that the *Platooning* specification is prone to ambiguity. Also, the deployment of the application required a lot of effort to overcome some lack of "intelligence" the chosen tools present - the constant trade-off between a more realistic application and the simulation performance caused some difficulties to evaluate the application behavior.

From the simulation, it is possible to conclude that the *PMP* works efficiently - maneuvers durations are within an acceptable interval, messages meet the hard communication requirements and the lane capacity is proven to be increased.

Regarding future work, we will consider gathering fuel consumption and emissions information using a more powerful emission model than the open source models available on *SUMO*. Additionally, we will consider using models that take into account road slopes. Finally, it may be interesting to test the protocol on a real implementation.

Acknowledgment. This work has been sponsored by the Portugal Incentive System for Research and Technological Development. Project in co-promotion n° 002797/2015 (INNOVCAR 2015–2018), and also by COMPETE: POCI-01-0145-FEDER-007043 and FCT - Fundação para a Ciência e Tecnologia within the Project Scope: UID/CEC/00319/2013.

References

1. Milanés, V., et al.: Cooperative adaptive cruise control in real traffic situations. IEEE Trans. Intell. Transp. Syst. **15**(1), 296–305 (2014)
2. Guvenc, L., et al.: Cooperative adaptive cruise control implementation of team mekar at the grand cooperative driving challenge. IEEE Trans. Intell. Transp. Syst. **13**(3), 1062–1074 (2012)
3. Segata, M., et al.: Supporting platooning maneuvers through IVC: an initial protocol analysis for the JOIN maneuver. In: 11th Annual Conference on Wireless On-demand Network Systems and Services (WONS), pp. 130–137. IEEE (2014)
4. Amoozadeh, M., et al.: Platoon management with cooperative adaptive cruise control enabled by VANET. Veh. Commun. **2**(2), 110–123 (2015)
5. Segata, M., et al.: Toward communication strategies for platooning: simulative and experimental evaluation. IEEE Trans. Veh. Technol. **64**(12), 5411–5423 (2015)
6. Fazio, P., et al.: Vehicular networks and road safety: an application for emergency/danger situations management using the WAVE/802.11p standard. Adv. Electr. Electron. Eng. **11**(5), 357 (2013)
7. Al Alam, A., et al.: An experimental study on the fuel reduction potential of heavy duty vehicle platooning. In: 13th International IEEE Conference on Intelligent Transportation Systems (ITSC), 2010, pp. 306–311. IEEE (2010)
8. Alam, A.: Fuel-efficient distributed control for heavy duty vehicle platooning. In: KTH Royal Institute of Technology (2011)
9. ETSI: ETSI TR 102 638 V1.1.1 Intelligent Transport Systems (ITS); Vehicular Communications; Basic Set of Applications; Definitions (2009)
10. Sommer, C., Häarri, J., Hrizi, F., Schüunemann, B., Dressler, F.: Simulation tools and techniques for vehicular communications and applications. In: Campolo, C., Molinaro, A., Scopigno, R. (eds.) Vehicular Ad hoc Networks, pp. 365–392. Springer, Cham (2015)
11. Ribeiro, B., Santos, A., Nicolau, M.J.: A survey on vehicular communication technologies. In: Intelligent Environments 2016, vol. 21. Ambient Intelligence and Smart Environments, pp. 308–317. IOS Press (2016)
12. Robinson, T., et al.: Operating platoons on public motorways: an introduction to the SARTRE platooning programme. In: 17th World Congress on Intelligent Transport Systems, vol. 1, p. 12 (2010)
13. Varaiya, P.: Smart cars on smart roads: problems of control. IEEE Trans. Autom. Control **38**(2), 195–207 (1993)

Research of Interaction Between Applications of Augmented Reality and Control Methods of UAVs

Maria Makolkina[1,2], Ruslan Kirichek[1(✉)], Valeria Teltevskaya[1], and Elisaveta Surodeeva[1]

[1] The Bonch-Bruevich State University of Telecommunications,
22 Pr. Bolshevikov, St. Petersburg, Russian Federation
malokina@list.ru, kirichek@sut.ru,
valeria-telt@yandex.ru, elisaveta.surodeeva@gmail.com
[2] Peoples' Friendship University of Russia (RUDN University),
6 Miklukho-Maklaya St, Moscow 117198, Russian Federation

Abstract. In this paper, the interaction between applications of augmented reality and methods of control the unmanned aerial vehicles (UAVs) is studied. During the experiment, the application of augmented reality was used to control the UAV and the camera. Assessment of quality of service of the network and subjective score of quality of experience are carried out. Hurst exponent is used to determinate the correlation between quality of service of the communication network and quality of experience.

Keywords: Augmented reality · Flying ubiquitous sensor networks · Unmanned aerial vehicles · Quality of service · Quality of experience · Hurst exponent

1 Introduction

The management of unmanned aerial vehicles is one of the most important problem, which should be solved for the widespread implementation of UAV systems. The flying touch networks use the UAVs as devices to collect data from land sensors and transfer it to the server for processing. Such networks can be used, for example, in industrial production or agricultural industry for monitoring the processes or the UAVs can be used as flying routers [1–4].

There are three types of management of the UAV: manual control, automated management, automatic control. In case of remote manual control, the pilot is guided by the image transferred from the camera. Such control can be exercised by means of technologies of augmented reality and the tactile Internet. Augmented reality (AR) represents addition of the surrounding physical world with virtual data with the help of special devices of display, for example, of glasses [5]. The main task of the tactile Internet is transfer information about impact on a remote subject and the return transfer of response of this subject to influence with the minimal delays [6].

© IFIP International Federation for Information Processing 2017
Published by Springer International Publishing AG 2017. All Rights Reserved
Y. Koucheryavy et al. (Eds.): WWIC 2017, LNCS 10372, pp. 186–193, 2017.
DOI: 10.1007/978-3-319-61382-6_15

The managing man has an opportunity to influence the UAV through the application of augmented reality turns of the head and a ducking, watching change of the image from the camera in the device of display of augmented reality.

Solving a problem of management of the UAV by means of applications of augmented reality, it is necessary to solve several subtasks:

- to provide transfer data about turn of the head from the device of augmented reality on the quadcopter;
- to provide transmission of a video image from the camera UAV on the AR device;
- to estimate quality of service on the network;
- to estimate quality of experience of the user in augmented reality at management of the UAV.

2   Features of Data Transfer

The pilot can control movements of the quadcopter or the camera mounted on it by means of turns and a ducking. As the suspension bracket of the camera provides rotation only on a vertical axis, for support of the maximum review it is necessary to turn the pilotless device. In the AR device, which is on the head of the pilot, display of a video stream from the camera is provided. Thanks to it, the pilot can understand location of the UAV and transfer information about desirable turn of the camera. For this purpose, high-quality information display from camera and a timely response of the UAV and camera to movements of the managing man should be provided.

During transmission of a video image, we can face a problem of noises in data transfer channel. Transfer of video information is influenced by such parameters of quality of service of a network as losses and time delays [6]. It influences on quality of experience and can lead failures in control of the UAV, because in case of control the pilot can possess information about location of the device proceeding from the arriving video information. In this regard, for research was selected the model of a network (Fig. 1), in which the device of augmented reality exchanges data with the quadcopter with use technology of wireless data transfer of Wi-Fi of IEEE 802.11n. This technology allows to transfer the large volume of information with throughput to 150 Mbps [7], as it is required for high-quality transmission of video information.

AR device

WiFi gateway

UAV

Fig. 1. Model of network for interaction between the AR device and UAV.

Within this paper, influence of quality of service of network on quality of perception of the user in the AR system at management of the UAV will be investigated.

3   Setting of Experiment

Purpose: A research of influence of quality of experience in systems of augmented reality on control of the UAV with use of the laboratory stand.

For this research the laboratory stand in laboratory of the Internet of Things of St. Petersburg State University of Telecommunications was developed [8, 9]. The hardware complex consists of the UAV (quadcopter 3D Robotics IRIS Plus) with the camera onboard. To capture video, an Intel Edison module connected to a Microsoft LifeCam HD-3000 camera is used, which allows to record HD video in 720p. Videostreaming is implemented by means of the FFServer library and using the RTP and RTSP protocols. Via the device of wireless access, the quadcopter is connected to AR glasses through Wi-Fi gateway. Epson Moverio BT-200 augmented reality glasses represent the transparent binocular video augmented reality glasses. They are equipped with such sensors as a gyroscope and the accelerometer, have an opportunity to interact through Wi-Fi access point. The AR glasses are equipped with the Android OS, which allowed us to use the LibVLC library and quickly develop an application for transmitting video from the quadcopter and managing its camera. The structural scheme of the stand is provided on Fig. 2.

AR device

Wi-Fi router   NetDisturb
                          Wi-Fi Direct   UAV

Fig. 2. Structure of the experimental stand

For collection of the experimental data and entering of additional noises into a network, the additional server with installed NetDisturb software was implemented between augmented reality glasses and the quadcopter. NetDisturb allows to make different noises and distortions in a network between the quadcopter and points, such as time delays, losses, capacity reduction [10]. NetDisturb was installed on a PC with two Gigabit Ethernet network cards. Two Wi-Fi access points were connected to this PC. The first AP was on channel 1 and the second AP was on channel 11, acting as router and repeater, correspondingly. Also software based on the pcap.net library for interception and the analysis of a traffic was developed to estimate influence of quality of service of a network on quality of experience of augmented reality in AR glasses in case of control of the quadcopter. The experiment was carried out in a room large enough to allow the UAV fly freely up to 7 m away.

The software, created for determination of influence of quality of service on quality of experience in systems of augmented reality, intercepts a traffic of data between the quadcopter and AR glasses. On base of received data, exactly time, when the packet was received, and packet size calculation of Hurst exponent is made. Hurst exponent is the measure, used in time series analysis [11–13]. Parameter will decrease, if the time delay between couple of identical changes of values of a time series increases. In this case the coefficient reflects a level of self-similarity of a traffic:

- while $0 < H < 0, 5$ – a time series is not self-similar, antipersistent, more probable for changing of the direction of a deviation, high definitions of a deviation follow for low and conversely;
- while $H = 0, 5$ – random time series, the following value don't depend on the previous values;
- while $H > 0, 5$ – time series is self-similar, persistent.
- The self-similar traffic is a traffic which looks equally at any temporal scales. In other words, the probability that the traffic on the following step will deviate average value in the same direction, as on the previous step, is so high as Hurst exponent is closer to one.

For clear determination of Hurst exponent, interception of packages will be carried out during one minute. For 1 min time series we have to calculate dispersion – a deviation of a random value from its average value among.

$$M\left[(R/S)_t\right] \sim cn^H, \text{when n } \to \infty \tag{1}$$

where $(R/S)t$ — the normalized assessment of width of a range, c — a constant, n — the size of the researched unit of observations, H — Hurst exponent, i.e. a level of self-similarity of the researched process. For the given finite time series of $X = X1, X2, ...,$ Xn we will calculate average value of m:

$$m = \frac{1}{n} \cdot \sum_{i=1}^{n} X_i \tag{2}$$

Then we will calculate a time series of deviations from average Y:

$$Y_t = X_t - m, \ t = 1, 2..., n \tag{3}$$

Calculate a time series of deviations Z:

$$Z_t = \sum_{i=1}^{t} Y_i, \ t = 1, 2..., n \tag{4}$$

Calculate a range series R:

$$R_t = \max(Z1, Z2, ..., Zt) - \min(Z1, Z2, ..., Zt), t = 1, 2..., n \tag{5}$$

Calculate a standard deviations series S:

$$\sqrt{\frac{1}{t}\sum_{i=1}^{t}(X_i - u)^2}, \quad t = 1, 2\ldots, n \tag{6}$$

where u — average definition of values of a row from X1 to Xt.

Calculate a normalized range series (R/S):

$$(R/S)_t = R_t/S_t, \quad t = 1, 2\ldots n \tag{7}$$

To average a row $(R/S)_t$ on areas [X1, Xt] in case of different values t on an interval from 1 to n, one usually takes not all n points, but some enough set, which is evenly distributed on all interval from 1 to n.

The received averaged values and corresponding to them block lengths of averaging of t, need to be marked in logarithmic axes. The received points need to be approximated the linear function, constructed by means of the least-squares method. The slope (an inclination tangent of angle to the positive direction of an X-axis) the received line according to a formula (1) will be assessment of Hurst's coefficient of an initial time series.

In this research Hurst exponent is used for determination of correlation between quality of service and quality of experience in AR systems in case of control of the UAV.

4   Description of Experiment

The examinee of augmented reality glasses, where information from the camera of the quadcopter is displayed, turns the head, thereby directing the camera, and subjectively estimates a response of the quadcopter on the done movements and change of the image in glasses. The experiment u be made several times, each time displays influence of different noises, such as

AR device   WiFi gateway   UAV

a time delay, losses and reduction of throughput. For correct subjective evaluation, the experiment without introduction of noises was taken for a standard, i.e. as close as possible to ideal conditions of data transfer.

5   Analysis of Results of Experiment

After experiment without introduction of noises, Hurst exponent was calculated. It was equal to 0, 61. It means that the traffic was self-similar and these results can be taken as a standard in case of further assessment of quality of experience, i.e. assessment of these results is 5. Further experiments with adding of a time delay were made. Results are provided in Table 1.

Table 1. Experiment with delays

Delay	Subjective score	Hurst exponent
Without delay	5	0, 61
10–30 ms	4	0, 60
50–150 ms	3	0, 59
150–250 ms	2	0, 56

From the table is seen, that in case of time delays less 100 ms, quality of experience of video remains at the satisfactory level, but there are a lot of difficulties in case of control with this delay. Because of delay the managing man doesn't know when it is necessary to stop movement, i.e. control is made at random, commands are transferred with delay, the response returns with a time delay. In this case Hurst exponent truly defines correlation between quality of service and quality of experience in the AR systems – the greatest value complies to the highest assessment of the testee. Thus, in case of time delays higher than 150 ms it is impossible to exercise control of the UAV by means of the application of augmented reality.

The next experiments were made with adding of random losses in link between the quadcopter and the AR device. Results of this experiment are provided in Table 2.

Table 2. Experiment with losses

Losses	Subjective score	Hurst exponent
Without losses	5	0, 61
0%–1%	4	0, 61
0%–3%	3	0, 60
0%–5%	2	0, 59
0%–7%	2	0, 53
0%–9%	1	0, 47

Proceeding from the received results, one may say, that losses significantly influence quality of experience. In addition to difficulties with control, there are also noises in recognition of the image on the device of augmented reality. Quality of experience of video promptly falls in case of increase in number of losses, it becomes difficult to sort the image, besides some timepoints "fall out" of video information, that exerts a negative impact on control of the quadcopter.

The last experiment was connected to throughput restriction, resulting in packet losses.

According to Table 3 it is possible to draw a conclusion that throughput restriction critically influences quality of experience of the user in systems of augmented reality. Also in case of capacity reduction, control of the quadcopter significantly becomes more difficult, because the managing man ceases to hold information about any movement of the aircraft. All data are transferred with big time delays, part of them is lost, in case of observation in the device of augmented reality begins the dizziness.

Table 3. Experiment with throughput restriction

Throughput	Subjective score	Hurst exponent
Not limited	5	0, 61
To 1700 kbps	5	0, 61
To 1500 kbps	3	0, 56
To 1000 kbps	2	0, 55
To 500 kbps	1	0, 49

6 Conclusion

For control of unmanned aerial vehicles, it is possible to use applications of augmented reality. Because control takes place in real time, it is necessary to impose certain requirements to quality of service of a network for support of high-quality and comfortable control of the UAV. In this paper, influence of quality of service of a network on quality of experience of the user in the device of augmented reality by transmission of a video image from the aircraft camera was considered. By the received results we will draw a conclusion that on a network with the minimal time delays to 100 ms it is possible to control the quadcopter by means of the application of augmented reality without loss of quality of experience and control.

Further, it is possible to continue a research in the area of influence of quality of service of a network on a quadcopter response (the tactile Internet) in case of control by means of the DR applications, and also to consider the AR applications as a method of management of other different robotic systems.

Acknowledgment. The publication was financially supported by the Ministry of Education and Science of the Russian Federation (the Agreement number 02.a03.21.0008), RFBR according to the research project No. 16-37-00209 mol_a "Development of the principles of integration the Real Sense technology and Internet of Things".

References

1. Furukawa, T., Bourgault, F., Durrant-Whyte, H.F., Dissanayake, G.: Dynamic allocation and control of coordinated UAVs to engage multiple targets in a time-optimal manner. In: IEEE International Conference on Robotics and Automation ICRA 2004, vol. 3, pp. 2353–2358 (2004)
2. Park, H.S., Kim, K.-H.: AR-based vehicular safety information system for forward collision warning. In: Shumaker, R., Lackey, S. (eds.) VAMR 2014. LNCS, vol. 8526, pp. 435–442. Springer, Cham (2014). doi:10.1007/978-3-319-07464-1_40
3. Fu, W.T., Gasper, J., Kim, S.W.: 2013 IEEE International Symposium on in Mixed and Augmented Reality (ISMAR), pp. 59–66. IEEE (2013)
4. Filonenko, A., Vavilin, A., Kim, T., Jo, K.-H.: Augmented reality surveillance system for road traffic monitoring. In: Huang, D.-S., Jo, K.-H., Wang, L. (eds.) ICIC 2014. LNCS (LNAI), vol. 8589, pp. 310–317. Springer, Cham (2014). doi:10.1007/978-3-319-09339-0_32
5. Bilton, N.: Google begins testing its augmented reality glasses, 4 April 2012
6. Aijaz, A., Dohler, M., Aghvami, A.H., Friderikos, V., Frodigh, M.: Realizing the tactile Internet: haptic communications over next generation 5G cellular networks. IEEE Wireless Commun. **24**, 82–89 (2016). doi:10.1109/MWC.2016.1500157RP. IEEE
7. IEEE 802.11-2012 IEEE Standard for Information technology–Telecommunications and information exchange between systems Local and metropolitan area networks–Specific requirements Part 11: Wireless LAN Medium Access Control (MAC) and Physical Layer (PHY) Specifications
8. Kirichek, R., Koucheryavy, A.: Internet of Things laboratory test bed. In: Zeng, Q.-A. (ed.) Wireless Communications, Networking and Applications. LNEE, vol. 348, pp. 485–494. Springer, New Delhi (2016). doi:10.1007/978-81-322-2580-5_44
9. Kirichek, R., Vladyko, A., Zakharov, M., Koucheryavy, A.: Model networks for Internet of Things and SDN. In: Proceedings of the 18th ICACT, pp. 76–79 (2016)
10. Koucheryavy, A., Vladyko, A., Kirichek, R.: State of the art and research challenges for public flying ubiquitous sensor networks. In: Balandin, S., Andreev, S., Koucheryavy, Y. (eds.) ruSMART 2015. LNCS, vol. 9247, pp. 299–308. Springer, Cham (2015). doi:10.1007/978-3-319-23126-6_27
11. Makolkina, M., Prokopiev, A., Paramonov, A., Koucheryavy, A.: The quality of experience subjective estimations and the hurst parameters values interdependence. In: Balandin, S., Andreev, S., Koucheryavy, Y. (eds.) NEW2AN 2014. LNCS, vol. 8638, pp. 311–318. Springer, Cham (2014). doi:10.1007/978-3-319-10353-2_27
12. Kirichek, R., Paramonov, A., Koucheryavy, A.: Flying ubiquitous sensor networks as a queueing system. In: Proceedings of the 17th ICACT, pp. 127–132 (2015)
13. Paramonov, A., Koucheryavy, A.: M2M traffic models and flow types in case of mass event detection. In: Balandin, S., Andreev, S., Koucheryavy, Y. (eds.) NEW2AN 2014. LNCS, vol. 8638, pp. 294–300. Springer, Cham (2014). doi:10.1007/978-3-319-10353-2_25

Energy-Efficient Power Control and Clustering in Underlay Device to Multi-device Communications

Mariem Hmila$^{(\boxtimes)}$ and Manuel Fernández-Veiga

Department of Telematics Engineering, University of Vigo, Vigo, Spain
{`meriame,mveiga`}`@det.uvigo.es`

Abstract. Underlay device to device multicast communication brings great benefits to cellular networks in term of energy and spectral efficiency, since a group of users can communicate directly by reusing cellular resources. In this paper, we propose a scheme to maximize network energy efficiency (EE) through transmission power control. In addition, to get a compromise between fairness and the overall EE, we analyse a second scheme with fairness factors to maximize minimum individual EE. The problem is formulated as a fractional programming optimization and solved with iterative algorithm. Two different EE metrics are analysed via extensive numerical simulations with a spatial Poisson process for the users' locations, and applying different clustering algorithms as K-nearest neighbour, distance limit and DBSCAN.

Keywords: Optimization · Fractional programming · D2D multicasting communication · 5G wireless networks

1 Introduction

The emergence of mobile multimedia rich services increases the number of connected devices and the requested data rate regularly. Consequently, the fifth generation (5G) supposes to have 1000× higher data volume, up to 100× more throughput and connected devices, 10× longer battery life, and low latency [8]. Underlay device to device communication (D2D) is a new paradigm introduced to realize 5G. It allows users in proximity to communicate directly by using resource allocated to cellular user (CUE). This has advantages as [9]: high data rate, energy and spectral efficiency, increase network capacity, low delay. However, it can cause harmful co-channel interference to CUE. The main techniques to mitigate interference are power control and resource allocation. Currently, they are joint to propose a more EE solutions. Several works proposed EE power and resource allocation scheme subject to QoS. In [3], a centralized solution had been conducted to minimize transmission power. The problem was formulated as

© IFIP International Federation for Information Processing 2017
Published by Springer International Publishing AG 2017. All Rights Reserved
Y. Koucheryavy et al. (Eds.): WWIC 2017, LNCS 10372, pp. 194–206, 2017.
DOI: 10.1007/978-3-319-61382-6_16

mixed integer linear programming (MILP) and solved through Hungarian algorithm. While in [14], the authors proposed a distributed solution to maximize users EE. The problem was formulated as a non cooperative game and solved by an iterative optimization algorithm. However, these works mainly consider unicast D2D communication where single transmitter and receiver communicate. Another interesting approach is to allow users with common content interest to form clusters where one device transmit to multiple receivers. This is called multicast D2D communication(D2MD). Compared to unicast, this mode reduces overhead signals and saves resources yet it is more challenging hence date rate is determined according to the weakest receiver so non fails to decode any of the transmitted data. Most of the available works target interference issue in D2MD communication focus on system throughput maximization subject to QoS constraints. The work in [5], investigate power control for D2D multicast communication. The authors first proposed a distributed scheme for group formation. Then, they studied single and multiple CUE channels re-usage and developed power allocation scheme based on swarm algorithm (PSO). The authors in [10] proposed a heuristic algorithm to solve mixed integer non-linear programming (MINLP) resource and power allocation problem. Moreover, they extended their work in [11] where D2D clusters can reuse the channel of multiple CUE instead of reusing single orthogonal channels and several D2D groups can share the same channel. They proposed greedy and heuristic algorithms and compared their performance. To this end, the paramount importance of green communication concept and the high potential of D2MD [12] motivated us to analysis spectral and energy efficiency in the scenario where underlay D2MD is applied in a cellular network. In this paper, we propose joint power and resource allocation model to maximize system and users EE. However, for analytical purpose we focus on a single channel sharing which lead us to EE power control schemes powered with stochastic geometry and clustering techniques. The rest of the paper is organized as follows. In Sect. 2, we introduce system model. Power control algorithm and problem formulation is discussed in Sect. 3. Finally, we discuss simulation results in 4 and conclude in Sect. 5.

2   System Model

We consider a single cell environment with one base station (BS) located in the centre and multiple uniformly distributed users. On the uplink, M CUE transmit on M orthogonal communication channels. Reusing downlink resources requires sophisticated coordination between UEs and the BS, and has been shown to be less effective than uplink resource sharing. Therefore, we assume the coexistence of K D2MD clusters $k = 1, ..., K$, that reuse the same channels allocated to CUEs to communicate directly. Each group has head cluster (transmitter) and $|\mathcal{D}_k|$ receivers where $|\mathcal{D}_k| = 1$ is a unicast case [11]. Here, the BS suffers from interference caused by the co-channel D2MD transmitters. Similarly, the $|\mathcal{D}_k|$ receivers of group k suffer from interference caused by the CUE and other transmitters of D2MD groups sharing the same resource block. The SINR $\gamma_{k,m,r}(\{\mathbf{p}_k\}_m, p_m)$ of a D2D receiver r in group k and channel m is given by

$$\frac{h_{k,m,r}p_{k,m}}{\sigma^2 + p_m\beta_{k,m,r} + \sum_{j\neq k} x_{j,m}p_{j,m}h_{j,m,r}} \tag{1}$$

where $h_{k,m,r}$ are the deterministic link gain factors from the transmitter in group k to receiver r on channel m, and $\beta_{k,m,r}$ is similarly the link gain factor from CUE transmitter m to receiver r in group k. Symbol $p_{k,m}$ denotes the transmission power of the D2MD transmitter in group k on channel m, and p_m is the transmission power of CUE user m. For a CUE user m, the SINR is similarly given by

$$\gamma_m(\mathbf{p}_k, p_m) = \frac{h_m p_m}{\sigma^2 + \sum_k x_{k,m}p_{k,m}h_{k,m}}, \quad m = 1, \ldots, M \tag{2}$$

where h_m is the link gain from user m to the base station, p_m is the transmitted power, $h_{k,m}$ is the link gain from the transmitter in D2D group k to the cellular base station on channel m and $x_{k,m}$ are binary variables defined for $k = 1, \ldots, K$, $m = 1, \ldots, M$ as $x_{k,m} = 1$ if D2D group k uses channel m, and 0 otherwise.

The normalized transmission rate (in bits/s/Hz) of CUE m is the channel capacity $r_m = \log_2(1 + \gamma_m)$, for $m = 1, \ldots, M$. For D2MD group k, the unique transmission rate is determined by the weakest receiver, i.e., by the receiver with the poorest channel quality. In addition, we account explicitly for the aggregated received rate in group k, which depends on the number of receivers per group $|\mathcal{D}_k|$. Thus,

$$R_k = \sum_{m=1}^{M} x_{k,m}|\mathcal{D}_k| \min_{r\in\mathcal{D}_k} \log_2(1 + \gamma_{k,m,r}), \quad k = 1, \ldots, K. \tag{3}$$

3   Problem Formulation

The energy efficiency (EE) of a given user (in bits/Joule) can be defined as the ratio of the achievable transmission rate and the total consumed power:

$$\eta_m \triangleq \frac{r_m}{s_{c,m} + p_m}, \quad m = 1, \ldots, M \tag{4}$$

for a CUE user; and

$$\zeta_k \triangleq \frac{R_k}{s'_{c,k} + \|\mathbf{p}_k\|_1}, \quad k = 1, \ldots, K. \tag{5}$$

In (4) and (5), $s_{c,m}$ (respectively, $s'_{c,k}$) is the transmitter circuit power, p_m is the power used by CUE transmitter m, $\mathbf{p}_k = (p_{k,1}, \ldots, p_{k,M}) \in \mathbb{R}_+^M$ is the allocated power vector of the head cluster over the M channels, and $||\cdot||_1$ denotes the ℓ_1-norm.[1] We assume that p_m and $\mathbf{p}_k$ satisfy individual power constraints $\|\mathbf{p}_k\|_1 \leq \bar{p}_k$

---

[1] For vectors $\mathbf{x} \in \mathbb{R}^n$, the ℓ_p-norm, for any $1 \leq p \leq \infty$, is $(\sum_{i=1}^n |x_i|^p)^{1/p}$. Hence, the ℓ_1-norm is $\|\mathbf{x}\|_1 = \sum_{i=1}^n |x_i|$, ℓ_2 is the usual Euclidean norm, and $\|\mathbf{x}\|_\infty = \max_i |x_i|$.

for $k = 1, \ldots, K$, and $p_m \leq P_m$ for all m. Moreover, we explicitly include the assumption that minimum transmission rates have to be satisfied both for the CUE and the D2MD users,

$$r_m \geq \underline{r}_m, \quad \text{and } R_k \geq \underline{R}_k \tag{6}$$

for all indexes k, m, where $\underline{r}_m$ (resp., $\underline{R}_k$) are the target rates of CUE (D2MD) user m (resp., k). The above definition for energy-efficiency is user-centric. The notation can be extended to present the *global network energy efficiency (GEE)* η by considering the ratio of the aggregated rate and the total consumed powers. More formally, if $\mathbf{r}$ and $\mathbf{R}$ are the vectors of rates for CUE and D2MD groups, respectively, then

$$\eta \triangleq \frac{||\mathbf{r}||_1 + ||\mathbf{R}||_1}{s_c + \sum_k ||\mathbf{p}_k||_1 + ||\mathbf{p}||_1} \tag{7}$$

Here, s_c is the total circuit power network devices. The GEE targets the total performance of the cellular network EE. This does not depend on users devices which might not be fair for limited battery life devices. For this reason, we introduce a second performance metric for maximizing the *minimum EE* among all the users in the system. The following definition captures this idea and introduces the notion of fairness between users.

Definition 1. *Let $\boldsymbol{\omega} = (\omega_1, \ldots, \omega_M) \in \mathbb{R}_+^M$ and $\boldsymbol{\theta} = (\theta_1, \ldots, \theta_K) \in \mathbb{R}_+^K$ be two arbitrary weight vectors. The $(\boldsymbol{\omega}, \boldsymbol{\theta})$-weighted energy efficiency (WEE) is*

$$\psi \triangleq \min\{\min_m \omega_m \eta_m, \min_k \theta_k \zeta_k\}. \tag{8}$$

The uniform choice $\boldsymbol{\omega}_2 = \boldsymbol{\theta}_2 = 1$, gives equal weight to every user, yields max-min fairness as the optimization criterion. With the above setting, the maximization of the global network energy efficiency can be mathematically formulated as (*problem GEE*): solve $\max_{\mathbf{p}, \mathbf{x}_k \in \mathcal{P}} \eta$, where η is equal to

$$\frac{\sum_m \log_2(1 + \gamma_m) + \sum_k \sum_m x_{k,m} |\mathcal{D}_k| \log_2(1 + \min_r \gamma_{k,m,r})}{s_c + \sum_k ||\mathbf{p}_k||_1 + ||\mathbf{p}||_1} \tag{9}$$

where $\mathcal{P}$ is the feasible set of power vectors; namely, the set defined by the constraints

$$\begin{array}{ll}
||\mathbf{p}_k||_1 \leq \overline{p}_k, \quad k = 1, \ldots, K; & p_m \leq P_m, \quad m = 1, \ldots M \quad (10) \\
\underline{R}_k \leq R_k, \quad k = 1, \ldots, K; & \underline{r}_m \leq r_m, \quad m = 1, \ldots, m \quad (11) \\
||\mathbf{x}_k||_1 \leq s & ||\mathbf{x}_{\cdot,m}|| \leq r \quad (12) \\
\mathbf{x}_k \in \{0, 1\}^M & (\mathbf{p}, \mathbf{p}_1, \ldots, \mathbf{p}_K) \in \mathbb{R}_+^{(K+1) \times M} \quad (13)
\end{array}$$

Here, constraints (10) bound the maximum transmission power per user; constraints (11) are the minimum rate conditions, where the rates have been defined previously; constraints (12) enforce the maximum split factor s for every D2MD group and the maximum reuse factor r per subcarrier; and finally (13) is simply the nonnegativity of all the power vectors. Clearly, (12) are the integer constraints, (11) are the coupling constraints on the transmission powers, and the set $\{\mathbf{p}_k\}$ are the coupling variables of the problem. Finally, note that the QoS constraints (11) are *user-specific*. In the same fashion and subject to the same constraints (10)–(13), the *minimum-EE* optimization problem can be formulated, for fixed weight vectors, as: solve $\max_{\mathbf{p}\in\mathcal{P}} \psi$.

To better understand the influence of D2MD communication on the network performance, we analyze in depth a special case when $M = 1$ or $x_{k,1} = 1$ for all k. This means a single CUE channel is shared among all uses D2D groups. This will give us an idea about maximum capacity of the channel and allows us to clearly see the impact of other system parameters. In such a case the problem turns to a power control problem lies under the fractional optimization class (14) where the decision part is absent, and has canonical form

$$\max_{\mathbf{x}\in\mathcal{C}} \frac{f(\mathbf{x})}{g(\mathbf{x})}. \tag{14}$$

Here, closed-form sufficient and necessary conditions for feasibility can be given, a result adapted from [13]. For single channel case, users are re-indexed such as 0 is the CUE, $|D_0| = 1$ is the BS and $j = 1, \ldots, K$ are the D2D transmitters.

Theorem 1. *Define* $\underline{\gamma}_k = 2^{r_j} - 1$ *for* $k = 0, \ldots, K$, *and the matrix*

$$W = [W]_{k,j} \triangleq \begin{cases} 0, & j = k \\ \frac{h_{k,j}\underline{\gamma}_k}{h_k}, & j \neq k. \end{cases} \tag{15}$$

A solution exists iff the spectral radius of W *is less than one and* $(I-W)^{-1}\underline{\mathbf{s}} \leq \overline{\mathbf{p}}$ *where* $\overline{\mathbf{p}} = [\overline{p}_0, \ldots, \overline{p}_K]^T$ *and* $\underline{\mathbf{s}}$ *has elements* $s_j = \sigma^2\underline{\gamma}_j/h_j$.

If the problem is feasible then it can be solved by finding the unique zero of $F(\lambda)$ where a point $\mathbf{x} \in \mathcal{C}$ solves (14) if and only if $\mathbf{x}^* = \arg\max_{\mathbf{x}\in\mathcal{C}}\{f(\mathbf{x}) - \lambda^* g(\mathbf{x})\}$, with λ^* being the unique zero of $F(\lambda) = \max_{\mathbf{x}\in\mathcal{C}}\{f(\mathbf{x}) - \lambda g(\mathbf{x})\}$. To do this, we use Dinkelbach's algorithm [4] (presented in Algorithm 2 jointly for GEE and MEE) to solve one convex problem in each iteration, where $f(\mathbf{x})$ and $g(\mathbf{x})$ are concave and convex respectively. However, in our case the feasible set is convex yet the numerator of (9) is non-concave thus we use a sequential convex programming approach given by $\log_2(1 + \gamma) \geq a\log_2\gamma + b$, where

$$a = \frac{\overline{\gamma}}{1 + \overline{\gamma}}, \quad b = \log_2(1 + \overline{\gamma}) - \frac{\overline{\gamma}}{1 + \overline{\gamma}}\log_2\overline{\gamma} \tag{16}$$

Putting all pieces together, we resume the solving procedure in Algorithm 1.

4   Simulations and Results

Stochastic geometry models have been commonly used to map the network into a collection of points over a spatial area so that its actual performance (spectral

---

Algorithm 1. EE maximization for $M = 1$

1: **if** Problem feasible (Theorem 1) **then**
2:     $i = 0$. Pick any $\mathbf{p}^{(0)} \in \mathcal{P}$. If $\mathbf{p}^{(0)}$ is feasible then
3:     **repeat**
4:         $i = i + 1$
5:         Maximize (9) or (8) with $a_k^{(i)}$ and $b_k^{(i)}$
6:         Set $p_k^{(i)} = 2^{q_k^{(i)}}$, where $q_k^{(i)} = \arg\max \tilde{\psi}_i$
7:         Set $\tilde{\gamma}_k^{(i)} = \gamma_k(\mathbf{p}^{(i)})$
8:         Update $a_k^{(i)}$ and $b_k^{(i)}$ with (16)
9:     **until** convergence
10: **end if**

Algorithm 2. Generalized Dinkelbach's algorithm. The case $I = 1$ is the simple Dinkelbach's algorithm.

1: $\epsilon > 0, \lambda = 0$
2: **repeat**
3:     $\mathbf{x}^* = \arg\max_{\mathbf{x} \in C} \min_{1 \leq i \leq I} \{ f_i(\mathbf{x}) - \lambda g_i(\mathbf{x}) \}$
4:     $F = \min_i f_i(\mathbf{x}^*) - \lambda g_i(\mathbf{x}^*)$
5:     $\lambda = \min_i f_i(\mathbf{x}^*)/g_i(\mathbf{x}^*)$
6: **until** $F \leq \epsilon$

---

efficiency, coverage, etc.) can be analyzed and characterized [1,2]. Here, we use a standard homogeneous Poisson point process (PPP) distribution to determine the number and locations of the cellular users and of the D2MD transmitters and receivers, with density λ. The received signal or interference power is assumed to vary due to the path loss resulting from the random spatial distribution. Specifically, the channel quality between a transmitter at $y \in \mathbb{R}^2$ is $P_r = P_t \cdot (1 + |y/d_0|^\alpha)$ where P_r is the received power, P_t is the transmitted power, d_0 is a reference distance (100 m in our case), α is the path loss exponent. Also, we chose the CUE with the best channel quality to share his RB with D2D groups [7]. This will allow us to focus on the effect of D2MD communications without

Table 1. System parameters.

Parameter	Values	Parameter	Values
Bandwidth	100 MHz	Max. tx. power	$[-15, 15]$ dBm
Cell size	500 m	Noise power density N_0	-100 dBm/Hz
Number of D2D groups	$[1, 11]$	Number of iterations	200
Network density (λ)	$[50, 250]$	Circuit power	10 dBm
Minimum tx. rate	$[0.1, 0.4]$ bit/Hz/s	Path loss exponent	2.5

considering the case of shared channel quality. Concerning the D2MD groups, the head cluster and group formation were done following three different algorithms presented and discussed in bellow. The parameters used for the numerical results reported here are listed in Table 1 and were taken or inspired by similar works [5,13,14].

Table 2. Global and minimum EE, rate in KNN (left) and DL (right).

Min rate	GEE	Avg rate	MEE	Min rate	GEE	Avg rate	MEE	Min rate
0.1	226.280	14.538	133.876	1.472	593.807	37.790	207.066	2.277
0.2	222.999	14.352	139.819	1.538	587.773	37.457	209.762	2.307
0.3	218.606	14.093	133.746	1.471	576.695	36.764	211.694	2.328
0.4	216.362	13.980	132.662	1.458	559.525	35.735	204.938	2.254

4.1 K-Nearest Neighbour Clustering (KNN)

This is the first algorithm used to classify users into K disjoint groups. The K head clusters are randomly selected among $\mathcal{S}$, the set of points randomly drawn from a homogeneous Poisson point process with density λ. The remaining users/points in $\mathcal{S}$ are then are assigned to the closest group head. Finally, only the groups that reach the target size $|\mathcal{D}_k|$ are retained.

Feasibility was tested for variates of $\lambda = 50, 300$ with 50 as step. The constraints were set to 0.2 b/s/Hz as minimum rate and 0 dBm transmission power for 5 groups of size 2 sharing CUE channel averaged over 200 feasible cases. Clearly, a solution exist for low λ values as 50 users and a relatively large average distance from the head cluster (approx., 120 m) and the weakest receiver, which is naturally decreasing down to 40 m as the density increases up to 300. The percentage of feasibility was high hence 0 infeasible case appeared during test cases. The problem also continuous to be feasible as we increase number of groups per channel yet that has opposite affect on EE. Increasing number of users from 1 up to 11 EE decrease from 303.3774 down to 144.2761 while rate increase from 6.6283 up to 53.5086. The main reason behind low EE is that the average consumed power increase to satisfy minimum rate constraint under high level of interference.

Sum-rate Capacity and EE were analysed while considering a wide range of available transmission power budget [−15, 15] dBm. The minimum rate were fixed to 0.2 b/s/Hz with 5 D2MD per channel of size 2. Figure 1 show global and maximum minimum rate respectively for different λ. Obviously, aggregate and minimum rate increases logarithmically as maximum transmission power increase to saturates to a maximum value hence the aggregate interference level prevents further improvement in data rate. This behaviour is confirmed by global and maximum minimum EE as illustrated in Fig. 2.

Rate Constraints were tested with range of $[0.1, 0.4]$ b/s/Hz. The number of groups per channel was set to 5 of size 2 and maximum transmission power 0 dBm averaged over 200 feasible cases. The results are shown in Table 2. Clearly, GEE and global rate as well as MEE and minimum rate decrease as minimum rate level increase. This is a clear indication that setting a higher value for the minimum transmission rates forces the devices to use proportionally higher power in order to satisfy the constraint. But, since the rate increases only logarithmically with the SINR in the low- or moderate SINR region, these increased rates do not compensate the extra energy expenditure.

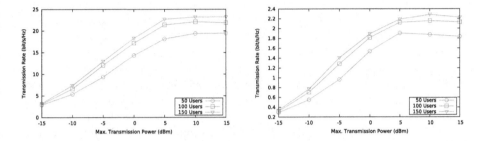

Fig. 1. Global and maximum minimum rate vs. transmission power in KNN.

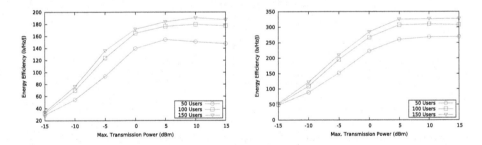

Fig. 2. Global and maximum minimum EE vs. transmission power in KNN.

4.2   Distance Limited (DL)

DL algorithm follows a similar concept to KNN in that we specify the number K of clusters to be formed in advance. Here, we introduce a new parameter called ($d_{\max}$) which is the maximum allowed distance between a transmitter and a receiver, specified as a fraction of the cell radius. This open the door to form heterogeneous groups with unicast and multicast communication simultaneously.

Feasibility is analysed with different λ and d_{max} values. The minimum rate is set to 0.2 bit/s/Hz and maximum allowed transmission power is 0 dBm with 5 groups. Taking an example $\lambda = 250$ and d_{max} ratios is [1/3, 1/10] average group size goes from 20 down to 2 with distance between 160 m and 40 m. Clearly, having bigger group did not affect problem feasibility as we still have 0 infeasible cases in total. The problem also continuous to be feasible as we increase number of groups per channel yet that has opposite affect on EE. Increasing number of users from 1 up to 11 EE decrease from 591.4391 down to 424.2723 while rate increase from 12.6849 up to 53.5086. The main reason behind low EE is that the average consumed power increase to satisfy minimum rate constraint under high level of interference.

Sum-rate Capacity and EE was tested in DL using similar constraints values as KNN. We set $\lambda = 150, 200$ and 250 to ensure multicast cast communication in minimum. Vales of d_{max} ratio were 1/5, 1/6 and 1/7 respectively with average group size 3. Figure 3 show global and minimum rate respectively for different λ. Obviously,we have similar behaviour as in KNN as aggregate rate or minimum rate increase logarithmically with maximum transmission up to saturates point hence the aggregate interference level prevents further improvement in data rate. This behaviour is confirmed by global and maximum minimum EE as illustrated in Fig. 4. Compared to KNN, higher values were attained here hence we have larger groups. We notice also small difference between values among various λ due to d_{max} control at this level.

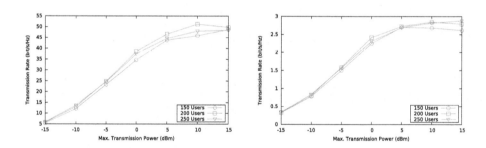

Fig. 3. Global and maximum minimum rate vs. transmission power in DL.

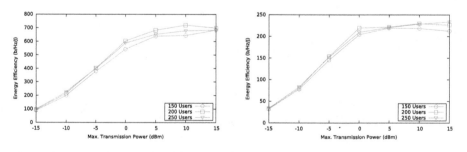

Fig. 4. Global and maximum minimum EE vs. transmission power in DL.

Rate Constraints were testes with $\lambda = 250$ and d_{max} ratio is $1/8$. The maximum transmission power was fixed to 0 dBm and minimum rate is in the range of $[0.1, 0.4]$ b/s/Hz with a step 0.1. The results are shown in Table 2. Again, we notice similar but higher values of GEE, global rate, MEE and minimum rate as in KNN. This confirm that setting a higher value for the minimum transmission rates forces the devices to use higher power to satisfy the constraint.

4.3   Density-Based Spatial Clustering of Applications with Noise

The DBSCAN algorithm [6] is used to identify dense zones by taking a reference point and searching over its neighbourhood within a limited distance d_{max}. If the density of points in this area is above a threshold, the area is identified as a potential group. The same process is applied to neighbours until all points are checked. If some point is not a neighbour of a group, it is regarded as a noise. In the original version of DBSCAN, a minimum number of neighbours $|\mathcal{D}_k|$ is identified to specify the core, border and noise points. Here, we follow a similar process (but varying d_{max}) and declare the core point of the discovered groups as the cluster heads.

Table 3. Global and minimum EE, rate in DBSCAN.

Min rate	GEE	Avg rate	MEE	Min rate
0.1	261.4748	53.2012	89.8905	0.9886
0.2	252.3485	51.0620	83.3020	0.9152
0.3	233.2863	47.0388	79.7355	0.8715
0.4	214.7058	44.1950	67.0430	0.7149

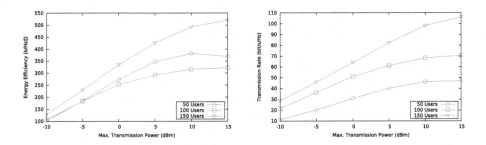

Fig. 5. Global rate and EE vs. transmission power in DBSCAN.

Feasibility. As in the previous cases, we start the performance analysis by assessing problem feasibility for some typical densities (here, $\lambda = 50, 100, 150$) and several d_{max} ratios $\{1/3, 1/19\}$. The minimum rate is set to 0.2 bit/s/Hz

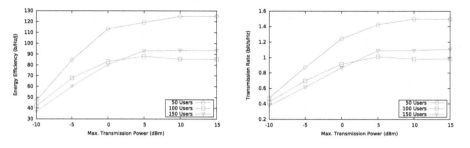

Fig. 6. Minimum rate and EE vs. transmission power in DBSCAN.

and maximum allowed transmission power is 0 dBm. In contrast to the previous clustering algorithm, DBSCAN allows us either to have many groups with moderated sizes, or few groups with large sizes. The unbalance (in the size of its groups) appears due to the indirect control of points number per given dense area. This fact explains why the number of infeasible cases is significantly larger than with the other clustering techniques (e.g., a maximum of 831 not solvable cases were found). For instance, for $\lambda = 100$ and ratio of 1/4, we had 2 D2MD groups of size 52 and a maximum distance inside a cluster of 350 m. Reducing d_{max} to 1/7 yielded more reasonable (and feasible) configurations, with 18 D2MD groups of size 3, a diameter equal to 71 m and without infeasible instances. As the transmission power budget decrease, some infeasible cases appear with -5 dBm and -10 dBm whereas -15 dBm generates extremely low feasibility percentage.

Sum-rate Capacity and EE. Both measures have been tested in DBSCAN using the usual parameters for the power and rate constraints. We tried $\lambda = 50, 100, 150$ to study the effect of density on this algorithm. For the d_{max} ratio, we chose 1/5 and 1/7, with 9 and 18 as the average number of groups and 2, 3 and 6 receivers per group, respectively. Figure 5 shows the global EE and aggregated rate, respectively, for different λ. We notice a similar performance to the results by the previous algorithms for the aggregate and individual rates. Similarly, Fig. 6 illustrates the minimum rate and EE. As proven previously, each channel has limited users capacity such as EE and minimum rate decrease while average rate increase. This can be seen clearly as low λ values as higher MEE and minimum rate are.

Rate Constraints. We repeated the numerical computations for assessing how a stricter rate constraint could change the fundamental trade-off between rate and energy efficiency. To this end, we pick $\lambda = 100$ and a configuration by design with 18 groups and 3 receivers per group. Now, the GEE decreases with the minimum acceptable rate. The same pattern happens for MEE, as detailed by Table 3.

Discussion. The EE and rate curves have similar shape in all the clustering algorithms. This means that the clustering technique is not determinant to the fundamental performance of this type of systems, if one ignores the practical issues of use a particular clustering technique in a real network, and with a distributed implementation. Nevertheless, the performance can be enhanced under certain conditions. The KNN algorithm is highly sensitive to the users density, λ. Its performance improves as λ increases, and this means a shorter distance between head cluster and the receivers. Clearly, since this distance is explicitly controlled in DL, the performance with DL is only slightly depending on the density. In addition, the flexibility of DL concept makes possible to have heterogeneous groups in area and number of UEs, and particularly the coexistence of unicast and multicast groups. Also, DL clustering offers higher EE and transmission rates, again as a immediate consequence of the closeness between the cluster head and a typical receiver in its group, shorter that the average distance observed with other clustering algorithms. The feasibility test shows that the problem can be solved for a wider distance, yet the fraction of feasible cases is largely influenced by the power budget.

5   Conclusion

In this paper, we proposed a general model to study global and users individual EE in D2MD. The problem is formulated as a joint power and resource allocation, yet for analytical tractability we limited the number of shared channel to one. Then, optimal power control was investigated. We proposed a combined frame work of optimization and stochastic geometry which allow us to assess a number of performance measures as D2D coverage, global and users EE and rate, or the capacity of a RB. The clustering algorithms do not have significant impact on EE or rate, yet can be used to slightly improve the fundamental performance. Also, under certain conditions a single resource block has a limited capacity where as more users sharing the channel as the EE decrease.

References

1. Ak, S., Inaltekin, H., Poor, H.V.: Gaussian approximation for the downlink interference in heterogeneous cellular networks. In: 2016 IEEE International Symposium on Information Theory (ISIT), pp. 1611–1615, July 2016
2. Ak, S., Inaltekin, H., Poor, H.V.: Tractable framework for the analysis of general multi-tier heterogeneous cellular networks. CoRR abs/1610.05617 (2016)
3. Alamouti, S.M., Sharafat, A.R.: Resource allocation for energy-efficient device-to-device communication in 4G networks. In: 2014 7th International Symposium on Telecommunications (IST), pp. 1058–1063. IEEE (2014)
4. Dinkelbach, W.: On nonlinear fractional programming. Manag. Sci. **12**(7) (1967)
5. Gong, W., Wang, X.: Particle swarm optimization based power allocation schemes of device-to-device multicast communication. Wirel. Personal Commun. **85**(3), 1261–1277 (2015)
6. Khan, K., Rehman, S.U., Aziz, K., Fong, S., Sarasvady, S.: DBSCAN: past, present and future. In: 2014 Fifth International Conference on the Applications of Digital Information and Web Technologies (ICADIWT), pp. 232–238. IEEE (2014)
7. Lin, X., Ratasuk, R., Ghosh, A., Andrews, J.G.: Modeling, analysis, and optimization of multicast device-to-device transmissions. IEEE Trans. Wirel. Commun. **13**(8), 4346–4359 (2014)

8. Ma, Z., Zhang, Z., Ding, Z., Fan, P., Li, H.: Key techniques for 5G wireless communications: network architecture, physical layer, and mac layer perspectives. Sci. China Inf. Sci. **58**(4), 1–20 (2015)
9. Mach, P., Becvar, Z., Vanek, T.: In-band device-to-device communication in OFDMA cellular networks: a survey and challenges. IEEE Commun. Surv. Tutor. **17**(4), 1885–1922 (2015)
10. Meshgi, H., Zhao, D., Zheng, R.: Joint channel and power allocation in underlay multicast device-to-device communications. In: 2015 IEEE International Conference on Communications (ICC), pp. 2937–2942. IEEE (2015)
11. Meshgi, H., Zhao, D., Zheng, R.: Optimal resource allocation in multicast device-to-device communications underlaying LTE networks. arXiv preprint arXiv:1503.03576 (2015)
12. Rebecchi, F., de Amorim, M.D., Conan, V., Passarella, A., Bruno, R., Conti, M.: Data offloading techniques in cellular networks: a survey. IEEE Commun. Surv. Tutor. **17**(2), 580–603 (2015)
13. Zappone, A., Björnson, E., Sanguinetti, L., Jorswieck, E.: Achieving global optimality for energy efficiency maximization in wireless networks. CoRR 1602.02923 (2016). http://arxiv.org/abs/1602.029023
14. Zhou, Z., Dong, M., Ota, K., Wu, J., Sato, T.: Distributed interference-aware energy-efficient resource allocation for device-to-device communications underlaying cellular networks. In: Global Communications Conference (GLOBECOM), pp. 4454–4459. IEEE (2014)

Adaptive-Segmentation and Flexible-Delay Based Broadcasting Protocol for VANETs

Houda Hafi[1(✉)], Wahabou Abdou[2], and Salah Merniz[1]

[1] MISC Laboratory, Abdelhamid Mehri University, Constantine, Algeria
{houda.hafi,salah.merniz}@univ-constantine2.dz
[2] LE2I UMR6306, CNRS, Arts et Métiers, Univ. Bourgogne Franche-Comté,
21000 Dijon, France
wahabou.abdou@u-bourgogne.fr

Abstract. A Vehicular Ad hoc Network (VANET) is an interconnection of vehicles that communicate through wireless technologies. It offers to road users a wide variety of applications which can be classified into four main categories: safety, road traffic, comfort and infotainment. This paper deals with safety applications. Their main goal is to detect critical road conditions (e.g. accidents, black ice, etc.) and/or send notifications to other vehicles in the network. An effective dissemination of such a message relies on multi-hop retransmissions. Thus an explicit or implicit cooperation between vehicles is needed in order to relay the message over a wide area. The main challenge is to avoid the broadcast storm problem. This paper proposes an efficient segment-delay based method that divides the road into several segments depending on the network density and utilises a waiting time update technique to expedite the dissemination process with respect to network performance.

Keywords: VANETs · Safety applications · Broadcasting protocol · Road segmentation · Delay adjustment

1 Introduction

Reducing the risk of road accidents is a major challenge. Throughout the world, several solutions are proposed to achieve this goal. Some of them take advantage of technological advances, particularly in the field of intelligent transportation systems (ITS) since some ITS's applications rely on interactions between smart vehicles and their environment (another vehicle, a road side unit or any other intelligent node). Compared to a simple car, a smart vehicle is equipped with a set of wireless communication devices such as sensors, radars, global navigation satellite systems (GNSS) like the Global Positioning System (GPS), human machine interfaces, etc. A collaborative multi-hop wireless communication between smart vehicles leads to a Vehicular Ad hoc Network (VANET).

© IFIP International Federation for Information Processing 2017
Published by Springer International Publishing AG 2017. All Rights Reserved
Y. Koucheryavy et al. (Eds.): WWIC 2017, LNCS 10372, pp. 207–218, 2017.
DOI: 10.1007/978-3-319-61382-6_17

Two main communication modes are possible. The first one is an ad hoc mode called vehicle to vehicle (V2V) communication, where vehicles do not use any pre-existing network infrastructure to communicate. In the second mode, vehicles communicate with a fixed devices installed along the road, forming a vehicle to infrastructure (V2I) or infrastructure to vehicle (I2V) communications.

VANETs differ markedly from other types of networks (mobile ad hoc networks - MANETs, sensor networks, mesh networks, etc.) on several points. The first difference rises on mobility features. In MANETs, the nodes speed is that the users walking, whereas, in VANETs the speed is that of the vehicle that can exceed one hundred kilometres per hour. High mobility makes a rapidly changing topology and frequent disconnections between nodes in the network. Moreover, the number of nodes in VANETs is very large compared to MANETs. Furthermore, displacement environment is quite different from that of MANETs [1].

Vehicular networks provide safety applications which aim to protect drivers from any road hazard. These applications need a very short end to end delay, because of the imminence of the danger. Moreover, after a while, the information will become obsolete [2]. To meet this requirement, inter-vehicle communication protocols must take into consideration the network topology and select appropriate relay nodes in order to avoid the broadcast storm problem which leads to an increase in the number of redundant messages, the latency and the radio interferences [3].

This paper proposes a novel broadcasting method which is based on road segmentation. The idea is to privilege the nodes that are farthest from the source without penalising those which are not far away from it if the former have not received the packet due to a collision or fading channel problem.

The remaining of this paper is organised as follows. Section 2 presents some related works. Section 3 introduces our broadcasting technique. Simulation results are presented in Sect. 4. And Sect. 5 concludes the paper and point out some future work.

2   Related Works

In literature, many solutions have been proposed to tackle the broadcast problems in VANETs. They can be classified into two categories: sender-oriented and receiver-oriented protocols. In the first class, the relay nodes are selected by the sender. In the second one, when a node receives a packet, it decides autonomously if it broadcasts the packet or no.

Several techniques are used to forward emergency packets: knowledge-based, counter-based, probabilistic based, segment-based, delay-based and distance-based. The simplest broadcasting method is the Simple flooding. Every packet is relayed exactly once by each node. An inconvenience of this method is that it may lead to many useless redundant packets since it does not take into account the network topology and density. To overcome this issue, some neighbor knowledge-based protocols have been proposed. These methods are based on a comparison of lists of neighbors: 1-hop neighbor list for Distributed Vehicular Broadcast (DV-CAST) [4] or 2-hop neighbor list for Scalable Broadcast Algorithm (SBA) [5].

These lists are included in the broadcast packets and help receivers to check if it is useful to retransmit the packets (if there exist additional nodes that may receive the packet). However, this makes the data packet size very large especially in a dense network.

Another category of broadcasting protocols is the counter-based methods. They rely on the idea that the more a node receives copies of the packet, the less likely it is useful to relay this packet. Upon reception of the first copy, the node initialises a counter and sets a timeout. During the waiting time, the counter is incremented upon reception of a copy of the packet. At the expiration of the waiting period, the packet is retransmitted if the counter of redundant copies is less than a threshold value. AckPBSM [6] and POCA [7] use this approach and set lower timeout to the farthest nodes from the source (or last-hop relay).

Probabilistic-based methods represent a further receiver-oriented dissemination technique to broadcast an emergency message in VANETs. In these schemes, the receiver calculates a dissemination probability based on a defined parameter. For instance, authors in [8] associate the forwarding probability of a node to its distance from the source so that the farthest node will have a high chance to rebroadcast the packet. In [9–11] the rebroadcasting probability depends on the node's local density, node's speed and redundancy ratio respectively. In [12] authors propose a protocol called E-ProbT that combines the number of common neighbors and the distance between the transmitter and the receiver to compute the probability of forwarding.

To resolve the broadcast storm problem and have a high reliability, authors in [13–15] use the segment-based technique. They divide the road into multiple segments and assign the responsibility of dissemination and acknowledgement of the broadcast message to the farthest vehicle in the last non-empty segment.

To deal with rebroadcast redundancy and provide an appropriate end to end delay which is a critical quality of service requirement in safety applications, several protocols that are based on delay-based schemes have been proposed. In this strategy, distant nodes from the source have the lowest waiting time. Therefore, they have the highest priority to rebroadcast the packet. Slotted 1-persistence [8] is a delay-based protocol where all nodes located in the same segment will have an identical waiting time. Although, it privileges the farthest nodes by giving them the shortest slot time, the collision problem can not be circumvented, on account of the simultaneous access to the radio channel by all the nodes that belong to the same segment.

Distance-based schemes represent the most used by all aforementioned techniques since all protocols have the same end, viz. reliable and fast data packet delivery with a few hop counts. The main idea behind this technique is that the source uses the information gained from periodic hello messages and choose the farthest node as a forwarder [16,17]. In [18] authors exhibit an amendment sender-oriented distance-based protocol, where the source pick the effective forwarders and incorporate them in the data packet header. Receiving the packet, the node checks whether it has been chosen as relay node. In the positive case, it calculates its relay waiting time which is defined as $\alpha \times i$, where i is the node's index in the list of forwarder candidates and α is a pre-defined slot time. In their work, they assume that α is 10 ms and the number of relay nodes is 12 (from 0 to 11). If the receiver is not part of the forwarder candidates, the packet is discarded.

3   Dynamic Segment-Delay Broadcasting Protocol

There are two approaches to broadcast a safety message in VANETs: sender-oriented and receiver-oriented methods. The reliability of each technique depends on the transmission conditions. In the case of obstacle-free environment that allows a direct vision (Line Of Sight) between the transmitter and the receiver, the sender-oriented method may be preferred. However, its performances degrade quickly in a complex environment where there are many obstacles that hinder the errorless reception of the message by the relay nodes falling further in distance from the source. In this case, it's better that each node decides in an autonomous way. Nevertheless, if all receivers decide to rebroadcast the packet at the same time, this involves many redundant packets which will saturate the bandwidth and consequently increase the collisions and the latency. Therefore, a hybrid technique is advisable to avail of the advantages of each one.

This paper introduces a new distributed broadcast technique called Segment-Delay Based Broadcast Protocol (SDBP) for vehicular ad hoc networks. Our proposed combines the sender-oriented and receiver-oriented schemes. SDBP is sender-oriented in the sense that the source helps the nodes with some information that incorporates in the data packet header, and receiver-oriented where each node acts autonomously after receiving the data packet.

3.1   An Overview of the Proposed Method

The aim of SDBP is to guarantee a high and fast dissemination of a safety message in a sparse and high-density network. It is based on segment and delay dissemination techniques. It gives the high priority of forwarding to the nodes located in the farthest segment. The novelty of our work relies on the dynamic adaptation of the waiting time of each node after the ending of the fixed period referred to "SlotTime" for which a packet will be received by the other nodes. We devote following sections below to delineate the different steps of SDBP.

3.2   Sending Phase

The sending process may be triggered by a vehicle that detects an unexpected road hazard. In such case, it should inform all its neighbors by broadcasting an emergency message. To ensure the reliability of message dissemination in a sparse and dense network, SDBP proposes a dynamic density-based segmentation technique. Most of the segmentation techniques proposed in literature produce the empty segment problem [8,13,15]. In general, the length of each segment is obtained by dividing the communication range of the source node by the desired segment number. In such case, if the nodes are not uniformly distributed, the farthest segments may be empty. Some techniques are proposed to remedy this problem. SDBP introduces a new approach that completely avoids the appearance of empty segments. In SDBP, the number of segment relies on the local density of a node (number of neighbors) and it does not depend on node's transmission range which is unknown by the sender in the real world since it is inconstant and varies swiftly depending on the signal propagation environment.

To better manage the groups of vehicles and facilitate the task of relay nodes selection, the source divides its transmission range into K segments depending on its number of neighbors (N).

$$K = \lfloor \sqrt{N} \rceil \tag{1}$$

All segments are uniform in terms of number of nodes $M_i, i \in \{1, 2, ..k\}$, excluding the farthest segment. Indeed, when N is not a multiple of K, the farthest segment will have a high number of nodes compared to the other segments. this will increase the number of nodes with a high priority in broadcasting. Equation 2 is used to determine the number of nodes in each segment.

$$M_i = \begin{cases} \dfrac{N}{K} + (N \bmod K) & \text{if i=1 for the farthest segment} \\\\ \dfrac{N}{K} & \text{for } i \in \{2, 3, ..k\} \end{cases} \tag{2}$$

In order to reduce the dissemination time of each message, priority of relaying messages should be given to nodes that are in the farthest segment. Therefore, each node must be aware of the segment it belongs to. The maximum and minimum boundaries of each segment are included in the data packet header (see Fig. 1). Equation 3, explains how to reckon the boundaries of each segment (Fig. 2).

$$\begin{cases} n_i = (N + 1) - \displaystyle\sum_{j=1}^{i} M_j \\\\ Dmin_i = n_i^{th} \ neighbor's \ position \\\\ Dmax_i = \begin{cases} Farthest \ neighbor's \ position & \text{if i=1} \\ Dmin_{i-1} & \text{if } i \in \{2, 3, ..k\} \end{cases} \end{cases} \tag{3}$$

Broadcaster ID	The number of segments	The farthest node's position	Dmin$_1$	Dmin$_2$	....	Dmin$_k$	DATA

Fig. 1. SDBP packet header

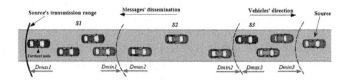

Fig. 2. Example of segmentation process

3.3 Forwarding Phase

Figure 3 summarises the main idea of SDBP that can be explained as follows: When a node receives a data packet for the first time, it initialises a counter to compute the number of redundant copies. Then, it determines to which segment it belongs to and calculates its waiting time WT according to Eq. 4.

$$WT_j = \alpha \times SlotTime \times \frac{d(Source, FarthestNode)}{d(j, Source)} \qquad (4)$$

where $\alpha \in \{1, 2, \ldots, K\}$ is the segment's number, d represents the distance between two nodes and $SlotTime$ is an approximate time for a packet to be thoroughly received by the other neighbors. In our work, we have taken the SlotTime value proposed in [11].

Afterwards, a timer is triggered which is the minimum between waiting time and SlotTime. At the timer's expiration, three cases may be distinguished:

- If the node has already received another copy of the same packet, this latter will be discarded.
- If no copy has been received by the node and its waiting time is expired ($WT = 0$), the node forwards the packet.
- If the waiting time of the node has not expired yet and it is always greater than $SlotTime$, the node updates its waiting time through the Eq. 5. Else, the minimum value between WT and $SlotTime$ is selected again and the process restarts.

$$WT_j' = \frac{WT_j}{2} \qquad (5)$$

The reasoning behind the waiting time adjustment is to hasten the dissemination process mostly in a network where there are many obstructions that prevent the good reception of the message. In actuality, when a node broadcasts a safety message, it does not know which nodes will receive the packet and which ones will lose it. For instance, in a network where the message is lost by all nodes falling farther from the source, the nearest neighbors to the source must wait a lengthy time before broadcasting the message. This approach enormously increases the end to end delay.

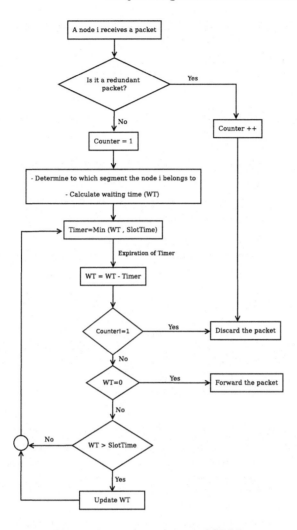

Fig. 3. Forwarding process of SDBP

4   Experimentation and Results

To assess the performance of SDBP, we carried out our simulations thanks to Network Simulator 2 (NS2, version 2.35) [19]. We have used the m-Nakagami propagation model and IEEE 802.11p as wireless communication standard. To generate mobility traces, we have used a microscopic traffic simulator called "SUMO" [20]. The simulation starts by broadcasting a safety message from the vehicle located at the extremity of the road. In order to evaluate SDBP under different density environments (sparse, moderate and dense), we vary the number and the speed of vehicles in the network according to Table 2 so that the denser the network the smaller the speed of vehicles. The maximum speed in each scenario is 110% of the minimum speed provided in Table 2. Each simulation scenario is run 10 times and the results presented in this section are the average values of the performance metrics detailed in Sect. 4.1. The detailed simulation settings are given in Table 1.

Table 1. Simulation scenarios parameters

Network Simulator	NS-2.35
Traffic and Mobility Generator	SUMO 0.28.0
Highway Length	8 Km
MAC protocol	IEEE 802.11p
Number of data packet sources	1
Slot Time	4 ms
Number of data packets	30
Propagation model	m-Nakagami

Table 2. Speed values

Vehicles density(vehicles/km)	10	20	30	50	60	90	120
Minimum speed of vehicles(m/s)	20	10	7	4	3	2	1.5

To validate the performance of SDBP, two protocols are chosen namely: the Simple Flooding which is a reference protocol and the Furthest Distance to show the behavior of a protocol based solely on the sender-oriented technique in a non-deterministic environment.

- Simple Flooding Protocol (SFP): the well-known technique where nodes broadcast each received packet only once (the first time) without any waiting time.
- Furthest Distance Protocol (FDP): a sender-oriented distance-based dissemination technique where the duty of forwarding is ascribed to the twelve farthest nodes from the source [18].

4.1 Performance Metrics

The comparison study among SDBP, SFP and FDP is carried out with respect to four performance metrics.

1. Dissemination time: the required time in order that all nodes in the network receive the packet.
2. Packet delivery ratio: the number of nodes that have successfully received the packet divided by the total number of nodes in the network.

3. Forwarders ratio: the percentage of nodes that participated in the rebroadcast operation of the packet.
4. Redundant packets ratio: the percentage of duplicated packets received with respect to the total number of packets.
5. Number of dropped packets: number of packets discarded at the physical layer by virtue of the following motives [21]:

   – Transmission Busy (TXB): this scenario occurs when a node in a transmission state receives another packet. Because a node can not send and receive at the same time, Therefore the packet which was supposed to be received will be dropped.
   – Reception Busy (RXB): in this case, a node receives a second packet while it is occupied by the reception of another one. This situation which will cause a collision.
   – Searching valid preamble (SXB): in this situation, the node which is in IDLE state drops the packet because it is searching for a valid preamble.
   – Receiving a frame preamble (PXB): as the previous case, the node is in IDLE state but it can not receive correctly the current packet because it is busy by receiving a valid preamble of another one.

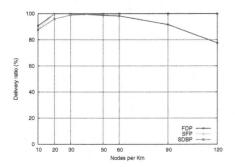

Fig. 4. Packet delivery ratio versus vehicle's density

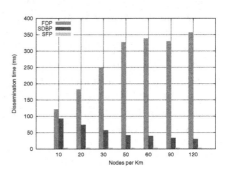

Fig. 5. Dissemination time versus vehicle's density

4.2   Simulation Analysis

Figure 4 shows the packet delivery ratio against the vehicle's density. Obtained results indicate that in a low density network the three protocols give roughly the same delivery ratio with a moderate rise of FDP and SFP. When the network starts to be crowded, the ratio reception of FDP falls, because of the loss of packet by the selected farthest nodes. However, SDBP retains a high reachability as SFP whether is a low-density or high-density network.

In terms of dissemination time, Fig. 5 shows that SDBP outperforms plenty the FDP protocol. As we can see, FDP's dissemination time increases proportionally with vehicle's density owning to the long waiting time of nodes nearby

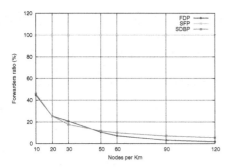
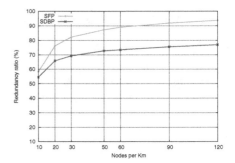

Fig. 6. Forwarders ratio versus vehicle's density

Fig. 7. Redundancy ratio versus vehicle's density

to the source. Unlike the SDBP where the dissemination time decreases proportionately with vehicle's density, because nodes tune their waiting time regularly if no reception is recorded, which allow to the nodes with a short distance to the source to rebroadcast quickly. As expected the SFP presents the smallest values since all nodes rebroadcast the received packets immediately without any delay.

Figure 6 compares the performance of the three protocols in terms of forwarders ratio. Clearly, SFP represents the highest rate (100%), seeing that all receiver nodes are effective forwarders. Both protocols SDBP and FDP exhibits approximately the same rating from 10 to 50 vehicles/km. After that, we observe that SDBP slightly overshoots the FDP because SDBP performs better that FDP with regard to the reception ratio.

For a fair comparison in terms of redundancy ratio, we have taken into account the protocols that present a complete reception in the network. As we have shown in Fig. 4, when the network become dense, SFP and SDBP always give a delivery ratio of 100% while FDP's reception rate falls down. Figure 7 shows that SDBP leads to a few number of redundant packets compared to SFP. It should be noted that a certain degree of redundancy must be maintained to ensure a good reception rate.

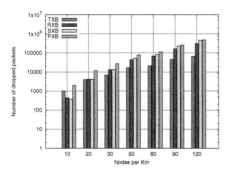
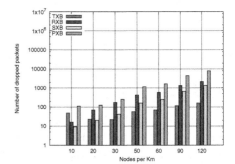

Fig. 8. Number of dropped packets of SFP versus vehicle's density

Fig. 9. Number of dropped packets of SDBP versus vehicle's density

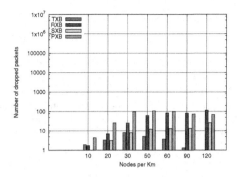

Fig. 10. Number of dropped packets of FDP versus vehicle's density

Figures 8, 9 and 10 show the number of dropped packets for SFP, SDBP and FDP owning to TXB, RXB, SXB and PXB causes. As is foreseen, SFP is ranked first in the packet loss and this for the four reasons. Although FDP gives better results in terms of the number of dropped packets compared with SDBP and SFP, it has the lowest delivery ratio and the highest dissemination time which are key parameters of messages in safety applications.

5   Conclusion

This paper introduced a novel efficient broadcasting protocol called SDBP, which allows delivering emergency messages in vehicular safety applications. The purpose is to achieve a high performance in terms of reachability and dissemination time in both sparse and dense network. For that, a hybrid technique which blends segment and delay dissemination methods is used. Simulations results show that SDBP outperforms two well-known protocols SFP and FDP. SDBP's good performances are mainly due to some mechanisms like the density-based segmentation and the dynamic adjustment of the waiting time. These mechanisms allow, respectively, a wide coverage of the network and a small dissemination time. The current version of SDBP uses a distance-based to compute the waiting time. In future work, it may be interesting to look at the benefit of adapting the waiting time in accordance with the network density and consider a real road topology in the evaluation process.

References

1. Naja, R. (ed.): Wireless Vehicular Networks for Car Collision Avoidance. Springer, Heidelberg (2013)
2. Javadi, M., Habib, S., Hannan, M.: Survey on inter-vehicle communication applications: current trends and challenges. Inf. Technol. J. **12**(2), 243 (2013)
3. Tseng, Y.-C., Ni, S.-Y., Chen, Y.-S., Sheu, J.-P.: The broadcast storm problem in a mobile ad hoc network. Wirel. Netw. **8**(2–3), 153–167 (2002)

4. Tonguz, O.K., Wisitpongphan, N., Bai, F.: Dv-cast: a distributed vehicular broadcast protocol for vehicular ad hoc networks. IEEE Wirel. Commun. 17(2), 47–57 (2010)
5. Peng, W., Lu, X.-C.: On the reduction of broadcast redundancy in mobile ad hoc networks. In: Proceedings of the 1st ACM International Symposium on Mobile Ad Hoc Networking & Computing, pp. 129–130. IEEE Press (2000)
6. Ros, F.J., Ruiz, P.M., Stojmenovic, I.: Reliable and efficient broadcasting in vehicular ad hoc networks. In: IEEE 69th Vehicular Technology Conference (VTC Spring 2009), pp. 1–5. IEEE (2009)
7. Nakorn, K.N., Rojviboonchai, K.: Poca: position-aware reliable broadcasting in vehicular ad-hoc networks. In: Proceedings of 2010 Second Asia-Pacific Conference on Information Processing (APCIP 2010) (2010)
8. Wisitpongphan, N., Tonguz, O.K., Parikh, J.S., Mudalige, P., Bai, F., Sadekar, V., et al.: Broadcast storm mitigation techniques in vehicular ad hoc networks. IEEE Wireless Commun. 14(6), 84–94 (2007)
9. Wegener, A., Hellbruck, H., Fischer, S., Schmidt, C., Fekete, S.: Autocast: an adaptive data dissemination protocol for traffic information systems. In: 2007 IEEE 66th Vehicular Technology Conference (VTC-2007 Fall), pp. 1947–1951. IEEE (2007)
10. Mylonas, Y., Lestas, M., Pitsillides, A., Ioannou, P., Papadopoulou, V.: Speed adaptive probabilistic flooding for vehicular ad hoc networks. IEEE Trans. Veh. Technol. 64(5), 1973–1990 (2015)
11. Achour, I., Bejaoui, T., Busson, A., Tabbane, S.: Sead: a simple and efficient adaptive data dissemination protocol in vehicular ad-hoc networks. Wirel. Netw. 22(5), 1673–1683 (2016)
12. Lima, S., Larces, D., Júnior, C., Larces, J.: E-probt: a new approach to mitigate the broadcast storm problem in vanets. In: Proceedings of the 31st Annual ACM Symposium on Applied Computing, pp. 709–715. ACM (2016)
13. Korkmaz, G., Ekici, E., Özgüner, F., Özgüner, Ü.: Urban multi-hop broadcast protocol for inter-vehicle communication systems. In: Proceedings of the 1st ACM International Workshop on Vehicular Ad Hoc Networks, pp. 76–85. ACM (2004)
14. Fasolo, E., Furiato, R., Zanella, A.: Smart broadcast algorithm for inter-vehicular communication. In: Proceedings of WPMC (2005)
15. Sahoo, J., Wu, E.H.K., Sahu, P.K., Gerla, M.: BPAB: binary partition assisted emergency broadcast protocol for vehicular ad hoc networks. In: Proceedings of 18th International Conference on Computer Communications and Networks (ICCCN 2009), pp. 1–6. IEEE (2009)
16. Jaballah, W.B., Conti, M., Mosbah, M., Palazzi, C.E.: Fast and secure multihop broadcast solutions for intervehicular communication. IEEE Trans. Intell. Transp. Syst. 15(1), 433–450 (2014)
17. Palazzi, C.E., Roccetti, M., Ferretti, S.: An intervehicular communication architecture for safety and entertainment. IEEE Trans. Intell. Transp. Syst. 11(1), 90–99 (2010)
18. Rehman, O., Ould-Khaoua, M., Bourdoucen, H.: An adaptive relay nodes selection scheme for multi-hop broadcast in vanets. Comput. Commun. 87, 76–90 (2016)
19. Network Simulator. "ns-2". http://www.isi.edu/nsnam/ns/
20. SUMO (2017). https://sourceforge.net/projects/sumo/
21. Hassan, A., Ahmed, M.H., Rahman, M., et al.: IEEE 802.11 p performance evaluation in a city environment (2011)

Information Technology

NetFlow Anomaly Detection Though Parallel Cluster Density Analysis in Continuous Time-Series

Kieran Flanagan[1,2](✉), Enda Fallon[1], Paul Connolly[2], and Abir Awad[3]

[1] Software Research Institute, Athlone Institute of Technology, Athlone, Ireland
`k.flanagan@research.ait.ie`, `efallon@ait.ie`
[2] The NPD Group, Inc, IDA Business Park, Athlone, Co. Westmeath, Ireland
`paul.connolly@npd.com`
[3] Faculty of Computing, Engineering and Science,
University of South Wales, Treforest, UK
`abir.awad@southwales.ac.uk`

Abstract. The increase in malicious network based attacks has resulted in a growing interest in network anomaly detection. The ability to detect unauthorized or malicious activity on a network is of importance to any organization. With the increase in novel attacks, anomaly detection techniques can be more successful in detecting unknown malicious activity in comparison to traditional signature based methods. However, in a real-world environment, there are many variables that cannot be simulated. This paper proposes an architecture where parallel clustering algorithms work concurrently in order to detect abnormalities that may be lost while traversing over time-series windows. The presented results describe the NetFlow activity of the NPD Group, Inc. over a 24-hour period. The presented results contain real-world anomalies that were detected.

Keywords: Anomaly detection · NetFlow · Clustering · Density analysis

1 Introduction

In recent years, research into new methods of anomaly detection within a network has increased in prominence. The need for a fast, reliable method to identify possible malicious activity has grown in response to emerging threats. Protecting confidential and proprietary data is of paramount importance to any organization to ensure that both legal and contractual obligations are kept. In addition, the data stored may not necessarily be the property of the company storing and handling the data. Malicious activity such as Botnets and Port Scans are increasing in frequency. These attacks, while simple, have the potential to allow for unauthorized access onto the network.

Within any organization, it is common place to use network monitoring and analysis tools to help with the detection of any anomalous behaviour on the network. Tools, such as McAfee ePO and Tipping point for example, are signature based models, which require a known example of a threat to be catalogued and a signature generated. The signature based model, while highly exact, fails if a novel attack occurs

Y. Koucheryavy et al. (Eds.): WWIC 2017, LNCS 10372, pp. 221–232, 2017.
DOI: 10.1007/978-3-319-61382-6_18

(e.g. zero-day vulnerabilities), since no previous signature exists. This limitation gave rise to anomaly based detection mechanisms. These methods require no signature database, but instead model the "normal" traffic on a network and alerts to any activity that happens outside of these normality bounds.

While much research has been conducted on various methods for anomaly based systems using a variety of approaches [1–5], key limitations apply when attempting to adapt these approaches to a real-time system. These include, most notably, computational cost. Within commonly used distance based outlier detection mechanisms, the need for distance based calculations for each new sample can be overwhelming for high volume data. This gave rise to optimized algorithms designed to mitigate this limitation. Algorithms such as Fast Local Outlier Factor (FastLOF) [6] and Micro-Cluster based Outlier Detection (MCOD) [7], reduce the overall cost of the range queries with varying degrees of success.

It has been shown that the application of time series can be beneficial in the detection of network anomalies. Applying time series over time-windows of increasing size has been shown to be capable of normalizing normal behaviours over time. However, at smaller time-intervals, it is possible for abnormal behaviour to traverse time windows, allowing for the possibility of becoming a false positive. This is particularly prevalent among anomalies that generate low numbers of NetFlow. It is possible for it to become hidden within other network traffic as time progresses, making detection increasingly unlikely.

Moreover, while it is possible that a large increase may occur, small deviations in established traffic behaviour may also be an indication of unauthorized activity. For example, an increase in failed login attempts may produce little difference with respect to NetFlow, it may be indicative of someone trying to guess a password. Detecting such an instance would be of paramount importance, particularly if followed by a successful login attempt [8]. This paper proposes a solution to this problem. By implementing parallel clustering algorithms, it is possible to gain a higher level of granularity while maintaining the normalization techniques gained from an incrementally increasing time window. Concurrent algorithms can detect minor deviations from established behaviour that can occur, regardless if they occur while traversing between time-windows.

In Sect. 2, an overview of related work is given. In Sect. 3, a brief overview of the technology used is presented. In Sect. 4, we propose a framework for the identification of anomalies within NetFlow data. The architecture is presented as well as an overview given on algorithms created and used. In Sect. 5, testing methodology is presented. In Sect. 6, results obtained from live data are presented and analysed. In Sect. 7, conclusions and future work are presented.

2 Related Works

Recent research into anomaly detection has largely focused on applying anomaly detection mechanisms on network data to successfully identify anomalous behaviour. Many problems still exist however. Performance is a key factor when trying to utilize anomaly detection techniques and there are many examples where this is apparent.

Methods such as Principal component analysis [3], K nearest neighbour [9] and ensemble techniques [10, 11] have been used to various degrees of success in this task.

However, there comparatively expensive operations have led to a rise in clustering techniques to mitigate the calculations need when associating anomaly detection with big data [12, 13]. Using aggregated data, such as NetFlow can be used to reduce the calculations further [14]. Limitations are present with these techniques however. Kumari et al. [15] looks at a clustering technique for the use of anomaly detection over a network, setting a distance based threshold as the 100th farthest data point from the obtained cluster centroids. This threshold is a common theme across multiple anomaly detection solutions [16–18]. However, it can be argued that using a common threshold over all clusters within real data is non-representative of the various forms of traffic created. E.g. Traffic from different applications do not act in a similar manner.

This brings forward an interesting problem. While distance based outliers have been shown to be of significance in a plethora of works [19–21], we propose another indicator of possible anomalous behaviour. By monitoring cluster density over a time series, changes in underlying behaviour can be detected. Rather than only focusing on samples that are anomalous via distance based calculations, changes in the density of activity over time are also monitored.

Asmuss et al. [18] demonstrates the use and effectiveness of utilizing a time series based approach over live data. The aggregation of traffic is highly beneficial in this case, as it reduces the computational sources needed. Furthermore, it also provides a tangible benefit when comparing results across clusters. This idea of time-aware analysis has been used elsewhere also [22], and has shown to be a valuable tool in mapping continuous behaviour.

This ability to generate a normalized view of traffic over time, practically speaking, has some limitations however. The potential for an anomaly to traverse though sequential time windows can lead to the anomaly threshold not being broken, thus leading to a false positive reading. Presented in Sect. 4 is an architecture that utilizes concurrent time windows in order to mitigate the risk of this happening. Anomalies can be gathered from individual instances of the clustering algorithm, while the correlation of clustering behaviours through instances can also indicate anomalous activity.

3   Technology Overview

3.1   Cisco NetFlow

Cisco NetFlow is a system that amalgamates network traffic information into a format that successfully describes communications occurring on a network. Through a Net-Flow enabled device (Fig. 1), packet traces are identified and stored as a single flow representation of a specific set of communications between two devices. These are used for multiple tasks such as network performance monitoring and used as a means of security evaluation when an incident has been detected. Visualization of the NetFlow has also proven to be of tangible benefit [23]. Using this aggregated data for anomaly detection has numerous benefits, such as data size being reduced for processing purposes and storage. For the analysis in this paper, NetFlow was used as it was found that using NetFlow for network monitoring purposes was highly common in the area [24], as well, in this case, the current infrastructure of NPD allowed for the collection of NetFlow with relative ease.

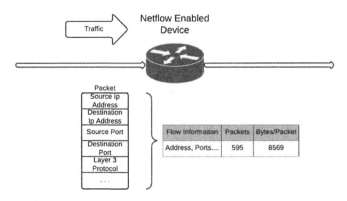

Fig. 1. NetFlow example

3.2   MCOD

MCOD is a distance based outlier detection mechanism that utilizes clustering to reduce the amount of distance based calculations needed to identify possible anomalies. This reduced performance cost of the algorithm makes it an ideal candidate for real-time anomaly detection over data streams when compared to other distance based algorithms such as Local Outlier Factor (LOF). As described in [7], MCOD uses a sliding window approach to identify outliers over a data stream. By using an expiring data set, the algorithm can be optimized to only use a data set that is large enough for satisfactory anomalies to be detected, while maintaining the low amount of calculations needed. Distance is calculated between cluster centroids and the NetFlow sample being queried. If the point is within this range of a cluster centroid and the cluster has the specified density, k, then the point is determined to be a non-anomaly, or inlier.

4   Proposed Framework

The architecture is a two-step approach that involves monitoring traffic at different levels of abstraction. Firstly, an adaptation of the MCOD algorithm is applied on the NetFlow data in sequential time windows (Fig. 2). This stage can outline distance based outliers contained within the NetFlow information. Following this, the clusters generated within each time-window are correlated to identify those representing similar traffic. The density values (how many input samples are contained within the cluster) are then gathered at the end of each window 5 min period.

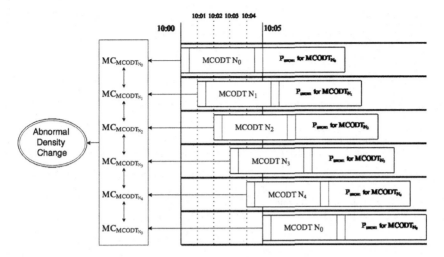

Fig. 2. Architecture overview

4.1   Anomaly Detection

When using algorithms such as k-Nearest Neighbour and MCOD, a common variable that must be tuned to the dataset is k. While it's exact use may change, the principal remains consistent. k is used to describe the limit of normality within anomaly detection frameworks. It is a single variable used to tune the classification or detection rate within an algorithm. Within MCOD, it is the value at which a micro cluster is generated and an outlier is classified as an inlier. Within the context of NetFlow anomaly detection, this is a severe limitation, as it assumes that all network traffic activity has an equal distribution across the network, which is an extremely unlikely assumption (Discussed further in Sect. 5).

In order to successfully mitigate this limitation, all cluster densities are monitored irrespective of k's value. This allows for the successful detection of abnormal increases and decreases in cluster densities with respect to the time window being analysed.

4.2   Density Normality Measurement Generation

Within the proposed architecture, MCODT is initialized with a time window of size t. MCODT clusters data within this window, identifying anomalies using distance based calculations. The clusters generated within this time window contain samples that correspond to a type of network behaviour (Table 5). In parallel, windows are initialized in time steps of St using the same configuration as the initial algorithm (Fig. 3).

The positions of the clusters generated are then correlated with each subsequent MCODT instance to successfully capture the clusters activity through the other MCODT instances. This correlative step is needed as, due to the cluster generation step of MCODT, a cluster might not be in the exact same position throughout the sequential time windows, even though they represent the same class of network traffic (Fig. 4).

Symbol	Meaning
q_i	the i-th query point.
S_q	stream of query points.
W_t	window of Size t-time.
p_i	i-th point p; $i = 1, ..., n$.
n_{W_t}	number of non-expired points in window W_t .
$p_i.arr$	arrival time of point p.
$p_i.exp$	expiring time of point p.
p_{anom}	point p declared as anomalous.
now	current time.
r	query range, $q.r$ is the distance parameter for query q.
k	number of neighbours parameter $q.k$ is the neighbours parameter for query q.
nn_{p_i}	number of neighbours for point p.
MC_i	i-th micro cluster, $i = 1, ..., n$.
D	micro cluster density, $MC_i.D$ is the density of the i-th microcluster.
$x.MC_i$	all time windows microcluster i is present in.
$y.MC_i$	all Density measurements for microcluster i

Fig. 3. Commonly used notation

Algorithm 1 Micro-Clustering Outlier Detection in Time-Series (MCODT)

Input: Query Point Stream S_q
Output: MC_i for all i, P_{anom}

  1: **while** (S_q) **do**
  2:    Obtain point q from S_q
  3:    $q.arr = now$
  4:    **if** $q.r < |MC_i|$ **then**
  5:      q is added MC
  6:      $MC.D + +$
  7:    **else if** $nn_q >= k$ **then**
  8:      new MC
  9:      $MC + q$
10:    **else**
11:      $p = p_{anom}$

Fig. 4. MCODT definition

Once the clusters have been correlated and shown to be representative of the same class of network traffic, the cluster is persisted and given an ID. At the end of each instance of MCODT, the clusters density is measured and compared to its own historical activity and its activity in the other instances (Fig. 5).

Algorithm 2 Parallel Cluster Corrolation

Input: MC_i for all i within $MCODT_{N_0}$
Output: $D.MC_i$ for all i within $MCODT_N$ for all N
  for MC_i for all i within $MCODT_{N_0}$ **do**
    for MC_i for all i within $MCODT_N$ where $N \neq 0$ **do**
      if $MC_iN_0 = MC_iN$ **then**
        Clusters Represent the Same Class
        $D.MC_i = D.MC_N$ for all N

Fig. 5. Cluster correlation

This allows for the identification of anomalies, using the 3-standard deviation rule, within the persisted cluster. Furthermore, when a cluster is not generated in all the instances of MCOD, it is indicative of non-homogenous network activity. This specific type of traffic (as shown in Sect. 6) is highly irregular, and corresponds to network traffic that is extremely uncommon within the testing environment (Fig. 6).

Algorithm 3 Residual Calculation For Cluster Density

Input: MC_i for all i within $MCODT_N$ for all N
Output: Residual of $D.MC_i$ for $MCODT_N$ for all n
  for $MCODT_N$ for all N **do**
    for MC_i for all i in $MCODT_N$ **do**

$$\bar{X}_n = n^{-1}[X_n + (n-1)\bar{X}_{n-1}]$$

$$s_n^2 = \frac{n-2}{n-1}s_{n-1}^2 + \frac{1}{n}(X_n - \bar{X}_{n-1})^2$$

    Residual $= D.MC_i - 3(s_n) + \bar{X}_n$
    if Residual> 0 **then**
      Flag as Anomaly

Fig. 6. Residual calculation

5 Methodology

5.1 Collected Data

To successfully test the proposed method, NetFlow was collected in a 24-hour period from within NPD. This was live data, and no previous insight about this 24 h period was held. It was unknown if it held anomalies or not, simulating realworld conditions. The NetFlow contained all communications, both internally and externally, during this period. A total of 151,995,634 NetFlow samples. From these samples, 8 attributes were extracted (Table 1). And from these, 6 attributes were selected to be used in the anomaly detection calculations.

- Source/Destination IP
- Destination Port
- Source Port
- Destination Bytes
- Source Bytes
- Protocol ID

These attributes were normalized using theoretical maximums as well as observed maximums over a 3-month period (Table 2).

Table 1. Selected NetFlow attributes

Destination Bytes	Volume of traffic sent from the Destination IP in bytes
Destination I.P	The destination I.P address of the NetFlow
Destination Port	The Destination port used for the NetFlow
Protocol I.D	The ID of the Protocol used. (6 = TCP, 17 = UDP)
Source Bytes	Volume of traffic sent from the Source IP in bytes
Source I.P	The Source IP of the NetFlow
Source Port	The Source port of the NetFlow
Start Time	The time at which the represented communiqué was initiated

Table 2. Maximum values used for normalization

Variable	Maximum value
Source/Destination Port	65535
Source/Destination Bytes	4294967270 (Bytes)
Protocol ID	255

The remaining collected attributes were excluded from the anomaly calculations due to various reasons. The IP addresses were excluded due to the IP address leases allocated by DHCP servers were inconsistent in both maintaining the allocated IP's, and time-out periods for leased IP's. This would lead to inconsistent results within networks, as IP addresses could be re-allocated in as little as 30 min, drastically changing their perceived normal traffic pattern. Instead, IP addresses were categorized as either internal or external, in order to develop separate clusters in feature space to represent internal-to internal and external-to-external traffic types. These attributes, along with the Start Time attribute, were collected for the investigation.

5.2   Program Configurations

For testing, a 24-hour example was chosen with no specific preference. No previous assumptions existed about this data before testing. The architecture was configured with an initial time window size of 5 min, and parallel instances were configured to run at one minute intervals after this, leading to a total of 5 MCOD instances processing the data in parallel. Configured variables are outlined in Table 3.

Table 3. Program configurations

Name	Symbol	Value
Minimum Density Required	K	50
Maximum range for Sample	R	.0025
Number of Algorithm Instances	N	5
Size of Window	T	360 s

6   Results

In this section, we discuss the results of the proposed method of anomaly detection. Anomalous samples that were identified at both stages of the proposed architecture are outlined and analysed. Examples of normal activity of various types will also be presented.

6.1   Point Anomalies

Due to the two-stage architecture of the proposed method, anomalies may be detected in two different manners. Firstly, anomalies outlined by the distanced based calculations are outlined at the end of every time window. An anomaly outlined in this window contains a point that never meets the required density irrespective of time. These are regarded as Point Anomalies. Due to the relatively small time window of the MCODT instances, the number of point anomalies detected within the first hour of processing was vast. The number of additional anomalies fell rapidly over the course of the analysis. Because of this, focus was placed on point anomalies that were detected after the initial 12 h of analysis. Table 4 outlines two such samples that were correctly identified as an anomaly.

Table 4. Sample point anomalies

Sample ID	Source Port	Destination Port	Source Bytes	Destination Bytes	Protocol ID
A	57838	53	116	262	17(UDP)
B	49886	1900	8428	0	17

Sample A represents a simple DNS request, which at first seemed like a false positive. However, upon investigation, it was shown that this DNS request was from an internal asset to an external DNS server. This incident was of interest to security technicians within the NPD Group. Sample B was an unauthorized UPnP (Universal

Plug and Play) device connected to the network. It has been well documented how network security can be effected by having a UPnP device hosted on a network [25]. Upon Detection, the device was disconnected from the network.

6.2   Cluster Density Analysis

Cluster densities were measured at regular intervals. Five instances of MCODT were run in parallel, each with the same configuration settings (Table 3) The initial instance, $MCODT_{N0}$, was initialized at 00:00am on the day in question. One minute after this, $MCODT_{N1}$, was initialized, followed by $MCODT_{N2}$ and so on. This low level of analysis allows for the detection of possible malicious activity in as little as one minute after an incident Table 5 outlines sample clusters, selected based on being classified as an anomaly, and their activity over the course of one hour within the scope of all the independent instances. This totals 1440 total densities measured for 1532 clusters generated and persisted over the course of testing.

Table 5. Detected anomalies

ID	Source Port	Destination Port	Source Bytes	Dest. Bytes	Protocol ID	N0	N1	N2	N3	N4
1	34701	6001	272	296	6	2	4	2	6	3
2	2598	6773	3486	3486	6	3	5	7	3	5
3	6188	41781	212	74	6	48	30	32	24	27
4	**54787**	**5355**	**376**	**0**	**17**	**5**	**NA**	**NA**	**NA**	**NA**
5	58544	2181	2840	1640	6	10	10	10	10	10
6	7858	443	1026	782	6	308	256	337	201	339
7	1720	61444	320	0	6	1418	1418	1418	1418	1418
8	45549	8879	22472	7580	6	755	755	755	755	755
9	**5925**	**5040**	**442**	**0**	**17**	**28**	**21**	**116**	**182**	**167**
10	1521	46172	3532	5624	6	10	15	9	13	14

Anomalies were shown in both the independent analysis and correlative analysis. Of interest is an anomaly detected (Table 5, Sample 9). This anomaly appears in all instances of the algorithm, and is shown to have significant divergence from observed normal behaviours. The rapid increase, once investigated, was attributed to a single asset. It was shown to be connected to an external IP. It proceeded to attempt to open a connection to the external asset, but never received any connection. This was of interest to the security team within NPD, and was swiftly resolved. Sample 4 was also anomalous within the test. The cluster only appeared in one window, showing the extremely temporal nature of the event. The other instances did not detect sufficient activity to generate a cluster. It represents an extremely short burst of activity to an external device.

7 Conclusions and Future Work

This paper proposed an architecture designed to detect anomalies within NetFlow data. To achieve this at a micro level, a clustering algorithm was run in parallel to determine anomalies in cluster activity in time-series. It was shown to be able to detect anomalies in live data without any previous knowledge on the data. These anomalies were investigated and shown to be of security interest. The result was interesting given that the testing was conducted on real world, live data, with actionable anomalies found. Future work would include refining the extensibility of the algorithm. Due to the abstraction of the density monitoring, it is possible to add attributes to MCODT's feature space in order to monitor changes in not only network traffic, but other metrics that could attribute to the risk of a malicious attack, such as the vulnerability of an asset determined by an external program.

References

1. Chen, Z., Yeo, C.K., Francis, B.S.L., Lau, C.T.: Combining MIC feature selection and feature-based MSPCA for network traffic anomaly detection. In: 2016 Third International Conference on Digital Information Processing, Data Mining, and Wireless Communications, DIPDMWC, pp. 176–181 (2016)
2. Lin, W.-C., Ke, S.-W., Tsai, C.-F.: CANN: An intrusion detection system based on combining cluster centers and nearest neighbors. Knowl. Based Syst. **78**, 13–21 (2015). doi:10.1016/j.knosys.2015.01.009
3. Fernandes Jr., G., Carvalho, L.F., Rodrigues, J.J.P.C., Proença Jr., M.L.: Network anomaly detection using IP flows with Principal Component Analysis and Ant Colony Optimization. J. Netw. Comput. Appl. **64**, 1–11 (2016). doi:10.1016/j.jnca.2015.11.024
4. Ciplinskas, R., Paulauskas, N.: Outlier detection method use for the network flow anomaly detection. Moksl - Liet Ateitis **8**, 327–333 (2016). doi:10.3846/mla.2016.928
5. Wankhede, R., Cholem V.: Intrusion detection system using classification technique. Int. J. Comput. Appl. **139**, 25–28 (2016). doi:10.5120/ijca2016909397
6. Goldstein, M.: FastLOF: An Expectation-Maximization based Local Outlier detection algorithm. In: 2012 21st International Conference on Pattern Recognition, ICPR, pp. 2282–2285 (2012)
7. Kontaki, M., Gounaris, A., Papadopoulos, A.N., et al.: Continuous monitoring of distance based outliers over data streams. In: 2011 IEEE 27th International Conference on Data Engineering, pp. 135–146 (2011)
8. Purwanto, Y., Kuspriyanto, H., Rahardjo, B.: Time based anomaly detection using residual polynomial fitting on aggregate traffic statistic. In: 2015 1st International Conference on Telematics, ICWT, pp. 1–5 (2015)
9. Iwok, P., Purwanto, Y., Suratman, F.Y.: Modified K-means algorithm using timestamp initialization in sliding window to detect anomaly traffic. In: 2015 International Conference on Control, Electronics, Renewable Energy, and Communications, ICCEREC, pp. 19–23 (2015)
10. Goeschel, K.: Reducing false positives in intrusion detection systems using data-mining techniques utilizing support vector machines, decision trees, and naive Bayes for off-line analysis. In: SoutheastCon 2016, pp. 1–6 (2016)

11. Uddin, M., Rehman, A.A., Uddin, N., et al.: Signature-based Multi-Layer Distributed Intrusion Detection System using Mobile Agents (2012)
12. Vijayakumar, V., Neelanarayanan, V., Balan, E.V., et al.: Big Data, Cloud and Computing ChallengesFuzzy Based Intrusion Detection Systems in MANET. Procedia. Comput. Sci. **50**, 109–114 (2015). doi:10.1016/j.procs.2015.04.071
13. Singh, K., Guntuku, S.C., Thakur, A., Hota, C.: Big Data Analytics framework for Peerto-Peer Botnet detection using Random Forests. Inf. Sci. **278**, 488–497 (2014). doi:10.1016/j.ins.2014.03.066
14. Carela-Español, V., Barlet-Ros, P., Cabellos-Aparicio, A., Solé-Pareta, J.: Analysis of the impact of sampling on NetFlow traffic classification. Comput. Netw. **55**, 1083–1099 (2011). doi:10.1016/j.comnet.2010.11.002
15. Kumari, R., Sheetanshu, Singh MK, et al.: Anomaly detection in network traffic using K-mean clustering. In: 2016 3rd International Conference on Advanced Information Technologies, RAIT, pp. 387–393 (2016)
16. Alsayat, A., El-Sayed, H.: Social media analysis using optimized K-Means clustering. In: 2016 IEEE 14th International Conference on Software Engineering Research, Management and Applications, pp. 61–66 (2016)
17. Velmurugan, T.: Efficiency of k-Means and K-Medoids algorithms for clustering arbitrary data points. ResearchGate **3**, 1758–1764 (2012)
18. Asmuss, J., Lauks, G.: Network traffic classification for anomaly detection fuzzy clustering based approach. In: 2015 12th International Conference on Fuzzy Systems and Knowledge Discovery, FSKD, pp. 313–318 (2015)
19. Abid, A., Kachouri, A., Mahfoudhi, A.: Anomaly detection through outlier and neighborhood data in Wireless Sensor Networks. In: 2016 2nd International Conference on Advanced Technologies for Signal and Image Processing, ATSIP, pp. 26–30 (2016)
20. Fu, P., Hu, X.: Biased-sampling of density-based local outlier detection algorithm. In: 2016 12th International Conference on Natural Computation, Fuzzy Systems and Knowledge Discovery, ICNC-FSKD. pp. 1246– 1253 (2016)
21. Tsiatsikas, Z., Fakis, A., Papamartzivanos, D., et al.: Battling against DDoS in SIP: Is Machine Learning-based detection an effective weapon? In: 2015 12th International Conference on EBus. Telecommunications, ICETE, pp. 301–308 (2015)
22. Gajic, B., Nováczki, S., Mwanje, S.: An improved anomaly detection in mobile networks by using incremental time-aware clustering. In: 2015 IFIP IEEE International Symposium on Integrated Network Management IM, pp. 1286–1291 (2015)
23. Wong, P.C., Haglin, D., Gillen, D., et al.: A visual analytics paradigm enabling trillion-edge graph exploration. In: 2015 IEEE 5th Symposium Large Data Analysis and Visualization, LDAV, pp. 57–64 (2015)
24. Li, B., Springer, J., Bebis, G., Hadi Gunes, M.: A survey of network flow applications. J. Netw. Comput. Appl. **36**, 567–581 (2013). doi:10.1016/j.jnca.2012.04.020
25. Zheng, H., Li, C., Chen, Z.: Petri Nets based modeling and analysis of UPnP security ceremonies. In: 2011 Third Pacific-Asia Conference on Circuits, Communications and System, PACCS (2011)

Investigation of Traffic Pattern
for the Augmented Reality Applications

Maria Makolkina[1,2(✉)], Andrey Koucheryavy[1],
and Alexander Paramonov[1]

[1] The Bonch-Bruevich State University of Telecommunications,
22 Pr. Bolshevikov, St. Petersburg, Russian Federation
makolkina@list.ru, akouch@mail.ru,
alex-in-spb@yandex.ru
[2] Peoples' Friendship University of Russia (RUDN University),
6 Miklukho-Maklaya Street, Moscow 117198, Russian Federation

Abstract. In this article, the interaction between augmented reality and flying ubiquitous sensor networks (FUSN) technologies is investigated. Such modern applications require development of the new traffic patterns, which can be used to establish a new approach to the further Quality of Experience assurance and estimation. The proposed new traffic pattern captures service space model, model of an environment of the user and behavior model.

Keywords: Augmented reality · Flying ubiquitous sensor networks · Unmanned aerial vehicles · Interaction model · Traffic pattern · Quality of experience

1 Introduction

Today there are many applications of augmented reality that can be classified into six large groups: medicine; assembly, maintenance and repair of the complex equipment; addition of the different information to the existing objects; control of robots, unmanned aerial vehicles, etc.; gaming and entertainment industry; military [1, 2]. In addition, the use of augmented reality for the management and monitoring of telecommunication networks is a special interest [3, 4]. Also, augmented reality is used to analyze traffic flows in the Vehicular Ad-hoc networks (VANET) [5–7] and other transport networks to detect congestions [8, 9]. There are a few applications that allow user to manage various engines and devices [10], informing drivers about the road situation [11], and control the UAVs [12]. Flying ubiquitous sensor networks (FUSN) based on UAVs is gaining more popularity with arising of the Industrial Internet of Things (IIoT). Among the industries that demonstrate the greatest interest in the introduction of the Industrial Internet, can be called mining, engineering, agriculture, and transport. It is widely believed that data collection from the devices and data analysis are the main ideas of the FUSN. At the same time the important aspect is missed, that the transfer of a rapidly growing raw data in processing centers requires new technological solutions and methods of the network planning [13, 14]. For some applications, for example, observing over the territory, cameras may be installed on the

© IFIP International Federation for Information Processing 2017
Published by Springer International Publishing AG 2017. All Rights Reserved
Y. Koucheryavy et al. (Eds.): WWIC 2017, LNCS 10372, pp. 233–246, 2017.
DOI: 10.1007/978-3-319-61382-6_19

UAVs. Such systems apply new restrictions on the application and impose new requirements to the telecommunication networks, because of high sensitivity of the UAVs to the network performance. The accuracy and maneuverability of UAV management depends on the quality of service and quality of experience.

Due to the fact that there are many fundamentally different services, it is necessary to develop models for the interaction of network elements while providing the services of the augmented reality, the traffic model, the user's behavior model, and the density model of both users and objects of augmented reality.

In this paper, we investigated traffic pattern for the augmented reality applications that use video camera for control, observation, monitoring, surveillance etc.

2   Related Works

By now, several works on new traffic patterns have been known in the context of the introduction of the concept of the Internet of Things (IoT). Thus, in [15] authors investigated the solutions for a smart city service based on the technology of augmented reality and Internet of Things infrastructure. They described the implementation of delivering the important information about the bus arrival times, tourist landmarks to the citizens, using bus-mounted IoT devices which transmit the data to the associated cloud servers. D2D communication that reduces the traffic load on the network and transfers data directly between the two devices is well suited for implementing such applications. It is also worth noting that today much attention is paid to models of downloading traffic D2D [16, 17]. In the paper [18] traffic modeling and simulation of multiplayer real-time games and M2M applications are presented. Authors evaluate the impact of additional simulated traffic on the performance of mobile wireless network. The researches from Japan in [19] review 5G network to perform augmented reality applications. They investigated the influence of the bandwidth and the latency on the development and implementation augmented reality services. In [20] the features of augmented reality applications researched. They consider network requirements, such as bandwidth, delay and propose to reevaluate the network infrastructure to support such applications. In this paper [21] traffic in Ubiquitous sensor networks is analyzed. The new on-off model for the source traffic simulating described. During the investigation authors determine how parameters of such model influence on the traffic at the sink.

These works are important and allow us to move forward in analyzing traffic, but for augmented reality there are features associated with the emergence of new parameters such as traverse speed, the angle of sector of the review, density of objects, which are planned to be taken into account in the developed model.

The goal of the investigation is the development a traffic pattern, depending on the UAV's position changes in the augmented reality applications.

3   Interaction Model

To develop an interaction model of the network elements, we chose as an example an application for the city area monitoring. In the observed area, the objects are people, their personal devices, buildings, cars, traffic conditions, etc. Installing the camera on the UAV allows the pilot to detect the obstructions, to control the UAV, collect data from land sensors and observe everything in the surveillance area. For example, the pilot can determine the object by the sensor located on it and get all the necessary information with the augmented reality glasses or visually identify the object independently if it does not have sensors.

The pilot controls the actions of UAV through the AR device (glasses or helmet) by means of turns and nods, Fig. 1. The camera is installed on the UAV, video stream displayed on the AR device that is on the head of the pilot. Based on the video stream, pilot can define the UAV location and control both the UAV itself and the camera to change the viewing angle. So, it is necessary to transmit two streams simultaneously with different requirements to quality of transmission; the first one is a video stream, the second is a control stream. Also, objects found in the field of view may transmit information to the AR device. Depending on the movement of the UAV or the camera number and type of objects in the field of view may change, which affects both the video stream itself and the control flow.

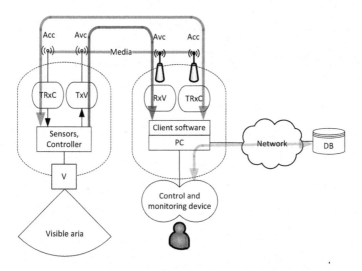

Fig. 1. Interaction of the main elements in the provision of AR services.

4   Traffic Pattern

For the description of the traffic made by service it is necessary to connect volume given by the user and the user of data in case of changes of his surrounding:

- service space model;
- user surrounding model;
- behavior model.

As a service space we will understand an information model of physical three-dimensional space in which there can be a user of service. The information model includes the description of some objects which are in this space of $X = \{\bar{x}_1, \bar{x}_1, \ldots, \bar{x}_n\}$, where n is total number of objects.

The model of a surrounding of the user is a subspace of service space, i.e. a part of space limited by perception opportunities (model of these opportunities). A surrounding is usually bound to position of the user in space of service and includes a set of objects of $X^U = \left\{\bar{x}_1^{(U)}, \bar{x}_2^{(U)}, \ldots, \bar{x}_n^{(U)}\right\}$, where k is a number of the objects, which are in the area of perception of the user.

The behavior model describes changes of position of the user and his surrounding in service space. Changes in a surrounding of the user can be caused by relocation of the user, and relocation of objects in service space. The change caused by appearance in a surrounding of the user of a new object $\bar{x}_i$, leads to a request of data on this object.

The algorithm of implementation of service shall provide performance of the following functions:

- identification of an event of change of a surrounding and computation of parameters of change;
- information request about surrounding change;
- receiving data and its display.

The possible diagram of a data interchange is provided on Fig. 2.

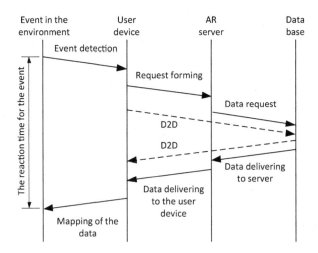

Fig. 2. Diagram of a Data Interchange by provision of AR service.

As a surrounding also as well as space of service is limited (area of perception) physical three-dimensional space, changes in it can be described as a stream of events connected to appearance of objects in it. Objects can enter through its boundaries owing to relocation of these boundaries or objects. In the first case, relocation of boundaries is connected to behavior of the user, and in the second to behavior of objects. In that and other case quality of functioning of system will depend on its ability to timely service events of this flow.

Thus, the task of support of quality of service can be considered as a choice of parameters of system (productivity, throughput, distribution of its functionality) from the characteristic of an event stream and load of the system made by this flow.

Properties of an event stream substantially define properties of a data stream between system elements. For example, in system of positioning on the district map such flow is defined by events of change of coordinates of the user and is defined by characteristics of his movement, in system with using AR glasses it will be determined by their orientation in space and, probably, by the events connected to transferring data about objects in field of view or their characteristics.

It is obvious that characteristics of a flow will depend on distribution and characteristics of objects in service space, and also characteristics of movement of the UAV.

Let's make an assumption that objects in space of service are distributed in a random way (form a Poisson field) and are fixed, only the UAV is mobile. Then, change of position of the UAV is equivalent to change of its surrounding. Taking into account properties of space of service and surrounding, this change can be described by the volume or the area.

Properties of the traffic generated by the UAV device, depends on the distribution of objects of the UAV surrounding and the UAV behavior (motion and rotation). Poisson field is a one of the possible distribution of the objects. This distribution may not very close to real world distribution, bat it is very convenient to get final solutions for the queuing system model. The arguments for the Poisson field are that we do not know for now the exact distribution of the objects in the real world, but we know exactly the solutions for the Poisson field. This model can be used for comparison and quality angling of the service system.

In case information about surrounding of the user represents the image, received by the videocamera, set on the unmanned aerial vehicle, for determination of field of restriction of a surrounding of the user it is necessary to consider features of movement of this device and the transferring video camera. Let's consider 2D option of a surrounding (terrestrial objects) and will describe a surrounding of the user by radius sector r. Such model is closer to a real situation, than model of a circle [22] since the video camera has limited viewing angle, and probably rather high line speed of movement restricts opportunities regarding the circle review. We will mean the line speed of relocation of the UAV v a constant. Then, during t change of a surrounding will be defined by number of new objects in the area defining a surrounding of the user.

As an example, when using the UAV, the district map with the conditional text and graphics images or designations of objects can be model of a surrounding. The high-speed link of video transmission is more subject to changes of conditions of reception, than low-speed link of signal transmission of control. In case of decline in quality of transmission channel of video, the image, represented to the user can be changed for the district map which is available on the local server.

Let's estimate quantity of new objects in a surrounding during t as

$$n(t) = \tilde{S}(L(t))\rho \qquad (1)$$

where $\tilde{S}(L(t))$ - is square of change of a surrounding;

ρ- density of objects (objects/sq.m). The density is equal to the number of objects to the service area ratio.

The model illustrating relocation of the user and change of its surrounding is given in Fig. 3. Offset of the sector representing a surrounding of the user from starting point on distance L is led to formation of area (the shaded area) which defines surrounding change. Objects in the field are identified according to a service provision algorithm, therefore requests for provision of additional information are created.

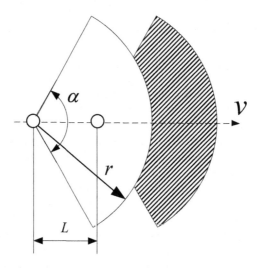

Fig. 3. Change of Surrounding in case of translational motion.

From the given figure, the area of the shaded area can be determined by a formula (2)

$$\tilde{S}(L) = \tilde{S}(r) - \tilde{S}(r - L) = \begin{cases} \frac{\alpha}{2}(2rL - L^2) & L \leq r \\ \frac{\alpha r^2}{2} & L > r \end{cases} \qquad (2)$$

The number of new objects in the area can be defined as

$$n(t) = \tilde{S}(L)\rho \qquad (3)$$

where ρ - density of objects (objects/sq.m),

α - the angle of sector of the review (radians).

Dependence of the number of new objects the area on the time, for different angle and velocity, is depicted on the Fig. 4.

The picture 4 shows the dependence of the number of new objects in the environment during the time t for two different viewing angles π/2 and π (radians), which

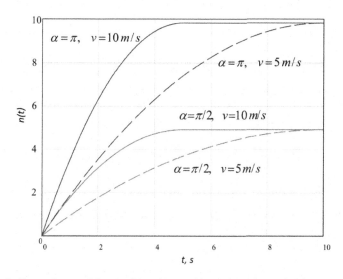

Fig. 4. Dependence of the number of new objects the area on the time (moving)

are close to the typical angle of sector of the review of the camera lenses (normal focal length, short focal length), and also for two values of the speed 5 and 10 m/s, which is close to the typical speed of UAV motion for video recording of the terrain.

As you can see from this picture, when the viewing angle or speed increases, the number of new objects in the area also rises over a time interval. Stabilization of the number of objects in the case as a speed exceeds over some value occurs when a complete change of all objects in the area takes place during the considered period of time. This is because their number is determined by the area of the sector.

Considering this process in progress, i.e. in case of movement of the user, there is the event stream (data requests).

Intensity of an event stream (data requests) can be defined as number of objects in a small increment of the area of the considered figure

$$\lambda_r = \frac{d\tilde{S}(L)}{dL} |L = 0 \; \rho v \tag{4}$$

where ρ - density of objects (objects/sq.m),

v - traverse speed (m/s).

Derivative of formula (2) in a point L = 0.

$$\frac{d\tilde{S}(L)}{dL} |_{L=0} = \alpha(r - L)|_{L=0} = \alpha r \tag{5}$$

Then, consider (4) и (5)

$$\lambda_r = \alpha \, r\rho v \tag{6}$$

Considering properties of the Poisson field accepted for model the quantity of objects in some limited area is accidental, distributed under the Poisson law and depends only on the area (or volume) of the considered area. Therefore, for the accepted model the flow of requests will represent the elementary flow for which the probability of arrival of k of requests for an interval of time of t will be defined as

$$p_k = \frac{(\lambda_r t)^k}{k!} e^{-\lambda_r t} = \frac{(\alpha \, r\rho v t)^k}{k!} e^{-\alpha \, r\rho v t} \tag{7}$$

Probability of k arrival requests during the time interval given in the Fig. 5.

With translational motion the device can make rotational motions. The model of rotational motion is given in Fig. 6.

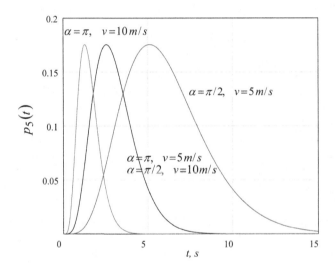

Fig. 5. Probability density of k requests during the time interval (moving)

The square of the shaded area can be determined by a formula (8)

$$\tilde{S}(\beta) = \tilde{S}(0) - \tilde{S}(\beta) = \begin{cases} \dfrac{\beta \, r^2}{2} & \beta \leq \alpha \\[2mm] \dfrac{\alpha \, r^2}{2} & \beta > \alpha \end{cases} \tag{8}$$

The number of new objects in the area can be defined as

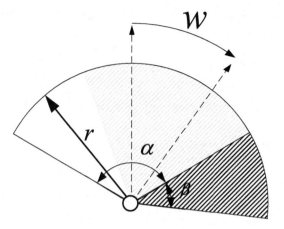

Fig. 6. Change of Surrounding in case of turn.

$$n(\beta) = \tilde{S}(\beta)\rho \tag{9}$$

where ρ - density of objects (objects/sq.m),

β - the turning angle (radians),

α - the angle of sector of the review (radians).

Dependence of the number of new objects the area on the time, for different angle, is depicted on the Fig. 7.

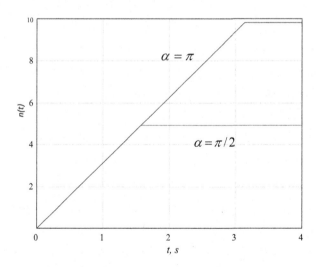

Fig. 7. Dependence of the number of new objects the area on the time (turn)

Considering this process in progress, i.e. in case of movement of the user the event stream (requests of data) takes place.

Intensity of an event stream (requests about data) can be defined as number of objects in a small increment of the area of the considered figure

$$\lambda_r = \frac{d\tilde{S}(\beta)}{d\beta}\Big|_{\beta=0} \rho\, w \tag{10}$$

where ρ - density of objects (objects/sq.m), w - angular speed of turn (rad/s).

Derivative of expression (2) in a point $\beta = 0$

$$\frac{d\tilde{S}(L)}{dL}\Big|_{\beta=0} = \frac{r^2}{2} \tag{11}$$

With (10) and (11)

$$\lambda_r = \frac{r^2 \rho\, w}{2} \tag{12}$$

Taking into account model of a Poisson field, the flow of requests will represent the elementary flow, for which the probability of arrival of k- requests for an interval of time t will be defined as

$$p_k = \frac{(\lambda_r t)^k}{k!} e^{-\lambda_r t} = \frac{\left(\frac{r^2 \rho w}{2} t\right)^k}{k!} e^{-\frac{r^2 \rho w}{2} t} \tag{13}$$

Probability of k arrival requests during the time interval given in the Fig. 8.

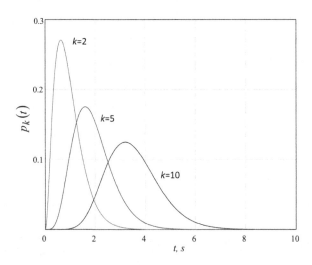

Fig. 8. Probability density of k requests for an interval of time (turn)

Figure 9 shows the ratio of angular speed of turn (rad/s) and the line speed of relocation for the equal traffic intensity and the angles of the review $\alpha = \frac{\pi}{2}$ and $\alpha = \frac{\pi}{4}$.

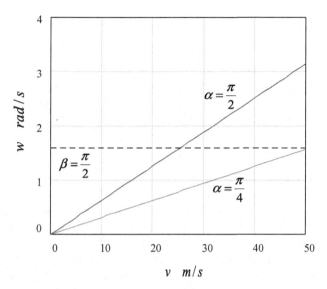

Fig. 9. The ratio of angular speed of turn (rad/s) and the line speed of relocation (m/s) for the equal traffic intensity.

For example, upon rotation $\beta = \pi/2$ for the one second traffic intensity is equivalent to the traffic intensity of the linear motion with speed of 50 m/s (180 km/h). In this example, the radius is selected to be 50 m. This ratio of produced traffic and UAV motion features should be considered when choosing a method of selection and implementation of data delivery.

The traffic flow made as a result of service provision is defined by a flow of replies to the data requests. Generally, both the single data packet, and a flow of packets (transmission of video or audio data) can be the response. Intensity of this flow can be described as

$$\lambda_s = \lambda_r \eta \tag{14}$$

where η - average quantity of the packets necessary for processing of a request.

By transmission of video data can exceed intensity of requests in tens and hundreds times. Taking into account requirements to quality it leads to essential growth of requirements to throughput of communication network.

The physical amount of surrounding of the user is, as a rule, commensurable with a radius of wireless technologies used for the PAN organization, for example group of Wi-Fi standards. Many objects of AR services (elements of city infrastructure, vehicles, household appliances) can be equipped with nodes of access and necessary data which can be presented to users. Therefore, use of D2D technologies can be the possible decision, providing essential lowering of a traffic on a communication network.

Intensity of this flow will be defined as

$$\lambda_s = \lambda_r \eta_{D2D} \tag{15}$$

where $\eta_{D2D} = (1 - \gamma)\eta$, γ - part of the objects of surrounding supporting D2D technology.

Certainly, application of D2D of technologies is possible only when objects of service are the physical entities mentioned above, which can be equipped with the respective communication centers. Rather wide range of services requires interaction with remote data bases and the solution of tasks of provision of quality.

5   Conclusion and Discussion

The model considered above allows analysis of the AR service traffic regardless of the service implementation methods, both on the server and client components. The specific method of implementation can significantly influence the nature of the traffic. Implementation is characterized by distribution of data handling functions between the client and server applications, and also methods of data selection. In particular, it is the organization of a buffer memory (cache) of the client application, determination of its size, speed of updating, formations of data requests with the forecast of movement. Control of these parameters allows to select the most acceptable usage mode of resources depending on requirements and behavior of the client application or device.

The article represents the investigation of the Augmented Reality scenario that uses UAV for data and video collection. This application may be widely used for the monitoring of the remote and inaccessible areas, restrained urban conditions with the busy streets and roads. The UAV with a video camera installed is used as an intermediate element. The user of the application through the AR glasses may see not only the picture from the video camera, but also an additional information about objects on the picture, due to the data collection from the sensors and online data analysis on the servers.

During the investigation, the service model of the AR application with the UAV was developed. From this service model, it appears that the characteristics of the created traffic depend on the UAV behavior, UAV surroundings, and the way of data transmission.

Further authors develop the traffic model that considers the UAV-based AR service characteristics, such as a limited lookout angle, speed of the UAV, and a number of objects in the service area.

The proposed model estimates traffic parameters of the new, previously not investigated application. For this reason, authors began the investigation with the Poisson field model for the object distribution, as it has known solutions, and the real objects distribution on the territory is unclear. In the future works authors are going to provide models for the other distributions.

Acknowledgment. The publication was financially supported by the Ministry of Education and Science of the Russian Federation (the Agreement number 02.a03.21.0008), RFBR according to the research project No. 16-37-00209 mol_a "Development of the principles of integration the Real Sense technology and Internet of Things".

References

1. Ong, S.K., Yeh, A., Nee, C.: Virtual and augmented reality applications in manufacturing. Springer Science & Business Media (2013)
2. Billinghurst, M., Clark, A, Lee, G.: A survey of augmented reality. Found. Trends Hum. Comput. Interact. **8**(2-3), 73–272 (2015)
3. Bergenti, F., Gotta, D.: Augmented reality for field maintenance of large telecommunication networks. In: Conference and Exhibition of the European Association of Virtual and Augmented Reality (2014)
4. Hui, M., Bai, L., Li, Y., Wu, Q.: Highway traffic flow nonlinear character analysis and prediction. Mathematical Problems in Engineering (2015)
5. Abdi, L., Ben Abdallah, F., Meddev, A.: In-vehicle augmented reality traffic information system: a new type of communication between driver and vehicle. Procedia Comput. Sci. **73**, 242–249 (2015)
6. Park, J.-G., Kim, K.-J.: Design of a visual perception model with edge-adaptive gabor filter and support vector machine for traffic sign detection. Expert Syst. Appl. **40**(9), 3679–3687 (2013)
7. Vinel, A., Vishnevsky, V., Koucheryavy, Y.: A simple analytical model for the periodic broadcasting in vehicular ad-hoc networks. In: 2008 IEEE GLOBECOM Workshops, pp. 1–5 (2008)
8. Hong-Bin, Z., Xiao-Duan, S., Yu-Long, H.: Analysis and prediction of complex dynamical characteristics of short-term traffic flow. Acta Physica Sinica **63**(4), 1–8 (2014)
9. Topór-Kamiński, T., Krupanek, B., Homa, J.: Delays models of measurement and control data transmission network. In: Nawrat, A., Simek, K., Świerniak, A. (eds.) Advanced Technologies for Intelligent Systems. SCI, vol. 440, pp. 257–278. Springer, Heidelberg (2013). doi:10.1007/978-3-642-31665-4_21
10. Ng-Thow-Hing, V., Bark, K., Beckwith, L., Tran, C., Bhandari, R., Sridhar S. User-centered perspectives for automotive augmented reality. In: IEEE International Symposium on Mixed and Augmented Reality 2013, Adelaide, SA, Australia, October 2013
11. de Winter, J.: Preparing drivers for dangerous situations: a critical reflection on continuous shared control. Systems, Man, and Cybernetics (SMC) 1050–1056 (2011)
12. Zollmann, S., Hoppe, C., Langlotz, T., Reitmayr, G.: FlyAR: augmented reality supported micro aerial vehicle navigation. IEEE Trans. Vis. Comput. Graph. **20**, 560–568 (2014)
13. Shafig, M.Z., et al.: A first look at cellular machine-to-machine traffic: large scale measurement and characterization. In: 12th ACM Sigmetrics Performance International Conference. June 11–15, London, England, UK (2012)
14. Dao, N., Koucheryavy, A., Paramonov, A.: Analysis of routes in the network based on a swarm of UAVs. In: Kim, K., Joukov, N. (eds.) ICISA 2016. LNEE, vol. 376, pp. 1261–1271. Springer, Singapore (2016). doi:10.1007/978-981-10-0557-2_119
15. Pokric, B., Krco, S., Pokric, M.: Augmented reality based smart city services using secure IoT Infrastructure. In: 2014 IEEE 28th International Conference on Advanced Information Networking and Applications Workshops (WAINA) (2014)

16. Andreev, S., Galinina, O., Pyattaev, A., Johansson, K., Koucheryavy, Y.: Analyzing assisted offloading of cellular user sessions onto D2D links in unlicensed bands. IEEE J. Sel. Areas Commun. **33**(1), 67–80 (2014)
17. Pyattaev, A., Johnsson, K., Surak, A., Florea, R., Andreev, S., Koucheryavy, Y.: Network-assisted D2D communications: implementing a technology prototype for cellular traffic offloading. In: 2014 IEEE Wireless Communications and Networking Conference (WCNC), pp. 3266–3271 (2014)
18. Drajic, D., et al.: Traffic generation application for simulating online games and M2M applications via Wireless Networks. In: 9th Conference on Wireless on-demand Network Systems and Services WONS 2012, Courmayeur, Italy, 9–11 January 2012
19. Orlovsky, J., Kiyokawa, K., Takemura, H.: Virtual and augmented reality on the 5G highway. J. Inform. Process. **25**, 133–141 (2017)
20. Westphal, C.: Challenges in networking to support augmented reality and virtual reality. In: ICNC 2017, Silicon Valley, California, USA, 26–29 January 2017
21. Vybornova, A., Koucheryavy, A.: Traffic analysis in target tracking ubiquitous sensor networks. In: Balandin, S., Andreev, S., Koucheryavy, Y. (eds.) NEW2AN 2014. LNCS, vol. 8638, pp. 389–398. Springer, Cham (2014). doi:10.1007/978-3-319-10353-2_34
22. Koucheryavy, A., Makolkina, M., Paramonov, A.: Applications of augmented reality traffic and quality requirements study and modeling. In: Vishnevskiy, V.M., Samouylov, K.E., Kozyrev, D.V. (eds.) DCCN 2016. CCIS, vol. 678, pp. 241–252. Springer, Cham (2016). doi:10.1007/978-3-319-51917-3_22

Benefits of Multiply-Cascaded TCP Tunnel with Network Coding over Lossy Networks

Nguyen Viet Ha[⊠], Kazumi Kumazoe, Kazuya Tsukamoto, and Masato Tsuru

Kyushu Institute of Technology, Kitakyushu, Japan
nvha@infonet.cse.kyutech.ac.jp

Abstract. Transmission Control Protocol (TCP) is still dominant for reliable end-to-end data transmission with congestion control over diverse types of networks although it does not perform well in goodput on lossy networks. To mitigate the goodput degradation of TCP on lossy networks, TCP with Network Coding (TCP/NC) was proposed. But it has not been well deployed because TCP/NC should be implemented in both sides of end-to-end connection; it requires considerable costs and is sometimes difficult in tiny end devices, e.g., with less memory and power. In this paper, to utilize the potential of TCP/NC more practically with no change on end-host TCP, we consider the TCP/NC tunnel that simply conveys end-to-end TCP sessions not only on a single TCP/NC session but also on cascaded TCP/NC sessions traversing a lossy network in the middle without per-session management. The simulation results by Network Simulator 3 clearly show the benefit of the multiply-cascaded TCP/NC tunnel. In congestion scenarios with a wide range of link loss rates, the end-to-end standard TCP with multi-cascaded TCP/NC tunnel can achieve a significantly higher goodput compared to both the end-to-end TCP/NC without tunnel and the end-to-end standard TCP with single TCP/NC tunnel.

1 Introduction

Transmission Control Protocol (TCP) is ineffective in lossy networks, e.g., wireless networks [1]. TCP always cuts down the sending rate for each loss because it recognizes all loss are interpreted as a congestion signal. To mitigate this performance degradation issue without change of end-host TCP, a variety of Performance Enhanced Proxy (PEP) approaches have been studied in either split type (e.g., TRL-PEP [2]) or snoop type (e.g., D-Proxy [3]). While their effectiveness has been shown in some conditions, they require complicated per-TCP session management on the proxy nodes. From a different viewpoint, IP over TCP (we call it TCP tunnel in this paper) in general is a kind of proxy to provide a reliable virtual link that encapsulates and transparently conveys IP packets over one or more TCP sessions between two (ingress/egress) entities, e.g., interfaces, routers, or gateways. TCP tunnel is used for diverse purposes, including security by encryption, performance improvement by session aggregation, flexible manageability by overlay, and so on. Since many applications rely

© IFIP International Federation for Information Processing 2017
Published by Springer International Publishing AG 2017. All Rights Reserved
Y. Koucheryavy et al. (Eds.): WWIC 2017, LNCS 10372, pp. 247–258, 2017.
DOI: 10.1007/978-3-319-61382-6_20

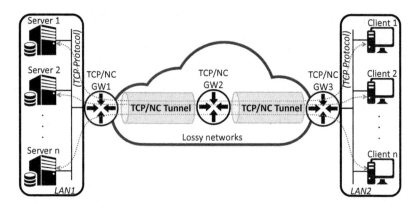

Fig. 1. The example of TCP/NC tunnel with two TCP/NC Gateways

on end-to-end TCP sessions, TCP over TCP tunnel can be seen commonly in various cases, although its performance depends on conditions due to the complex interaction between upper-layer TCP and lower-layer TCP [4]. In addition, since TCP itself is ineffective as mentioned above, TCP tunnel also does not perform well in lossy networks.

As an alternate solution for TCP goodput degradation in lossy networks, TCP with Network Coding (TCP/NC) was presented in 2009 [5]. The sink recovers all data even though some of packets are lost by allowing the source to send the data as random linear NC combination packets (referred to as combination packets) to the sink. Although TCP/NC is shown to have certain benefits in lossy networks, TCP/NC is not easy to be deployed because of several reasons. First is the incompatibility with the existing TCP protocol; thus, TCP/NC is required to be implemented at both ends of connection. Second, TCP/NC is costly to be implemented in some end devices e.g., with less memory and power.

To take advantage of TCP tunnel and TCP/NC, we propose TCP/NC tunnel system to mitigate the end-to-end TCP performance degradation in lossy networks without any change at end-host TCP. TCP/NC tunnel system consists of at least two gateways running TCP/NC protocol called TCP/NC gateways. In this paper, by extending the simplest TCP/NC tunnel with two gateways [6], we develop and evaluate the multi-cascaded TCP/NC tunnel which convey end-to-end TCP sessions on multi-cascaded TCP/NC sessions traversing multiple loss channels in the middle. An example of TCP/NC tunnel system is shown in Fig. 1. Data transmissions by end-to-end TCP sessions between LAN1 and LAN2 are encoded, decoded, and/or retransmitted at GW1, GW2, and GW3 to mask the packet losses happening in the lossy networks.

In TCP/NC tunnel system, adjacent TCP/NC gateways establish TCP/NC sessions together which can have the different NC-related parameters (NC parameters) based on the condition of each loss channel. The TCP/NC gateway of the source side (e.g., GW1 in Fig. 1) receives an IP packet from an end-host which runs the original TCP protocol. After that, the gateway encapsulates this packet, and forwards it to the next TCP/NC gateway through TCP/NC tunnel with the packet loss recovery capability. The TCP/NC gateway of the sink side (e.g., GW3 in Fig. 1) forwards the received packet to an end-host as original IP packet after recovering the packet if necessary. Besides, some intermediate TCP/NC gateways (e.g., GW2 in Fig. 1) can be placed in the middle which has different lossy networks. The TCP/NC gateways do not interfere to the TCP establishment phase as well as the ACK returning process among TCP end-hosts. When the packet losses happen in local networks (before or after the tunnel), the end-to-end TCP manages the lost packet recovery by a simple retransmission.

In contrast to PEP approach, the proposed "tunneling" approach does not require a complicated per-session management on each gateway. On the other hand, the tunneling approach must involve the encapsulation overhead (e.g., header space and processing time) in general. In addition, the problem of TCP over TCP tunnel should be taken into consideration.

TCP/NC tunnel system has been implemented and validated in Network Simulator 3. In the proposed system, to eliminate some limitations of original TCP/NC, a reinforced version of TCP/NC is used, which includes a dynamic estimation and a change of NC parameters (TCP/NCwLRLBE [7]) and an efficient retransmission of unrecoverable lost packets (TCP/NCwER [8]). They were previously developed by the authors as reviewed later in Sect. 2.2.

The remainder of this paper is organized as follows. In Sect. 2, TCP/NC is briefly described. The details of proposed TCP/NC tunnel is presented in Sect. 3. Simulations and results are described in Sect. 4 and the conclusions are discussed in Sect. 5.

2   Overview of TCP/NC

2.1   TCP/NC Scheme

TCP/NC protocol [5] was proposed to implement a NC into the protocol stack with a minor change by adding a new NC layer between TCP and IP layer. The sender-side NC layer allows the source to send m combination packets (C) created from n original packets (p) $(m \geq n)$ using Eq. (1) where α is the coefficient on a certain Galois Field, e.g., $GF(2^8)$. When the number of the lost combination packets is no more than $k = m - n$, the sink-side NC layer is expected to recover all the original packets using the remaining combination packets without retransmission. Therefore, TCP layer is unaware of loss events and maintains the Congestion Window (CWND) appropriately to improve the goodput performance. The processes of creating m combination packets and regenerating n original packets are called encoding and decoding, respectively.

$$C[i] = \sum_{j=1}^{n} \alpha_{ij} p_j ; \quad i = 1, 2, 3, ..., m \tag{1}$$

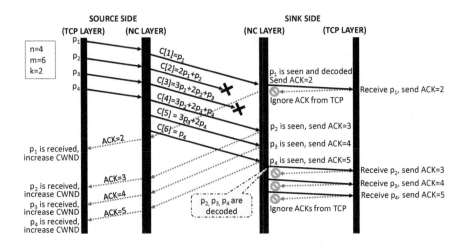

Fig. 2. NC process example

Besides executing the encoding/decoding process, NC layer allows a new interpretation of ACKs by using the degree of freedom concept and the seen/ unseen definition. ACK number in ACK packet is set to the sequence number of the oldest "unseen" packet, which can be decoded when the sink receives the additional combination packets. Example of the coding process is shown in Fig. 2. The packets p_1, p_2, p_3 and p_4 are encoded to the combination packet $C[1]$, $C[2]$, $C[3]$, $C[4]$, $C[5]$ and $C[6]$. When a new packet comes to NC layer, the combination packets will be created and transported immediately. Due to the two lost combinations, the NC layer cannot decode any combination packets until receiving the combination packet $C[6]$. For each received combination packets, NC layer returns an ACK packet whose ACK number corresponds to the smallest "unseen" packet. During the process, TCP layer totally unawares with any loss events; thus, the CWND keeps increasing and the performance is stable.

If the number of lost combination packets exceeds the recovery capability, one or some packets will be "unseen" in all received combination packets. Then TCP layer will receive duplicate ACK numbers from NC layer and retransmit the "unseen" packets to NC layer; NC layer simply forwards them to lower layer, i.e., IP layer.

Definition 1 (seeing a packet). *A node is said to have seen a packet p if it has enough information to compute a linear combination of the form $(p + q)$, where q is itself a linear combination involving only packets that arrived after p at the sender.*

2.2 Reinforced Version of TCP/NC

The TCP/NCwLRLBE was developed in [7] to solve the issues of the original TCP/NC which are how to choose the appropriate NC parameters (n and m)

and how to change them in an online fashion. TCP/NCwLRLBE considers the channel burst loss channel; thus, the link loss rate (r) and the length of continuous losses (l) are estimated from continuous observation of the packet transmission between the source and the sink. The probability of successful recoverable transmission (Pr) for each pair n and m is calculated based on the loss rate, loss burstiness conditions. Finally, n and m are selected based on Pr which is minimum value and greater than or equal 0.9.

Another problem is retransmission of the unrecoverable lost packets. In the original TCP/NC, the packets which cannot recovered by redundant combination packets in NC layer at the sink will be retransmitted by TCP layer at the source. The retransmitted packets are transported one by one in each Round Trip Time (RTT), resulting in a poor goodput performance. In response to this problem, TCP/NCwER [8] was developed in which NC layer helps retransmission in an efficient way. Multiple lost packet can be retransmitted in one RTT and the all of them are also encoded to avoid the repeated loss. In TCP/NC tunnel system, therefore, the reinforced version of TCP/NC, which is a combination of TCP/NCwLRLBE and TCP/NCwER, is used instead of the original TCP/NC.

3   Masking Packet Losses with Cascaded TCP/NC Tunnel

The TCP/NC tunnel system requires at least two special TCP/NC gateways at the border of each networks which run the specific application called tunnel handler. TCP/NC gateways can also be installed in the middle networks to increase the performance. The TCP/NC gateways at border aggregate and transfer end-to-end TCP sessions between end-hosts into a single TCP/NC session or cascaded TCP/NC sessions. TCP/NC tunnel system does not interfere the returning ACK process between the sinks and the sources; thus, this process is completely transparent with the tunnel handler. Note that, only one direction data transfer and only packet losses on this direction are considered in this paper to make validation and evaluation simple.

We investigated the benefit of single TCP/NC tunnel [6], i.e., with only two TCP/NC gateways, and showed that it could support tiny end devices which are unable to run TCP/NC on a lossy network. More specifically, in a wide range of link loss rates, the standard end-to-end TCP with single TCP/NC tunnel (Single TCP/NC tunnel) outperforms in goodput significantly compared to the standard end-to-end TCP without tunnel (E2E-TCP) and performed comparably to the end-to-end TCP/NC without tunnel (E2E-TCP/NC). On the other hand, in this paper, we focus on more a general case, i.e., multi-cascaded TCP/NC tunnel with more than two TCP/NC gateways, and will show that the standard end-to-end TCP with multi-cascaded TCP/NC tunnel can significantly outperform Single TCP/NC tunnel and E2E-TCP/NC in congestion cases on a lossy network. Moreover, we focus on the application of a large file transfer in this paper; hence, we evaluate the goodput performance only. Consideration on the end-to-end delay for other applications will be our future work.

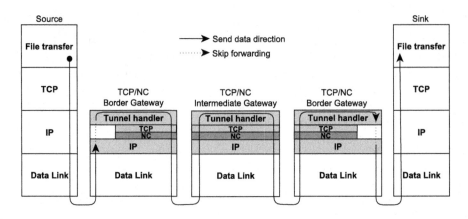

Fig. 3. Tunnel handler

3.1   The Operation of the TCP/NC Gateway

There are two type of TCP/NC gateway. Border TCP/NC gateway connects to the local networks and the intermediate TCP/NC gateway located in the middle. Each TCP/NC gateway can be equipped two interface types, an internal interface and an external interface to distinguish the packets which receive in the local network or external network. The internal interface is connected to the local network and the external interface is connected to the external network. Consequently, the intermediate TCP/NC gateway has only external interfaces.

The protocol stack and structure of TCP/NC tunneling are illustrated in Fig. 3 and the packet processing at the TCP/NC gateway is shown in Fig. 4. When an IP data packet from end-hosts arrives at internal interfaces of the border TCP/NC gateway, it is moved to the tunnel handler to become the transferred data to forward to TCP layer and NC layer. At NC layer, all the segments are encoded to the combination packets and sent to an adjacent TCP/NC gateway via a TCP/NC session. When the combination packets arrive at the external interface of the adjacent TCP/NC gateway, the decoding process is performed by NC layer to recover the lost combinations if needed. A new decoded packet is forwarded to TCP layer for reordering. Data of the packet in the correct sequence in terms of tunnel TCP session is pushed to the tunnel handler. After that, if this is an intermediate TCP/NC gateway, the tunnel handler converts the received data to the packets and sends to the next TCP/NC gateway into another TCP/NC tunnel. This process is like the process at the border TCP/NC gateway described above. Otherwise, this is a border TCP/NC gateway. The tunnel handler converts the received data to an original TCP segment to be sent to the sink based on IP address of the data. Finally, when the sink receives the packet, it returns an ACK packet with null data to the source, which is transparently forwarded through the TCP/NC tunnel because only the single directional data transfer is considered. In case of the bi-directional data transfer, the system needs to handle an ACK packet with data on an opposite directional TCP/NC tunnel. However,

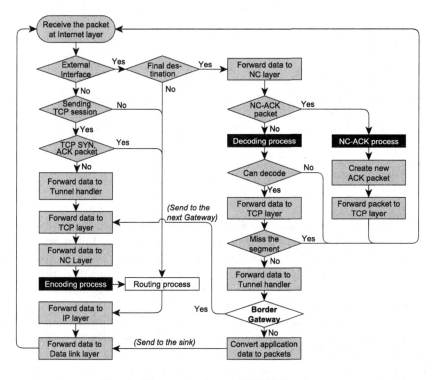

Fig. 4. The processing at TCP/NC gateway

in any case, the system can maintain the end-to-end TCP ACK semantics for the retransmission process by end-hosts responsible to packet losses that happen outside the tunnel.

3.2   Congestion Control

The TCP/NC gateway includes two different buffers in which some type of congestion can happen. Those are TCP sending buffer and link buffer. First, the TCP sending buffer of the TCP/NC gateways (e.g., GW1 and GW2 in Fig. 1) accumulates all packets from end-to-end TCP sources or the adjacent TCP/NC gateway and keeps on-the-fly packets for TCP retransmission. Therefore, when the non-ACKed packets cannot be released from the TCP sending buffer due to packet loss, the congestion can still occur, even if the total incoming throughput into GW1 and the incoming throughput into GW2 are less than the bandwidth of the inter-gateway link. Second, the incoming packets can be amplified to the combinations for redundancy by encoding process when TCP/NC gateways communicate together via TCP/NC tunnel. If the amplified data exceeds the bandwidth of the intermediate link, the congestion will happen at the link buffer of external interface of the GW1 and GW2. Besides, the link buffer of the internal interfaces of GW3 can be congested if a number of lost packets belonging to the same end-to-end TCP session are burstly recovered and forwarded.

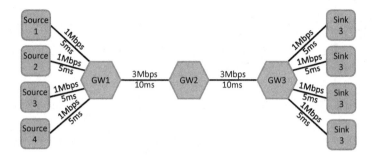

Fig. 5. The network topology

To mitigate congestions in the first case that will impact the performance, the TCP sending buffer size is set to 64 KB plus the link buffer size of the external interface. Note that, the actual congestion window size is limited up to 64 KB because the TCP window scaling option is not used in this paper. In the preliminary comparison, a very large size of the TCP sending buffer decreases the goodput of end-to-end TCP sessions.

Another issue to be considered is the TCP retransmission timeout (RTO). Retransmission timeout is unavoidable in heavily lossy network or network congestion. If the RTO timer of an end-to-end session is smaller than that of the TCP/NC session, the end-to-end retransmission of a packet happens before the TCP/NC tunnel recovers the packet by in-tunnel retransmission. In such cases, the same packets are stored in the TCP sending buffer multiple times (dead packets). Therefore, the minimum RTO timer value of each TCP/NC tunnel session should be set so that the sum of those values is less than the value that is used for each end-to-end TCP session. On the other hand, the minimum RTO value of each TCP/NC tunnel should not be too small to avoid unnecessary time out. From those conditions, the maximum number of cascaded gateways is limited based on the minimum RTO requirement of each application. To reduce the deployment cost, a small number of gateways is also important. However, the optimal number of gateways remains as future work. In the simulation below, the minimum RTO of all the TCP/NC tunnel sessions is set to 400 ms and the minimum RTO of end-to-end TCP session is set to 1000 ms.

4   Simulation and Result

The simulation of TCP/NC tunnel was accomplished using Network Simulator 3 (ns-3) [9]. The topology is a tandem network with three routers/gateways connect to at most four sources and four sinks, as shown in Fig. 5. Each edge link connects an end-host and a router has a bandwidth of 1 Mbps and a propagation delay of 5 ms. The intermediate links connecting between routers has a bandwidth of 3 Mbps and a propagation delay of 10 ms. The link buffer size is set to 100 packets, and the packet size is 1000 bytes. The size of TCP sending buffer

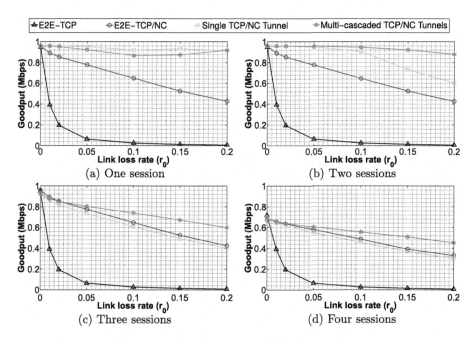

Fig. 6. The goodput comparison

in TCP/NC gateway is 164 packets. The transferred data size is 100 Mbytes. The TCP type is NewReno. The intermediate link is considered as lossy channel of random loss channel. Losses happen at GW2 and GW3 in the direction of transferred data. The link loss rate in each link is set from 0.0 to 0.3 (r_0). Therefore, the total link loss rate from GW1 to GW3 equals $r_0 + r_0 \times (1 - r_0)$. Note that, the link loss rate parameter in X-axis in the result figures is r_0. In all scenarios, each simulation was performed 10 times to obtain the average value. The simulation is run in four cases, which has one, two, three and four active sessions. The sessions are started at the same time with the same data size and run the same protocol. There are four protocols which are used to compare:

- E2E-TCP: all sources and sinks run TCP.
- E2E-TCP/NC: all sources and sinks run TCP/NC.
- Signal TCP/NC tunnel: all sources and sinks run TCP but over a single TCP/NC session by configuring two TCP/NC gateways at GW1 and GW3.
- Multi-cascaded TCP/NC tunnel: all sources and sinks run TCP but over two cascaded TCP/NC sessions between GW1 and GW2, GW2 and GW3 by configuring three TCP/NC gateways at GW1, GW2 and GW3.

The simulation result is shown in Fig. 6, the goodput performance is calculated by the average of the goodput of all sessions. Both the congestion and non-congestion cases are considered in this simulation. In all cases, the goodput of E2E-TCP/NC and two types of TCP/NC tunnel with the packet loss recovery capacity are always better than that of E2E-TCP over the lossy networks. Therefore, it is shown that implementing TCP/NC tunnel can mitigate the goodput degradation of TCP sessions on lossy networks without any change on end-host TCP.

E2E-TCP/NC and TCP/NC tunnel are different in the cause of congestion and the reaction to it. In E2E-TCP/NC, the congestion happens when total throughput of all sessions exceeds the bandwidth of intermediate link. All packet losses caused by congestion are aware and retransmitted by TCP/NC end-host through Triple-Duplicate ACK and TCP timeout mechanisms. In contrast, the congestion in TCP/NC tunnel mainly happens at TCP sending buffer, as investigated in Sect. 3.2. TCP/NC gateway is unaware of the packets lost by the TCP sending buffer congestion; such lost packets should be retransmitted from TCP end-host after TCP timeout.

The goodput of E2E-TCP/NC does not change in the case of the number of sessions less than four because the total throughput of all end-to-end sessions (from 1 Mbps link) does not exceed 3 Mbps bandwidth of intermediate link. As the link loss rate increases, the number of packet losses likely exceeds the recovery capacity of NC layer, resulting in retransmission and sending rate reduction by TCP layer. Thus, the goodput is decreased. In case of 4 sessions, the congestion happens. NC parameters are also increased to mitigate these losses.

When comparing the goodput between E2E-TCP/NC and Single TCP/NC tunnel, two situations are seen. First, the performance of TCP/NC tunnel is clearly better than that of E2E-TCP/NC in case of one or two end-to-end sessions. This is because TCP/NC tunnel can fully utilize 3 Mbps bandwidth of intermediate link to transmit and retransmit the data including redundancy for one or two end-to-end sessions. Meanwhile, E2E-TCP/NC is limited to 1 Mbps link for each end-to-end session. Second, the performance of E2E-TCP/NC is slightly better than that of Single TCP/NC tunnel in case of three or four end-to-end sessions. In this situation, the congestion on the TCP/NC tunnel happens. This leads to the goodput performance decrease of TCP/NC tunnel to nearly the same level of E2E-TCP/NC. More precisely, an encapsulation overhead (4%) of TCP/NC tunnel makes its goodput slightly lower than E2E-TCP/NC.

Next, the goodput performance of Single TCP/NC tunnel and Multi-cascaded TCP/NC tunnel are compared. In cases of one session, the goodput performance are similar in general but some interesting observations are seen. First, in one session case, the goodput of Single TCP/NC tunnel is slightly better than that of Multi-cascaded TCP/NC tunnel. Second, the goodput of Multi-cascaded TCP/NC in two sessions case is better than in one session case. Both issues mainly come from choosing the value of n. In NC process, TCP/NC gateway must receive enough n original packets to finish one encoding process (to generate m combination packets). But the TCP/NC gateway is passive in receiving n original packets because this depends on the end-host or the preceding TCP/NC gateway. In one session case, only one source end-host provides original data. In addition, when it does not receive enough ACK packets due to packet losses, the packet sending rate is decreased. Hence, the number of packets received at TCP/NC gateway becomes sometimes insufficient compared with n

and this "incoming packet suspending" happens more frequently with a larger n. In Single TCP/NC tunnel, the gateway of the source side estimates the total link loss rate r to choose n while Multi-cascaded TCP/NC chooses n based on r_0. Thus, n in Single TCP/NC tunnel is less than n in Multi-cascaded TCP/NC. Consequently, the incoming packet suspending less happens in Single TCP/NC tunnel than Multi-cascaded TCP/NC tunnel. In fact, at link loss rate (r_0) of 0.1, the estimated (n, m) of GW1 in Single TCP/NC tunnel is (25, 35) while the estimated (n, m) of GW1 and GW2 are (40, 47) and (30, 40), respectively in Multi-cascaded TCP/NC tunnel. The packets from GW1 to GW2 do not send consecutively; thus, GW2 does not estimate an accurate (n, m).

In cases of two, three, and four sessions, the goodput advantage of Multi-cascaded TCP/NC tunnel to Single TCP/NC tunnel is clearly shown. In two sessions case with two end-hosts, for example, the probability of continuously and timely receiving enough n original packets is double compared to the one session case. At each TCP/NC gateway, the incoming packet suspending will happen less and an appropriate (n, m) and thus an appropriate redundancy factor $R = m/n$ can be estimated. In such cases, Multi-cascaded TCP/NC tunnel is always better than that of E2E-TCP/NC and Single TCP/NC tunnel in goodput simply because the each link loss rate (r_0) to be responded by the former is lower than the total link loss rate (r) to be responded by the latter, which allows the former to use a smaller redundancy factor R. For example, in case of three sessions, the estimated (n, m) of E2E-TCP/NC, Single TCP/NC and Multi-cascaded TCP/NC tunnel are (25, 35), (25, 35) and (40, 47), respectively at r_0 of 0.1. In case of four sessions, the estimated (n, m) of E2E-TCP/NC, Single TCP/NC and Multi-cascaded TCP/NC tunnel are (23, 33), (25, 35) and (40, 47), respectively at r_0 of 0.1. As the loss rate increases, the goodput decreases gradually but the goodput advantage of Multi-cascaded TCP/NC tunnel increases as expected. Note that the goodputs of both Single and Cascaded TCP/NC tunnels with four sessions are significantly lower than those with three sessions because a sever congestion happens even in no link loss case.

In this paper, for simple and fair comparison between Single TCP/NC tunnel and Multi-cascaded TCP/NC tunnel, we used a homogeneous link scenario in which the same bandwidth and the same loss rate are set on the link between GW1 and GW2 and that between GW2 and GW3. Since the Multi-cascaded TCP/NC tunnel can choose suitable NC parameters for each link, it is expected to take more advantage of Multi-cascaded TCP/NC tunnel in case of more heterogeneous links. Therefore, the presented results can be considered as the baseline advantage of Multi-cascaded TCP/NC tunnel.

5   Conclusions

In this paper, the TCP/NC tunnel system was preliminarily implemented and evaluated on ns-3 simulator, which simply conveys end-to-end TCP sessions on a single TCP/NC session between two TCP/NC gateways or cascaded TCP/NC sessions involving more than two TCP/NC gateways traversing a lossy network in the middle without per-session management. The simulation results showed that by using TCP/NC tunnel, TCP end-hosts can take advantage of the recovery capacity of NC without running TCP/NC on each end-host.

In particular, we showed the benefit of multi-cascaded TCP/NC tunnel. More specifically, in congestion scenarios with a wide range of link loss rates, the end-to-end standard TCP with multi-cascaded TCP/NC tunnel can achieve a significantly higher goodput compared to both the end-to-end TCP/NC without tunnel and the end-to-end standard TCP with single TCP/NC tunnel. Those results suggest the potential of the TCP/NC tunnel in goodput performance without change at the end-hosts as well as no per-session management at the gateways.

As future work, more sophisticated sizing method of TCP sending buffer at each TCP/NC gateway and more sophisticated "concatenation" in multi-cascaded tunnel should be investigated to decrease the number of packets dropped at the TCP sending buffer and the number of the dead packets that are stored multiple times in the TCP sending buffer. In this paper, we assume enough resources of each gateway. For practical use, the implementation and deployment costs of our proposed system should be estimated carefully.

This work is partly supported by JSPS KAKENHI (16K00130) and KDDI Foundation.

References

1. Lefevre, F., Vibier, G.: Understanding TCP's behavior over wireless links. In: Proceedings of IEEE Symposium on Computers and Communications, pp. 123–130 (2000)
2. Ivanovich, M., Bickerdike, P., Li, J.: On TCP performance enhancing proxies in a wireless environment. IEEE Commun. Mag. **46**(9), 76–83 (2008)
3. Murray, D., Koziniec, T., Dixon, M.: D-Proxy: Reliability in wireless networks. In: Proceedings of 16th Asia-Pacific Conference on Communications (APCC), pp. 129–134 (2010)
4. Honda, O., Ohsaki, H., Imase, M., Murayama, J.: Understanding TCP over TCP: effects of TCP tunneling on end-to-end throughput and latency. In: Proceedings of SPIE, 6011, 9 pages (2005)
5. Sundararajan, J.K., Shah, D., Medard, M., Mitzenmacher, M., Barros, J.: Network coding meets TCP. In: Proceedings of the IEEE International Conference on Computer Communication (INFOCOM), pp. 280–288 (2009)
6. Ha, N.V., Kumazoe, K., Tsukamoto, K., Tsuru, M.: Masking lossy networks by TCP tunnel with network coding. In: Proceedings of 22nd IEEE Symposium on Computers and Communications (ISCC), 6 pages (2017)
7. Ha, N.V., Kumazoe, K., Tsuru, M.: TCP with Network Coding meets loss burstiness estimation for lossy networks. In: Proceedings of 11th International Conference on Broad-Band Wireless Computing, Communication and Applications (BWCCA), pp. 303–314 (2016)
8. Ha, N.V., Kumazoe, K., Tsuru, M.: TCP network coding with enhanced retransmission for heavy and bursty loss. IEICE Trans. Commun. **E100–B**(2), 293–303 (2017)
9. Network simulator (ns-3). https://www.nsnam.org/. Accessed 1 Mar 2016

Circuit Design

A Broadband Power Amplifier Applied in GSM/TD-SCDMA/WLAN System

Wenyuan Li[✉], Yan Ding, and Hui Luo

Institute of RF-&OE-ICs, Southeast University, Nanjing 210096, China
lwy555@seu.edu.cn, dingyan0052@hotmail.com, mianhuahui@sina.cn

Abstract. A broadband power amplifier operating from 0.8 GHz to 2.4 GHz is designed in 0.13-µm SiGe HBT process. The power amplifier adopts pseudo-differential structure, adaptive bias control technique, broadband matching network and compensated matching technique to optimize linearity, efficiency and bandwidth. The simulation results show that the maximum power gain is 25 dB, 3-dB bandwidth is 690 MHz - 2470 MHz. P1 dB, P_{sat} and PAE are better than 26 dBm, 29 dBm and 38%, respectively. The chip area of DAC occupies 2.56 mm^2 with pads.

Keywords: SiGe-HBT · Broadband power amplifier · Adaptive bias control · Pseudo-differential

1 Introduction

In past few decades, GaAs HBT (heterojunction bipolar transistor) has been a proper technology to design power amplifier(PA) which has excellent efficiency and linearity [1], but it is hard to integrate with CMOS(Complementary Metal Oxide Semiconductor) process. SiGe HBT has good linearity and efficiency and is much cheaper compared with GaAs, so power amplifiers designed by SiGe process are widely applied in a variety of applications [2, 3]. At the same time, the traditional PAs are generally designed for narrow band, which cannot be applied in various applications. So it is significant to design a multi-mode multi-frequency power amplifier.

There are various structures applying in broadband power amplifier [4], such as balance structure, power synthetic structure, distributed active transformer structure, traditional power amplifier structure. The bandwidth of the balanced amplifier is better than that of the other amplifier. However, at the relatively low frequency, the quarter wavelength transmission lines with 3 dB coupler are not easy to integrate, so we abandon balance amplifier and synthesis power structure. The distributed active transformer structure can obtain good performance, but the Q value of inductance in this process is not high, and it is difficult to guarantee consistency of time delay. So we don't choose this structure. Finally, we chose the traditional structure. Gain flatness is more important in designing broadband PA. Considering frequency features of |S21| which will fall with

Y. Koucheryavy et al. (Eds.): WWIC 2017, LNCS 10372, pp. 261–270, 2017.
DOI: 10.1007/978-3-319-61382-6_21

increasing frequency, so it is necessary to legitimately design the matching network and feedback network [5].

This paper is organized as follows. Section 2 describes the characteristics of the adopted temperature sensor. Details of the circuit implementation is discussed in Sect. 3. Section 4 shows the simulation results of the chip and compares with previous PAs.

2   Process Technology

IBM 0.13-μm SiGe HBT technology has high gain, large current density and perfect substrate thermal conductivity. Moreover, the base-emission open voltage and saturation voltage are low which lead this technology is more suitable for low voltage application. This process not only provides high-performance NPN transistor with cut-off frequency up to 200 GHz and breakdown voltage to 1.8 V, but also provides high-breakdown NPN transistor with cutoff frequency to 57 GHz and breakdown voltage (BV_{ceo}) to 3.5 V. In this paper, the width of emitter is 120 nm, length of emitter is 18um. Because of PAs will process large sign and high output power. It needs large output voltage swing, so we choose high-breakdown transistor. However, BV_{ceo} is measured when base is open-circuit. BV_{cer} usually applies to decide breakdown voltage. Here BV_{cer} is 7 V, so the supply voltage is 2.5 V.

3   The Circuit Design

In this paper, a two-stage 0.8–2.4 GHz broadband MMIC (Monolithic Microwave Integrated Circuit) PA isdesigns for GSM, TD-SCDMA, WLAN systems. This circuit is shown in Fig. 1. Broadband matching network applied in input, which will be impedance conjugate match with the input transistor of the first stage, so that power can be

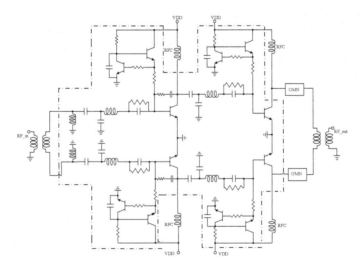

Fig. 1. Structure diagram of the power amplifier

effectively transmitted to drive stage. Negative feedback technology used in drive stage and compensate technology to increase stability, expand bandwidth and obtain good input matching [6]. A low-pass low Q multi-stage LC is adopted in output matching network to achieve optimal load and maximum output power. Considering modulation in different systems, so power stage is biased in class AB to make a good compromise between linearity and efficiency [7].

3.1 The Overall Structure of Circuit

Since there is no through silicon via (TSV) in this process, and all ground wires must connect to ground through a bonding wire. Parasitic inductance of the bonding wire has great impact on the performance of PA. So pseudo-differential structure is adopted, because of the common emitter node can act as AC virtual ground to reduce influence of bonding wires [8]. At the same time, differential structure can increase voltage swing, reduce current limit. Since bandwidth is wide, second harmonic of low-frequency will be in band, using differential structure can filter out second harmonic to a certain extent. As show in Fig. 1, the PA adopts common emitter using a two-stage pseudo-differential structure. All components are integrated on-chip except the one outside the dotted line.

The number of transistors in power stage is determined by output power, breakdown voltage and maximum current which single tube can withstand. In order to obtain enough output power, the number of transistors in output stage will be much more. The parasitic of those transistors can make output impedance become lower, which increases the difficult of designing output matching network. Finally, we chose the number of transistors of power stage and driver stage are 128 and 36 respectively in half-circuit. And current in half-circuit is 72 mA and 270 mA in driver stage and power stage respectively. Adopt a series resistor in the transistor base to increase stability, as well as in parallel with a capacitor to reduce power loss of resistors.

3.2 Adaptive Bias Control Circuit

Since PA mainly works under large signal condition, clamping feature of diode makes forward voltage and negative current signal of the power transistor is clipped when input power increases. So average current increases and average voltage decreases, which results in the loss of trans-conductance and gain reduction and phase distortion. In order to solve gain compression and phase distortion under large-signal condition, it is necessary to compensate for power transistors to make consistent trans-conductance between small signal and large signal conditions as far as possible. To improve efficiency and linearity and HBT device is a current-controlled device, so we adopt current mirror biasing circuit which can be adaptively change the bias current to raise the efficiency and linearity [9, 10].

As shown in Fig. 2, transistors Q1 and Q2 act as current mirror which provide base bias current of the power transistor Q0. The bias current is controlled by VDD and R1. There is the relationship as follows:

$$V_{BE0} + I_{R3} \cdot R3 = V_{BE1} + I_{R2} \cdot R2 \tag{1}$$

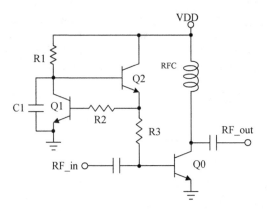

Fig. 2. Adaptive bias control circuit

The value of R2 and R3 are associated with emitter area ratio of Q0 and Q1. Assumed that $S_{Q0}: S_{Q1} = n: 1$, then $I_{B0}: I_{B1} = n: 1$, $V_{BE0} = V_{BE1} = V_{BE2} = V_{BE}$. We have equation like this:

$$\frac{R2}{R3} = \frac{I_{R3}}{I_{R2}} = \frac{I_{B0}}{I_{B2}} = n \tag{2}$$

After selected the value of R2 and R3, R1 can be calculated using this formula. I_{C0} is static bias current of the power transistor.

$$R1 \approx \frac{VDD - 2V_{BE}}{I_{C1}} = n\frac{VDD - 2V_{BE}}{I_{C0}} \tag{3}$$

The linearization mechanism is constituted by base-emitter junction of Q2 and bypass capacitor C1. C1 makes RF signal short, so that base voltage of Q2 can maintain a constant value. The impedance of linear bias decreases at RF frequencies due to function of C1. Therefore, RF signal leaks to bias part increases which makes V_{BE2} decline and I_{C2}

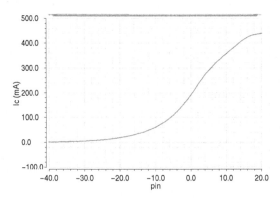

Fig. 3. Bias current changes with the input power

increases to compensate with decline of V_{BE0} and increase of I_{C0} with the increasing input power. It makes bias current dynamic varies from input power, which can increase average efficiency. Figure 3 gives the bias current changes with the input power.

3.3 Broadband Matching Network

In order to integrate the proposed PA to broadband communication systems, the bandwidth of output- and input- matching network should be wide enough. To achieve broad band, we use a broadband matching technology, including matching compensation technology and low Q multistage LC matching network. The basic idea of matching compensation at inter-stage is be mismatch at low-frequency and match at high-frequency to suppress low-frequency gain and compensate high-frequency gain which can compensate transistors' gain varies from frequency characteristics and achieve gain flatness. Multi-stage broadband matching technique is adopted in input/output matching network to achieve maximum power transform over entire frequency range. The basic principle is to limit the maximum Q value of matching network in accordance with operating frequency and bandwidth. Any impedance transformation doing inside the constant curve of Q can meet the requirement and complete impedance matching. The maximum value of Q can be calculated as follows:

$$Q = f_o / BW \tag{4}$$

Here f_o is center frequency, $f_o^2 = f_H \times f_L$, BW is bandwidth. The load matching is applied in output and the optimum load impedance is obtained from load-pull test. Since the band is wide, we need to simulate the optimum load at multiple frequency points, and the best load at each frequency will be different. But the impedance value changes slightly, so we choose average value as Z_{opt}. Then design a matching network between 50Ω and Z_{opt} inside the constant Q contour [11]. Here the optimum load shows in Fig. 4 is about 10.5 + j * 1.25. Figure 5 shows impendence transformation and the

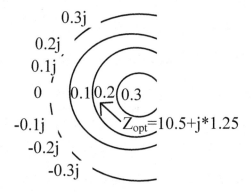

Fig. 4. Optimum load

matching network designed in this method. Figure 6 shows the impedance value after transformation.

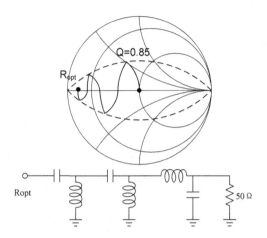

Fig. 5. Multi-stage broadband matching

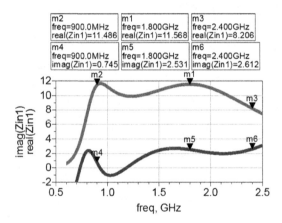

Fig. 6. The impedance after transformation

4 Layout and Simulation Results

PA will flow large current and is achieved by many cell transistors. It is significant to carefully design the arrangement of transistors. To guarantee power with same phase, the arrangement of transistors is tree structure. Figure 7 is the layout of the PA. The chip size is 1.56 mm × 1.70 mm.

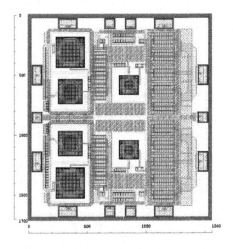

Fig. 7. The layout of power amplifier

The post-simulation shows the S parameter as Fig. 8. The maximum gain is 25.6 dB at 781.6 MHz, 3 dB bandwidth is 690 MHz to 2470 MHz. Input VSWR (Voltage Standing Wave Ratio) is less than 2.2:1 as shown in Fig. 9. The 1 dB compression point (P1 dB)at 0.9 GHz, 1.9 GHz and 2.4 GHz are shown as Figs. 10, 11 and 12. P1 dB are 26.38 dBm, 26.49 dBm, 26 dBm respectively. Saturation output power ($P_{out,sat}$) is greater than 29 dBm with the power added efficiency (PAE) better than 38%. Its bandwidth, Saturation output power and power added efficiencymeets general requirement for GSM/TD-SCDMA/WLANsystem, so the proposed PA can be integrated to corresponding electronic systems.

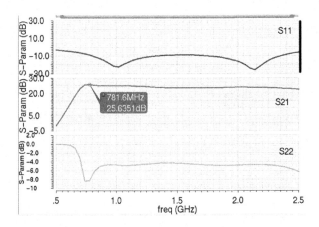

Fig. 8. S parameter

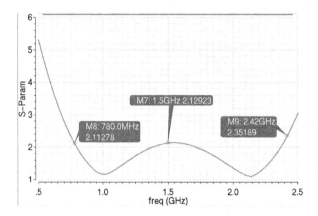

Fig. 9. Input VSWR

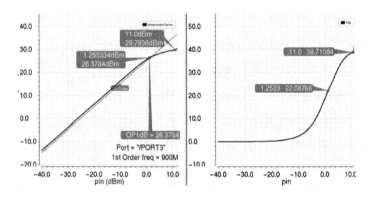

Fig. 10. P1 dB/Pout and PAE@0.9 GHz

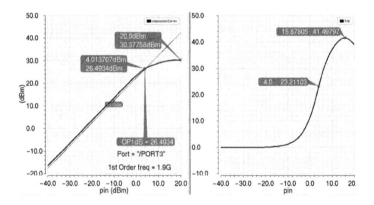

Fig. 11. P1 dB/Pout and PAE@1.9 GHz

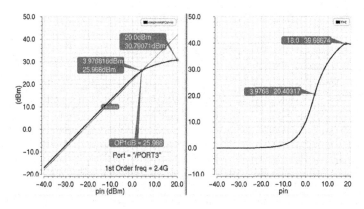

Fig. 12. P1 dB/Pout and PAE@2.4 GHz

The accomplished performance is compared with the earlier in Table 1.

Table 1. state-of-the-art of PA performance

Ref	Technology	Freq (GHz)	Gain (dB)	P1 dB (dBm)	PAE %	Size (mm²)
[12]	CMOS	3~7	12	7.21	38.5	0.75
[13]	SiGe-HBT	0.7–1.9	20	25	23	3.15
[14]	GaAs-HBT	1.96	30	28	22	NA
This work	SiGe- HBT	0.8–2.4	25.6	26	38	2.65

5 Conclusion

A 0.8-2.4 GHz cascade pseudo-differential architecture broadband power amplifier is demonstrated in this paper. Compensated matching, broadband matching, and adaptive bias control technique are employed to optimize linearity, efficiency and bandwidth. The simulation results of S-parameter and power gain show excellent feature. P1 dB and PAE at Saturated output power are better than 26 dBm and 38%.

Acknowledgements. We are sincerely thankful for the support from the Project Funded by the Priority Academic Program Development of Jiangsu Higher Education Institutions (PAPD, No. 1104007003), Natural Science Foundation of China (No. 61471119), Topnotch Academic Programs Project of Jiangsu Higher Education Institutions (TAPP) PPZY2015A035 and Academic Degree Postgraduate Innovation Project of Jiangsu Regular University (SJLX16_0085).

References

1. Bacon, P., Mohan, C., Fryklund, D., Zampardi, P.: Semiconductor trends in wireless handsets. Microwave J. **46**(6), 22–56 (2005)
2. Kim, J.H., Kim, K.Y., Park Y.H., Chung, Y.K., Park, C.S.: A 2.4 GHz SiGe bipolar power amplifier with integrated diode linearizer for WLAN IEEE 802.11b/g applications. In: Radio and Wireless Symposium, pp. 267–270. IEEE (2006)
3. Zhao, J., Wolf, R., Ellinger, F.: A SiGe LTE power amplifier with capacitive tuning for size-reduction of biasing inductor. In: 9th Conference on Ph.D. Research in Microelectronics and Electronics (PRIME), pp. 313–316 (2013)
4. Zhang, H., Gao, H., Li, G.P.: Broad-band power amplifier with a novel tunable output matching network. IEEE Trans. Microw. Theory Tech. **53**(11), 3606–3614 (2005)
5. Nellis, K., Zampardi, P.J.: A comparison of linear handset power amplifiers in different bipolar technologies. IEEE J. Solid-State Circuits **39**(10), 1746–1754 (2004)
6. Tajima, J., Yamao, Y., Sugeta, T., Hirayama, M.: GaAs monolithic low-power amplifiers with RC parallel feedback (short paper). IEEE Trans. Microw. Theory Tech. **32**(5), 542–544 (1984)
7. Cripps, S.: RF power amplifiers for wireless communication. Circuit Design RF Transceivers **20**(1), 145–184 (1999)
8. Bakalski, W., Simburger, W., Thuringer, R., Vasylyev, A.: A fully integrated 5.3-GHz 2.4-V 0.3-W SiGe bipolar power amplifier with 50-Ω output. IEEE J. Solid-State Circuits **39**(7), 1006–1014 (2004)
9. Kim, J.H., Kim, J.H., Noh, Y.S., Park C.S.: High linear HBT MMIC power amplifier with partial RF coupling to bias circuit for W-CDMA portable application. In: International Conference on Microwave and Millimeter Wave Technology, pp. 809–812 (2002)
10. Hu, Q.Z., Liu, Z.H., Yan, L., Zhou, W.: A SiGe power amplifier with power detector and VSWR protection for TD-SCDMA application. In: Proceedings of the International Conference Mixed Design of Integrated Circuits and System, pp. 214–217 (2006)
11. Chen, Y.J.E., Yang, L.Y., Yeh, W.C.: An integrated wideband power amplifier for cognitive radio. IEEE Trans. Microw. Theory Tech. **55**(10), 2053–2058 (2008)
12. Gadallah, A., Allam, A., Mosalam, H., Abdel-Rahman, A.B., Jia, H., Pokharel, R.K.: A high efficiency 3~7 GHz class AB CMOS power amplifier for WBAN applications. In: International Symposium on Radio-Frequency Integration Technology, pp. 163–165. IEEE (2015)
13. Li, W., Zhang, Q.: A 0.7–1.9 GHz broadband pseudo-differential power amplifier using 0.13-μm SiGe HBT technology. In: International Conference on Microwave and Millimeter Wave Technology, pp. 1–4 (2012)
14. Ledezma, L.M., Vysyaraju, R.V.: High efficiency quadrature HBT power amplifier optimized for use with digital predistortion. In: 16th Annual Wireless and Microwave Technology Conference, pp. 1–3. IEEE (2015)

IBIS-AMI Based PAM4 Signaling
and FEC Technique for 25 Gb/s Serial Link

Yongzheng Zhan, Qingsheng Hu[⊠], and Yinhang Zhang

Institute of RF- & OE-ICs, Southeast University, Nanjing 210096, China
sdzyz1989@163.com, qshu@seu.edu.cn

Abstract. This paper investigates Input/Output Buffer Information Specification Algorithmic Model Interface (IBIS-AMI) model extension for 25 Gb/s PAM4 (4-level Pulse Amplitude Modulation) serial link to improve the development efficiency. By using the ADS (Advanced Design System) Channel Simulator, the effects of device package, jitter and crosstalk on the actual performance are studied at first. Then, for forward error correction (FEC) technique, the bit error rate (BER) performance and the bathtub curves are analyzed in detail. Simulation results show that device package, jitter and crosstalk can make the link performance worse. And much better performance can be obtained by using the combination of equalization and FEC techniques compared with using the equalization technique separately.

Keywords: IBIS-AMI model · PAM4 · FEC · Reed-Solomon (RS) code · Bit error rate (BER)

1 Introduction

To meet the increasing demand of data rate and overcome the bandwidth limitation of channel, PAM4 (4-level Pulse Amplitude Modulation) signaling [1, 2], as an alternative of NRZ (non-return-to-zero), has drawn more and more attention in high-speed serial link systems, especially for backplane applications. For example, it has been adopted for some aspects of the 400 Gb/s Ethernet standard [3]. However, the high complexity of PAM4 transceiver contributes to the low development efficiency, as well as the increasing simulation time. Furthermore, this may pose a challenge to the whole system simulation since system engineers may not have a lot of experience with PAM4 link design.

An effective approach to shorten the developing time of PAM4 serial link system is to adopt Input/Output Buffer Information Specification Algorithmic Model Interface (IBIS-AMI) [4, 5], which allows an encapsulated transceiver model by defining a common serial model interface. Furthermore, AMI simulation allows designers to run millions of bits to predict a link performance accurately at low BER level since an efficient convolution method which can be used to calculate signal waveforms at channel output is employed in it.

This paper investigates the IBIS-AMI model extension for PAM4 serial link. Not only the device package [6] but also the jitter and crosstalk [7] are considered in the model to evaluate their impacts on the actual performance. Furthermore, Forward Error

© IFIP International Federation for Information Processing 2017
Published by Springer International Publishing AG 2017. All Rights Reserved
Y. Koucheryavy et al. (Eds.): WWIC 2017, LNCS 10372, pp. 271–281, 2017.
DOI: 10.1007/978-3-319-61382-6_22

Correction (FEC) technique, which is commonly combined with certain advanced equalization techniques in the serial link, is also introduced to improve the bit error rate (BER) performance.

The rest of the paper is organized as follows. In Sect. 2, we construct the IBIS-AMI model for PAM4 link. Section 3 introduces FEC technique to improve BER performance. In Sect. 4, we present the simulation parameter and platform for PAM4 link. Section 5 analyzes the performance of our proposed link. Finally, we draw conclusions and discuss future work in Sect. 6.

2   IBIS-AMI Modeling for PAM4 Link

Figure 1 presents a simplified end-to-end serial link system. It can be seen that a pseudo random binary sequence (PRBS) is first modulated into PAM4 signaling by a modulator (MOD). Then, a feed forward equalizer (FFE) is adopted to compensate the high frequency loss of channel at the transmitter side (Tx). For the receiver (Rx), decision feedback equalizer (DFE) is employed to equalize the receive signal with inter-symbol interference (ISI), outputting equalized data into a de-modulator (DeMOD). Although some equalization techniques have been applied to remove ISI, it is hard to achieve the desired BER, *e.g.* 10^{-12} or below. To improve the BER performance, some FEC techniques such as Reed-Solomon (RS) or BCH code can also be employed.

Fig. 1. An end-to-end serial link system

In order to accurately simulate the serial link, IBIS and AMI should be modeled for Tx and Rx separately as illustrated in Fig. 2, where IBIS defines termination electrical characteristics for Tx output and Rx input buffers, while AMI concerns the algorithm model employed in Tx and RX, such as modulation, FFE and DFE.

Fig. 2. IBIS-AMI modeling of link system

2.1   IBIS for Tx and Rx

Generally, IBIS model mainly concerns input/output buffer electrical characteristics and package information. For IBIS buffer there are three data tables: (*i*) Voltage-Time (V-T) tables for transition speed, (*ii*) Current-Voltage (I-V) tables for nonlinear termination resistance and PowerClamp/GroundClamp for clamping feature, (*iii*) C_comp section for lumped capacitance.

As shown in Fig. 3, we can see that RisingRamp/FallingRamp, Pullup/Pulldown, PowerClamp/GroundClamp and C_comp are considered for Tx buffer, while PowerClamp/GroundClamp and C_comp are included for Rx buffer. It can also be observed that device package is modeled as a network of resistance (R), inductance (L) and capacitance (C).

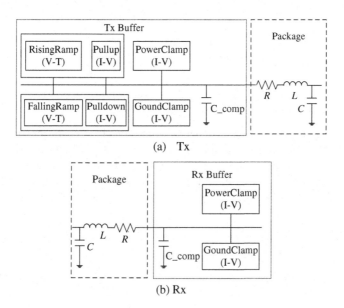

Fig. 3. IBIS buffer and package

2.2 AMI Parameter and Simulation Mode

Different from IBIS, AMI mainly concerns the algorithm models in the transceiver. Therefore apart from a section Reserved_Parameter which is used to describe some pre-defined parameters, another section Model_Specific for user-defined parameters is also included in Tx/Rx AMI parameter. Figure 4 only indicates Tx AMI parameter list. The Boolean values of Init_Returns_Impulse and GetWave_Exists in the Reserved_ Parameter depend on whether the algorithm model is linear time-invariable (LTI) or not. For example, for Tx AMI, the values of these two parameters are true and false respectively since FFE is a linear element, while they are false and true for Rx AMI because DFE is a nonlinear one.

Meanwhile, several optional parameters in the Reserved_Parameter such as Tx_Jitter and Tx_DCD are also provided to model various Tx jitters. Use_Init_Output and Max_Init_Aggressors are used to define the AMI_Getwave input and the maximum number of aggressor, respectively.

In the second section, *i.e.* Model_Specific, the items FFE coefficients and PAM4 define the tap coefficients of FFE and modulation scheme, respectively.

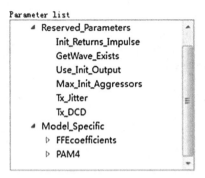

Fig. 4. Tx AMI parameter list

The AMI simulation mode also depends on the algorithm characteristic of FFE and DFE. See Table 1, when the algorithm is LTI, both statistical and bit-by-bit are supported in the function of AMI_Init. Otherwise, only bit-by-bit mode is supported by AMI_GetWave. In the latter case, AMI_Init is only used to set up the parameters and allocate memory for AMI_GetWave. As a result, bit-by-bit simulation mode is chosen in ADS Channel Simulator.

Table 1. IBIS-AMI simulation mode

Algorithm characteristic	Init_Returns_Impulse	GetWave_Exists	Simulation mode	Interface function
LTI	True	False	Statistical & Bit-by-Bit	AMI_Init
non-LTI	False	True	Bit-by-Bit	AMI_Init and AMI_GetWave

2.3   AMI Model Extension for PAM4 Signaling

Let's consider Tx first. A 4-tap FFE is used which can be modeled as a four-tap finite impulse response (FIR) filter in AMI_Init function, *i.e.*:

$$y[n] = \sum_{i=0}^{M-1} w_i x[n - iN] \tag{1}$$

where $x[n]$ and $y[n]$ denote input and output sample data, respectively, w_i and M denote tap coefficients and tap number, respectively. N is the number of samples per bit, which is passed through the SamplesPerBit in the AMI_Init function.

Default NRZ stimulus uses $[-1/2 \mid 1/2]$ to represent logic low and high, respectively. For PAM4, however, four stimulus levels are needed. So some current IBIS-AMI standards need to be extended for PAM4 signaling. We use $[-0.5 \mid -0.5/3 \mid 0.5/3 \mid 0.5]$ to represent logic levels $-3, -1, 1$ and 3, respectively. Thus, by converting

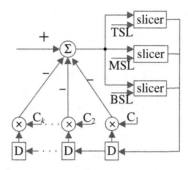

Fig. 5. Block diagram of PAM4 DFE

the original NRZ bit pattern to a PAM4 one, the simulator can generate a stimulus square wave according to the above mapping scheme.

Another modification is about Rx DFE slicer levels [8, 9]. We need to add TSL, MSL and BSL (top/middle/bottom slicer level) to the reserved parameter list. Figure 5 shows the block diagram of a PAM4 DFE with TSL, MSL and BSL. For simplicity, MSL can be fixed at 0 and TSL = −BSL = 0.5 * 2/3 = 1/3. As mentioned earlier, when considering its nonlinearity, Rx AMI is required to return TSL and tap coefficients (C_i) through AMI_Parameter_Out string for each AMI_GetWave call.

3 Forward Error Correction (FEC)

As required bandwidth increase, the increasing link rate poses a challenge for the serial interface communication [10]. Therefore, data rate 400 Gb/s [11] attracts the attention of some groups for next-generation Ethernet development, such as IEEE and OIF. In the research process of 400 GbE, a number of FEC options have been proposed and discussed with the aim of achieving the desired BER performance. See Table 2, BCH (2858, 2570) can provide a coding gain of 3.8 dB at BER of 10^{-12}, while the coding gain for RS (528, 514), RS (536, 514) and RS (544, 514) over GF (2^{10}) are 5.28 dB, 5.97 dB and 6.39 dB at 10^{-13} BER, respectively. Obviously, RS codes are more attractive for their high coding gains compared with BCH code.

Table 2. Coding gain comparisons

FEC scheme	Coding gain (dB)	Data rate (Gb/s)	Target
BCH (2858, 2570)	3.8	111.875	400 GbE@10^{-12} [12]
RS (528, 514)	5.28	25.78	400 GbE@10^{-13} [13]
RS (536, 514)	5.97	26.17	
RS (544, 514)	6.39	26.56	

In this paper three RS codes are employed for high-speed serial link to evaluate the improvement in BER performance.

4 System Simulation

4.1 Simulation Parameters

In this paper, two backplane channels A and B are simulated. Figure 6 depicts the frequency response of the two channels and their combinations with a package model in which the equivalent R, L and C value at the Nyquist frequency is 40 mΩ/1.1 nH/0.7 pF, respectively. In addition, Fig. 6 also shows far end crosstalk (FXET) and next end crosstalk (NEXT) for channel B. We find that with the frequency increasing, the crosstalk especially the NXET interference has a more remarkable influence on the transmission link. Table 3 lists their insertion loss (IL) for PAM4 at 25 Gb/s and 50 Gb/s.

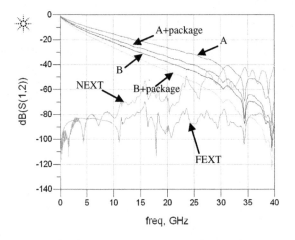

Fig. 6. Frequency responses of channel

Table 3. Channel insertion loss

Channel	Insertion loss (dB)	
	6.25 GHz	12.5 GHz
A	10.98	18.2
B	15.7	26.1
A + package	14	23
B + package	18.7	31

Table 4 summarizes the simulation parameters. The symbol rate and the peak-to-peak magnitude of NRZ, as the launching signal, are 12.5 Gbaud and 1 V, respectively. Then, the modulation scheme [2/3, 0, 1/3] can realize the signal conversion. For the device package and the crosstalk, they are given in the form of S-parameter. As for the jitter, the Tx duty cycle distortion (DCD) and random jitter (RJ) and the Rx RJ are 0.04 UI, 0.01 UI, 0.01 UI, respectively.

Table 4. Simulation parameter

Data pattern	PRBS31
Symbol rate	12.5 Gbaud
Tx launch	1 V diff p2p (0.5 V diff pk)
Modulation scheme	[2/3, 0, 1/3]
Tx/Rx package	Pkg35mm_T21mm115ohmHiXtalkBGAHiXtalk.s8p
Tx DCD	0.04 UI
Tx RJ	0.01 UI
Rx RJ	0.01 UI
NEXT	TEC_Whisper42p8in_Meg6_NEXT_B5B6_C8C9.s4p
FEXT	TEC_Whisper42p8in_Meg6_FEXT_B5B6_C8C9.s4p

4.2 PAM4 Simulation Platform

An IBIS-AMI serial link simulation platform based on ADS is established which contains the transmission channel and crosstalk channel, shown as Fig. 7. In the transmitter, Tx_AMI module generates a PRBS31, and maps the signal into PAM4 pattern, and then sends it to FFE. Following the Tx_AMI module is the package. In Rx_AMI, attenuated signal is received and equalized with DFE. An eye probe is attached to the Rx_AMI component to display the eye diagram as an oscilloscope. Various jitters can also be added by AMI reserved parameter Tx_Jitter and Rx_Jitter.

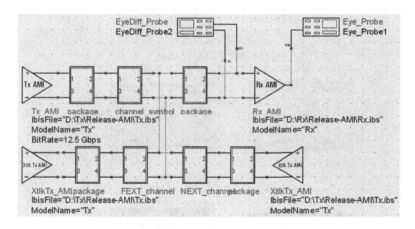

Fig. 7. IBIS-AMI simulation platform

5 Results Analysis

5.1 Eye Diagrams

Figure 8 gives the simulation results of eye diagram, in which Fig. 8(a)–(d) represent the case of channel B, channel B with package, channel B with package and jitter, and channel B with package, jitter and crosstalk, respectively. We can see that when only channel loss is considered, the output eye diagram is the best since ISI introduced by channel is well mitigated by equalization. After DFE, the horizontal and vertical opening of eye diagram can be up to 45.4 mV and 37.96 ps.

When only device packages are added into the link, the horizontal opening and the vertical opening reduce to 36 mV and 36.4 ps in the receiver. It is because that device package can aggravate ISI, making the eye worse. When jitter is also injected into the link, the eye becomes smaller further with a horizontal and vertical opening of 32.8 mV and 34.6 ps, respectively. Finally, when all these impairments are present, more ISI is

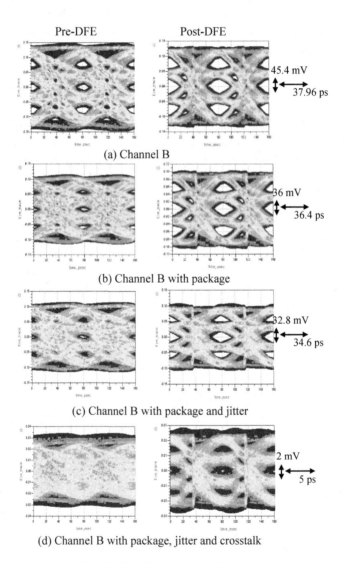

(a) Channel B

(b) Channel B with package

(c) Channel B with package and jitter

(d) Channel B with package, jitter and crosstalk

Fig. 8. Eye diagram simulation results

introduced, making the eye almost closed. In this case only FFE and DFE cannot satisfy the BER requirement and FEC can be applied to improve the link performance.

5.2   BER Performance

Figure 9 shows BER versus SNR (signal-to-noise ratio) for RS codes (528, 514, 7), (536, 514, 11) and (544, 514, 15). The y-axis of Figs. 9, 10 and 11 in the 5.3 section is base 10 logarithmic. From Fig. 9, we learn that RS code can significantly lower the output BER at the same SNR, namely achieving a better performance in the receiver. We can also see that RS codes with error correcting capability $t = 7, 11, 15$ can provide approximately 6 dB, 6.75 dB, 7.25 dB coding gain at the BER of 10^{-15}, respectively. This explains that RS codes with larger t can always obtain larger coding gain than those with smaller t.

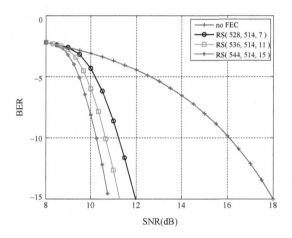

Fig. 9. BER performance

5.3   Bathtub Curves

Based on the previous analysis, the equalizer and FEC techniques are employed to evaluate the link performance through the bathtub curve. Shown as Fig. 10 and Fig. 11, their voltage bathtub curve and timing bathtub curve with three RS codes are plotted for channel A and B respectively. It is obvious that the better performance margin can be achieved by RS code with larger t. This explains the combination of the equalization technique and RS code performs better than the equalization technique separately.

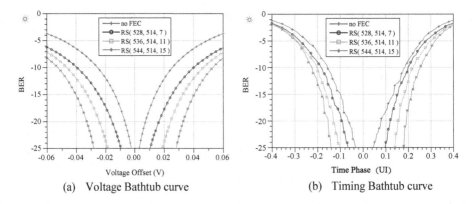

(a)   Voltage Bathtub curve   (b)   Timing Bathtub curve

Fig. 10. Bathtub curves for channel A

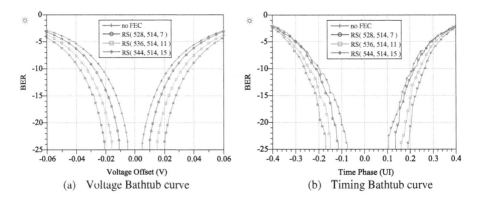

(a)   Voltage Bathtub curve   (b)   Timing Bathtub curve

Fig. 11. Bathtub curves for channel B

6   Conclusions and Future Work

In this paper, the simulation link of a 25 Gb/s PAM4 link system over backplane channel is constructed with IBIS-AMI model. By using the ADS Channel Simulator, the effects of device package, jitter and crosstalk on the actual performance are studied, which is shown to continually decrease the eye opening. Meanwhile, the combination of the equalization and FEC techniques are studied with the bathtub curve. As expected, their combination performs better than the equalization technique separately.

In the future, a trade-off between complicated equalization and FEC coding will be studied for the optimization of the link performance. Moreover, transcoding [14] will be considered to reduce total overhead, as well as discuss the trade-off between the overclocking and the link performance margin. This can provide a design guide on improving signal reliability for 400 GbE.

References

1. Dikhaminjia, N., He, J.,Tsiklauri, M., et al.: PAM4 signaling considerations for high-speed serial links. In: IEEE International Symposium on Electromagnetic Compatibility (EMC), pp. 906–910 (2016)
2. Dikhaminjia, N., He, J., Hernandez, E., Tsiklauri, M.: High-speed serial link challenges using multi-level signaling. In: IEEE 24th Electrical Performance of Electronic Packaging and Systems (EPEPS), pp. 57–60 (2015)
3. Chiang, P.-C., Hung, H.-W., Chu, H.-Y.: 60 Gb/s NRZ and PAM4 transmitters for 400 GbE in 65 nm CMOS. In: IEEE International Solid-State Circuits Conference Digest of Technical Papers (ISSCC), pp. 42–43 (2014)
4. John, Y., Arash, Z.-Y.: IBIS-AMI modelling of high-speed memory interfaces. In: IEEE 24th Electrical Performance of Electronic Packaging and Systems (EPEPS), pp. 73–75 (2015)
5. I/O Buffer Information Specification (IBIS), Version 6.0, copy right IBIS Open Forum 2013, September 2013
6. Musah, T., Jaussi, J., Balamurugan, G., Hyvonen, S.: A 4–32 Gb/s bidirectional link with 3-Tap FFE/6-Tap DFE and collaborative CDR in 22 nm CMOS. IEEE J. Solid State Circuits 49(12), 3079–3090 (2014)
7. Chastang, C., Gautier, C., Amedeo, A., et al.: Crosstalk analysis of multigigabit links on high density interconnects PCB using IBIS AMI models. In: IEEE Electrical Design of Advanced Packaging and Systems Symposium (EDAPS), pp. 223–226 (2012)
8. Elhadidy, O., Roshan-Zamir, A., Yang, H.-W., et al.: A 32 Gb/s 0.55 mW/Gbps PAM4 1-FIR 2-IIR tap DFE receiver in 65-nm CMOS. In: Symposium on VLSI Circuits (VLSI Circuits), pp. C224–C225 (2015)
9. Lee, J., Chiang, P.C., Peng, P.J., Chen, L.Y.: Design of 56 Gb/s NRZ and PAM4 SerDes transceivers in CMOS technologies. IEEE J. Solid State Circuits 50(9), 1–13 (2015)
10. Groumas, P., Katopodis, V., Choi, J.H., Bach, H.G.: Multi-100 GbE and 400 GbE interfaces for intra-data center networks based on arrayed transceivers with serial 100 Gb/s operation. J. Lightwave Technol. 33(4), 943–954 (2015)
11. IEEE P802.3bs Task: IEEE 802.3 400 Gbps Ethernet (400 GbE) study group materials (2014). http://www.ieee802.org/3/bs/
12. Cole C: Optical specifications of SMF PMDs study (2014). http://www.ieee802.org/3/bs/public/14_09/cole_3bs_02a_0914.pdf
13. Gustlin, M., et al.: Investigation on technical feasibility of stronger RS FEC for 400 GbE (2015). http://grouper.ieee.org/groups/802/3/bs/public/15_01/wang_x_3bs_01a_0115.pdf
14. Teshima, M., Kobayashi, S., Yamamoto, T., Ishida, O.: Bit-Error-Tolerant (512 * N)B/(513 * N + 1)B Code for 40 Gb/s and 100 Gb/s Ethernet Transport. In: IEEE INFOCOM Workshops, pp. 1–6 (2008)

Spur-Free MASH DDSM
with Eliminable Dither

Yilong Liao[⊠] and Xiangning Fan

School of Information Science and Engineering, Institute of RF & OE-ICs,
Southeast University, Nanjing, China
{yilongliao,xnfan}@seu.edu.cn

Abstract. This paper presents a new dither adding method for multistage-noise-shaping (MASH) digital delta-sigma modulator (DDSM), to reduce the output spurious tones. In this method, the additive dither signal is added to two different nodes of any preceding stage of the MASH DDSM, without using dither shaping filter. Then, those dither signals are sent to the error cancellation logic (ECL), where they are eliminated by each other, avoiding appearing in the output spectrum. Simulation results show that, for the MASH DDSM, the new dither adding method can guarantee a spur-free spectrum for all digital constant inputs without raising the noise floor.

Keywords: Digital delta-sigma modulator (DDSM) · Dither · Eliminable · Multistage-noise-shaping (MASH) · Spur-free

1 Introduction

In order to obtain a good performance and spectral purity, digital delta-sigma modulator (DDSM) is widely used in modern wireless communication subsystems, such as fractional-N frequency synthesizers and digital to analogue converters [1, 2]. Functionally, a DDSM oversamples a discrete-time discrete-amplitude input signal and produces a lower-resolution and noise-shaped output [3]. In general, there are two types of DDSM, which are multistage-noise-shaping (MASH) DDSM and single loop DDSM. However, due to the inherent stability, the MASH structure is much preferred in most applications [4].

In the case of constant input, MASH DDSM is a deterministic finite state machine (FSM), whose output is periodic [5]. When the cycle length is not long enough, its output spectrum shows high-power spurious tones, which will deteriorate the performance of the whole communication system.

In order to reduce the spurious tones, deterministic technique and stochastic technique were both presented in the past decades to extend the cycle length effectively.

For the deterministic technique, it can inherently extend the output cycle length of MASH DDSM. The most commonly used methods include setting the odd initial conditions [6, 7], using prime modulus quantizer [8, 9], and some other modified structures, such as HK-MASH [10] and SP-MASH [11].

© IFIP International Federation for Information Processing 2017
Published by Springer International Publishing AG 2017. All Rights Reserved
Y. Koucheryavy et al. (Eds.): WWIC 2017, LNCS 10372, pp. 282–291, 2017.
DOI: 10.1007/978-3-319-61382-6_23

As to the stochastic technique, it is realized by injecting an additive random dither signal to DDSM to break up the periodic output cycles [12, 13]. In the traditional dither adding method, the additive dither signal added to the circuit cannot be eliminated and the order of dither shaping filter cannot go beyond $(l - 2)$ for a conventional l-th-order MASH DDSM [13]. Thus, though this technique reduces high-power spurious tones effectively, the noise floor of the output spectrum is also raised inevitably. Then, a modified second-order error feedback modulator (EFM2) was introduced in [3, 14]. Compared with the conventional first-order error feedback modulator (EFM1), it contains an extra delay in the feedback loop, as shown in Fig. 1. Using this modified structure, a MASH 1-2-2 DDSM was constructed in [14], which can increase the order of the dither shaping filter to that of the modulator, without causing spurious tones in the spectrum. Therefore, adopting the EFM2 can alleviate the noise raising problem to some extent. However, as pointed out in [3], compared with the conventional MASH 1-1-1 DDSM without EFM2, the output spectrum power of MASH 1-2-2 DDSM is also raised about 12 dB in the lower frequency band.

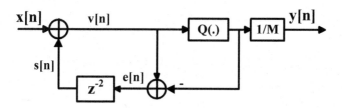

Fig. 1. Block diagram of modified second-order error feedback modulator (EFM2)

In this paper, we consider the stochastic technique and propose a new dither adding method for MASH DDSM to produce a spur-free spectrum, without raising the shaped quantization noise power in the output spectrum.

This paper is organized as follows. In Sect. 2, we review and analyse the structure of the previous dithered MASH DDSM briefly. Section 3 introduces the new method of the dither adding. Simulation results of MASH DDSM with the new dither adding method are presented in Sect. 4. At last, we summarise the whole work in Sect. 5.

2   Previous Dithered MASH DDSM

In a MASH DDSM, the most basic block is the first-order error feedback modulator, which quantises the summation of input and the quantization error of preceding moment to yield the output, as shown in Fig. 2. Mathematically, we write the quantization function as

$$y[n] = \frac{1}{M} Q(v[n]) = \begin{cases} 1, v[n] \geq M \\ 0, v[n] < M \end{cases}, \tag{1}$$

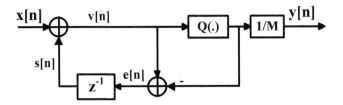

Fig. 2. Block diagram of a first-order error feedback modulator (EFM1)

where $v[n]$ is the input to the quantizer and M is the quantization interval. When the input word length is set as n_0, the corresponding quantization interval is $M = 2^{n_0}$.

Cascading l EFM1 blocks and combining their outputs to the error cancellation logic (ECL) circuit, we can construct an l-th-order MASH DDSM, as presented in Fig. 3. The role of ECL is to eliminate the intermedia stage noise and yields the final output. In the z-domain, the transfer function of l-th-order MASH DDSM can be expressed as

$$Y(z) = \frac{X(z)}{M} - \frac{E_l(z)}{M}(1 - z^{-1})^l, \tag{2}$$

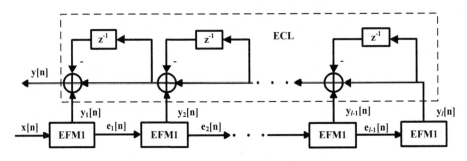

Fig. 3. Block diagram of an l-th-order MASH DDSM

Where $X(z)$, $Y(z)$, and $E_l(z)$ represent the input signal, output signal, and the quantization error of the last stage in the z-domain, respectively. From (2), we can see that, since the quantization error of the intermedia stages are eliminated by ECL, only the input signal with an all-pass filter and the quantization error of the last stage with an l-th-order high-pass filter are remained. The filtering functions related to the input signal and the quantization error are called signal transfer function (STF) and noise transfer function (NTF), respectively. In (2), they are $1/M$ and $(1 - z^{-1})^l/M$, respectively.

When the filtered dither is added, as shown in Fig. 4, the output can be derived as

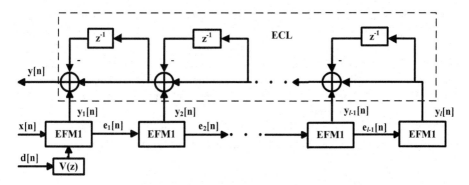

Fig. 4. Block diagram of MASH DDSM with additive filtered dither

$$Y(z) = \frac{X(z)}{M} - \frac{E_l(z)}{M} \left(1 - z^{-1}\right)^l + \frac{D(z)}{M} V(z), \tag{3}$$

where $V(z)$ is normally in the form of $(1 - z^{-1})^{l_d}$, with $l_d \leq (l - 2)$ [13], and $D(z)$ is the dither signal in the z-domain.

In order to illustrate the effectiveness of the stochastic technique, the output PSD plots of the MASH 1-1-1 DDSM with first-order shaped dither and the un-dithered MASH 1-1-1 DDSM are presented in Fig. 5. The simulation conditions are input word length $n_0 = 9$, quantization interval $M = 2^9$ and input $x[n] = M/2$.

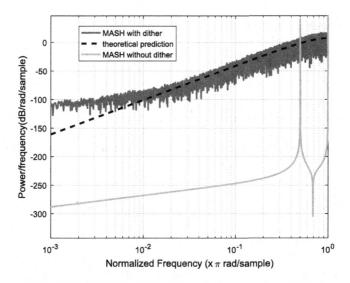

Fig. 5. Output PSD of 9-bit MASH 1-1-1 DDSM with first-order shaped dither and un-dithered MASH 1-1-1 DDSM, with constant input 256

Figure 5 shows that, for an un-dithered MASH 1-1-1 DDSM, when the input is $M/2$, its output cycle length is very small and the output spectrum has only two high-power spurious tones. However, when it comes to the MASH 1-1-1 DDSM with first-order shaped dither, a smooth output spectrum is obtained and no obvious spurious tones can be observed. Note that, compared with the theoretical prediction result of the output spectrum, we can find the MASH 1-1-1 DDSM with first-order shaped dither raised the noise floor inevitably.

The MASH 1-2-2 DDSM presented in [14] is redrawn in Fig. 6. With the same reasoning for the traditional MASH DDSM, its transfer function can be derived as

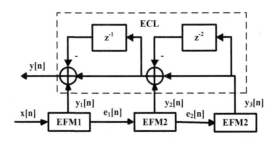

Fig. 6. Block diagram of MASH 1-2-2 DDSM

$$Y(z) = \frac{X(z)}{M} - \frac{E_3(z)}{M}\left(1 - z^{-2}\right)^2\left(1 - z^{-1}\right). \tag{4}$$

Similarly, with the shaped dither, the transfer function becomes

$$Y(z) = \frac{X(z)}{M} - \frac{E_3(z)}{M}\left(1 - z^{-2}\right)^2\left(1 - z^{-1}\right) + \frac{D(z)}{M}V(z). \tag{5}$$

Observing Eqs. (3) and (5), we can easily find that, in the traditional dither adding method, the dither signal appears in the output, raising the noise floor inevitably. In order to avoid this problem, we introduce a new dither adding method in the following section. Without losing generality, the new method is mainly analysed in MASH 1-1-1 DDSM.

3   MASH DDSM with New Dither Adding Method

The MASH 1-1-1 DDSM with the new dither adding method in the first stage (referred to as MASH 1D-1-1 DDSM) is illustrated in Fig. 7, which shows that the dither signal is added to two different nodes of the first stage of the MASH 1-1-1 DDSM, without dither shaping filter. Thereby, the input-output relationship of the first stage in the z-domain can be derived as

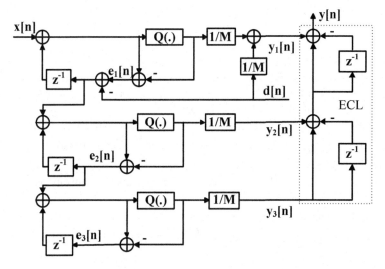

Fig. 7. MASH 1-1-1 DDSM with the new dither adding method in the first stage (MASH 1D-1-1 DDSM)

$$Y_1(z) = \frac{X(z)}{M} - (1 - z^{-1})\frac{E_1(z) - D(z)}{M}, \tag{6}$$

Where $Y_1(z)$ and $E_1(z)$ represent the output $y_1[n]$ and quantization error $e_1[n]$ of the first stage in the z-domain, respectively.

Since the negative dither signal is also sent to the next stage, the transfer function of the second stage can be written as

$$Y_2(z) = \frac{E_1(z) - D(z)}{M} - (1 - z^{-1})\frac{E_2(z)}{M}, \tag{7}$$

where $Y_2(z)$ and $E_2(z)$ represent the output $y_2[n]$ and quantization error $e_2[n]$ of the second stage in the z-domain, respectively. Then, the input-output relationship of the third stage and ECL can be expressed as

$$Y_3(z) = \frac{E_2(z)}{M} - (1 - z^{-1})\frac{E_3(z)}{M}, \tag{8}$$

$$Y(z) = Y_1(z) + Y_2(z)(1 - z^{-1}) + Y_3(z)(1 - z^{-1})^2, \tag{9}$$

where $Y_3(z)$ and $Y(z)$ represent the output of the third stage $y_3[n]$ and the final output $y[n]$ in the z-domain, respectively. Substituting Eqs. (6), (7), and (8) into (9), the transfer function of MASH 1D-1-1 DDSM is derived as

$$Y(z) = \frac{X(z)}{M} - \frac{E_3(z)}{M}(1 - z^{-1})^3. \tag{10}$$

Compared with (3) and (5), (10) states that, with the new dither adding method, the output of MASH 1D-1-1 DDSM is free from the dither signals. Equivalently, since the additive dither signals are eliminated in ECL, no noise floor rising phenomenon can be observed in the output of MASH 1D-1-1 DDSM.

Furthermore, from (10), we know that the shaped quantization noise of MASH 1D-1-1 DDSM is $\frac{E_3(z)}{M}(1 - z^{-1})^3$. For ease of reading and comparison, the shaped quantization noise of dithered MASH 1-2-2 DDSM is written as $\frac{E_3(z)}{M}(1 - z^{-1})(1 - z^{-2})^2$ [14]. The power of the each shaped quantization noise can be calculated as

$$P_{D\_dB} = 20\log\left|\frac{E_3(z)}{M}(1 - z^{-1})^3\right|, \tag{11}$$

$$P_{T\_dB} = 20\log\left|\frac{E_3(z)}{M}(1 - z^{-1})(1 - z^{-2})^2\right|, \tag{12}$$

where P_{D_dB} and P_{T_dB} represent the power of shaped quantization noise of MASH 1D-1-1 DDSM and dithered MASH 1-2-2 DDSM, respectively. Substituting $z = \exp(j2\pi f)$ into (11) and (12), when f is small enough, we can get

$$P_{T\_dB} - P_{D\_dB} = 20\log\left(\frac{2\pi f}{\pi f}\right)^2 \approx 12 \text{ dB}, \tag{13}$$

where f is the normalized frequency. Obviously, the computing result in (13) is consistent with the simulation result in [3]. In other words, compared with dithered MASH 1-2-2 DDSM, the shaped quantization noise power of MASH 1D-1-1 DDSM is reduced by 12 dB in the lower band.

It is worth noting that, the proposed dither adding method can be applied in any preceding except the last stage of a MASH DDSM. Since (6) has clearly stated that, in the new dither adding method, the dither signal can be treated as the quantization noise of the corresponding stage, and it always can be eliminated in ECL.

4   Simulation Results

The output PSD plots of MASH 1-1-1 DDSM with first-order shaped dither, MASH 1-2-2 DDSM with third-order shaped dither, and MASH 1D-1-1 DDSM are simulated in Simulink, which are illustrated in Fig. 8. In addition, the theoretical prediction results are also labelled in the output PSD plots. The simulation parameters are listed as follows: input word length $n_0 = 9$, quantization interval $M = 2^9$ and input $x[n] = M/2$.

Figure 8 presents that the spur-free spectra are achieved in all those three structures. But MASH 1-1-1 DDSM with first-order shaped dither raises the noise floor obviously.

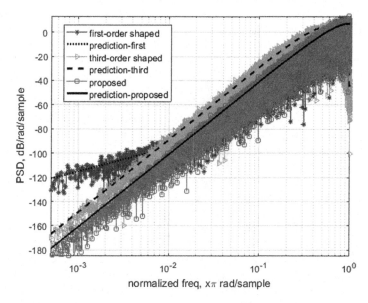

Fig. 8. Output PSD of 9-bit MASH 1-1-1 DDSM with first-order shaped dither, MASH 1-2-2 DDSM with third-order shaped dither, and MASH 1D-1-1 DDSM, with constant input 256

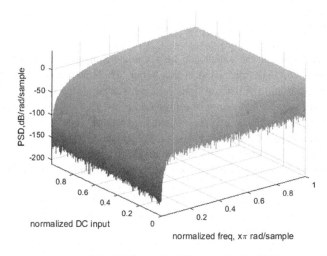

Fig. 9. Output spectra of MASH 1D-1-1 DDSM for all 512 DC inputs with $n_0 = 9$

Moreover, in the lower band, though a slope of 60 dB/decade is both obtained in MASH 1-2-2 DDSM with third-order shaped dither and MASH 1D-1-1 DDSM, the latter one further reduces the shaped quantization noise power about 12 dB, as expected.

Besides, For all 512 DC inputs with $n_0 = 9$, the output PSD plots of MASH 1D-1-1 DDSM and MASH 1-1-1 DDSM with the proposed dither adding method in the second

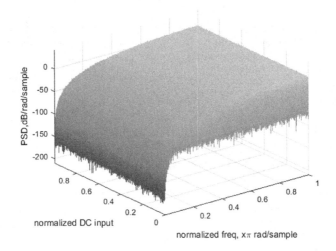

Fig. 10. Output spectra of MASH 1-1-1 DDSM, with the proposed dither adding method applied in the second stage, for all 512 DC inputs with $n_0 = 9$

stage are shown in Fig. 9 and Fig. 10, respectively. As can be seen, the spur-free spectra are achieved for all digital constant inputs in both cases.

5   Conclusion

A new dither adding method which can be applied in any preceding except the last stage of a MASH DDSM is proposed in this paper. Theoretical analysis states that, in the new method, the additive dither signal can be treated as the quantization noise of the corresponding stage. Thus, it can be eliminated in the ECL. Simulation results show that spur-free spectra are achieved for all constant digital inputs. Furthermore, compared with conventional MASH 1-1-1 DDSM with first-order shaped dither and MASH 1-2-2 DDSM with third-order shaped dither, the MASH 1-1-1 DDSM applying the new dither adding method can avoid noise floor rising problem and acquire better spectrum performance.

Acknowledgment. This paper is supported by the Priority Academic Program Development of Jiangsu Higher Education Institutions.

References

1. Norsworthy, S.R., Schreier, R., Temes, G.C.: Delta-Sigma Data Converters: Theory, Design, and Simulaion. IEEE Press, New York (1997)
2. Schreier, R., Temes, G.C.: Understanding Delta-Sigma Data Converters. Wiley, New York (2005)

3. Fitzgibbon, B., Pamarti, S., Kennedy, M.P.: A spur-free MASH DDSM with high-order filtered dither. IEEE Trans. Circuits Syst. II Express Briefs **58**(9), 585–589 (2011)
4. Hosseini, K., Kennedy, M.P.: Minimizing Spurious Tones in Digital Delta-Sigma Modulators. Springer, New York (2011)
5. Friedman, V.: The structure of the limit cycles in sigma-delta modulation. IEEE Trans. Commun. **36**(8), 972–979 (1988)
6. Kozak, M., Kale, I.: Rigorous analysis of delta-sigma modulators for fractional-N PLL frequency synthesis. IEEE Trans. Circuits Syst. I Reg. Pap. **51**(6), 1148–1162 (2004)
7. Borkowski, M.J., Riley, T.A.D., Hakkinen, J., et al.: A practical $\Delta\Sigma$ modulator design method based on periodical behavior analysis. IEEE Trans. Circuits Syst. II Express Briefs **52**(10), 626–630 (2005)
8. Hosseini, K., Kennedy, M.P.: Mathematical analysis of a prime modulus quantizer MASH digital delta-sigma modulator. IEEE Trans. Circuits Syst. II Express Briefs **54**(12), 1105–1109 (2007)
9. Level, P., Camino, S.R.L.: Digital to digital sigma-delta modulator and digital frequency synthesizer incorporating the same. Patent US 6 822 593 B2 (2004)
10. Hosseini, K., Kennedy, M.P.: Maximum sequence length MASH digital delta-sigma modulators. IEEE Trans. Circuits Syst. I Reg. Pap. **54**(12), 2628–2638 (2007)
11. Song, J., Park, I.C.: Spur-free MASH delta-sigma modulation. IEEE Trans. Circuits Syst. I Reg. Pap. **57**(9), 2426–2437 (2010)
12. Pamarti, S., Welz, J., Galton, I.: Statistics of the quantization noise in 1-bit dithered single-quantizer digital delta-sigma modulators. IEEE Trans. Circuits Syst. I Reg. Pap. **54**(3), 492–503 (2007)
13. Pamarti, S., Galton, I.: LSB dithering in MASH delta-sigma D/A converters. IEEE Trans. Circuits Syst. I Reg. Pap. **54**(4), 779–790 (2007)
14. Fitzgibbon, B., O'Neill, K., Grannell, A., et al.: A spur-free MASH digital delta-sigma modulator with higher order shaped dither. In: European Conference on Circuit Theory & Design, pp. 723–726 (2009)

A 20 Gb/s Wireline Receiver
with Adaptive CTLE and Half-Rate DFE
in 0.13 μm Technology

Yinhang Zhang, Qingsheng Hu[(⊠)], and Yongzheng Zhan

Institute of RF- & OE-ICs, Southeast University, Nanjing 210096, China
736671385@qq.com, qshu@seu.edu.cn

Abstract. This paper presents a 20 Gb/s receive equalizer including an adaptive continuous time linear equalizer (CTLE) and a 2-tap half-rate decision feedback equalizer (DFE) in 0.13 μm BiCMOS technology for high speed serial link. The CTLE can adjust the ratio of high frequency and low frequency components adaptively by detecting the energy at both ends of a slicer and then generating a control signal by an integrator. Following the CTLE is a half-rate DFE which can get a better trade-off between the working speed and design complexity especially for the case of 20 Gb/s or above. The chip area including pads and chip guarding is about 0.72×0.86 mm^2 and the power consumption is about 528 mW. Post simulation results show that the horizontal eye opening of the equalized data can be up to 0.9 UI at 20 Gb/s.

Keywords: CTLE · DFE · Serial link · Design complexity

1 Introduction

The requirement of high data rate in wire-line communications has been becoming more and more intense. The chip-to-chip and board-to-board communication are moving towards 20 Gb/s or above. The channel loss, jitter, cross-talk and noise will become more and more serious with the increase of velocity [1–3]. In order to compensate channel loss or combat the inter-symbol interference, a variety of equalization schemes are widely used at the near or far end. Partial response maximum likelihood equalization based on sequence detection can find the most probable transmission sequence from all possible sequences and get the lowest bit error rate [4, 5]. Because the structure of Viterbi decoder is too complex, and difficult to implement with high speed circuit, it is seldom used in high speed serial link.

In the receiver, the feed forward equalizer (FFE) has a simple structure and can cancel pre-cursor ISI and post-cursor ISI simultaneously. At high speed, e.g. 20 Gb/s or beyond, it is difficult to design high precision delay line which is easily affected by the process, voltage, temperature (PVT) [6–8]. Similarly, the continuous time linear equalizer (CTLE) can also eliminate the pre-cursor and post-cursor by increasing the high-frequency components of the signal. But the noise and crosstalk is potentially amplified by the CTLE [9, 10]. DFE is a nonlinear structure and it is the most effective equalizer to eliminate the post-cursor. In order to eliminate the influence of the previous

© IFIP International Federation for Information Processing 2017
Published by Springer International Publishing AG 2017. All Rights Reserved
Y. Koucheryavy et al. (Eds.): WWIC 2017, LNCS 10372, pp. 292–303, 2017.
DOI: 10.1007/978-3-319-61382-6_24

symbol on the current symbol, the previous symbol is fed back and subtracted from the current symbol. Since the feedback signals are hard decision signals, the feedback signals do not enhance crosstalk and noise. The structure of DFE equalizer is simple and easy to operate at relatively high rate [11–14].

The reminder of the paper is structured as follows. We review the principle of the adaptive CTLE based on the slope detection and the half-rate DFE. Then, the circuit design of the key modules is introduced in Sect. 3. We give the circuit layout and post-simulation results in Sect. 4. Finally, we draw conclusions in Sect. 5.

2   Architecture

The overall structure consists of an adaptive CTLE and a half-rate DFE, as shown in Fig. 1. Adaptive CTLE can provide high frequency gain and compensate the loss caused by channel bandwidth degradation. In addition, CTLE can not only make up for some of the shortcomings of DFE, but also reduce the number of taps, which reduces power consumption [15–17]. Due to the inherent drawbacks of linear equalizers, it is necessary to follow a half-rate decision feedback equalizer.

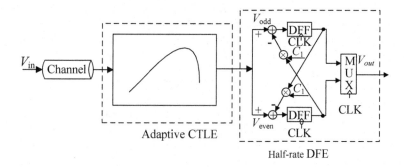

Fig. 1. A typical equalization architecture with CTLE and Half-rate DFE

Due to the change of the environment, the different backplane materials and the change of the data rate, the improvement of the adaptive ability of CTLE is absolutely necessary. For the adaption CTLE based on spectrum balancing method, the power detector consumes large power. In order to solve these problems, the adaptive CTLE based on slope detection is presented in this paper, as shown in Fig. 2. The signal transmitted through the channel is first sent to a linear equalizer which has two paths: high-pass path and all-pass path. The high-pass path is used to compensate the high-frequency loss by high-frequency peaking, and the all-path is employed to adjust the low-frequency gain. The optimum proportion of high frequency and low frequency is adjusted by feedback control voltage V_{ctrl}. The output of the linear equalizer is adopted to produce a fixed swing and slope signal by the slicer. Slope detector &integrator are used for detecting the slope (energy)deviation between the slicer input and its output.

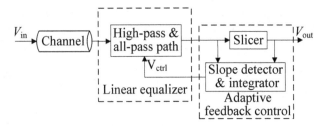

Fig. 2. Adaptive CTLE

Figure 3 shows a simplified structure of half-rate DFE, which is composed of odd path and even path. Each path consists of an adder and two Flip-Flops. The rate of clock signal for odd path data and even path data is half of input data, which is illustrated by Fig. 4. The multiplexer restores half-rate data to full-speed data. The advantages of half-rate structure can be described as follows: firstly, the time constraint of the half-rate DFE is the same as the full-rate DFE, but the data duration of half-rate DFE is doubled, so it is easier for the adder to complete the operation accurately. Secondly, the architecture of half-rate DFE can reduce design difficulty of the CDR circuit and clock buffer.

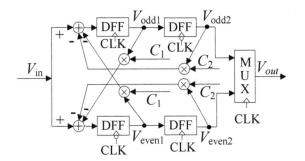

Fig. 3. Half-rate DFE

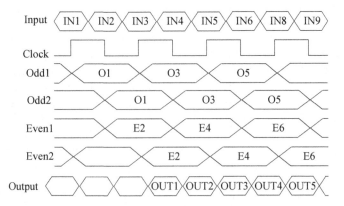

Fig. 4. Timing diagram of half-rate DFE

3 Circuit Design

3.1 Linear Equalizer

Linear equalizer is mainly used to compensate the loss caused by channel bandwidth degradation. The design of linear equalizer must consider two issues: (1) bandwidth, which determines the range of frequency compensation; (2) boost factor, which is determined by the loss of the channel [17]. The linear equalizer shown in Fig. 5 employs a high-path and an all-path path to compensate the loss of the channel. The bandwidth of high-path is completed by the inductance peaking technique and the bandwidth of the all-path is expanded by pole zero cancellation. The ratio of high frequency and low frequency is determined by the bias voltage of the tail transistor. In other words, the adaptation of the linear equalizer is performed by the feedback control voltage V_{ctrl}, which is produced by the slope detector and integrator. Figure 6 shows the frequency response curve of the linear equalizer with different V_{ctrl}.

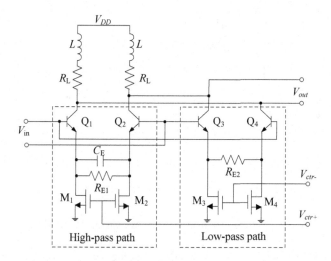

Fig. 5. Linear equalizer

3.2 Slope Detector and Integrator

Figure 7 shows the slope detector & integrator. Two coupled difference pairs, M_1 and M_2, M_3 and M_4, are used to detect the energy of the slicer input and output, respectively. The total current flowing through the coupled differential pair M_1 and M_2 can be expressed as follows:

$$I_{\text{out1}} = I_{\text{ds1}} + I_{\text{ds2}} = \frac{\mu_n C_{\text{ox}}}{2}\left(\frac{W}{L}\right)\left(2\left(V_{\text{in,cm}} - V_{\text{in}}\right)^2 + \frac{V_{\text{in,dm}}^2}{2}\right) \qquad (1)$$

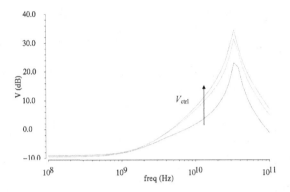

Fig. 6. Frequency response of linear equalizer with different V_{ctrl}

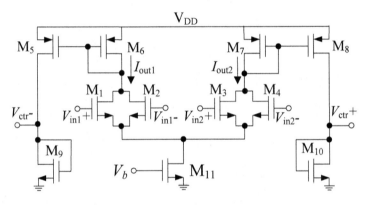

Fig. 7. Slope detector and integrator

where the I_{ds1} and I_{ds2} are the drain current of transistor M1 and M2, respectively. $V_{in,com}$ is the common mode input voltage and $V_{in,dm}$ is the differential mode input voltage. The square term in the formula shows that the energy of different slope signal waveforms can be measured by I_{out1}. In Fig. 7, M_6 and M_7 are active load transistor, M_5 and M_6 are mirror current source, similarly, M_7 and M_8 are mirror current source. Therefore, the feedback control voltage generated by the integrator can be described as follows:

$$V_{ctrl} = I_{out2}R_{L} - I_{out1}R_{L} = \frac{\mu_{n}C_{ox}}{4}\left(\frac{W}{L}\right)\left(V_{in2}^2 - V_{in1}^2\right)R_{L} \qquad (2)$$

According to Eq. (2), V_{ctrl} is closely related with the difference of slicer both ends signal energy. The V_{ctrl} feeding back to the linear equalizer adjusts the frequency response of the linear equalizer.

3.3 Slicer

Slicer implemented by two cascaded current mode logic (CML) structure is shown in Fig. 8. The slicer is a limiting amplifier so that it processes the edge and amplitude of the input signal and produces fixed swing and slope signal for the feedback loop. The slicer is a high resolution comparator. The edge of the input signal is processed into an approximate ideal binary signal, so that the slope of the slicer output is almost independent of the slope of the equalizer output signal.

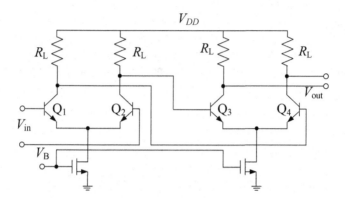

Fig. 8. Slicer

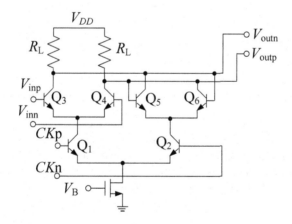

Fig. 9. SCFL based Latch

3.4 SCFL Based Latch

The sensitivity of latch has a great influence on the performance of DFE. The D Flip-Flop consists of two stages latches. Each stage latch contains three pairs of transistors, as shown in Fig. 9. Q_1 and Q_2 are input clock transistors, Q_3 and Q_4 consist of sampled transistors, Q_5 and Q_6 are latch transistors. When the CK_p/CK_n is high/low, the Q_1 is turned on and the Q_2 is turned off, the current I_{ss} flows through the Q_1, and the data is sampled. When CK_p/CK_n is low/high level, the output signal is latched by the latch transistor, the data remains intact.

For latch, firstly, the size of clock signal must be large enough to ensure that the Q_1 or Q_2 can be turned off completely. Secondly, the performance of the latch is determined by the proportional relation between the latch transistor and the sampling transistor. Considering the operating speed, data retention capability and bandwidth, the proportional relation adopted in this design is 0.8.

3.5   Summer

The summer based on CML is shown in Fig. 10. The input signal V_{in} and its feedback signal are summed up in the form of current, and then converted into the output voltage V_{out}. The V_{out} can be expressed as follows:

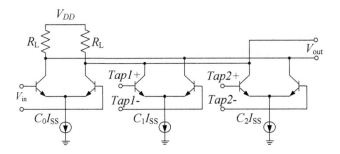

Fig. 10. Summer

$$V_{out} = [G_0 V_{in}(t) - G_1 V_{in}(t - T) - G_2 V_{in}(t - 2T)]R_L = [C_0 - C_1 - C_2]I_{SS}R_L \quad (3)$$

where G_i (i = 0, 1, 2) are the input trans conductance, C_i (i = 0, 1, 2) are the tap coefficients. In order to effectively eliminate the post-cursor and achieve a good equalization effect, it is important to select the appropriate tap coefficients C_i (i = 1, 2). Typically, it can be obtained by the impulse response of the channel or the adaptive least mean square (LMS) algorithm.

3.6   Multiplexer

Figure 11 shows the architecture of multiplexer. The 2:1 multiplexer based on SCFL is mainly composed of two cross coupled differential pair transistor. This circuit is driven by half-rate clock, which is same as the master slave flip-flop. The half-rate data can be

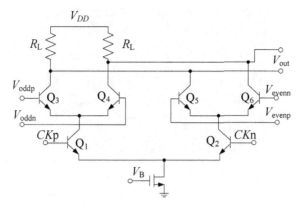

Fig. 11. Multiplexer

recovered to full rate data through this circuit. When the CK_p is high, the odd path is selected. When the CK_n is high, the even path is selected. In order to improve the stability of current source, the gate length of the tail current transistor should be larger.

3.7 Buffer

To drive external 50 ohms load resistance, the buffer based on CML logic was implemented in this work, as shown in Fig. 12. It is composed of multi-stage CML logic. It has the advantage of simple structure and enough bandwidth. In order to improve the driving ability, this paper adopts 3 stages. The size of tail current transistor and difference input transistor should be gradually increased, and the size of load resistance should be reduced gradually.

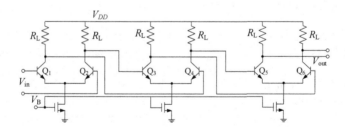

Fig. 12. Buffer

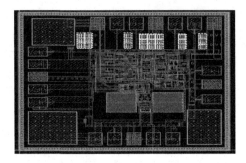

Fig. 13. Layout of the proposed equalizer

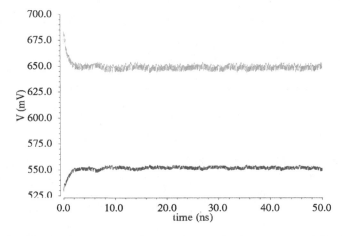

Fig. 14. Simulation results of feedback control voltage (V_{ctrl+} and V_{ctrl-})

4 Layout and Post Simulation

Figure 13 shows the layout of the proposed equalizer including adaptive CTLE and half-rate DFE. The total area including pads and chip guarding is 0.72×0.86 mm^2. The circuit has been submitted for fabrication. Figure 14 shows the simulation results of feedback control voltage V_{ctrl+} and V_{ctrl-}. It can be seen that the feedback control voltage can be stable after 5 ns.

Figure 15(a) gives the input eye diagram. The output eye diagram of adaptive CTLE and half-rate DFE are given in Fig. 15(b) and (c), respectively. It is can be seen that the eye opening is less than 0.6UI after adaptive CTLE equalization, and the eye opening can be further widened by half-rate DFE at the rate of 20 Gb/s.

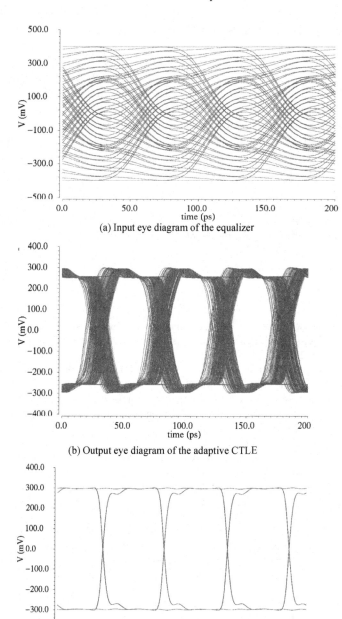

(a) Input eye diagram of the equalizer

(b) Output eye diagram of the adaptive CTLE

(c) Output eye diagram of half-rate DFE

Fig. 15. Simulation results of 20 Gb/s

5   Conclusions and Future Work

In this brief, in order to deal with higher channel loss, a half-rate DFE combined with an analog adaptive CTLE based on slope detection is employed at the receiver. The adaptive CTLE can adjusts the range of high-frequency peaking and compensate the channel loss. It can effectively reduce the burden of DFE and cut down the number of taps. Eye opening is up to 0.9 UI after the CTLE and half-rate DFE equalization at 20 Gb/s. It improves that the half-rate DFE can further improve the signal integrity of serial link at the rate of 20 Gb/s.

In future work, on the one hand, because the ISI is mainly caused by the post-cursor, we will focus on the adaption performance of DFE. On the other hand, when the loss of the link reaches up to 35 dB attenuation at Nyquist frequency at 25 Gb/s or above, higher order modulation mode (such as PAM4), or other modulation methods (such as ENRZ) should be deeply studied.

References

1. Yuan, G., Alaa, R., Taee, A.: Design techniques for decision feedback equalization for multi-giga-bit-per-second serial data links: a state-of-the-art review. IET Circ. Devices Syst. **52**(8), 118–130 (2014)
2. Bulzacchelli, J.: Equalization for electrical links: current design techniques and future directions. IEEE Solid State Circ. Mag. **7**(4), 23–31 (2015)
3. Wang, X., Hu, Q.: Analysis and optimization of combined equalizer for high speed serial link. In: 2015 IEEE 9th International Conference on Anti-counterfeiting, Security, and Identification, pp. 43–46, Xiamen (2015)
4. Pervez, M., Cathy, Y., Adam, H.: Partial response maximum likelihood equalization and detection for DSP based SerDes with cross talk and practical equalization. In: DesignCon 2014, pp. 1–27, Santa Clara (2014)
5. Pervez, M., Cathy, Y., Adam, H.: Partial response and noise predictive maximum likelihood (PRML/NPML) equalization and detection for high speed serial link systems. In: DesignCon 2013, pp. 1160–1184, Santa Clara (2013)
6. Boesch. R., Zheng. K., Murmann. B.: A 0.003 mm² 5.2 mW/tap 20 GBd inductor-less 5-tap analog RX-FFE. In: IEEE Symposium on VLSI Circuits, pp. 1–2, HI (2016)
7. Kocaman, N., Ali, T., Rao, P.: A 3.8 mW/Gbps quad-channel 8.5–13 Gbps serial link with a 5 tap DFE and a 4 tap transmit FFE in 28 nm CMOS. IEEE J. Solid State Circ. **51**(4), 881–892 (2016)
8. Kao, S., Liu, S.: A 7.5-Gb/s one-tap-FFE transmitter with adaptive far-end crosstalk cancellation using duty cycle detection. IEEE J. Solid State Circ. **48**(2), 391–404 (2013)
9. Preibisch, J., Reuschel, J., Scharff, K.: Impact of continuous time linear equalizer variability on eye opening of high-speed links. In: 2016 IEEE 20th Workshop on Signal and Power Integrity, pp. 1–4, Turin (2016)
10. Feng, Z., Hu, Q.: A 6.25 Gb/s decision feedback equalizer in 0.18 μm CMOS technology for high-speed Ser Des. In: 2011 7th International Conference on Wireless Communications, Networking and Mobile Computing, pp. 1–4 (2011)

11. Yuan, S., Wang, Z., Zheng, X.: A 10 Gb/s speculative decision feedback equalizer with a novel implementation of adaption in 65 nm CMOS technology. In: IEEE International Conference on Electron Devices and Solid-State Circuits, pp. 1–2, Chengdu (2014)
12. Parikh, S., Kao, T., Hidaka, Y., Jiang, J.: A 32 Gb/s wireline receiver with a low-frequency equalizer, CTLE and 2-tap DFE in 28 nm CMOS. In: IEEE Solid State Circuits Conference, pp. 28–29, Lisbon (2013)
13. Navid, R., Chen, E., Hossain, M.: A 40 Gb/s serial link transceiver in 28 nm CMOS technology. IEEE J. Solid-State Circ. **50**(4), 814–827 (2015)
14. Zhang, G., Chaudhair,P., Green, M.: A BiCMOS 10 Gb/s adaptive cable equalizer. In: IEEE Solid State Circuits Conference, pp. 149–152, Bangkok (2003)
15. Jiang, C., Hu, Q.: A 6.25 Gb/s adaptive analog equalizer in 0.18 μm CMOS technology for high-speed Ser Des. In: 2012 2nd International Conference on Computer Science and Network Technology, pp. 266–270, Changchun (2012)
16. Kim, Y., Lee, T., Kim, L.: A 21-Gbit/s 1.63-pJ/bit adaptive CTLE and one-tap DFE with single loop spectrum balancing method. IEEE Trans. Very Large Scale Integr. Syst. **24**(2), 789–793 (2016)
17. Ibrahim, S., Razavi, B.: Low-power CMOS equalizer design for 20-Gb/s systems. IEEE J. Solid-State Circ. **46**(6), 1321–1336 (2011)

Spur-Free and Stable Digital Delta-Sigma Modulator via Using HK-EFM

Xiangning Fan[✉], Pengpeng Shi, Yilong Liao, and Jian Tao

School of Information Science and Engineering,
Institute of RF-&OE-ICs, Southeast University,
Nanjing 210096, China
xnfan@seu.edu.cn

Abstract. This paper presents a new multi-stage noise-shaping (MASH) digital delta-sigma modulator (DDSM), denoted as HJ-MASH DDSM which can remove spurs in the output spectrum and has long sequence lengths than Jinook structure and HK-MASH in the worst input case by applying HK-EFM in the first stage error feedback modulator (EFM) of the DDSM. In addition, the proposed HJ-MASH DDSM lowers the difficulty of constructing higher order MASH DDSMs compared to HK-MASH DDSM. While the performance and stability are all superior to Jinook structure for all constant inputs, especially for the input which correspond to minimum cycle lengths. The digital delta-sigma modulator applied in fractional-N frequency synthesizers ameliorates the synthesizer's spectral purity apparently by verification.

Keywords: Delta-sigma modulator · MASH · HK-EFM · Stability

1 Introduction

The frequency divider is one of the most significant components of frequency synthesizer, which can support frequency synthesizer to generate multiple high-precision frequency signals. According to divisor, it can be divided into integer divisor and fractional-n divisor. The fractional-n frequency divider can be constructed by using two integer dividers, a divide-by-n divider and a divide-by-(n + 1) divider [1, 2].

The digital delta-sigma modulator (DDSM) is extensively analyzed and used in modern wireless communication subsystems, such as fractional frequency synthesizers, analog-to-digital and digital-to-analog converters, and switched-mode power supplies to acquire an excellent performance and spectral purity. Delta-sigma modulator translate a fine input sequence that should be represented in m bits to a coarse output sequence represented in n bits, where n is significantly less than m. Delta-sigma modulator is a technique for improving the effective resolution of a quantizer by oversampling and noise shaping.

© IFIP International Federation for Information Processing 2017
Published by Springer International Publishing AG 2017. All Rights Reserved
Y. Koucheryavy et al. (Eds.): WWIC 2017, LNCS 10372, pp. 304–314, 2017.
DOI: 10.1007/978-3-319-61382-6_25

The oversampling ratio OSR is defined as:

$$OSR = \frac{f_s}{2f_B} \tag{1}$$

where f_s is the sampling frequency and f_B is the largest frequency component in the signal spectrum. $2f_B$ corresponds to the Nyquist frequency. Besides, the low frequency part of the rest of its spectrum is attenuated and its high frequency part is amplified. In that case, the oversampling and the noise shaping property of the DSM can be used together to achieve a high signal-to-quantization-noise ratio using a relatively coarse quantizer [3, 4].

Delta-sigma modulator (DSM) is widely used to select a clock divider in the fractional-N frequency synthesizer. As shown in Fig. 1, the conventional first–order DSM consists of a digital accumulator, a register, a quantizer and feedback loop. Since the DSM is a finite-state machine (FSM), its output sequence is periodic when the input is a constant value. More importantly, the quantization noise sequence is also periodic, and the noise sequence period or the sequence length is strongly dependent on the input value and the DSM structure. If the sequence length is short, the quantization noise power is spread over a small number of tones, resulting in spurs in the noise spectrum.

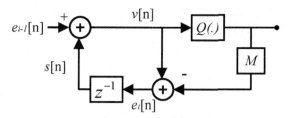

Fig. 1. Block diagram of the EFM1

The first-order EFM is widely used in implementing the first-order DSM, since the error feedback modulator (EFM) has a relatively low hardware cost and low power consumption. We show the block diagram of a first order EFM1 that used a multi-bit quantizer. The input to the modulator is a digital word with n bit. When the $v[n]$ is greater than M (2^n), the quantizer overflows and the output signal $y[n]$ (the carry out) will be one. Otherwise, the quantizer does not overflow and $y[n]$ will be zero as follow:

$$y[n] = \begin{cases} 0, & v[n] < M \\ 1, & v[n] < M \end{cases} \tag{2}$$

The rest of this paper is organized as follows. Section 2 summarizes previous works and describes the architecture and performance of HK-MASH and Jinook MASH, respectively. Section 3 presents the proposed MASH structure, and describes the simulation results and comparisons with other works. Concluding remarks are made in Sect. 4 after acknowledgment. Additionally, simulation results are verified by Simulink & MATLAB.

2 Previous MASH Architecture

By contrast with the SQ-DDSM and EFM, both of which use a single quantizer, the multistage noise shaping (MASH) technique allows one to realize high order noise shaping using lower modulators. In MASH DDSM, one can use lower order modulators (with orders as low as 1) in a cascade. If first order stages are available, L stages can be combined to form an Lth order MASH modulator. A MASH DDSM with 1-bit internal first order modulators is a feedforward structure and is unconditionally stable; this is the principal advantage of the MASH modulator over the SQ-DDSM topology. Furthermore, in a MASH DDSM, the stable input range is equal to the full scale while the stable input range is only a fraction of the full scale in an SQ-DDSM. The MASH DDSM is widely used in commercial fractional-N frequency synthesizer products.

2.1 HK-MASH Architecture

The basic building block of the HK-MASH DDSM [5] is the first order HK-EFM1 shown in Fig. 2, it is very similar to the convention EFM1. The main difference compared to the conventional EFM1 shown in Fig. 1 in that it includes a feedback block denoted as az^{-1}. Therefore, the cycle lengths of conventional EFMs are maximized by introducing a feedback path from the output of each EFM to its input using a delay block with a particular choice of coefficient a, where a is a small integer that is chose such that $M - a$ is primer.

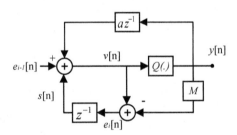

Fig. 2. Block diagram of the HK-EFM1

$$STF(z) = \frac{1}{M}\frac{1}{1 - \alpha z^{-1}} \text{ and } NTF(z) = \frac{1}{M}\frac{1 - z^{-1}}{1 - \alpha z^{-1}} \qquad (3)$$

The parameter α is the normalized version a of given by

$$\alpha = \frac{a}{M} \qquad (4)$$

Figure 3 show a block diagram of an Lth order MASH DDSM comprising a cascade of n-bit HK-EFM1 blocks and an error cancellation network. As in the conventional MASH structure, the negative of the quantization error from each stage ($-ei[n]$) is once again fed to the next stage and the output of each stage ($yi[n]$) is fed to the error cancellation network, which eliminates the intermediate quantization noise terms. The output of the Lth order HK-MASH DDSM can be expressed in the Z-domain as:

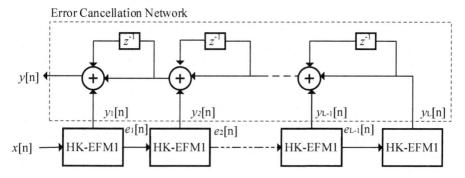

Fig. 3. Block diagram of an Lth order HK-MASH DDSM incorporating a cascade of HK-EFM1

$$Y(z) = \frac{1}{M}\frac{1}{1-\alpha z^{-1}}X(z) + \frac{1}{M}\frac{(1-z^{-1})^L}{1-\alpha z^{-1}}E_L(z) \qquad (5)$$

By contrast with a conventional modulator ($\alpha = 0$), a pole at $z = \alpha$ is added to both the STF and the NTF. If α is sufficiently small, this pole is very close to the origin in the z plane; equivalently, it is a distant pole which does not significantly affect the overall operation of the modulator. In order to illustrate this point, consider the magnitude response of the multiplying factor $G_{hk}(z) = \frac{1}{1-\alpha z^{-1}}$ which appears in the STF and the NTF. Substituting $z = e^{jw}$ into $G_{hk}(z)$ and calculating the resulting magnitude yields

$$20log_{10}\left(\left|G_{hk}\left(e^{jw}\right)\right|\right) = 20log_{10}\left(\frac{1}{\sqrt{1+\alpha^2 - 2\alpha cos(w)}}\right) \qquad (6)$$

Figure 4 shows (6) for different values of, namely $0, \frac{1}{2^5}, \frac{3}{2^9}, \frac{3}{2^{19}}$. As α decreases, the resulting spectrum approaches that of $\alpha = 0$. When $\alpha = \frac{3}{2^9}$, the magnitude of G_{hk} at low frequencies is only 0.05 dB.

In our example, we consider a 9-bit HK-MASH DDSM3, a 19-bit HK-MASH-DDSM3 and a 20-bit HK-MASH DDSM3. Therefore, the value of a has been set to 3, 1, 3, respectively, which corresponds to a carry in bit and simplifies the implementation. The output of HK-MASH DDSM3 is given by

$$Y(z) = \frac{1}{M}\frac{1}{1-\alpha z^{-1}}X(z) + \frac{1}{M}\frac{(1-z^{-1})^3}{1-\alpha z^{-1}}E_3(z) \qquad (7)$$

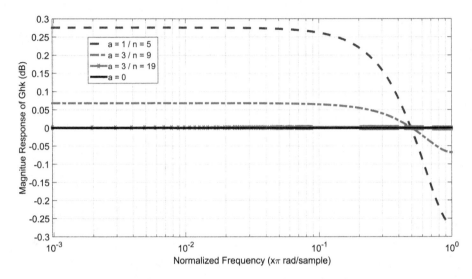

Fig. 4. Magnitude response of the multiplying factor $\frac{1}{1-\alpha z^{-1}}$

The sequence length of the Lth HK-MASH DDSM have been proven mathematically to be equal to $(M-a)^L$. Therefore, the sequence length of the HK-MASH DDSM3 is $(M-a)^3$.

Figure 5 shows the simulated power spectrum of the HK-MASH DDSM3 when the input is half-scale, once again with zero initial condition and no dither. Note that the spectrum is close to the ideal white noise case, and no individual tones can be seen.

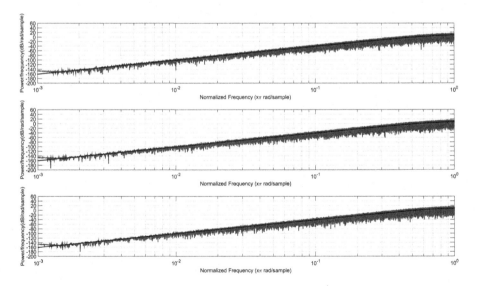

Fig. 5. Simulated power spectrum for 9-bit, 19-bit, 20-bit HK-MASH DDSM3 (top - down)

2.2   Jinook Structure

The basic building block of the Jinook MASH structure [6, 7] is the first order MEFM1 shown in Fig. 6, it is very similar to the convention EFM1. The main difference compared to the conventional EFM1 shown in Fig. 1 in that it takes two inputs and generates two ouputs to be fed to the next EFM. In the MEFM1, the output is delivered to not only the noise cancellation network but also the subsequent MEFM1. Therefore, the Jinook MASH structure links the EFMs by connecting the output and the quantization error signal of an EFM to the input of the next-stage EFM.

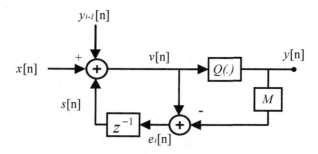

Fig. 6. Block diagram of the MEFM1

Figure 7 show a block diagram of an Lth order Jinook MASH DDSM with EFM1 block, MEFM1 blocks and an error cancellation network. The Jinook MASH DDSM totally stands in matching the input value and the output average and that provides long sequence lengths for the full input range. Besides, it's significant to note that the block of the first stage is a conventional EFM1, therefore, the input of EFM1 is a pure dc signal and not a perturbed one. In the MEFM1, the output and the quantization error signals that are to be connected to the next stage have the same sequence length. Since two periodic inputs can be regarded as one periodic signal, the MEFM1 is functionally equivalent to the traditional EFM, and it generates a periodic output signal.

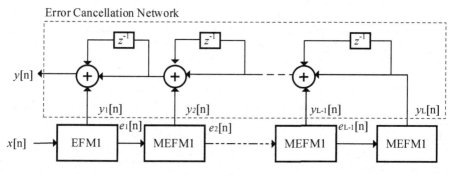

Fig. 7. Block diagram of an Lth order Jinook MASH DDSM

The output of the Lth Jinook MASH DDSM can be expressed in the Z-domain as:

$$Y(z) = \frac{1}{M}X'(z) + \frac{1}{M}\left(1 - z^{-1}\right)^{L}E'(z) \tag{8}$$

$$X'(z) = \{1 + \frac{1}{M}\left(1 - z^{-1}\right) + \cdots + \frac{1}{M^{L-1}}\left(1 - z^{-1}\right)^{L-1}\}X(z) \tag{9}$$

$$E'(z) = E_{L}(z) + \frac{1}{M}E_{L-1}(z) + \cdots + \frac{1}{M^{L-1}}E_{1}(z) \tag{10}$$

In our example, we consider a 9-bit Jinook MASH DDSM3, a 19-bit Jinook MASH-DDSM3 and a 20-bit Jinook MASH DDSM3. The output of these Jinook MASH DDSM3 is given by

$$Y(z) = \frac{1}{M}\{1 + \frac{1}{M}\left(1 - z^{-1}\right) + \frac{1}{M^{2}}\left(1 - z^{-1}\right)^{2}\}X(z) + \frac{(1 - z^{-1})^{3}}{M}\{E_{3}(z) + \frac{1}{M}E_{2}(z) + \frac{1}{M^{2}}E_{1}(z)\} \tag{11}$$

Now, let us derive the sequence length of the Jinook MASH DDSM3. Firstly, the sequence length N_1 of the first stage is explicitly related to the constant input. The sequence lengths of the second and the third stages of the Jinook MASH DDSM3 is $N_1 \cdot M$ and $N_1 \cdot M^2$, respectively, if the input signal is constant. Therefore, the sequence length of the Lth Jinook MASH DDSM is $N_1 \cdot M^{L-1}$ if the signal is constant.

Figure 8 shows the simulated power spectrum of the Jinook MASH DDSM3 when the input is half-scale in the left column and the input is only one-tenth of M in the right column, once again with zero initial condition and no dither. Note that the spectrums of the right column are superior to the left ones, because the Jinook MASH DDSM gets

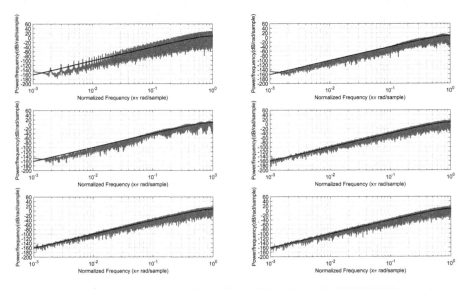

Fig. 8. Simulated power spectrum for 9-bit, 19-bit, 20-bit Jinook MASH DDSM3 (top - down), the input of left subgraph and right subgraph is $\frac{M}{2}$ and $\frac{M}{10}$, respectively

the minimum sequence length and the performance of structure is not stable when the input is equal to half-scale in the left column. Due to the unstable performance, it is necessary to advance a new structure which can ameliorate the stability and do not improve the complexity of structure.

3 Proposed MASH Structure

Although the noise shaping effect of HK-MASH is amazing, it is complicated to construct the hardware implementation of HK-MASH and the input is not exactly equal to the output. Besides, the noise shaping effect of the Jinook structure exhibits instabilities in some input cases and the minimum output sequence length is dependent on the output sequence length of the first-stage EFM cell. In this section, we proposed a new MASH structure shown in Fig. 9 that can totally make a trade-off between complexity and performance. The structure is similar to the Jinook structure but the first-stage EFM cell replaces with HK-EFM, which can effectively increase the sequence length and lower the whole complexity of hardware implementation, so we denote our structure as HJ-MASH.

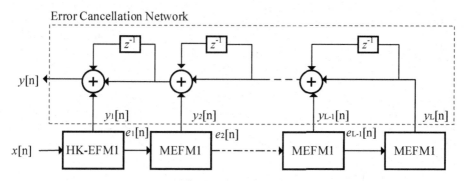

Fig. 9. Block diagram of an Lth order proposed HJ-MASH DDSM

In our example, we consider the 3rd-order MASH DDSM, The output of the proposed HJ-MASH DDSM3 is given by

$$Y(z) = \frac{1}{M}\frac{1}{1-\alpha z^{-1}}X'(z) + p_1(z)E_1(z) + \frac{1}{M}\left(1-z^{-1}\right)^3 E'(Z) \qquad (12)$$

$$p_1(z) = \frac{\alpha z^{-1}(1-z^{-1})}{M(1-\alpha z^{-1})} + \frac{\alpha z^{-1}(1-z^{-1})^2}{M^2(1-\alpha z^{-1})} + \frac{(1-z^{-1})^3}{M^3(1-\alpha z^{-1})} \qquad (13)$$

$$X'(z) = \left(1 + \frac{1-z^{-1}}{M} + \frac{(1-z^{-1})^2}{M^2}\right) \qquad (14)$$

$$E^{'}(z) = E_3(z) + \frac{1}{M}E_2(z) \tag{15}$$

Now, let us derive the sequence length of the proposed HJ-MASH DDSM3. Firstly, the sequence length N_1 of the first stage is exactly equal to $(M - a)$ for all constant inputs and for all initial condition. The sequence lengths of the second and the third stages of the HJ-MASH DDSM3 is $N_1 \cdot M$ and $N_1 \cdot M^2$, respectively. Therefore, the sequence length of the Lth proposed HJ-MASH DDSM is $N_1 \cdot M^{L-1}$ if the signal is constant. In that case, the sequence length of the HJ-MASH DDSM3 is exactly equal to $M^2(M - a)$, which is higher than the sequence length of HK-MASH DDSM3 and Jinook MASH DDSM3 for most input. Therefore, the sequence length of the Lth proposed HJ-MASH DDSM is $(M - a) \cdot M^{L-1}$ if the signal is constant.

Figure 10 shows the simulated power spectrum of the proposed HJ-MASH DDSM3 when the input is half-scale, once again with zero initial condition and no dither. Note that the spectrum is close to the ideal white noise case, and no individual tones can be seen except the first sub-graph. According to Fig. 3, If α is sufficiently small, this pole is very close to the origin in the z plane; equivalently, it is a distant pole which does not significantly affect the overall operation of the modulator.

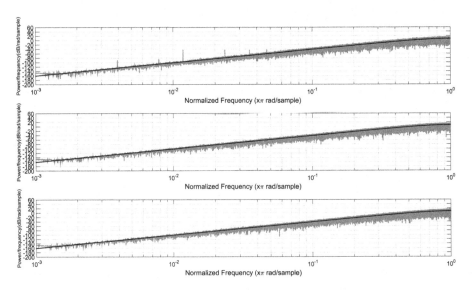

Fig. 10. Simulated power spectrum for 9-bit, 19-bit, 20-bit proposed HJ-MASH DDSM3 (top - down)

Figure 11 shows the comparison of simulated power spectrum between the proposed HJ-MASH DDSM3 and the Jinook structure. The input of the first subgraph is half-scale, once again with zero initial condition and no dither. while the input of second subgraph is one-tenth of M. According to this, it can be easily concluded that the performance and stability of proposed HJ-MASH structure are all superior to Jinook structure.

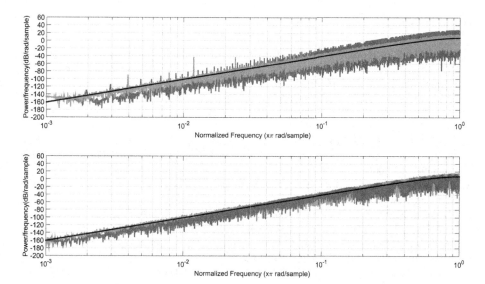

Fig. 11. Simulated power spectrum for 9-bit, 19-bit proposed HJ-MASH DDSM3 and Jinook DDSM3 (top – down)

4 Conclusion

A new MASH DDSM (denoted as HJ-MASH DDSM) has been presented to remove spurs in the output spectrum. In addition to the spur-free property, when the number of input bits n is large enough, the deviation between input and output resulted from the feedback loop of first-stage EFM can be ignored, and it can be assumed that the input is approximately equal to the output. Meanwhile, the output sequence length of the proposed structure is $M^{L-1}(M - a)$, the length is higher than Jinook structure and HK-MASH in the worst input case. Besides, the simulation shows that the noise shaping effect of the proposed structure is better than Jinook structure, while almost catch up with HK-MASH, the complexity is decreased and the stability is improved. At the same time, it can be proved that the hardware consumption of the proposed structure is close to the conventional MASH structure, less than HK-MASH [8].

Spur suppression technique are significant to fractional-N frequency synthesizers. Conventional HK-MASH requires extra hardware and has a high complexity to accomplish, and Jinook MASH has a terrible performance while the input is half-scale. The proposed HJ-MASH structure in this paper can perform stable and excellent in any input while just take little hardware overhead as compared with HK-MASH.

Acknowledgment. This paper is supported by the Priority Academic Program Development of Jiangsu Higher Education Institutions.

References

1. Heydarzadeh, S., Torkzadeh, P.: 12 GHz programmable fractional-n frequency divider with 0.18 um CMOS technology. In: 5th Computer Science and Electronic Engineering Conference, Colchester, pp. 29–33 (2013)
2. Jin, J., Liu, X., Mo, T., Zhou, J.: Quantization noise suppression in fractional- PLLs utilizing glitch-free phase switching multi-modulus frequency divider. IEEE Trans. Circuits Syst. I: Regular Papers **59**, 926–937 (2012)
3. Hosseini, K., Kennedy, M.P.: Mathematical analysis of digital MASH delta-sigma modulators for fractional-N frequency synthesizers. In: Proceedings of PRIME 2006, Lecce, Italy, pp. 309–312 (2006)
4. Hosseini, K., Kennedy, M.P.: Minimizing Spurious Tones in Digital Delta-Sigma Modulator. Springer, New York (2011)
5. Hosseini, K., Kennedy, M.P.: Maximum sequence length MASH digital delta sigma modulators. IEEE Trans. Circuits Syst. I **54**, 2628–2638 (2007)
6. Song, J.: Hardware reduction of MASH delta-sigma modulator based on partially folded architecture. IEEE Trans. Circuits Syst. II **62**, 967–971 (2015)
7. Song, J., Park, I.-C.: Spur-Free MASH delta-sigma modulator. IEEE Trans. Circuits Syst. I **57**, 2426–2437 (2010)
8. Yao, C.-Y., Hsieh, C.-C.: Hardware simplification to the delta path in a MASH 111 delta-sigma modulation. IEEE Trans. Circuits Syst. **56**, 270–274 (2009)

Compression Method to Remove Unnecessary MSBs of IQ Data Frames in C-RAN

HoJun Kwak[1], SungKwon Park[1(✉)], JoonYoung Jung[2], Eunhui Hyun[2], and JeWon Lee[2]

[1] Hanyang University, Seoul, Republic of Korea
{incom35,sp2996}@hanyang.ac.kr
[2] Electronics and Telecommunication Research Institute, Daejeon, Republic of Korea
{jungjy,ehhyun,jw_lee}@etri.re.kr

Abstract. Smart phones are growing rapidly with the support of Over the Top (OTT) service and multimedia streaming service as well as existing Internet service. In the conventional Distributed-RAN (D-RAN) structure, a Base Band Unit (BBU) and a Remote Radio Head (RRH) are configured at one cell site. However, C-RAN, which is a new RAN structure, is composed of separated base stations in which BBU and RRH are separated. RRH is left in cell sites where radio signals are transmitted and received, and BBUs are collected and managed in different places. When the bandwidth of the LTE signal is 20 MHz and the 2×2 Multiple Input Multiple Output (MIMO) antenna is used, the CPRI requires 2.5 Gbps transmission. Since there is a limit to handle mobile traffic that is continuously increasing with the current transmission rate, several techniques for compressing IQ data before transmission have been proposed. In this paper, we apply the compression technique to remove unnecessary parts in the Most Significant Byte (MSB) of a basic frame after applying the existing Up/Down sampling and Non-linear Quantization. We measured the error vector magnitude (EVM) to measure the compression rate and the quality of the signal after compression to confirm the compression performance. Also, it was confirmed whether the experimental results satisfied the compression requirement of Open Radio Interface (ORI).

Keywords: CPRI · C-RAN · Compression · Up/down sampling · Non-linear quantization · ORI

1 Introduction

In the past, the mobile phone was simply a mobile phone with only a call function, but today's smart phone is born with various functions added to the mobile phone. Smartphones with various functions such as TV, camera, Internet, etc., have steadily increased penetration, usage, and dependency. In addition, the smart phone supports OTT services such as YouTube, Mobile IPTV, and multimedia streaming services along with existing Internet services. For this reason, mobile traffic has rapidly increased, and a new RAN structure, C-RAN, has emerged in order to efficiently distribute mobile traffic [1].

© IFIP International Federation for Information Processing 2017
Published by Springer International Publishing AG 2017. All Rights Reserved
Y. Koucheryavy et al. (Eds.): WWIC 2017, LNCS 10372, pp. 315–322, 2017.
DOI: 10.1007/978-3-319-61382-6_26

In the conventional Distributed-RAN (D-RAN) structure, a Base Band Unit (BBU) and a Remote Radio Head (RRH) are configured at one cell site. However, C-RAN, which is a new RAN structure, is composed of separated base stations in which BBU and RRH are separated. RRH is left in cell sites where radio signals are transmitted and received, and BBUs are collected and managed in different places. Figure 1 shows the structure of D-RAN and C-Ran.

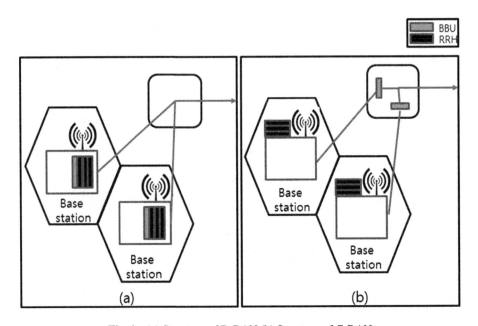

Fig. 1. (a) Structure of D-RAN (b) Structure of C-RAN

BBU and RRH exchange user data, CPRI control and management data, and synchronization information of CPRI frame through CPRI interface. User data is transmitted in the form of baseband digital IQ stream in IQ data block in CPRI basic frame. Control, management data and synchronization information are transmitted using CPRI subchannel which is control word in CPRI basic frame. Each basic frame that constitutes a subchannel consists of 1 byte of control word and 15 bytes of payload.

When the bandwidth of the LTE signal is 20 MHz and the 2 × 2 MIMO antenna is used, the CPRI requires a transmission rate of 2.45 Gbps [2]. There is a limit to the amount of traffic currently available to handle ever-increasing mobile traffic. One of the currently proposed methods is to increase the number of antennas, but this method is disadvantageous in that it is costly. Therefore, several techniques have been proposed to compress IQ data before transmission.

Currently, compression methods such as Up/Down sampling, Non-linear Quantization, and Block Scaling are available. In this paper, we apply the compression method to remove unnecessary parts in the MSB of the basic frame after applying the existing Up/Down sampling and non-linear quantization. We measured the error vector magnitude (EVM) to measure the compression rate and the quality of the signal after compression to confirm the compression performance. Also, it was confirmed whether the experimental results satisfied the compression requirement of ORI.

2 Compression Method

2.1 Up/Down Sampling

In LTE environments, the sampling rate of ADC, DAC, and BBU processing exceeds the signal bandwidth [3]. For example, the sampling rate at 10 MHz LTE is 15.36 MHz and 1/3 of the spectrum does not convey LTE related information.

Therefore, when transmitting IQ data, up sampling the analog signal by K, and down sampling by L after low-pass filtering. On the receiver, perform up sampling by L and down sampling by K after low-pass filtering. Generally, because L is set larger than K, When compressing, it is called down sampling by decrementing by K/L, and it is called up sampling because it increases by L/K when reconstructing.

2.2 Non-linear Quantization

Unlike linear quantization, which divides the quantization level Q_q by a constant amount, non-linear quantization narrows the quantization level at a lower level and makes the quantization level wider at a higher level. [4] Applying quantization with an optimized distance between quantization levels reduces quantization noise and improves signal quality. Figure 2 shows linear quantization and Non-linear quantization.

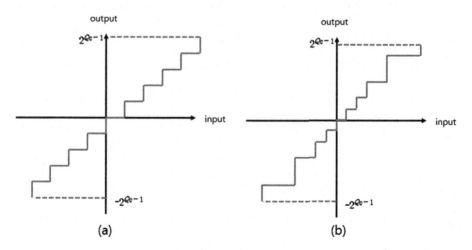

Fig. 2. (a) linear Quantization (b) Non-linear quantization

3 Proposed Compression Method

3.1 Remove the Unnecessary Part in MSB

When nonlinear quantization is performed, the analog value changes to a digital value consisting of only 0 and 1. Therefore, after nonlinear quantization, a frame with the same bits as the Q_q level is generated. If a small value is quantized, the value information can express the value by only the bits of the LSB part. Therefore, it can be concluded that the data of the MSB part is unnecessary when viewed from the receiver.

For example, assuming that the sender sends a value of 105, the 15 bits frame will consist of 00000001101001. However, the receiver does not need to receive all 15 bits value. Even if only 1101001 is received, It can know data is 105.

Therefore, before transmitting data from the transmitter, first determine whether the first bit of the MSB is 0 or 1, and then check how many times the same value as the first bit is repeated continuously. Then, the MSB part removes the repeated bits and transmits information on how many bits are removed and the remaining LSB data together.

On the receiver, first confirms whether the bit of the MSB part is 0 or 1, and confirms the number of bits removed. After that, by adding the same value as the first bit by the number of bits removed between the first bit and the LSB data, the data before compression is restored. Figure 3 shows the process of removing the MSB from the transmitting side and restoration from the receiving side.

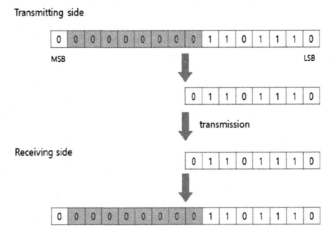

Fig. 3. The process of removing the MSB from the transmitting side and restoration from the receiving side

Most compression methods have EVM. For example, quantization generates EVM because it replaces existing values with quantization level values and substitutes them with approximate values when they are not the same value. But the compression method presented has the advantage of lossless compression without EVM. Therefore, when this compression method is applied to the conventional compression method, the compression rate can be increased while maintaining the EVM.

Also, for existing linear or nonlinear quantization, the range of quantization is $[-2^{Qq-1}, 2^{Qq-1} - 1]$. However, when we apply the proposed method, we set $[1, 2^{Qq-1}]$. When using the existing range, the first bit is necessary because the quantized value is negative or positive. Therefore, we have specified the range so that the quantized values are all positive. If all the quantized values are positive, the first bit is unconditionally zero. If the transmitter and receiver know the first bit is 0 in advance, the first bit can be removed as well when the unnecessary MSB is removed. By changing the range in this way, the compression rate can be further increased.

4   Experimental Process and Result

In this paper, to analyze the performance of the compression method that removes the unnecessary MSB part from the frame of IQ data, we simulate using MATLAB as follows.

According to the 3GPP standard, a 10 MHz channel frequency bandwidth was used and IQ data was generated with 15 bits according to the CPRI standard, and 16-QAM was used for modulation. The generated IQ data is passed through an inverse fast Fourier transform and a cyclic prefix is added. Next, after applying the down sampling and nonlinear quantization, we measure and remove the unwanted parts of the MSB.

On the receiver, the number of removed bits is checked, and the number of bits removed by the same value as the first bit is restored at the beginning of the LSB data, and then de-linear quantization and up sampling are applied. Figure 4 shows the process of compressing and restoring IQ data.

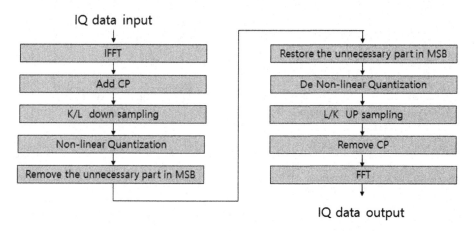

Fig. 4. The process of compressing and restoring IQ data

In the Up/Down sampling process, K is set to 2, L is set to 3, window size N_W is set to 64, low pass filter index I is set to $[-(N_W/2), (N_W/2) - 1]$ and the window function used for low pass filtering is the hamming window function [5]. The hamming window function is advantageous in that the processing time is short because of simplicity in comparison with other window functions. The Hamming window function $W(I)$ is as in

$$W(I) = 0.54 - 0.46 \cos \left(\frac{2\pi \left(I + \dfrac{N_W}{2} \right)}{N_W} \right) \tag{1}$$

In the Non-linear Quantization process, the Quantization level Q_q is set to 6, 8, 10, 12 and Quantization range is set to $[1, 2^{Q_q-1}]$. Figure 5 shows the values before and after quantizing the IQ data. The quantized values show that all values are positive.

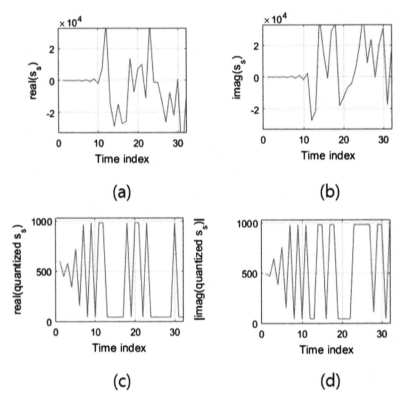

Fig. 5. (a) I data before quantization (b) Q data before quantization (c) I data after quantization (d) Q data after quantization

4.1 Experimental Process

With the advent of various compression technologies, ORI standardization organizations have introduced a standard that includes IQ data compression technology applicable to C-RAN. Requirements for compression set by ORI should be compressibility 50% or more, EVM 3% or less, latency 100 μs or less [6]. If these three requirements are satisfied, it means that even if compression technology is applied, there is no significant change from the previous data, and latency does not affect the operating system. EVM is as in

$$EVM = \sqrt{\frac{E\left[|\bar{x} - x|^2\right]}{E\left[|\bar{x}|^2\right]}} \times 100[\%]$$ (2)

Compression rate is measured by comparing the input signal before down sampling and the signal after removing MSB. When EVM is measured, it is compared with IQ data before passing IFFT and IQ data after FFT.

Table 1 the result of applying UP/Down sampling and non-linear quantization, which are conventional compression methods. it can be seen that as the nonlinear quantization level Q_q gradually increases from 6 to 12, the compression rate decreases from 77% to 50%, but the EVM also decreases from 0.98% to 0.70%. Latency was measured to be approximately 22.2 μs.

Table 1. Compression rate, EVM and Latency result

Q_q level	Compression rate (%)		EVM (%)	Latency (μs)
	I data	Q data		
6	77.2984	77.5928	0.9820	22.2472
8	67.3284	67.1239	0.9265	22.1058
10	58.3351	58.2959	0.8527	22.3819
12	49.9967	49.9896	0.7015	22.2824

Table 2 shows the compression ratio, EVM, and latency after adding the proposed compression method.

Table 2. Compression rate, EVM and Latency result

Q_q level	Compression rate (%)		EVM (%)	Latency (μs)
	I data	Q data		
6	82.1139	82.1125	0.9820	29.2922
8	73.1244	73.0694	0.9265	29.1947
10	64.1148	64.0686	0.8527	29.2679
12	55.0015	55.0324	0.7015	29.2250

From the results, it can be seen that as the nonlinear quantization level Q_q gradually increases from 6 to 12, the compression rate decreases from 82% to 55%, but the EVM also decreases from 0.98% to 0.70%. In other words, the higher the compression ratio, the greater the error between the original signal and the original signal. Latency was measured to be approximately 29.2 μs. Compared to the three ORI requirements, we can see that Q_q is satisfied in both 6, 8, 10, and 12.

Comparing the existing approach with the proposed approach, adding the MSB removal method increases the latency from 22.2 μs to 29.2 μs, but it can increase the compression rate by 5% for each Q_q level without generating additional EVMs.

5   Conclusion

There is a limit to the amount of traffic currently available to handle ever-increasing mobile traffic. Therefore, one of the ways to solve this problem is to transmit IQ data. Conventional compression methods include up/down sampling, nonlinear quantization, block scaling, etc.

In this paper, we propose a compression method that calculates and removes unnecessary MSBs in data frames after applying Up/Down sampling and Non-linear quantization.

As a result of experiments using MATLAB, we found that as the Q_q increases, the compression rate decreases, but the EVM decreases and it is restored close to the original signal. Latency was also measured almost constantly. Also, it was confirmed that these experimental results satisfied the compression conditions required by ORI.

Compared with the conventional compression schemes, the latency increased by 7 μs, but the EVM was the same and the compression rate was improved by 5% for each Q_q level.

Acknowledgment. This work was supported by Institute for Information & communications Technology Promotion (IITP) grant funded by the Korea government (MSIP) (No. 2016-0-00106, Development of the RF-signal over IP Technology for the Smart Media Services based on Optical IP Network) and This research was supported by the MSIP (Ministry of Science, ICT and Future Planning), Korea, under the ITRC (Information Technology Research Center) support program (IITP-2017-2012-0-00628) supervised by the IITP (Institute for Information & Communications Technology Promotion).

References

1. de la Oliva, A., Hernández, J.A., Larrabeiti, D., Azcorra, A.: An overview of the CPRI specification and its application to C-RAN-based LTE scenarios. IEEE Commun. Mag. **54**(2), 152–159 (2016)
2. Tayq, Z., Quere, A., Anet Neto, L., Chanclou, P., Saliou, F., Grzybowski, K.: Performance demonstration of real time compressed CPRI transport. In: 42nd ECOC (2016)
3. Samardzija, D., Pastalan, J., MacDonald, M., Walker, S., Valenzuela, R.: Compressed transport of baseband signals in radio access networks. IEEE Trans. Wirelless Commun. **11**(9), 3216–3225 (2012)
4. Guo, B., Cao, W., Tao, A., Samardzija, D.: LTE/LTE-A signal compression on the CPRI interface. Bell Labs Tech. J. **11**(2), 117–133 (2013)
5. Priya, K., Swethaanjali, N., Arthi Bala Lakshmi, M.: Comparison of various filtering techniques USDE for removing high frequency noise in ECG signal. IJSRTM **3**, 211–215 (2015)
6. ORI Specification, V. 4. 1. 1 October 2014

Author Index

Printed in the United States
By Bookmasters